D0160515

Critical Acclaim for this book

'This is such an up-to-the-feminist-minute book. If one ever imagines that radical feminist thinkers or feminist cultural studies scholars can leave "women in development" to those who know about digging wells and sampling soil, think again. Kriemild Saunders and her savvy, worldly contributors make one realise that "development" is about the gendered constructions of desire, romanticism, icons, co-optation, consumerism and green tourism.'
– Cynthia Enloe, author of *Bananas, Beaches and Bases* (new edition)

'In this landmark volume, world-class feminists undo Western thinking on gender, development, and modernity. Women's empowerment over materialism, sociality over relentless progress, and sustainability over biological invasion are some of the post development alternatives proposed. Indeed, the lively theory and vivid examples show that the well being of women in the South is tied up with the fate of the planet itself. This indispensable resource will appeal to scholars and activists in many fields.'
– Aihwa Ong, author of *Flexible Citizenship: the Cultural Logic of Transnationality* and *Buddha in Hiding: Refugees, Citizenship, and the New America* (forthcoming)

'Here is a challenging set of inquiries about "development" from various feminist perspectives, particularly the questions of progress and post-development alternatives. This anthology is a noteworthy contribution to current discussions about globalization, survival, the ecological crisis and strategies for action.'
– Lourdes Beneria, Professor of City and Regional Planning and Women's Studies Director, Cornell University

Zed Books on Women and Development

Zed Books has a reputation as the leading publisher of critical, intellectually innovative and important books in the fields of Women's Studies and of Development. Amongst the many titles across both categories that we have published in recent years are:

Cultural Transformation and Human Rights in Africa
Abdullahi A. An-Na'im (ed.)

The Strategic Silence: Gender and Economic Policy
Isabella Bakker

Feminist Futures: Re-imagining Women, Culture and Development
Kum-Kum Bhavnani, John Foran and Priya Kurian (eds)

Victims and Heroines: Women, Welfare and the Egyptian State
Iman Bibars

Capital Accumulation and Women's Labour in Asian Economics
Peter Custers

Women, Gender and Development in the Caribbean: Reflections and Projections
Pat Ellis

Gender and Technology: Empowering Women, Engendering Development
Saskia Everts

Balancing the Load: Women, Gender and Transport
Priyanthi Fernando and Gina Porter (eds)

Macro-economics: Making Gender Matter. Concepts, Policies and Institutional Change in Developing Countries
Martha Gutierrez (ed.)

Feminist Perspectives on Sustainable Development
Wendy Harcourt (ed.)

Gender, Education and Development: Beyond Access to Empowerment
Christine Heward and Sheila Bunwaree (eds)

Silent Invaders: Pesticides, Livelihoods and Women's Health
Miriam Jacobs and Barbara Dinham (eds)

The Elusive Agenda: Mainstreaming Women in Development
Rounaq Jahan

Institutions, Relations and Outcomes: A Framework and Case Studies for Gender-aware Planning
Naila Kabeer and Ramya Subrahamian (eds)

The Violence of Development: The Political Eonomy of Gender
Karin Kapadia (ed.)

Patriarchy and Accumulation on a World Scale: Women in the International Division of Labour
Maria Mies

Gender, Development and Identity: An Ethiopian Study
Helen Pankhurst

Feminists Doing Development: A Practical Critique
Marilyn Porter and Ellen Judd (eds)

Feminist Post-Development Thought: Rethinking Modernity, Postcolonialism and Representation
Kriemild Saunders (ed.)

Staying Alive: Women, Ecology and Development
Vandana Shiva

Continent of Mothers, Continent of Hope: Understanding and Promoting Development in Africa Today
Torild Skard

The Women, Gender and Development Reader
Nalini Visvanathan, Lynn Duggan, Laurie Nisonoff and Nan Wiegersma (eds)

Women and Land in Africa: Linking Research to Advocacy
L. Muthoni Wanyeki (ed.)

Feminist Post-Development Thought

Rethinking modernity, postcolonialism & representation

Edited by

Kriemild Saunders

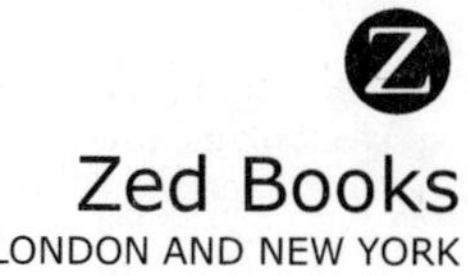

Zed Books
LONDON AND NEW YORK

Feminist Post-Development Thought was first published in 2002 by
Zed Books Ltd, 7 Cynthia Street, London N1 9JF, UK,
and Room 400, 175 Fifth Avenue, New York, NY 10010, USA
zedbooks@zedbooks.demon.co.uk
http://www.zedbooks.demon.co.uk

Cover designed by Andrew Corbett.
Set in 10½/13 pt Adobe Garamond
by Long House, Cumbria, UK.
Printed and bound in the United Kingdom
by Bookcraft, Midsomer Norton.

Distributed in the USA exclusively by Palgrave,
a division of St Martin's Press, LLC,
175 Fifth Avenue, New York, NY 10010

A catalogue record for this book
is available from the British Library.

Library of Congress Cataloging-in-Publication Data
has been applied for

ISBN 1 85649 946 4 (hb)
ISBN 1 85649 947 2 (pb)

Contents

Abbreviations

AAWORD	Association of African Women for Research and Development
ACLS	American Council of Learned Societies
Alt-WID	Alternative Women in Development
APEC	Asia–Pacific Economic Cooperation forum
ARAWOC	Association for Research on Algerian Women and Cultural Change
AWID	Association for Women in Development
Campfire	Communal Areas Management Programme for Indigenous Resources
BGH	Bovine growth hormone
BKU	Bharatiya Kisan Union (India)
BSE	Bovine spongiform encephalopathy
BST	Bovine somatrophin
CAIPACHA	(NGO, Bolivia)
CIDA	Canadian International Development Agency
CML	Center for Mutual Learning
CRIAW	Canadian Research Institute for the Advancement of Women
CUFTA	Canadian–United States Free Trade Agreement
DAWN	Development Alternatives with Women for a New Era
DNC	Democratic National Conference
ELN	Ejército de Liberación Nacional (Bolivia)
EPR	Einstein–Podolsky–Rosen argument
EPZ	Export processing zone
EU	European Union
FAO	Food and Agriculture Organization
FCE	Fondo de Cultura Económica, Mexico
FDA	Food and Drug Administration
FTAA	Free Trade for the Americas
GAD	Gender and Development
GATT	General Agreement on Tariffs and Trade
GCC	Global commodity chain
GIRE	Grupo de Información en Reproducción Eelgida
GNP	Gross national product
GR	Green Revolution
ICPD	International Conference on Population and Development
ICTs	Information and communication technologies
IIA	Instituto de Investigaciones Antropológicas (Mexico)
IIH	Instituto de Investigaciones Históricas (Mexico)
ILO	International Labour Organization
IMF	International Monetary Fund
INAH	Instituto Nacional de Antropologia et Historia
INI	Instituto Nacional Indigenista

INS	Immigration and Naturalization Service (USA)
IPPF	International Planned Parenthood Federation
ISEC	International Society for Ecology and Culture
KRRS	Karnataka Rajya Raitha Sangha (India)
LEDeP	Ladakh Ecological Development Project
LPYT	Ladakh Pume Yarketh Tsokpa (Ladakh Women's Development Society)
MCH	Mother–child health programmes
NAFTA	North American Free Trade Agreement
NGO	Non-governmental organization
NRI	Non-resident Indian
OECD	Organization for Economic Cooperation and Development
OPEC	Organization of Petroleum Exporting Countries
PMPD	Postmodern post-development
POEA	Philippines Overseas Employment Administration
PRA	Participatory Rural Appraisal
PRATEC	Proyecto Andino de Tecnologias Campesinas
PRC	People's Republic of China
PRONAR	National Programme for Irrigation (Bolivia)
RBM	Results-based management
RFP	Requests for proposal
RMALC	Red Mexicana de Acción Frente al Libre Comercio
SAP	Structural adjustment programme
SEWA	Self-Employed Women's Association (India)
SID	Society for International Development
SNDR	Secretaria Nacional de Desarrollo Rural (Bolivia)
SSRC	Social Science Research Council
TNC	Transnational company
UN	United Nations
UNAM	Universidad Nacional Autónoma de México
UNCED	United Nations Conference on Environment and Development
UNDP	United Nations Development Programme
UNESCO	United Nations Educational, Social and Cultural Organization
UNFPA	United Nations Family Planning Association
UNRISD	United Nations Research Institute for Social Development
US(A)	United States of America
USAID	United States Agency for International Development
WID	Women in Development
WIDE	Women in Development Europe
WAD	Women and Development
WAL	Women's Alliance of Ladakh

Acknowledgements

I would like to acknowledge the organizers of and participants in the conference on *Which Way for Women and Development? Debating Concepts, Strategies and Directions for the Twenty-first Century* at the Graduate School, City University of New York (1998). I would especially like to thank the organizing committee (Electa Arenal, Joycelyn Boryczka, Patricia Clough, Jennifer Disney, Hester Eisenstein, Kimberly Flynn, Yvonne Lasalle and principal organizer Mitu Hirshman) and the Graduate School for hosting and supporting the conference. It was the starting point for conversations on women and development that brought into focus a dialogue between mainstream and postcolonial perspectives. Even though this anthology deviates substantively from it in themes and contributors, the conference was a stimulus for reflection. I would also like to acknowledge the enthusiastic support of Robert Molteno (Zed editor). Finally, I would like to thank my family, especially Carolyn Couch.

Contributors

Ravina Aggarwal is an Associate Professor of Anthropology and part of the Women's Studies Program at Smith College, Massachusetts. She is the co-founder of *Meridians: Feminism, Race, Transnationalism*. She has edited and translated *Forsaking Paradise*, an anthology of short stories from Urdu (Katha Press) and has completed a book manuscript entitled *Border Lines: Performance and Power in Ladakh*.

Frédérique Apffel-Marglin is Professor of Anthropology at Smith College, where she directs the Center for Mutual Learning (CML). She has done fieldwork in Eastern India for 25 years, publishing several books based on this work, but gave up fieldwork in 1992 for ethical/political reasons. Since 1994 the CML has collaborated with several Andean non-governmental organizations (NGOs). Her latest book, in association with PRATEC, is *The Spirit of Regeneration: Andean Culture Confronting Western Notions of Development* (London: Zed Books). She is currently working on a book on gender, regeneration and biodiversity with Loyda Sanchez.

Tani E. Barlow is an intellectual historian of modern China and works in the Department of Women's Studies, University of Washington, Seattle. *The Question of Women in Chinese Feminism* will be published by Duke University Press. She is founder and senior editor of *Positions: East Asia cultures critique.*

James Bever is an Assistant Professor in the Department of Biology at Indiana University. His work on the ecological and evolutionary consequences of the interactions of plant and soil organisms has shown that soil community dynamics can be strong determinants of plant community processes.

Piya Chatterjee is Associate Professor in Women's Studies at the University of California, Riverside. She is a historical anthropologist who also researches women's activism in the global South. She is currently helping to set up a small community-based NGO in North Bengal which will assist rural tea plantation women with self-help initiatives. *A Time for Tea: Women, Labor and Postcolonial Politics* (North Carolina: Duke University Press, 2002).

Patience Elabor-Idemudia is an Associate Professor in the Department of Sociology at the University of Saskatchewan, Canada. She has published a number of articles and book chapters on gender and development, diasporan African women, and immigrant women in Canada. She is also a feminist engaged in anti-racism activism.

Wendy Harcourt joined the Society for International Development (SID), Rome, Italy in 1988 and has contributed to its work in the fields of gender in development, alternative economics, sustainable development, culture, health, globalization and reproductive health and rights. She is currently Director of Programmes and editor of *Development.* She has edited three Zed Books titles: *Feminist Perspectives on Sustainable Development* (1993), *Power, Reproduction and Gender* (1997) and *Women@Internet: Creating New Cultures in Cyberspace* (1999).

Marnia Lazreg is Professor of Sociology and Women's Studies at Hunter College and the Graduate School of the City University of New York. She is a former fellow of the Pembroke Center (Brown University) and the Bunting Institute (Harvard University). She has published extensively on feminist theory, cultural movements, social class and development. In addition to her teaching and research, she has led gender and development workshops in Africa, Asia and the Middle East. She is the director of the Association for Research on Algerian Women and Cultural Change (ARAWOC) and has published numerous articles and books, most recently *Eloquence of Silence: Algerian Women in Question* (New York: Routledge, 1994).

Marianne H. Marchand is a senior lecturer in international relations at the University of Amsterdam. She has recently accepted a position as Professor of International Relations at the Universidad de las Américas-Puebla in Mexico. Her publications include *Femininsm/Postmodernism/Development* (with J. L. Parpart, London: Routledge 1995); *Gender and Global Restructuring* (with Anne Sisson Runyan, Routledge 2000); and her contribution (with Morten Bøås and Timothy M. Shaw) to the *Third World Quarterly* Special Issue on 'New Regionalisms' (20, 5 [1999]). She is co-editor of the *Ripe Series in Global Political Economy* (Routledge) and associate editor of the *International Feminist Journal of Politics* (Routledge); she also acts as a consultant on development issues for various NGOs.

Sylvia Marcos is Visiting Professor of Mesoamerican Religions at Claremont School of Religion, a practising clinical psychologist and a Research Associate of the Gender in Anthropology permanent seminar at the Institute for Anthropological Research, National Autonomous University of Mexico. She has published extensively on indigenous and rural women, with a focus on healing and sexuality in ancient and contemporary Mexico. Her latest book is *Gender/Bodies/Religions* (Mexico City: IAHR-ALER Publications, 2000).

Meera Nanda is an ACLS fellow in the Philosophy Department at Columbia University. She holds a doctorate in Science and Technology Studies from Rensselaer Polytechnic Institute and the Indian Institute of Technology, New Delhi. Her *Prophets Facing Backward: Postmodern Critiques of Science and the Rise of Reactionary Modernism in India* will be published by Rutgers University Press.

Jane L. Parpart is Professor of History, International Development Studies and Women's Studies at Dalhousie University. She has had extensive experience with gender and development issues in Asia and Africa. Her primary interest has been the connection between development theorizing, gender issues and development as practice. She is co-editor with Marianne Marchand of *Feminsm/Postmodernism/Development* (London: Routledge 1995) and is currently co-editing (with Kathy Staudt and Shirin Rai) *Rethinking Empowerment: Gender and Development in a Global/Local World* (Routledge, forthcoming). She has a long-standing interest in urban problems, particularly the impact of urbanization on attitudes towards modernity and development. She is currently exploring the way the emerging middle class in Bulawayo, Zimbabwe has constructed notions of modernity and progress in their daily social, material and spatial lives.

Ramona Pérez is an Assistant Professor of Anthropology at San Diego State University. Her work and publications focus on the negotiation of gender and community identity among Oaxaqueños in Mexico, Mexican migrants in the US and Mexican Americans in the Southwest. Her most recent book, *Molding Our Lives From Clay: Gender and Community Identity in Oaxaca,* is under review by the University of Texas Press.

Loyda Sanchez is a Bolivian who studied economics at the Universidad Mayor de San Andres in La Paz and pedagogy in Cochabamba. In 1970 she was a militant of the ELN, the guerrilla movement founded by Che Guevara. Later she was exiled to Chile, Argentina and Peru, and imprisoned in 1976–8 by the Peruvian military government. In the 1980s she worked as a member of several Bolivian NGOs, with indigenous peasant communities in the valleys around Cochabamba. Sanchez is currently the coordinator of CAIPACHA, an NGO dedicated to Andean/Amazonian cultural affirmation and mental decolonization.

Saskia Sassen is the Ralph Lewis Professor of Sociology at the University of

Chicago and Centennial Visiting Professor at the London School of Economics. Her most recent books are *Guests and Aliens* (New York: New Press 1999) and *Globalization and its Discontents* (New Press 1998). A new updated edition of *The Global City* came out in 2001. She is the editor of *Cities and Their Cross-Border Networks* (London: Routledge 2001). Her books have been translated into ten languages. She is co-director of the Economy Section of the Global Chicago Project and is the chair of the newly formed Information Technology, International Cooperation and Global Security Committee of the SSRC.

Kriemild Saunders is a visiting lecturer in the Women's Studies Program at the University of Massachusetts, Amherst. Her wide-ranging interests include sexuality, queer practices, gender, development, race and class relations. In the Bahamas she is a long-standing activist against the subjugation of sexual minorities, and against class and gender subordination. She is currently working on a manuscript on women, gender and sexuality in the South, tentatively titled 'Engendered Subjects: Deconstructing Discourses on Women, Gender and Development'.

Kathleen Staudt is Professor of Political Science and Director of the Center for Civic Engagement at the University of Texas at El Paso. Her research areas include gendered 'development' bureaucracies, women's politics, and US–Mexican border studies, with a focus on political economy and social/nationalist/civic education in public schools. Among her books are *Free Trade?* and *Women, International Development and Politics: the Bureaucratic Mire* (both Temple University Press, 1998, 1997) and *Policy, Politics and Gender: Women Gaining Ground* (Kumarian Press 1998).

Peggy Schultz is a Research Associate in the Department of Biology at Indiana University. She studies the relationship between arbuscular mycorrhizal fungi and associated plant species in a variety of habitats. Her work includes restoration of native plant communities.

Vandana Shiva is a world-renowned environmentalist and the director of the Research Foundation for Science, Technology and Natural Resource Policy, New Delhi. Her many books include *Protect or Plunder? Understanding Intellectual Property Rights* (Zed Books 2001), *Stolen Harvest* (Zed Books 2000), *Biopiracy: the Plunder of Nature and Knowledge* (South End Press 1997) and *Staying Alive* (Zed Books 1989). In 1993 she received the Alternative Nobel Prize (the Right Livelihood Award).

Banu Subramaniam is an Assistant Professor of Women's Studies at the University of Massachusetts, Amherst. Her primary research focus is on the relationships between gender, race, colonialism and science, and how these histories have shaped and been shaped by each other.

Esther Wangari is an Associate Professor in the Women's Studies Program and Director of the Women's Studies Graduate Program at Towson University. Her ongoing research is on the effects of rice irrigation production on health and environment in Kenya. She is a co-editor of *Feminist Political Ecology: Global Issues and Local Experiences* and a contributing author to *The Heritage of African People: Ameru*; she has also published numerous journal articles and book chapters. Dr. Wangari's research topics are gender, development and the environment.

Introduction
Towards a Deconstructive Post-Development Criticism

Kriemild Saunders

Women, gender and development: the opening of a subfield

Women in Development (WID) remains hegemonic at the level of feminist developmental practices. It is characterized by increasing legitimacy and deepening integration within major bilateral and multilateral development agencies.[1] WID emerged initially as a women's caucus within the Society for International Development (SID) to promote professional employment opportunities for women in development agencies, and to compile data which explored the intuition that development was having an adverse effect on impoverished Third World women. The matrix that allowed for the emergence of WID is multifaceted, but two powerful currents were the broader institutionalized field of modernization and development, and the feminist movement in the West in the 1970s.[2]

The will to realize a programme of development to address poverty in the Third World was announced by President Truman in 1949. He pledged that the old imperialism of exploitation for foreign profit was to be replaced with a democratic development programme of 'fair dealing'. The target of this programme was the poverty and misery of 'underdevelopment', which was viewed as threatening to the security of both the Third World and the First World (Rist 1997: 249–50). Thus poverty was highlighted as the weak link in the new tripartite world order, revealing an anxiety that the ever-growing body of sovereign Third World states was open to the seductions of communism.[3] Prior to this moment, the colonial powers deemed it appropriate to 'develop' raw materials and administrative structures subject to their political control – but not Third World *people*, who were defined by an inherent racial inferiority. The minimal colonial educational programmes were part of a civilizing effort to indoctrinate the natives into Western values, which touched a small fraction of the communities in which they were situated. 'National development' eventually surpassed the colonial imperatives of direct political subjugation to the empire. This disarming rhetoric should be grasped in the context of the Marshall Plan which raised $19 billion in US assistance, exempted from profiteering, for the economic reconstruction of post-war Europe between 1945 and 1950. An array of institutions – the International Bank for Reconstruction and Development (World Bank), the International Monetary Fund (IMF), a number of UN agencies and programmes, major multilateral and bilateral agencies, and ubiquitous educational and research centres – grew rapidly into a powerful development apparatus. The ideology of this apparatus was predicated on a faith in the value of a planned, managerial and interventionist approach to growth and national development, an expression of lessons learned from the Great Depression, the New Deal and the discursive assertions of Keynesianism and neoclassical economics. This represented a major displacement of the hegemonic liberal view of the market as self-regulating and orderly.

Truman's programme was represented as a promise to support democratic economic relations between the USA and the Third World. However, the unfair protectionist trading practices and the debt trap that were initiated and reproduced by America and its Western allies, with the aid of the IMF, the World Bank and major lending institutions, betrayed such a promise. Western economists were fully cognizant that fair dealings would require accepting goods from the Third World, equivalent to the debt owed; but this, they discerned, would undermine production in America and other core countries. Hence arose the imperative to export huge amounts of capital as loans to cover the interest accrued in pyramid-like schemes, legitimated by formal contracts and enforceable by economic sanctions on Third World governments (Payer 1975; 1991). This economic structure, imposed by powerful capitalist states, manifestly destroyed the abstract possibility of the realization of 'development' in general in the Third World. What this meant, in effect, was that war by other means was instituted against the Other to the advantage of people of European descent, and fully enforced.

The 1970s and early 1980s witnessed an upsurge of feminist activism against male domination and oppression. This was accompanied by theorizing on patriarchy in which the broad outlines of the most widely recognized theoretical perspectives – liberal, radical and Marxist/socialist feminisms – could be discerned. Politically, feminists in the West (white) saw the value of organizing separately from men in consciousness-raising groups with so-called leaderless structures. Liberal Feminism had an advantage: its ideological position gave it the greatest level of coherence with liberal modernization and development theory and practice, albeit with a tension around male bias. For functionalist scholars (for example: Becker 1981: 14–37; Parsons 1960) the emergence of the nuclear family model under Western industrialization and modernization, with its accompanying sexual division of labour at home, was deemed rational and advantageous to the reproduction of the family unit. Hence, the normative conventions within communities of people of European descent, whereby women were expected to specialize in domestic labour and men in wage labour, were upheld. However, Arthur Lewis (1955: 422) asserted that modernization would deliver even greater benefits to women than men, permitting freedom from household drudgery and seclusion in the household. Woman would be free to exercise her talents and join the human race. D. McClelland (1976: 404–95) saw the emancipation of women as crucial to the inculcation of new norms and the breaking of the hold of tradition in the Third World, because women played a central role in the upbringing of children. On the relationship of modernization to sex roles in society, male scholars articulated both conservative and liberal perspectives.

The seminal empirical work of liberal feminist Esther Boserup (1970) on the status of women in the Third World marked an aperture in the general field; it would eventually become a monument in the subfield it opened up. Where and to whom was this intuition that development was detrimental to women addressed? Why take this intuition seriously? The history of women's location in the development process in the West embodied the recurrent process of extrusion from industry, under the ideological alibi of protective legislation and the enforcement of the bourgeois ideal of woman's identity and place as properly the home, until the new-wave feminist outburst in the late 1960s. It is for this reason that Western feminists responded immediately to the early indications about the declining status of impoverished women in the Third World. Within development agencies dominated by men, this bourgeois ideal of what it is to be a woman, and her essential identity as wife and mother, had framed welfare strategies that were defined as appropriate for impoverished Third World women.[4]

Boserup's (1970) work helped to produce a distinctive feminist vision of the development process which challenged the assumption that the benefits of development would automatically trickle down to the poor; she pointed to women's declining status as a clear indication to the contrary. She also identified some general developmental tendencies in pre-modern societies from the standpoint of gender. In sparsely populated regions with shifting agriculture (commonly utilizing a long fallow method and hand-held implements) women did most of the agricultural work. Men did more agricultural work in densely populated areas utilizing the plough. Areas employing intensive irrigation systems tended to rely on the labour of both men and women.

Boserup employed the modernist designation of some societies as in transition from traditional to modern forms. They were divided dichotomously into subsistence and modern sectors. While scholars such as Arthur Lewis spoke of the advantageous movement of surplus labour from the subsistence to the modern sector, on the assumption that the marginal utility was virtually nil, Boserup identified the tendency to utilize male labour in paid employment in the modern sector to the relative detriment of women. The few opportunities available to women in the modern sector meant that they were bound to a large extent to the subsistence and informal sectors. In the urban sector women were concentrated in the informal realm, typified by petty trading and prostitution, while men were disproportionately located in the formal waged sector, a function of the prevailing norms of male privilege in training and access to credit. Men were characterized as advancing in the modern sector, while women were depicted as languishing in the backward, poverty-inducing rural and informal sectors that were seen as reproducing women's dependence on men, rather than the liberal feminist ideal of autonomy and self-empowerment.[5]

Welfarism was the first approach to address itself to women's needs in the development enterprise. Existing prior to WID, it was an extension of liberal Western ideologies of relief aid and addressed itself to the needs of extremely vulnerable groups: it was natural that women would become major clients. Caroline Moser (1989) identified three types of welfare programmes. The first addressed itself primarily to physical survival through the provision of food aid on a short-term basis after 'natural' disasters; typically, women and children were targeted as the most vulnerable. Programmes to combat malnutrition in the Third World through food and nutritional education were designed and implemented, targeting children of less than five years and pregnant or nursing mothers. In the 1960s the mother–child health (MCH) programmes were initiated, focusing on the reproductive role of women and the mother–child dyad, especially nutritional education and additional food to promote the survival of the most vulnerable group, namely children. Family planning for population control was also included as part of the welfare approach to women. Population control was simply viewed as a rational function of the dissemination of birth control information and contraceptives. The failure of this approach, and the inverse relationship between women's status and fertility, has led to a consideration of the complexity of fertility differentials in the context of broader socio-economic conditions.

From the 1970s the welfare approach was criticized by WID for its paternalistic perpetuation of existing gender roles and its dependence on the patriarchal power of the state and the family rather than individual autonomy.

The focus of WID on the productive labour of women, its invisibility and fundamental place in Third World development, supported an articulate, efficiency-based argument for the integration of women into development with access to training and resources. In addition, they advocated legal rights and administrative intervention to combat gender discrimination from a liberal, modernizing perspective (Rogers 1980; Boserup and Liljencrantz 1975; USAID 1982). Welfarism was seen as the expression of a sexist, sex-role socialization, and of a stereotyping that defined women's nature as biologically wired to nurture rather than rational, aggressive and competitive. These androgynous subjective qualities were deemed essential to participation within public life and productive (waged) labour. The capacity to reason and engage in productive labour, and the ability to exercise a will independent of patriarchal power, is the mark of a womanly subject conscious of her location within patriarchal power.[6] Feminist professionals fought for such self-recognition, but continued to perpetuate images of impoverished Third World women as helpless victims of patriarchy, since such representations authorized their right to organize a planned liberation of this client population, construed as lacking the sovereign power to liberate themselves.

Key monuments in the founding of women and development were the official UN conferences that historically have played a crucial role in mobilizing women internationally. They also legitimized the broad platforms of feminist activists at the national and international levels. During the first major conference in Mexico City in 1975, women collectively articulated their concerns and crafted a World Plan of Action, spearheading the UN Decade for the Advancement of Women (1976–85). The Programme of Action for half the decade was adopted at the Copenhagen conference in 1980. The international development strategy for the Third UN Development Decade (1980) affirmed the World Plan of Action and the recommendations of the Copenhagen conference. The first World Survey on the Role of Women in Development arose out of a demand for basic empirical information on the socio-economic and political conditions of women *vis-à-vis* men, and it required a disaggregation of the data by sex. These surveys have continued to serve the demand for updated information. This involved governments not only in responding to questionnaires and in preparations for world conferences, but in making a commitment to address the plans and recommendations from these conferences. The world conferences (Mexico City 1975, Copenhagen 1980, Nairobi 1985 and Beijing 1995), with parallel NGO fora, attracted 4,000, 7,000, 16,000 and more than 30,000 participants respectively. They also facilitated the ratification of declarations and conventions (such as the Convention on the Elimination of All Forms of Discrimination against Women), offered assessments and prepared forward-looking strategies for the advancement of women. In a catalogue of other UN world conferences, those on world population and world food held prior to the conference on women in Mexico City (1975) were heralded for paving the way for the recognition of women's role in development as a whole. Women did not have a voice within conferences with male-dominated delegations unless a few women took the initiative in well-articulated presentations. Hilkka Pietilä and Jeanne Vickers (1990: 86) concluded that 'the recognition of women was a matter of chance' until the end of the 1970s.

In the struggle to articulate a women's viewpoint, competing ideologies engaged each other at the Copenhagen conference. Women from core countries stressed equality between men and women, while developing countries stressed the satisfaction of basic material needs as a pressing issue in the context of a disadvantageous international economic order. Women from socialist states claimed that equality between men and women already existed. These ideological differences and the emergence of general political issues (such as Palestine and Zionism or racial discrimination) were interpreted as a reflection of official governmental positions. This was contrasted with the free fora at Mexico City and Copenhagen, where women's *true* voices were said to be more clearly audible (*ibid.* 1990: 78–9) in spite of political and cultural differences.

A look at a few of the commentaries on the Wesley conference on Women and Development: the Complexities of Change (1976) also gives the flavour of differences between the voices of Western and Third World women. Vina Mazumdar (1977) maintained that American women were disappointed by an ostensible lack of feminist ideology on the part of Third World women, who appeared too identified with their local establishment perspectives. May Ahdab-Yehia (1977) lamented the imposition of stereotypes of Arab women – concerns with the harem, the veil, seclusion, sexual asymmetry, polygamy, divorce, inheritance laws, or codes of honour and shame – rather than those individual and social differences that show the real complexities of women's roles and statuses. Achola O. Pala (1977) attempted to look at women and development from an African perspective: she deplored the fact that priorities were set from the outside, and that Africa is viewed as a testing ground for the investigation of ideas that originate elsewhere – Paris, London, New York and Amsterdam. She went on to problematize the notion of the integration of women in development and questioned the supposed benefits to men, arguing that historically African women have been active in provisioning for their families, and that they are well integrated into their dependent national economies. Such dependent integration was thought to produce 'apathy', 'indifference' and resistance to change, so that for the majority of African people the questions of autonomy and self-determination remain crucial.

AAWORD, a network of African researchers (1985: 28–9; Steady 1986: 15), rejected the gynocentric privilege of sex inequity as the fundamental problem facing all women, pointing instead to the importance of class and national hierarchies in determining access to resources. They astutely identified the heterogeneity of interests among women, which was counterposed to the gynocentric grounding of Western notions of sisterhood. Development Alternatives with Women for a New Era (DAWN), a network of activists, policy makers and researchers in the Third World, also decried the Western centring of sex equality and likewise a notion of sisterhood as defined by the First World and by local Third World élites (Sen and Grown 1987).

What is clear is that from the very founding of women, gender and development the 'women's point of view' was not singular but heterogeneous and multiple. This continues to constitute a challenge to the dominant Western feminist will to enforce a gynocentric philosophy and practice, which centres and magnifies patriarchal power and marginalizes other vertical social relations.[7]

Neo-Marxist criticism

In a reflection on the typical narrative of feminist discourses on this field, a differentiation is made between Women and Development (WAD) and Gender and Development (GAD). Given the fact that the presentations of scholarly ideas are typically narrow in focus, and do not really set out to construct theoretical foundations *per se*, the discursive creation of WAD entails a considerable discursive effort. In the light of this manifest difficulty, it is appropriate to ask what value or function such a differentiation makes in feminist narratives. In the first place, it marks a distinction between a class- and a gender-centred analysis. In other words, such an operation inscribes an incision between what is *properly* feminist and what is not – a gesture of *non-recognition*.[8]

WAD is regarded as contesting WID claims that women have been excluded from development, a justification for a programme of inclusion. The terms 'inclusion' and 'exclusion' differ in their meanings in both the liberal WID and neo-Marxist perspectives. For WID inclusion refers to the location of women *vis-à-vis* the modern sector – inside or outside. WID is concerned with maximizing women's access to the modern sector, opening the border between the traditional and the modern sectors, to allow for an equal proportion of women within the latter. The structural determinations of the exclusion of women from development or the modern sector (for example, male bias) are not of grave concern, since science and enlightened reason are regarded as antidotes to the vestiges of biased patriarchal superstition and ignorance, which locates women outside what is properly human – a rational and sovereign subjectivity. However, the neo-Marxists refer 'inclusion' and 'exclusion' to the hierarchical spatialization of the capitalist global economy (center–semi-periphery–periphery, urban–rural, subsistence–capitalist sectors, etcetera). Within these structural forms the peripheral spaces are not outside development, but proper to development, part of the structural principle of its local and global formations. It is from this perspective, rather than one growing out of WID initiatives in the early 1970s, that neo-Marxists claim that Third World women have always been an integral part of an exploitative developmental process. Hence, sectoral designations correspond to differing levels, intensities and forms of exploitation, misrecognized as traditional (backward) versus modern (advanced). This misrecognition by WID representatives is understood as unfolding from their national and class interests and alliances, which are thought to preclude them from seeing the *real* social relations in which impoverished Third World women are located. Most significantly, WID assessments presuppose that a gradual process of reform will eventuate in gender equity.

WAD underscores the idea that global capitalism, with its inequitable gender relations and prioritization of global capitalist dynamics, is also inimical to Third World men. GAD in turn charges WAD with non-recognition – inattention to gender relations, cross-gender alliances and divisions within classes. Nash and Safa (1980) are often referenced in connection with WAD, since they are among the few scholars associated with this perspective to attempt an explanation of male domination and violence. They contend that it is the structure of capitalism that keeps women at home, not men. In a discussion of male domination in Latin America, it is the pervasive sex-role ideology that is distinguished in prescribing the wife's deference to the husband. Frustration at the class system is regarded as the determining factor in men's abuse of women. They point to the fact that women typically see men as their oppressors, and direct their hostilities toward them rather than the class system (Nash and Safa 1980: xi, 25, 78). Kabeer (1995: 49) contends that even though dependency feminists acknowledge the ideological subordination of women in the home, they're not inclined to recognize that men benefit from women's domestic labour. While it is important to appreciate such benefits, it is necessary to acknowledge the extent to which women benefit from men's labour, and the complexities of economic exchanges at the domestic level within such analyses.[9]

Overall, WAD is charged with a privileging of class over gender, since gender inequities are framed in terms of the accumulation process of global capitalism, rather than patriarchal domination *per se*. However, a central prop in the hierarchical relations between gender and class is the problematic base–superstructure building metaphor, where gender ideology is consigned to the superstructural realm in a partitioning of the economic from the ideological, where economic determinism has a privileged place in the architecture. In spite of the fact that neo-Marxist feminists within development generally affirmed women's labouring activities as creating value and surplus value *vis-à-vis* the accumulation process, thereby locating such activities at the foundational level of the base, the rigidity of the base–superstructure model and the privileged place of economics and class (local and global) relations remained an inherent difficulty. It is largely as a result of the impact of the theoretical innovations of Louis Althusser (1977) – his hysteresial concept of the determination of the economic in the last instance (which never arrives), and his account of the ideological state apparatus – that the rigidity of the building metaphor began to lose its discursive force. In addition, Jacques Derrida (1981: 32) takes up the question of the relationship of the text to the real, and of the boundary between the one and the other, in a compelling inquiry. In a discussion of Marx's positing of the absolute exteriority of the real to the concept, Derrida speaks of it metaphorically as a formalism indefinitely confined to its own preface. This gesture confines the building metaphor by announcing it as a starting point, a provisional abstraction, in order to articulate the notion of the materiality of the text.

Maria Mies (1986) developed a sophisticated theoretical position to address this stumbling block – the subordination of gender to class – by developing a theory of patriarchy that was grounded on a materialist perspective. Mies's innovation lay in her elaboration of a theory of masculine and feminine subjectivity, premised on a Marxist philosophical anthropology that defined labouring activities as the essence of being. There is an examination of the place of the sexual/gender division of labour in the subordination of subsistence to a predatory (masculine) mode of production, characterized essentially by the subordination of women. This predatory mode is comprehended as constitutive of all forms of natural and social domination and exploitation. She identified a fundamental distinction between women's labouring activities in bio-social reproduction – sensuous, burdensome and self-fulfilling (non-alienating) – and men's activities, seen as mediated by tools and inherently alienated in industrial societies. The subsistence-based mode of production is construed as liberating, promoting wholeness of body and mind for both sexes, especially men (*ibid.*: 52–4, 216–35). Women are regarded as revolutionary due to their non-alienating labour.

Patriarchal social relations are not defined as universal, but the narrative presents patriarchy as existing throughout history, from hunting and gathering to socialist societies (*ibid.*: 66). Mies describes behaviour that imitates Big White Men, expressed as the Big Men–Little Men syndrome, and the pervasive exploitation and domination of the weak by the strong. This notion of imitation does not appear to erase the agency of other subjects in the duplication and replication of dominative and exploitative strategies by the strong over the weak. However, this attempt to grasp the heterogeneity of power makes Big White Men the centrifugal force through which all other forms of power are articulated.

Such a formulation tends towards a further reduction and homogenization of the concept of power, which defeats the search for its heterogeneity.

Fundamentally, Mies relies on essential subjects to ground a theory of social domination and exploitation that has its ultimate basis in a predatory (masculine) mode, thereby privileging patriarchal relations over class and all other vertical relations. Is this simply a problem of the universalizing tendency of grand theories, and another manifestation of the problematic of the essential, sovereign, revolutionary subject, prototypically represented by the proletariat? More recently the reticence towards grand theories has meant that patriarchy (or male domination), a fundamental feminist category, continues to circulate but flounders in a theoretical vacuum. Feminists appear to be in a quandary about how to address this theoretical crisis around grand theories and sovereign subjects. It is especially evident in development discourses.

The question of the materiality of power, most specifically patriarchy, need not be posited at the level of essential subjects, or relegated to the realm of ideology in a reinforcement of the base–superstructure building metaphor. The material manifestations of power can be theorized in its myriad expressions at both the micro and macro levels. However, it seems crucial to think the heterogeneity of power, the multiplicity of forms of its presence. The insistence of feminist speculations that centre on an essential/genetic dominative male subject is a problematic binding of (phallic) power to the male body; it *disavows* the heterogeneity of violent forms of power.[10] The critical issue is whose interest is served in such a disavowal. Moreover, I am not suggesting we abandon substantial nominal references such as women–men, worker–ruling class, North–South, which are necessary strategic risks that indicate the bodily marks of the articulation of diverse forms of power. Gayatri Spivak (1994: 66–71) challenges a poststructuralist notion that the network power/desire/interests is so heterogeneous that its articulation into a coherent narrative is counter-productive, requiring a persistent critique. She charges Foucault and Deleuze with ignoring ideology and the global articulations of power. Spivak invokes Marx's concept of the divided subject, the notion of false consciousness and the problematic of representation in the double sense of representative (liberal subject) and representation (semiotic object). I believe that it is important to think power as coherent in spite of the risks of any such representation; at the same time a critical vigilance ought to be observed to avoid the trap that we've grasped a transparent reality.

In the first place, GAD addresses itself to the fundamental structures of inequity between men and women. Ideologically, GAD sees itself as centring gender and class relations rather than women *per se*. Kabeer (1995: 65) sees the shift from women to gender relations as an extension of analysis from men and women as isolated categories, to broader interconnected relationships through which women are subordinated in the division of resources and responsibilities. However, it would be fallacious to view WID as not addressing itself to the socio-economic relations between men and women. Both WID and GAD are concerned with women's positioning *vis-à-vis* men, and both are equally gynocentric at the philosophical level. In the most general sense of the term gender is defined as 'the social meanings given to sex differences' within a given socio-cultural context. Ideologically, one of GAD's most distinguishing characteristics is its socialistic (state welfare) orientation, which is to be differentiated from conventional welfarism. This partiality to state welfare arises out of its redistributive role, and the significance of state subsidies in such areas as education, healthcare, childcare, housing and pensions, the reduction of which augments the reproductive work burdens of women. It identifies the special responsibility of the state to provide programmes to aid the work of social reproduction. Most neo-Marxists in WAD and GAD continue to be bound by an unquestioned commitment to an enlightened vision of socialistic development, entailing industrialization and modernity for the South.

While WID assumes the withering away of patriarchal ideology under the force of feminist enlightenment, GAD is concerned to unearth gender as an ideological construct in its culturally varied expressions. Gender ideology is regarded as permeating all aspects of life including material (socio-economic) practices such as work, the distribution of wealth, income and other resources, decision making, political power, rights and entitlements among others. Rather than simply asserting women's sovereign subjectivity, GAD seeks to grasp the construction and reproduction of gender identities, and the role of gender ideologies in the reproduction of unequal power relations between men and women. At the level of feminist practice this concern with gender ideology ought to encourage reflections on the impact of gender ideology on the construction and reconstruction of institutional practices and gender inequality. Gender mainstreaming has become a strategy increasingly associated with GAD, for assessing the potential and actual effects of policies and programmatic action for men and women.[11] Empowerment conceived as the harnessed, self-generating power of women to act in their own interest has become a by-word within the subfield as a whole. In spite of GAD's self-representation as gender- and class-centred, it is decidedly gynocentric.

Southern perspectives

DAWN (Sen and Grown 1987) remains a primary reference in the registration of Southern perspectives. It privileges poor, Third World women, which is in line with the imperatives of feminist developmentalism. Within developmentalism as a whole, poor bodies become the object of interventions. DAWN proffers itself as a legitimate representative of the interests of impoverished Third World women. It states:

> It is the experience lived by poor women throughout the Third World in their struggles to ensure the basic survival of their families and themselves that provides the clearest lens for an understanding of development processes. And it is *their* aspirations and struggles for a future free of the multiple oppressions of gender, class, race, and nation that can form the basis for the new visions and strategies the world now needs. (Sen and Grown 1987: 9–10)

The correspondence claimed between 'experience' and 'visions', and the centring of the Third World woman as a theoretical category, is not a materially grounded standpoint perspective in a strict sense – since from such a vantage point *labouring* activities are the essence of being – but the reference to the relationship of experience to vision, and the manifest centring of the Third World woman, creates the *effect* of a standpoint.[12] It produced a rash of feminist anxieties and reactions to the apparent installation of a sovereign, revolutionary subject (Goetz 1991).[13]

The perspective of poor women is grounded in their social location and is regarded as centred on the problems of poverty and inequality. DAWN articulates the desire of Third World women as tied to a yearning to be free from class, gender, racial and national inequalities, with a privileging of basic needs as basic rights. They envision a world in which one can maximize one's potential. DAWN criticizes the emphasis on liberal capitalism and the marginalization of basic needs which makes survival for the masses of Third World people extremely difficult.

DAWN stresses that empowerment entails a critical reflection and conceptualization of a feminist perspective.[14] They reject a monolithic viewpoint, affirming heterogeneity and diverse feminisms but recognizing the common opposition to gender oppression. Concern with other forms of oppression appears to be rhetorically hitched to being a woman, which constitutes this concern as legitimate and necessary. In other words, it seems that *difference*, grounded in experience, rationalizes the concern with other forms of oppression. I would like to look more carefully at the reference in question.

> For many women, problems of nationality, class and race are inextricably linked to their specific oppression as women. Defining feminism to include the struggle against all forms of oppression is both legitimate and necessary. In many instances gender equity must be accompanied by changes on these other fronts. But at the same time, the struggle against gender subordination cannot be compromised during the struggle against other forms of oppression or relegated to a future when they may be wiped out. (Sen and Grown 1987: 18)

This experiential justification for the necessity to address other oppressions marks a crucial Third World *difference*, a re-mark that holds to the gynocentric foundations of feminism, but simultaneously threatens to implode its limitations. The Western feminist anxiety about the figure of the Third World Woman tends to concentrate conceptually on the sovereign, revolutionary possibilities of the subject. There is an 'instinctive' sense that this new figure has the potential to displace the gynocentric figure of Woman (white, middle-class) with whom Western feminists identify. Yes! this re-mark portends the 'death' of Woman: she was recognized as a limitation from the very founding of the subfield, but Western feminism has continued to enforce her enthronement anyway, in a disavowal and non-recognition of the desire of the Other. This is not to say that the name Woman has not been significant in confronting gender oppression and exploitation globally; what is being re-marked is how such a frame obstructs the ability to tackle other forms of oppression.[15]

Should this displacement of Woman be viewed as permitting the installation of another sovereign subject, another centring? The Western feminist anxiety over the privileging of the name Third World Woman, and resistance to the new potential sovereign, ironically arose when feminism began to face the epistemological crisis of its inability to account for the Other, who took the appellation 'Woman of Colour'.[16] It is at this point that poststructuralism became attractive, since it appeared to promise a new mode of addressing this discursive problem (for example, the decentred or dispersed subject, or the non-subject). However, Woman is not a simple misnomer, catechesis or paleonymy for heterogeneous subjects in resistance, but a gynocentric disregard and repression of other forms of domination and exploitation.

No! The new name Third World Woman or other substitutes ('gender relations', for example) cannot stand in for other oppressions. Rather than thinking the impoverished Third World Woman as a sovereign, having a privileged insight into development processes, it may be more appropriate and cogent to see her positioning as a symptom of the overdetermined effects and resistances to multiple oppressions and exploitative processes. This delineation definitively takes away the authority of a sovereign, revolutionary subject posture or a self-centring, and normalizes her *vis-à-vis* other subjects, but it opens up something else. It enables a registration of the call to recognize the necessity and legitimacy of other oppressions, as a call to the wholly Other – a call to be just, an ethical imperative that transcends all specific frameworks.

Postcolonial narratives have taken up the thorny question of representation, which has had an ongoing influence on the discourse of development. Gayatri Spivak (1988) initiated a focus on the difficult issue of mediation and the representation of the subaltern woman, articulated through the double connotation of the term representation – representative (liberal subject) and representation (semiotic object). This sparked a sustained reflection on the representation of the Third World woman in Western feminist discourses and political practices. For example, Marnia Lazreg (1988) addressed the tendency to see gender relations as determined by Islam, which has the effect of stripping Algerian women of self-presence; their real existence is displaced by ahistorical signifiers of tradition such as the veil, seclusion or clitoridectomy. Chandra Mohanty (1988) contests an inclination to reduce the heterogeneity of Third World women into a single monolithic subject, a habit that is conceived of as a discursive colonization. In this practice Third World women are defined as victims of male violence, while Western feminists are positioned as the true subjects of counter-history. For Aihwa Ong (1988: 79–90) feminism unconsciously echoes a masculine will to power *vis-à-vis* the non-Western Other. The lives of Third World men and women are seen as construed in essentialist terms (as labour and reproductive power, for example). She calls for the abandonment of accustomed ways of looking at non-Western women to enable better understanding.

The essential monolithic Third World Woman who has been the object of increasing criticism is inherent to gynocentric feminism, with its centred woman subject and centred gender relations. To be sure, the woman subject is a subjective construct that White, Western middle-class women identify with, since it is the devalued aspect of their identity. What the aforementioned discourses miss is that woman is not a 'real' but a political subject, and the development discourse is part of a broader feminist discourse that is loaded with political stakes. One of the key discursive moves within feminism has been to posit woman as victim in both the North and South; such a signification is principally intended to mark the gravity of patriarchal violence that feminists are forced to resist, in an affirmation of woman's humanity. Even the idea that the Western woman is identified as liberated, while the woman in the South is seen as oppressed, is an exaggeration: the figure of the liberated woman in the North is theoretically contentious. This is not a denial of troubling representations of poor women in the South (for example, as backward, tradition-bound, illiterate, beasts of burden or victims of a barbaric patriarchy). The figure of the poor woman in the South is well suited to a victimology narrative that rationalizes the planned management and liberation of women in the South by Westernized professionals in the development apparatus. These depictions simultaneously designate a hierarchical distinction between Western and non-Western women. The side-effect of such a displacement has typically been an erasure of woman as an empowered and powerful subject, especially in view of the commanding position and forceful campaigns of Western feminism in general. The strategic discursive exhibition of the empowered Third World woman is no more 'real' than her twin, the contrary figure of the victimized woman. Since the 1970s the critiques of the discursive practices of exclusion and erasure advanced in the major industrialized countries of the world by women of colour (and by working-class and lesbian women to a lesser extent) entailed a similar call to address the heterogeneity of class, race, gender, generation, sexual orientation and so on. Going unanswered, these critiques eventually triggered a manifest political and theoretical crisis within Western (white) feminism. Many feminists of colour in the South and North expected an analysis of heterogeneity to present a truer conception of social life and subjectivities.[17]

Evidently, gynocentric femininism is constituted through modernist discourses aimed at the enlightenment of major social institutions within the South, through reform in the case of liberal feminism, and resistance/revolutionary struggle for neo-Marxists. In liberal, neo-Marxist and Southern world views, women continue to be constituted as sovereign subjects with the capacity to realize progress and development through social reform or revolutionary transformations in patriarchal social relations and societies. This enlightened, modernist legacy that installs a privileged subject – Woman, with a sovereign/revolutionary agency – has a vision of progress and development that challenges gender subordination and oppression, but like its proletarian counterpart, its centred, self-affective parameters are exclusionary and limit the possibilities for justice.

Post-development and the ordeal of the undecidable

Major development agencies have made commitments to ecological management and the neoliberal policies of structural adjustment, economic growth and capitalist accumulation. In the mid-1980s there was an intensifying focus on the link between industrialization and environmental degradation, due in part to a noticeable trend towards global warming, and the Bhopal and Chernobyl disasters. The most immediate and significant ecological limitation in the fossil age involves the capacity of biospheric sinks (soil, atmosphere and ocean) to absorb the gases and toxins emitted by industrial societies. The greenhouse effect is associated with climate turbulence, crop failures and losses in biodiversity. It is the long-term availability of resources, especially those that are non-renewable, that is perhaps the source of greatest apprehension in the long run (Bennholdt-Thomsen and Mies 1999; Sachs 1999: 166–7).

Stark images of poor Third World women burdened with fodder, fuel and water against barren landscapes – frequently published by aid agencies and NGOs in the early 1980s – dramatized the notion of their victimization by the ecological crisis in the South. Simultaneously, on the basis of a sexual division of labour in which poor women predominate in subsistence, the case was put for their special role in environmental management amidst rising environmental degradation.[18] Some feminists impugned such instrumentalism and agitated for education, training, family planning and women's control over resources to negotiate a place for them within the strategy of sustainable development.

In a discussion of the 1991 Beijing Declaration of the Group of 77 and the United Nations Conference on Environment and Development (UNCED), Wolfgang Sachs (1999: 27–33) pointed out that the South bargained for increased aid allocation (to 0.7 per cent of GNP), clean technologies and access to bio-industrial patents in exchange for good environmental behaviour. He underscored the untenability of 'catching-up' development, and how such demands reinforced the cultural hegemony of the West and the utopian ideal of Western lifestyles.

Women from various ecological perspectives and institutions from the North and South were drawn into the preparatory proceedings for UNCED. The Women's Action Agenda 21 asserted the need for a sustainable, people-centred development process. This historic collaboration between women from North and South in various preparatory proceedings – such as the World Women's Congress for a Healthy Planet (1992) and Planeta Femea (1992) – highlighted the global nature of the ecological crisis and created a feeling of global sisterhood. There was a diversity of ideological positions, from liberal feminist demands for equity on environmental concerns to a repudiation of development and modernity, but with little engagement of such differences. Feminists opted for a power bloc strategy featuring common agreements on sustainability and women's rights to inclusion (grounded on their caring sensibility), rather than an ideological war. With hindsight, feminists have questioned the effectiveness of such a strategy, which appeared to allow for easy ideological incorporation into the mainstream agenda of sustainable development, premised on economic growth and efficiency rather than sufficiency. Hence, the ideological constitution and contradiction of the fundamental category of sustainable development was not attacked, but sheltered in the compromised form of a people-centred development, an open and highly contested concept subject to diverse appropriations. An outright assault on the ruse of the marriage of development, economic growth and accumulation, sustainability and modernity would in all likelihood have fractured the new alliance, provided a stronger resistance to incorporation, but afforded an alibi for 'extremist' isolation. Preparing the ground for post-development requires that one rise to the difficult and risky task of challenging the faith of the faithful.

DAWN (Wiltshire 1992: 18–25) articulated for UNCED one standpoint of poor women in the South on the environment and development, which was grounded in local experiences of ecological strain on their basic survival. It disputed a pervasive misconception that population growth is a principal determinant, and the poor the essential agent of environmental destruction. On the contrary, DAWN argued, the poor have the greatest stake in environmental protection for their immediate survival. This viewpoint framed the ecological problem as arising from practices of global economic growth accompanied by state collusion with capital in export-oriented production, and over-consumption of resources and goods by élites from the North and South. There was a demand for a sustainable development that is locally controlled, affirmative of civil rights, and of material, spiritual and socio-cultural well-being. DAWN enunciated a claim that the poor and women in the South have the best knowledge of their local environments, problems, needs and solutions. This is the basis of a demand for the inclusion of women in environmental decision making and management.

The general coordinator of DAWN, Peggy Antrobus (1992: 3), identified the key distinction at Rio as between those espousing a 'technological fix' and those advocating alternative approaches to development. The ambiguous term 'alternative development' typically implies that there is an alternative path to what is proper to development – qualitative industrial growth and progress that produces gains comparable to those realized in the West. DAWN has been engaged in a project to elaborate a people-centred alternative development framework.[19] The DAWN debates (1995: 11–14, 22–5) on alternative development produced a schema of key components, which ranged from support for the realization of creative and fulfilling lives to the overcoming of socio-economic and cultural inequities, and the transformation of globalization and economic growth into a means to the ends of human development and a sustainable environment. What ought to be confronted is the fundamental contradiction of global capitalism and economic growth with the goals of equity, empowerment and a sustainable environment. There are notions of development that entail the fantasy that development can be something other than what it is (as in sustainable development or alternative development), a substitution of *ought* for *is*, an idealization and purification of the term development. Preserving the term development expresses an *attachment* to and faith in development. What is required is a critical operation that produces a *separation* from the notion of development, enabling a vision that fully grasps the radical import of its own critiques, drawing a line between development and post-development. A full recognition that development cannot be universalized, is environmentally destructive and grounded in exploitative social relations closes the door on recuperation by an environmental management approach that promotes efficiency and economic growth, rather than a strong demand for efficiency based on sufficiency and social justice in general. The developmental logic of global capitalism cannot accommodate such exigencies.

DAWN organized a Coalition for Alternative Development during Planeta Femea to formulate an alternative socio-economic framework and programme in which Northern networks were asked to offer critiques of their own countries' development. Braidotti *et al.* (1994: 120–1) pointed out that poor women in the South are seen as the source of the new alternative because of their central place in the balance between land, population, reproduction and production, ecological disaster and sustainable development, and multiple oppressions. They are apprehensive that the impoverished Third World woman as construed by DAWN could become the 'ultimate Other' that supports a totalizing perspective and a reversal of hierarchies, not their transcendence. They accept the materialist postulate that vision is better from below, adding that it does not guarantee superior vision. However, it is forgotten that the materialist standpoint is a strong power move that grounds a privileged, totalizing perspective.

Clearly, DAWN acts as a representative of poor women in the South, some of whom may claim the status of organic intellectuals, but the vanguard occupies a precarious position within any genetic narrative – an intellectual class standing in for poor, 'illiterate' Southern women. Representative political practice is what we cannot as yet do without, although its genetic foundations can be eclipsed. DAWN imitates a strong, problematic and risky Western gynocentric feminist move, in articulating a centred Third World woman subject, one who is thought to be in the truth – a revolutionary subject. Braidotti *et al.* exhibit an anxiety about the displacement of Northern feminists and the potential emergence of a totalizing perspective, and contest the claim of Southern representatives to speak for impoverished Third World women, a surprising gesture given the continued hegemonic power of Western (white) feminists within the field as a whole. One should be clear that the revolutionary subject is a theoretical and political fiction, not actually essential or genetic. This subject ought to be reduced to a nominal banner, albeit burdened by paleonymy and hence sedimented and overdetermined in multiple locations.[20] One can abandon the essential or genetic subject, but not the subject *per se*, a category we cannot as yet do without. The intellectual class could benefit by unburdening itself from the bonds of a Western, modernist, gynocentric fiction – the essential Third World Woman – and a self-affective, woman-centred politics, in spite of its seeming advantages, thereby unleashing the radical potential for justice beyond all frameworks, a vigilant attunement to the call to the wholly Other.[21]

I shall now consider a few works that articulate post-development perspectives, and attempt to indicate how each displays a 'trace' of the undecidable, a characteristic of decision making.[22] The ordeal of the undecidable arises out of the condition that a decision transcends its discursive supports – empirical evidence and conceptual frameworks. Making a responsible decision, since it is not bound strictly by rationality, entails a leap of faith. Whether one stands on the side of development or post-development, such a decision often entails going through the ordeal of the undecidable. Much ink has gone into thinking about what development is and whether it is happening – development as not yet or in the process of becoming, or development as myth and illusion. Wrestling with such issues often entails a moment of *aporia*: a paralysis, a quandary, a condition in which one does not know where to go – the ordeal of the undecidable.[23] The outcome of such a risk, the decision, determines whether one opts to position oneself on the side of development, post-development or somewhere else.

Maria Mies and Vandana Shiva (1993: 55–68) expound a post-development standpoint that highlights the mythology of 'catching-up' development strategies for Third World countries and gender relations. The impossibility of catching up is thought to be bound up with a colonizing logic of accumulation and growth that is based not only on an inequitable consumption of resources but also on a widening disparity between core and periphery in the face of ecological limitations. They identify colonial relationships – between core and peripheral nations, urban and rural regions, man and nature and men and women – that make it difficult for the colonized to overcome their enchantment with the lifestyle of the colonizer.[24]

Mies and Shiva (*ibid.*: 64–8) ask if 'catching-up development liberate[s] women', criticizing ineffective liberal feminist policies of equal rights for women based on affirmative action (for example, special quotas for women), in the face of the actuality of women's continuing socio-economic and political marginalization. They show that the liberal rights of freedom, equality and self-determination are premised on economic means that cannot be extended to all women in the world, but only to a small privileged class. The humanist model of emancipation for women is defined as a catching-up strategy in which men are the measure of what is properly human, and women are expected to overcome a feminine bodily existence that binds them to nature, in a pursuit of transcendence within the cultural realm.

Shiva (*ibid.*: 25–34, 70) calls for an overturning of a colonial mentality stamped by an overvaluation of industrial societies and a devaluation of subsistence-based communities, through an account of poverty creation and environmental degradation. She critiques the control of self-generating nature and regenerative life, and its manipulation into inert and fragmented raw materials in commodity production. This process is seen as transforming native values into non-value, labour into non-labour, creativity into passivity, and destruction into production through an appropriation of human and plant reproduction. Shiva advances an approach that contextualizes production and reproduction within a regenerative ecology, which is the basis of an ontology of the world as active subject not mere resource. Activation entails an overcoming of estrangement from nature's rhythms, and becoming a conscious participant within them. The project for a new anthropology and cosmology aims precisely at such an activation.[25]

The new cosmology entails an ontology of the interconnectedness of life, a consciousness of life's sacredness, necessary to the preservation of life on earth, which is identified with the feminine principle – a life force with a substantial presence. Shiva and Mies (*ibid.*: 19–20) affirm that women in the South respect the diversity and limits of nature and celebrate life's sacredness, which is conceived as grounded in the immanence of their everyday life and work in subsistence. The metaphors of proximity and distance are employed to differentiate subjects along a gendered and geographical axis, within a feminist ecological perspective. In this regard women are seen as nearer than men, and women in the South – struggling for their existence – as nearer than urban men and women in the North, but all humans are viewed as having an investment, because of their natural bodily existence. Clearly, this materialist ecological standpoint proffers a being/knowing relation with a privileged centre, Woman, with the Third World Woman at its core. This problematic modernist, materialist legacy that posits a Woman subject with an ecological consciousness inevitably runs up against the incongruence between subject position and putative consciousness, which exposes its fictive foundation. This ecologically grounded, feminist, post-development perspective can choose to ignore or address its shaky materialist subjectivity. The insistent focus on this subject has become an avoidance strategy for critics, a means of turning away from the radicalism of this standpoint. The abandonment of such a subject would undercut such an attack.

Frédérique Apffel-Marglin and Suzanne L. Simon (1994: 39–41) problematize a modern notion of self that is interpreted as determinant in the ecological crisis, and seek to affirm an ecological self and a regenerative approach rather than a productive (utilitarian) relationship to nature. They discuss the four-day festival of the menses celebrated in coastal Orissa in India, in which Apffel-Marglin spoke with a woman, Sisulata Devi, and a man, Bhikari Parida, about the nature of the identity between mothers, women and the earth. They are presented as forms of the same substance. In this festival the Earth and Mother bleed and women follow the rules pertaining to menstruation in a regeneration of the community.

Apffel-Marglin and Simon resist the reduction of the goddess to a symbol of the earth or women, defining the ontological significance as one in which the goddess is regarded as embodying the reality of the identity of women and the earth, while the generation and regeneration of the world is seen as a human, natural and divine process. This is placed in sharp contrast to the nature/culture dualism that typifies Western thought. They see the modern notion of self (autonomous and productive), and the utilitarian and exploitative relationship of modern folk to their bodies and nature as determinant in the ecological crisis, calling instead for an abandonment of modernist conceptions of liberation, the valorization of regeneration and the formation of an ecological self. This repudiation of the modernist self and affirmation of regeneration places this conceptualization within post-development.

Critical feminist engagements with developmentalism that seek inspiration in 'traditional' societies articulate a criticism from the margins of enlightenment discourses in a valorization of modes of life devalued by modernity. Because such a rationality is constituted through an encounter with modernity, enlightened discourses are neither eclipsed nor transcended: no such transcendence or absolute exteriority is as yet realizable. However, modernity and Western discourses and categories are the object of a persistent and interminable critique. The objection to the use of enlightenment categories draws attention to the limits they place on our thinking. Such categories are not easily displaced, but the difficult creative work of developing deconstructive concept-metaphors that resist hierarchical categories and Western metaphysics lends hope for a more effective theoretical and social practice of post-development.[26]

These critics are typically dismissed as espousing a regressive culturalism that naively celebrates tradition, denying the violence of such societies. I agree that there is a problematic tendency to de-emphasize the violence of 'traditional' cultures, but even when vertical social relations are acknowledged, they are typically overlooked. The insistence that there is no desire for a simple return to 'tradition' seemingly appears as a rhetorical deference to political correctness. This disavowal allows the spectre of a primitive barbarism to terrify modernist scholars and activists, and upholds the privilege of modernity. These works appropriately resist the right of modernity over 'tradition', Western over non-Western, enlightened reason over alternative modes of reasoning and faith. They attack the command and cultural hegemony of industrial production and its social relations over subsistence and all the attendant categories (for example, the valuing of productive relations over relations of reproduction/generation and regeneration; or the defining of industrial production as value and subsistence as non-value). In this critical endeavour there is an interrogation of Western notions of selfhood and a search for new 'models' of the self, 'models' that may ultimately gesture towards a process of the erasure of the subject itself, rather than its renovation. The marks of the ordeal of the undecidable are evident in the challenge to Western rationality and the appeal to notions of responsibility, faith and the sacred, and in the embracing of the gift of death – the absolute risk of an encounter with the Other and the call to the wholly Other.

Serge Latouche (1993: 115), in identifying the non-universality of modernity, points to the fact that, in spite of repeated failures, the myth of development continues to be perpetuated and failures are given circumstantial explanations. He continues to think that development and underdevelopment need to be thought in terms of a world system of asymmetrical regions, but breaks with orthodox Marxism by arguing in favour of the primacy of culture, seeing culture as prior to and alongside economic domination. Development is seen fundamentally as a Western cultural invention that has been poorly grafted in the South. Underdevelopment is construed as an effect of the collision of different cultural universes – Western and non-Western. This is not a denial of the fact that the desire for development has penetrated the South, especially among the élites. Given the extensive environmental destruction and the level of human alienation, Latouche questions whether development will have long-term viability for the West (O'Connor and Arnoux, 1993: 4–6).

Post-development is conceived as a post-Western world after the disintegration of Western civilization. Latouche takes the speculative risk of imagining this new phase as arising out of the nebula of the 'informal' society, typified by creativity and vitality. There is an emphasis on the pretence of the universality of modernity and the failure of opulence. The other side of modernity is seen as a violent systemic dereliction suffered by billions of excluded people, labelled 'castaways': these radical outcasts are subject to early death, while billions of others survive under degrading conditions without work (*ibid.*: 26–36). Development hasn't happened and the Marxian Third Worldism – the ideology of the revolutionary Third World proletariat – is pronounced dead (*ibid.*: 39). In a counterposing of the informal society to modernity, the former is defined as a paradoxical mark of difference that shakes the presumption of progress, and the sensibility of history, into an unreadable elsewhere. While modern society is seen as detaching the economic from the social, the informal society is regarded as embedding the economic with the social by reactivating networks of solidarity and reciprocity (*ibid.*: 50). This represents a premature impulse towards transcendence, the designation of a post-Western world – an unreadable elsewhere that is simultaneously a presence, that has its genesis in the informal economy and alternative social relations. It is a transcendence that seeks to break with the development narrative. One ought to exercise caution against moving too fast in pursuit of transcendence; maybe this unreadable elsewhere is indeed elsewhere.

It is argued that the concept of relative pauperization captures the dynamics of the development game, since it delineates placement and status (*ibid.*: 80). Thus, even though the poorest country can have greater quantities of roads, ports, factories, schools, hospitals and literate people, such goods are not *the* good, nor is it development (*ibid.*: 116). In the Western socio-economic mythology, 'more is better', and there is an ongoing drive against the stinginess of nature (*ibid.*: 75–88). Life is seen as a supreme, universal value expressed in the fact that it is the most fundamental human right, and the grand society has extended life, but it is valued in purely quantitative terms, with a disregard for the meaning of life in traditional cultures (*ibid.*: 91–2). The trace of the undecidable is indicated in the speculative risk of imagining a post-Western world, given that the ultimate end of the ecological crisis is unknowable, beyond calculation. In addition, the counterposing of the derelection of billions to the steady quantitative increases in goods and services, identified as the proof of the presence of development, is made to demonstrate that development is indeed a myth.

Wolfgang Sachs (1999: x–xi) sees the Western development model as an obstacle to the realization of justice and the reconciliation of humankind and nature. He advances the proposition that sophisticated, moderate-impact technologies should be created and deployed, while growth economics should be relinquished and replaced by a programme of economic efficiency (employing efficient technologies) and sufficiency (limited economic growth) based on simple living. He contends that the environmental crisis constitutes a serious blow to the notion that development through economic growth is compatible with justice, since growth can no longer be construed as inclusive (trickling down) or open-ended, as the reality of ecological limitations imposes itself. There is a criticism of the developmentalist conceptualization of 'equitable' strategies in terms of raising the socio-economic level of the poor, rather than lowering the position of the upper strata. He notes that modern optimism about human initiatives has been shattered by the ecological crisis. Sachs (*ibid.*: 170) suggests that paths to social improvement should be invented that do not overstep the limits of nature, but adds that 'a certain level of technology is necessary for overcoming chronic scarcity'. He advocates a retreat from the exploitation of the resources of the South and the use of a disproportionate share of the global commons (for example, the atmosphere and the oceans) as an important move towards global responsibility. Sachs's commitment to moderate-impact technologies and a programme of efficiency and sufficiency, abandoning growth economics, denotes a break with development and a resistance to modernist values, but not a radical turn towards regeneration nor the renunciation of industrialization. Faith in technology to alleviate chronic scarcity grounds a drive for the perpetuation of industrialization. Would moderate-impact technologies overstep the limits of nature under negotiated conditions of sufficiency? This faith is an absolute risk to harmonize responsibility to others and register the call to the wholly Other. On this question of privileging technological and industrial societies, it may be prudent to resist the modernist impulse to reinforce the existing hierarchy of modernity over 'non-modern' societies.

Development or post-development: which way for women in the south in the 21st century?

The posing of the development problematic as development or post-development invites contributors to draw a line and take a position that either reinforces developmentalism, or rejects it for a post-developmental practice (theoretical, political and socio-economic) that we are just beginning to imagine. For many scholars and activists who are grappling with this difficulty at this formative moment, such clear-cut divides constitute a near impossibility. A compelling example is Wolfgang Sachs's (1999) support for industrial production – in the context of a civilizational transformation in Western society and values, premised on a sustainable approach entailing efficiency and sufficiency – to make possible a more just and equitable relationship to the masses of people in the South. It shakes the linear developmental approach through a break with existing growth models and global capitalism, but holds on to an enlightened faith in the capacity of industry to overcome scarcity.

Post-development is not a distinct spatial region constituted through a self-conscious post-developmental mode of life, (in the future such self-conscious expressions of social organizing may well emerge); post-development is thus currently limited to a form of criticism or deconstructive practice that is just beginning to emerge. As a deconstructive practice it is an interminable criticism of developmentalism. Deconstruction is not limited to a questioning of development as theory and practice, but ought to take the risk of judgment, the risk of a decision, braving aporia and the undecidable in the call to the wholly Other.

This is precisely the risk that the contributors to this collection have taken. When you read these chapters you will be impressed by the enormity of the task and the risk, given what is at stake: the continuity of life on our planet, intricately bound up with the question of justice for all. I am writing this in New York in the immediate aftermath of the destruction of the twin towers of the World Trade Centre, a phallic American icon of global socio-economic power, the fall of which compels one to reflect on the urgency of the question of justice for the 'South', and the weight of injustice that we have had to bear. Why? What we have here is rage at an unbearable violence, which implodes in terrorism in America of an unprecedented magnitude, disrupting the normal routines of life that insulate Americans from the devastation the masses of the South endure daily.

Regardless of where contributors ultimately stand on the question of development, you will be struck by the immense effort to take up and engage a necessary but impossible question – development or post-development: which way for women in the South in the twenty-first century? It has not been an easy task: activists and scholars have come to this problematic from oblique, tentative and definitive positions. In all cases you will encounter the evidence of the undecidable – gaps, silences and the eruption of judgments reached by a logic which is not transparent but opaque, weighted in what is typically unseen, aporia and the ordeal of the undecidable. What follows is a summary of each chapter in the collection.

Part I: Aiding development or post-development

Part I addresses the theoretical and socio-economic practices that are concerned with aiding development. In Chapter 1, Jane Parpart examines the case of Participatory Rural Appraisal (PRA) in thinking the possibilities and limitations of empowerment, and ends up advocating an eclectic, more interactive and grounded approach to enlightenment values, and the use of universal Western norms to attack patriarchal values. She notes that the language of empowerment that emerged within small populist groups and NGOs has spread to mainstream aid agencies, asking what this means for gender, empowerment and participation. Parpart sees significant limitations to the PRA's emphasis on the local, and the belief that local inequities can be transcended through the powers of persuasion, discussion and inclusion. In looking at the case of women in mixed-sex organizations, she points to a continuing tendency towards the marginalization of women. Parpart maintains that transforming gender inequities requires attention to national and global power structures, and their differential impact on men and women. In respect to post-development she divides this discourse into two wings – the alternative popularist and the anti-development wings. The former is regarded as preoccupied with bottom-up participation and empowerment. Parpart cautions against anti-development approaches that abandon modernity and development, and embrace the local and traditional, as a romanticism that ignores the complexities of social change.

Kathleen Staudt's discussion of the dismantling of the master's house in Chapter 2 focuses on whether non-masters should disengage or marginally commit themselves to the masters' houses – major development organizations. She differentiates between a conflict and a collaborative model, arguing that outsiders draw lines that polarize social relations. Staudt maintains that outsiders are reluctant to acknowledge advances, while the insiders manipulate institutional mechanisms that both insiders and outsiders can exploit, which often involves compromises. She underscores the importance of recognizing a common ground between insiders and outsiders. However, Staudt cautions against post-development and post-revolutionary worlds that rarely live up to their promises, especially for women, asking whether non-masters in this post-development set see through a gender lens.

In Chapter 3 Ravina Aggarwal's 'Trails of Turquoise' challenge an exploitation of the Ladakh tradition that claims to have uncovered women's collective power and indigenous knowledge, a force capable of contesting Western development. She argues that grassroots movements are often appropriated by the middle and upper classes. There is a reflection on developmentalist initiatives within the twentieth century under nationalist and postcolonial Indian governments. Ladakh, on India's northern frontier, was the site for infrastructural and industrial agricultural projects entailing male-dominated transactions. Women's subsistence activities have been overlooked to this day and development for women centres on welfare schemes. Aggarwal notes that *perag*-clad women have made a comeback as icons of tradition in a postcolonial tourist economy. The region has become a site for 'green travel' and sustainable development, due in part to the initiatives of Helena Norberg-Hodge's (1991) essay on Ladakh. She depicted precolonial times as a period in which women had much greater social and political power over resources, while development is construed as destroying self-sufficiency, producing fragmentation and degrading the environment. Norberg-Hodge organized Women's Alliance of Ladakh (WAL) which promoted reality tours to demystify the glamour of modernity, defining women as guardians of the earth, family and community. WAL has been attacked for lacking a historical and a class analysis, and for the presumption of an authentic Ladakhan past. Aggarwal advocates a pragmatic agenda with public policies on sustainability and collective action that accounts for complex gender and class positions.

Part II: The feminization of the global economy

Part II looks at women's place within waged and non-waged labour and the impact of globalization. Saskia Sassen's analysis of counter-geographies of globalization in Chapter 4 traces a variety of cross-border profit circuits, reproduced on the backs of disadvantaged women from the South struggling to survive in formal, informal and illicit labour markets, typified by rapid growth and globalization. They are facilitated by a growth in unemployment, the closure of small- and medium-sized enterprises oriented to national markets, and large government debt. Sassen proposes that there is a systematic link between the growing presence of women in such circuits and the rise of unemployment, shrinking male employment opportunities, debt and falling government revenues, which have given rise to the significance of alternative ways of making a living, profit making and government revenue making. Key circuits are the prostitution of women and children, and the predominantly female labour market migrations. She suggests that there is a partial feminization of survival in which households, marginal 'licit' enterprises, governments and whole communities are becoming increasingly dependent on women for survival. This formulation departs from the prototypical analyses of globalization that tend to render gender-specific dynamics invisible. Sassen focuses on strategic sites where globalization can be studied from a feminist perspective. Her emphasis on survival in the context of globalization and a Northern development that undermines the conditions for development in the South represents a break with conceptual metaphors that present the South as developing.

In Chapter 5 Marianne Marchand unpacks aspects of the dominant discourse on globalization, showing the multidimensional, mediated and unequal effects of global restructuring. She engages a relational approach to look at ideological constructions, social relations and sexed bodies. First Marchand addresses the main tenets of globalization, and the gendered and interlocking transformations of the global political economy. Then she concentrates on the gender dynamics of globalization in the South. Finally she examines specific transformations in Mexico's maquiladora industry and their relationship to the re-articulation of space and identities linked to an emerging cosmopolitanism.

This last section of her essay advances the key proposition that a triple process of feminization is taking place: a feminization of the labour force, both female and male; a feminization of Mexico's politicians and political economy; and a symbolic feminization. Marchand identifies the development of both a global and a regional civil society. At the regional level in North America, she points to an élite-led regionalism connected to an exclusive cosmopolitanism, and an oppositional regionalism with an ethics based on a regional identity that seeks an inclusive cosmopolitanism aimed at social and environmental justice. The significance of these practices of resistance is thought to lie not only in an alternative vision and identity, but also in the construction of a regional civil society.

Part III: More worldly feminisms

Part III entails a critical reflection on feminist theories and practices of development and post-development. In Chapter 6 Marnia Lazreg ponders the limitations of postmodern/post-development (PMPD) thinking on development, especially the dismissal of the liberatory aspects of enlightened rationality (in Marxism, for example). She sees the empowerment approach as an expression of PMPD perspectives, arguing that its confessional mode aims to give Third World women a voice, a romantic feminist act of creationism. She laments the transformation of women's lives into a discourse, and the indignity of making other women speak for us. What seems to be signalled is the Western philosophical tension between the uncovering of subjugated knowledge by one who is suppose to be 'in the truth' – the Third World woman – and the confessional mode of speech. Lazreg points out that postmodernism does little to problematize the researcher's own investments in development.

Lazreg charges postmodernists with reifying globalization as a natural or irreversible process, adding that PMPD advocates are absorbed with the discursive management of globalization, and that management through gender requires canvassing the world, access to international funding and the distribution of dwindling aid. Lazreg identifies a shift from women in development as beneficiaries to 'participants' and to agents of civil society. She objects to the encouragement of locals in decision making that simultaneously precludes access to the knowledge and means to change their positioning in the global economy. Lazreg argues that a postmodern analysis cannot account for women's poverty and struggles to survive, pointing to the limits of discourse analysis and its inability to resolve the modernist view that female subjectivity is socially constructed. She contends that people of the South want commodities and development. Lazreg concludes with an assertion that 'posted' feminist development theory is conservative, and that the will to knowledge may have reached a point of no return in a postmodern cul-de-sac.

In Chapter 7 Tani Barlow rethinks the development discourse, and the question of access to the desire of the Other and the issue of mediation. She insists that one cannot encounter the desire of a subaltern Chinese woman without engaging the mediated subjects of a complex, situated, revolutionary historical formation. Three feminist formations of the subject 'Chinese women' are considered: woman as biogenetic agent, revolutionary subject and eroticized consumer.

The biogenetic agency of woman was rationalized in support of a eugenics programme aimed at advancing the national biological matrix. The constitution of woman as revolutionary subject entailed an identification of her as second class, slave-like and underdeveloped, with the goal of transforming her into a full subject, the social equal of man. Woman as eroticized consumer was directed towards a valorization of a sacrificed feminine difference under neoliberalism. Barlow concludes with a look at Chinese revolutionary agency, understood as encompassing a desire to end injustice, and mediated through an often-failed but extraordinarily potent vision of socialist revolution in which gender is a vector of power and injustice.

Frédérique Apffel-Marglin and Loyda Sanchez criticize the blind deployment of a feminist development apparatus in Andean communities in Chapter 8. It examines the case of the Bolivian state and the operations of the Ministry of Gender, Generation and Family Affairs with its programmes and projects directed at the development and emancipation of women in the *campesino* community. The state is recognized as having a hidden agenda to control women's fertility, since the right to choose is regarded as an indication of the level of development of the nation at the international level.

The need to discipline the body is questioned, and so is the presumption that the existing gender relations are detrimental to women. The authors question Western conceptualizations of the body – its unicity, essentiality and variable gender – and define the application of sex/gender categories as a neocolonial operation. The notion of personhood in the Andean context is comprehended as radically non-essential. This is thought to be evident in the notion of the body as a duality – male and female. There is a conception of being such that one can be a seed, a mountain, an animal: such an ontology provides an alternative to the anthropocentrism of the West. Development is conceived as producing individuals and citizens for the Bolivian state, which violates indigenous community and cosmology.

Part IV: The science question in development

Part IV focuses on the tension between local knowledge and Western science and asks whether Western science is a regime of domination or an objective body of knowledge and practices in demystifying repressive local ideologies, and an ally in the realization of a sustainable environment. In Chapter 9 Vandana Shiva raises fundamental questions about our responsibility to other species, and the integrity of boundaries between species. She challenges the transgression of such boundaries by patriarchal capitalists, and denounces the intellectual support of postmodern feminists. There is a reflection on the place of cows in Indian cosmology and the sustainability of Indian agriculture, identifying these animals as a source of energy, fertility, nutrition and leather, in contrast to the green and white revolutions, which are defined as inefficient and wasteful. In addition, trade liberalization is seen as promoting the slaughter of cows for meat exportation, threatening the small farmers' integrated livestock–crop production systems. The demand for Indian beef is prompted by the elimination of cows infected by mad cow disease. The genesis of mad cow disease is located in the processing of dead animals to feed healthy cattle, and the denial of authorities that the disease can jump the species barrier. Furthermore, there was a lifting of the ban to sell infected beef to the South in 1996. Shiva explicates this case to demonstrate that there are ecological boundaries that ought to be respected. Shiva envisions mad cows as symbols of a world view that perceives no difference between machines and living beings, herbivores and carnivores among others – an anti-ecological, industrial civilization. She concludes that the challenge of liberating strategies is to include other races, genders and species.

In Chapter 10 Banu Subramaniam, James Bever and Peggy Schultz take up the issue of sustainable development by examining the expression of the ideology of development in the discourse of invasion biology. These scientists situate themselves between the conventional norms of science that define it as objective, value-neutral and epistemologically pure, and radical critiques that view science as inherently reductionist, dominative and epistemologically violent. They oppose a monolithic conception of science in which it is seen as uniform in its methodology, epistemology and ideology. There is a rejection of nature as an idyllic and benign object of exploitation by science and global capitalism, and an identification of nature as including natural toxins, pathogens and parasites that can produce negative feedback cycles that do not facilitate a sustainable ecology, conditions often denied by ecofeminism. In addition, there is a repudiation of binary categories – exalting either science or local knowledge, or the primacy of the global or the local – in favour of the negotiated space 'in between' such binaries.

These scholars look at invasion biology because it exemplifies the effects of not only biological processes, but cultural and political dynamics. Hence, the ideological complexities of development are shown to manifest themselves in a narrative of political panic around exotic plants. Exotic or 'immigrant' species that enter new habitats are believed to have an adverse impact on desirable native species and degrade the ecosystem, producing a national crisis in America. This is deduced as a displacement of anxiety around alien people on to plants and animals. There is a critique of a managerial approach that polices borders rather than analyzing the ecological conditions, produced by development, that foster the reproduction of 'foreign' plants and animals. This case study leads to a fundamental questioning of ecological practices and such categories as native and foreign, natural and unnatural. This form of analysis is regarded as allowing for the possibility of understanding the natural world in a way that sees humans as participants and co-creators of natural life.

Meera Nanda examines the limits and the dangers of local knowledge in an affirmation of Western science in Chapter 11. She castigates postcolonial intellectuals who approach the West from a presumption of radical difference, and who reject modernity and development. She contrasts such intellectuals with subjugated populations (for example, untouchables) who embrace a humanist vision precisely because science is thought to allow them to penetrate the mystification of their local knowledge and power structures. She raises fundamental questions such as how deep is the difference between a *dalit* woman and a Westernized Indian woman, and whether we can assume the consent of subalterns in embracing their local knowledge. Nanda is disconcerted by postcolonial and post-development critics who see development as a source of violence, both real and symbolic. She notes that in India ecofeminism has been coopted by rich upper-caste rural males. Nanda concludes that a critique of development must engage patriarchy, caste and other inequities rationalized by traditional cosmologies, and cannot therefore accept the terms of local knowledge, pointing to the value of modern science in this regard.

The debates around science and its place in the reproduction of a sustainable ecosystem are crucial to the emerging discourses on post-development. This is clearly evident in the complex, multifaceted dialogue and competing perspectives that emerge from the various contributing authors within this section on science.

Part V: Stories from the field

Part V is structured in part around ethnographic narratives and the complex local dynamics of fieldwork. In addition, it seeks to theorize fieldwork as an intricate part of a participatory practice. In Chapter 12 Patience Elabor-Idemudia examines the possibilities and limitations of participatory research (PRA, for example) as a strategy for the production of knowledge and alternative development. The value of development research is deemed questionable, since 'advances' in knowledge do not typically improve the material conditions of local people. There is a criticism of the denigration of indigenous knowledge, and top-down knowledge production characterized by asymmetrical power relations between researchers and subjects in the research process.

Elabor-Idemudia advances a feminist participatory approach in which she catalogues the core features of the participatory approach – political action, individual consciousness raising, democratic relationships and decision making, skill acquisition and the inclusion of local knowledge. The feminist perspective starts from the experiences of women and legitimizes their contributions to development. It strives towards openness, egalitarian relationships, reciprocity, mutual disclosure and self-disclosure. Elabor-Idemudia raises such issues as who will participate in what activities, given an emancipatory orientation. She condemns international aid agencies for settling for the political and economic management of underdevelopment, rather than attempting to transform such conditions. In a discussion of an alternative vision Elabor-Idemudia points out that Eurocentric strategies have failed to realize sustainable economic development, and underscores the need for a development approach that is centred on and directed towards the putative beneficiaries. She identifies the need to look at indigenous models to protect the environment and promote sustainability.

In Chapter 13 Piya Chatterjee's analysis centres on the contradictions of her fieldwork practice in an examination of the history and politics of women and labour on the tea plantations of North Bengal, India, in the 1990s. She asks how and why *adivasi* and Nepali women emerge as primary workers, identifying a feminization of the commodity and the labour involved in tea production. She begins by pinpointing her authorial location and power – ethnic Bengali, Brahmin, upper-middle-class and female (subordinate) – at the apex of socio-political power in North Bengal. There is a cataloguing of the place of gender and status in her positioning as a *memsahib*. Chatterjee is conscious of the significance of the gift of time by the women workers, and the extent to which her research was dependent on leisure. Second, she thinks such contradictions through the questions posed by the subjects of her study. For example, Chatterjee was interrogated by elders of the Santhali community about the purpose and the benefits of the study and the book for the community, given that it would be written in the English language. Third, Chatterjee reflects on the efforts of the plantation women to organize a self-help group and its significance for thinking through the possibilities and limitations of doing collaborative work. In this regard the women rejected the offer for funding to start a clinic because they did not want 'charity'. Hence, 'development' is not conceived simply as material gain, since empowerment overrides socio-economic 'progress' in resistance to a neo-colonial re-territorialization.

The women of the plantation started an organization, opened a savings account and began a small piggery. The organization focused on small enterprises and building trust within the group around monetary matters. Later, there was a discussion about opening a clinic which was sorely needed, but it was beyond the means of the group. In a debate about receiving significant outside funding, the women opted to resist what they saw as charity in favour of autonomy.

In Chapter 14 Ramona Pérez seeks to understand the ritualized public violence, predominantly by men towards women, during fiestas within the community of Atzompa, a primary tourist destination outside Oaxaca, Mexico. Atzompa has become less dependent on subsistence agriculture and male wage labour, and increasingly dependent in the last thirty years on crafts and petty commodity production, and female wage labour in formal and informal economies. Pérez thinks the fiestas as an ideological and physical space where religion, social roles and formal political relations are reaffirmed and contested.

Pérez articulates a materialist, base–superstructural formulation of male abuse of women during the fiestas. It is construed as a release of suppressed hostilities during alcoholic binges that arose from women's emerging socio-economic and political power within the community. She argues that women consciously or unconsciously perpetuate the patriarchal structure of the fiestas to contain and control a more general violence and subordination through the reproduction of a symbolic subordination. Women are thought to accept domestic violence as a natural reaction to their increasing autonomy. During the fiestas drunken individuals are allowed to air their feelings, and are not held accountable for violent behaviour that is condemned in other contexts.

It seems to me that if the women of Atzompa feel compelled to accept male violence as a reaction to men's displacement within a tourist-based service sector, then this indicates a complex 'developmental' process in which economic benefits for women are *offset* by an intensification of patriarchal violence. This dynamic problematizes the very category of development with its notion of progress, since material 'progress' entails a regression – an escalation in male violence.

Part VI: Other bodies

Part VI critically evaluates the ideology of overpopulation and the population establishment, and the pursuit of empowerment and women's reproductive rights. It also examines non-Western constructions of gendered bodies and 'subjectivity'. In Chapter 15 Wendy Harcourt discusses a paradigm shift in population and development, evident at the International Conference on Population and Development (ICPD) in Cairo in 1994. It was characterized by a shift in concern from population expansion to women's rights and empowerment. However, this ideological turn has not produced significant transformations in the concrete approaches to medicine, health and cultural practices, but has been mired within entrenched bureaucratic systems and deteriorating socio-economic conditions. She insists that in spite of this Cairo opened up a space for negotiation that is crucial to any debate on development or post-development for women. What is implied is that the political projects and strategies to realize empowerment and reproductive rights for women, and the crisis of development that constitutes their context, are highly significant for an alternative development or a post-development alternative. This discursive breakthrough is seen as emerging out of the interplay of knowledge and power structures, and is important to women's empowerment, but it obfuscates mechanisms of disempowerment.

In an analysis of the difficulties of implementing the universal agreement on reproductive rights and health at the local level, she notes that such agreements are subject to diverse interpretations in different cultures and geopolitical contexts. Harcourt points to the emergence of a post-Cairo people-centred reproductive health framework aimed at a local rather than an externally imposed agenda. There is a recognition of the risks that women face under conservative/repressive political regimes. She underscores the importance of gender approaches to body politics, and the broader economic and political processes that entail a politics of place that responds to globalism. Place-based strategies are defined as encompassing work at three sites (women's bodies, the environment and socio-public spaces), but also entail a questioning of hierarchies, a resistance to male domination and the development of confidence in one's own creativity.

Esther Wangari engages in a critique of the population establishment and feminist support for problematic planning policies in Chapter 16. She underlines the ideological embeddedness of theoretical perspectives that tend to racialize putative cultural differences to explain social problems, in so doing obscuring the ideological hegemony of the West. Hence, Western culpability for such problems as high fertility rates and the spread of HIV is erased, and these issues are framed in terms of local cultural practices.

The notion that fertility rates determine resource depletion is challenged by pointing to the place of Westernized patterns of consumption, corruption and Western macro-level policies at the local level, and the global demands on local resources to satisfy Western consumption needs. The pervasive ideology that high fertility rates limit economic growth – rather than global capitalism with its unequal exchange, austere SAP policies, high debt and so on – is soundly criticized. Wangari persuasively undermines this ideology which continues to legitimize the violent imposition of reproductive technologies on the bodies of impoverished women in the South, disregarding health, consent and 'free' choice in the pursuit of the higher goal of sustainable development. Taking up the case of invasive birth control in her native Kenya, Wangari reconceptualizes the politics of reproductive technologies, shifting the focus from abstract individual rights that support general notions of bodily autonomy and empowerment to rights located within class and gendered forms of socio-economic power. She questions the tendency to rate women's access to reproductive technologies as empowering in itself, without comprehending the local and global socio-economic context, and the distinctions in health care, forms of technology and modes of programme deployment that produce widely divergent effects.

Wangari points to the silencing of women in the South who frame their concerns in terms of class, gender equity and the collusion of state power with global capitalism, the International Planned Parenthood Federation (IPPF) and international aid agencies. She calls on Western feminists to situate themselves in respect to such practices, and to assess institutional policies critically. Wangari is interested in racist ideologies of population control, and in the deployment of reproductive technologies alongside an abstract rights discourse to reduce populations in the South while ignoring Westernized consumption patterns at the local and global levels, and their effect on resource depletion in the South. These concerns place her contribution squarely within the parameters of a post-development criticism that centres on environmental degradation, the rapid depletion of resources, and the question of justice for people in the South.

In Chapter 17 Sylvia Marcos's analysis presents a representation of Mesoamerican corporeality as distinct from Western notions of the body. It is in line with other feminist post-developmentalist reflections on 'indigenous', 'traditional' and alternative constructions of community, bodies and 'subjectivity' that stimulate a critical engagement with Western notions of self, culture and philosophy. She takes a look at ancient Mexico, most especially the ideas and beliefs of the Nahuas of central Mexico, and thinks the relevance of such concepts as duality, equilibrium and fluidity in perceptions and constructions of 'gendered' bodies. For example, a masculine–feminine duality is fundamental to the creation, regeneration and sustenance of the cosmos. Marcos identifies a fluidity and reversibility of the terms of the concept, giving rise to a bipolarity: femininity is always in transition to masculinity, and vice versa.

Another core concept is that of a fluid equilibrium, a dynamic conceptualization of equilibrium. It modifies dual opposite pairs, promoting a constant movement towards balance, and the preservation of order in the everyday life of the cosmos. She makes a case for the centrality of the feminine within the symbolic realm, evident in the foundational conceptualization of the feminine as the originary force of the universe that gives rise to a masculine and feminine duality. In addition, women owned and administrated property. In contrast to Western body–mind dualisms, in the Mesoamerican tradition exterior and interior are not separated by skin; inside and outside are subject to a continuous exchange, and the body is open to the cosmos. In a discussion of the metaphors of pleasure and eroticism, Marcos surmises that women in Aztec society were venerated not only for their fertility and reproductive capacity, but as subjects of desire.

Although the essays in this collection are located within specific sections, most of them are conceptually broad and overlap multiple section categories. They are all in critical dialogue with each other on the question of development. For example, within Part I (Aiding Development) Staudt properly asks whether post-developmentalists see through a gender lens, and cautions that post-revolutionary worlds rarely live up to expectations. Parpart takes up the challenge to formulate a postmodern post-development empowerment perspective that takes account of women, but continues to acknowledge enlightenment values and universal, Western norms. Aggarwal confronts the exploitation of Ladakh's tradition, and the myth making of feminist post-developmentalists who misrepresent 'indigenous' women and 'traditional' societies as empowering to women, ignoring the inequities and élite power of both traditional and modern societies. In Part II (Locating Women/Locating Work), Sassen and Marchand separately put forth theses that globalization entails a feminization of labour. Marchand sees this dynamic manifested in the spread of maquiladoras, in the feminization of male labour and at the symbolic level of the state in Mexico. However, Sassen articulates the provocative thesis that feminization appears to be a general spatial operation of globalization in the South. Politically, Marchand points to the emergence of a regional civil society. It is unclear what the political implications of a general feminization could be. In either case, any post-development theoretical or political practice ought to think the significance of the feminization of the current global restructuring process. Within Part III (More Worldly Feminisms) there are manifest tensions between, on one hand, Lazreg's critique of 'posted' feminism and her affirmation of an enlightened developmentalism, and, on the other, Apffel-Marglin and Sanchez's critique of developmentalist feminism and its impact on the *campesino* community. Barlow's reiteration of the difficult issue of mediation, which underscores the mediated access to the Other, is a call for vigilance to all activists and scholars regardless of their positions on development.

In Part VI (Other Bodies) Harcourt discusses the topic of population and development, and the shift from a preoccupation with population expansion to women's rights and empowerment, underscoring the value of the space for negotiation opened by the ICPD in 1994, even though she recognizes the extensive obstacles to the realization of such an agenda. Wangari presents a contrast at the level of the concrete practices of the population establishment and its racist ideologies. In an explication of the Kenyan case, she problematizes the abstract reproductive rights discourse, and a notion of empowerment that likewise fails to account for real-life conditions. Another sharp contrast exists between the essays by Shiva and Nanda in Part IV (The Science Question in Development). Shiva challenges the violence of Western industrial science and the development enterprise; in contrast, Nanda sees many postcolonial or postmodern intellectuals as misguided and preoccupied with radical difference. Nanda affirms the value of a conventional notion of Western science and humanism in opposing the authority of local knowledge and power, while Shiva articulates the virtues of local knowledge for environmental and cultural sustainability. It is left to Subramaniam, Bever and Schultz to take a position that embraces both Western science and local knowledge in the realization of a sustainable ecosystem.

Notes

1 See G. Koczberski (1998: 395–409) and Eva Rathgeber (1990: 495–6) for a discussion of the extent to which WID remains entrenched within aid agencies.

2 See Margaret Snyder (1995: 18–19) on the determinate role of Third World feminist activism in the formation of the field. She highlighted four factors: the multiplication of member states in the United Nations with the decline of colonialism; disillusionment with modernization theories of the 1960s; evidence of Third World women's productive activities; and the rebirth of feminism in industrialized countries.

3 Arturo Escobar (1995) sees the underdevelopment–development dichotomy and the ranking of the world into First, Second and Third Worlds as expressing a mode of Western representation, rather than the reality of social life, while Serge Latouche (1993) views underdevelopment as a collision of different cultural universes. DAWN (1995: 6) conceives of the Third World as comprising both the slowest- and the fastest-growing economies.

4 However, in the early 1970s, Margaret Bruce (UN secretariat head for the women's commission) stated that most governments and NGOs felt that development would be beneficial to women (Irene Tinker 1990: 29).

5 See P. Richards (1983); J. Guyer (1984); M. Mbilinyi (1990) and A. Whitehead (1990) for a challenge to an oversimplifying tendency that locates women within subsistence and men in the modern sector, thereby underestimating women's participation within cash cropping.

6 The concept-metaphor of recognition is in debt to the broader discourse of the master–slave relation. See G. W. F. Hegel (1977); G. Bataille (1991); J. Derrida (1978) and J. Benjamin (1988) among others.

7 I. M. Young (1985: 173–83) defines gynocentrism as the privileging of feminine values such as interdependence, caring and nurturance, playfulness and poetic expressions. Women's oppression is construed as the devaluation of the feminine. It entails a rejection of masculine/humanist valorizations of autonomy, individualism, abstract rationality, instrumentalism and so on. She rightly identifies the limits and value of both gynocentrism and humanism. However, I think that gynocentrism, as she understands it, entails as strong a notion of victimization and outrage as humanism against women's oppression. Even though there is a tendency to tie 'feminine' values to the private domain, it is entirely appropriate for gynocentric values to contest masculinist values in the public political realm. Young (*ibid.*: 181) sees gynocentrism as being especially open to analyses of other structures (such as racism and classism), but that is mere wishful thinking; it is immanently woman-centred. I have appropriated the term gynocentrism to define a *woman-centred* theoretical discourse and political practice, wholly conscious that this has been the defining characteristic of feminism as a whole. In all likelihood feminism as a discursive form is too restrictive and self-affective to allow for the inclusion of others and other relations of domination and exploitation on an equal footing to gender relations.

8 Georges Bataille (1991) and Jacques Derrida (1978) identify sovereignty with non-recognition and death. However, I am using the concept of a sovereign consciousness to refer to a consciousness that is conceptualized as independent and excellent, with power and authority. It can confer recognition or non-recognition. Jacques Lacan (1977: 41–2; 1981: 74–6) sees misrecognition as tied up with the mirror stage, narcissism, aggressivity and the imaginary, while recognition emerges in relationship to the Other.

9 Time-budget studies and studies of expenditure of income emphasize the fact that women's working day tends to be longer, and that a greater proportion of their income and resources are devoted to the family. What is often forgotten is the extent to which participation in networking for men (and increasingly for women) is crucial to status, employment opportunities and promotions, not leisure *per se*.

10 This idea of disavowal entails the idea of a repression, something that is held back, namely, the representatives of heterogeneous power. See Lacan (1981: 162, 216–18, 251).

11 Gender mainstreaming is bound up with the gynocentric drive for gender equity within development. Feminists expect this approach to transform development, alleviate poverty and correct deficiencies and inefficiencies at the socio-economic level, which are assumed to be produced by an inattention to gender within development projects and programmes. It is difficult to comprehend how adherents could have such high expectations.

12 S. Harding (1991: 120, 124) interprets the Marxian standpoint as defined by human activity (not merely labouring activity) which structures and limits consciousness. She goes on to make a distinction between a mere claim and a standpoint, arguing that a standpoint begins from women's experiences or perspectives, but is characterized by articulated observations and theories about nature and social relations. This represents a very broad or general conceptualization of a standpoint which is pervasive within feminism, and in debt to the being/knowing relationship.

13 However, even before DAWN's centring of the Third World woman, she constituted an underlying symptom/anxiety, since she is arguably the heiress apparent in a feminist epistemological logic in debt to materialism that privileges subjugated positions and knowledge(s). See B. Burris *et al.* (1973: 329–37) and Donna Haraway (1988) for expressions of anxiety. This anxiety is attached to an envious resistance and fear of the displacement of the category woman with whom white middle-class intellectuals identify, and the enthronement of the other woman. See Goetz (1992), Braidotti *et al.* (1994), and Hirshman (1995) for other expressions of anxiety. See Sigmund Freud (1989: 72–74, 101–102) on fear of castration, and anxious expectation in which the combination of realistic and neurotic anxiety is in disproportion to the 'danger'.

14 I am concerned about the emergence of a developmentalist conceptualization of empowerment that expounds a liberal idealist notion of power, whereby power, like the proverbial layered cake, grows continuously with few if any losers. Equally dismaying is a psychologistic conceptualization of empowerment in which power is about self-perceptions and feelings – a feel-good term. The emerging politics of empowerment is becoming a Western project for the building up of the Third World woman, from object to empowered subject – ironically, a subject that is still an object of and subject to Western, gynocentric feminism: a perverse practice of empowerment indeed. This sovereign, juridical subject is fast becoming a privileged feminist project of development, one that has the advantage of being non-threatening to global capitalism.

15 See T. M. Simone's (1989) discussion of the end of racism as knowing how to 'die', and resistances against 'death'. Also Derrida (1993) on 'death', border-crossings and limitations.

16 In the American context bell hooks (1984) called for a movement by minority women from the margins to the centre of feminism, while G. Spivak (1988b) resisted the marginal designation which shores up the centre, underscoring the structural relationship between the margin and centre, and challenging the assumed boundary between the one and the other. The margin–centre relation signifies hierarchical power. Although some margins may always exist, pushing back the margins in the pursuit of justice is an imperative.

17 *Feminism/Postmodernism/Development* (Marchand and Parpart 1995) elaborates this thematic of representation and calls for a deconstruction of the development discourse, while acknow-

ledging the real problems facing poor women in the South, and a need to address development questions rather than reject development altogether. Such a move precludes a sceptical attitude towards development *per se*.

18 The significant work of I. Dankelman and J. Davidson (1988) depicts poor women in the South as victims and simultaneously identifies the organizing initiatives of women in resistance to environmental degradation. The emergence of the concept of empowerment, popularized by DAWN and other grassroots organizations, has forced a decisive shift away from the language of victimization.

19 Popular or people-centred development stresses empowerment and participation (Brohman 1996: 345). R. Munck (1999: 202) defines this approach as socialistic. The participatory approach is burdened by the democratic problem of mediation in respect to the representative subject, power and knowledge, and an underestimation of the effects of regional and global dynamics on local initiatives.

20 A. M. Goetz (1991: 134–50) critically engages the sceptical contestation of all claims to knowledge that emphasizes its mediated and particularistic quality. She advocates a more rigorous, materialist analysis and a claim to know that recognizes the partiality and situatedness of knowledge, identifying a necessity to take a position and be responsible. More rigorous, refined and elaborate frameworks are necessary, but are simply guardrails; they cannot protect against the mediated, partial and situated quality of all knowledge under consideration, however provisional. The will to be just should entail a recognition of the limits of the frame and a willingness to take the risk of travelling beyond it in the pursuit of justice.

21 For a discussion of the call to the wholly Other see Derrida (1992: 19–27; 1995: 82–115). Here he speaks of the relation of alterity to the Other, justice as absolute alterity, being *juste* with justice, singularity, responsibility, undecidability and faith, and much more besides.

22 Gilbert Rist (1997) sees development as an ideology with no basis in reality. He identified three clear *alternative* paths: first, the management of a perverse socio-economic system, regarded as both obligatory and impossible; second, the invention of new forms of social relations inspired by tradition that privilege autonomy, entailing an abandonment of productionist accumulation; third, a speculative approach encompassing the destruction of the ideology of development, a critique of the prevailing socio-economic imagery and the development of new basic concepts. He sees all these strategies as not only transgressive, but preparing the ground for 'post-development'. Other scholars (Munck 1999; Pieterse 2000) make a distinction between an anti-development or counter-development approach and a postmodern development. Arturo Escobar (1995: 199) cautions against the emergence of a postmodern development perspective and practice that attempts to recuperate development within the global ecological crisis.

23 Derrida (1992: 24) stresses that the ordeal of the undecidable (suspenseful impasse) cannot be surpassed or sublated but is lodged as a ghost in every decision.

24 Modernist feminist sympathizers who see their role as representing the desire of the Other/ 'subaltern', often assert that the South wants modernity and development, without asking themselves about the place from which they or the Other speaks. How can the Other not want commodities (translated as development), if their social life is commodified, their immediate survival dependent on it? Western and Southern scholars have the most difficulty defining what development is, but this does not shake the assurance that the Other wants it. How is this certainty that the other wants development mediated by a modernist lens?

25 The distinction between a critique of science and anti-science, where science is under the ideological hegemony of a violent global capitalism, is a small one indeed, a critical opening and abstract potentiality at the level of concrete socio-economic practices. See Banu Subramaniam, James Bever and Peggy Schultz (in this volume) and J. N. Pieterse (2000: 178–9) for perspectives that support such a discrimination.

26 See R. Munck (1999) for a discussion of the failure of post-development to transcend Western categories. J. N. Pieterse (2000: 175–91) presents a facile distinction between what is Western and what is not. Geography has too much significance, and qualitative markers in this distinction are virtually absent.

Part I

Aiding Development or Post-Development

1

Lessons from the Field
Rethinking Empowerment, Gender and Development from a Post-(Post-?)Development Perspective

Jane Parpart

Empowerment has become a 'motherhood' term, embraced by development practitioners from the World Bank to the smallest NGOs. It seems that empowering the poor (including women) to improve their lives has become a stock practice and an uncritically accepted goal of most of the development community. While the language of empowerment first surfaced among small, populist NGOs with their preference for small-scale, grassroots development interventions, by the mid-1990s even the World Bank had taken up the term. Indeed, the *World Development Report* 2000/2001, which calls for a concerted attack on world poverty, has an entire section devoted to empowerment.

Of course, empowerment tends to mean different things to different players – mainstream development agencies such as the World Bank generally look to empowerment to improve efficiency, while more alternative agencies[1] frequently see (or at least claim) it as a metaphor for fundamental social transformation. Yet empowerment as praxis has for the most part been seen as a very localized and personal issue, one that requires individuals and groups to struggle towards new consciousness and actions. Consequently practitioners concerned with empowerment, including the empowerment of women, have tended to be those who *do* rather than those who *theorize about* development.

It is not surprising, then, that development practitioners of all persuasions have found Participatory Rural Appraisal (PRA) an attractive means for facilitating empowerment of the poor, including women. PRA emphasizes hands-on, accessible techniques for gathering information and involving the marginalized in description, analysis and solutions to development problems. While acknowledging the influence of populist development critics such as Robert Schumacher

(1989) and Paulo Freire (1970), the primary architect of PRA, Robert Chambers, insists that PRA is a practical rather than theoretical endeavour, which has little to learn from theoretical debates. This stance undoubtedly has contributed to PRA's popularity, as it obscures potential contradictions with a mass of methods and techniques.

This chapter argues that empowerment cannot simply be read off a set of practices like Participatory Rural Appraisal (PRA). It requires both theoretical as well as practical considerations and inputs. Lessons from the field have much to tell us, but so do theoretical debates. Indeed, the various debates have much to learn from each other as well. Much of the scholarship on empowerment has emerged from the critiques of feminists, environmentalists and poststructuralists who have quarrelled with the top-down, Western-centric approach of mainstream development (Crush 1995; Pieterse 1998; Rowlands 1998). Ironically, the move towards the language of empowerment by mainstream agencies does not seem to have bridged this divide. The lengthy bibliography published in the most recent *World Development Report* lists almost no references to this literature, including the extensive scholarship on women, gender and empowerment (see Afshar 1998; Kabeer 1994; Parpart, Rai and Staudt 2002; and Rowlands 1997, 1998). Moreover, critiques of post-development approaches such as anti-development and alternative development[2] (Cooper and Packard 1997; Corbridge 1998 ; and Pieterse 2000) as well as the issues raised by political economists (Payne 2001) throw up crucial questions about the possibilities and limitations of both post-development and mainstream approaches to empowerment and development.

This chapter calls for a more interactive, grounded approach to empowerment and development, one that draws on the lessons from both praxis and theory, from the South as well as the North (Mama 2001). Using gender as an entry point for rethinking empowerment as a tool for development (however one defines it), this chapter tries to think in new ways about empowerment, gender and development by bringing theory(ies) and practice together in ways that permit us to explore the possibilities and limitations of empowerment as a means for improving the lives of women and men in a highly gendered world.

Debating development: new voices, new approaches

Before the late 1980s, the path to development may have been contested, but the end goal – development – came in for little criticism. Although not established as a professional subject or practice until the 1930s, ideas about development were rooted in Enlightenment thinking, with its belief in progress, science and modernity (Cowen and Shenton 1995). Development was seen largely as a technical problem, wherein Northern 'experts' helped Southern governments to introduce Western technology, institutions and practices. As long as states followed the 'rules' their transformation was practically guaranteed (Rostow 1960). When these promises did not bear fruit in the 1960s, some academics and activists in Latin America and other parts of the South blamed underdevelopment on Northern political and economic power (Amin 1974; Frank 1967). These dependency critics, however, never questioned the equation between development and Western notions of modernity and economic growth (Hirshman 1995).

The failure to question the fundamental goal of development does not mean policies and approaches remained the same. In fact, mainstream development thinking and practice proved remarkably responsive to various pressures. The dependency critique inspired a much publicized World Bank commitment to providing Basic Human Needs for the world's poor. In the 1970s, the failure of most Third World states to cope with the oil shock and the growing debt burden undermined mainstream development agencies' faith in state-led development. They moved towards a more neoliberal emphasis on the market, implemented through structural adjustment programmes (SAPs) which sought to reduce the role of the state, encourage privatization and off-load welfare burdens to private citizens and NGOs. However, the equation between development and Western notions of progress and economic growth remained intact. Indeed, strict adherence to these new 'rules' was once again presented as a virtual guarantee of development (or economic growth) (World Bank 1980, 1990).

The issue of women and development entered the development discourse in the 1970s, but remained tied to the terms of the larger debates. Whether adopting the liberal, mainstream women in development (WID) approach, or the more socialist and feminist gender and development (GAD) critique, the advocates of women's development for the most part focused on improving women's economic capacity and their participation in the drive for economic prosperity (Connelly *et al.* 2000). Some scholars in the South, most notably the DAWN group (Sen and Grown 1987) called for women-centred, grassroots development to empower women, but the preoccupation with women's role in the economy went largely unquestioned (Hirshman 1995).

By the late 1980s, however, new voices and critiques entered the fray and development discourse began to splinter in a number of interesting and important ways. Development along Western lines came increasingly into question, both in the South and the North. Environmentalists warned of unsustainable growth and devastated ecologies (Shiva 1988). Feminists questioned the patriarchal nature of development discourse and practice (Batliwala 1994; Mohanty 1995; Moser 1993). Poststructuralists argued that development discourse was designed to silence Southern voices, to control knowledge and spread Western capitalism around the globe (Escobar 1995). Indeed, by 1993, many were openly agreeing with F. Schuurman (1991) that development had reached an impasse.

Some scholars and activists have taken these critiques to their logical conclusion, coming out openly against development. This anti-development position has been equated with post-development (Pieterse 2000). Certainly scholars such as Arturo Escobar (1995) and M. Rahnema (1997) see development discourse as simply another version of Western hegemony, which the poor countries of the South would do well to avoid. Others, however, while sympathetic to these critiques, recognize that development problems cannot simply be wished away. This alternative or populist wing of post-development thinking is deeply critical of the top-down, hegemonic character of most mainstream development discourse and practice, calling for a more bottom-up, participatory approach – one where development 'experts' become 'facilitators' working with the poor rather than directing them (Munck 1999). Development, from this perspective, cannot be 'given' to the poor. It requires attention to local knowledge and accumulated wisdom, respectful partnership and participatory practice that will empower the poor so that they can define their own development problems, goals and solutions (Freedman 2000; Friedmann 1992). Thus, participation and empowerment, from this perspective, are the essential building blocks for grassroots, people-oriented transformative development.

This perspective has influenced, and been influenced by, many feminists concerned with gender equality and development. The focus on everyday life, the poor and the powerless resonates with the concerns of many gender and development theorists. Some have drawn on poststructuralist critiques of Western universalism, development discourse and modern disciplinary power (Marchand and Parpart 1995; Rowlands 1997), while others have been more attracted to the populist, grassroots emphasis of this perspective (Afshar 1998; Kabeer 1994). However, all see participation and empowerment as critical requirements for women to develop and challenge patriarchal structures and assumptions.

In contrast, mainstream development agencies initially responded to these debates with considerable hostility, fiercely defending SAPs and the wonders of the market. By the mid-1990s, however, the mounting evidence about SAPs' negative impact on the poor, especially women, began to undermine this certainty in some quarters. Some mainstream institutions, most notably within the United Nations, began to call for policies that would mitigate the worst aspects of structural adjustment, especially for the very poor (Payne 2001; Therien and Lloyd 2000). The language of empowerment and participation even began to appear in World Bank documents (World Bank 1995). The 1999 *World Development Report* calls for 'more attention to the voices and learning of the poor' (World Bank 1999: 153). The 2000/2001 *World Development Report* argues that 'poverty amid plenty is the world's greatest challenge' (World Bank 2001: v). The text is liberally sprinkled with the 'voices' of the poor, albeit rarely with much attention to context. An entire section is devoted to empowerment, which, while emphasizing economic growth, admits growth will require more participation of the poor in global forums and development programmes as well as more responsive state institutions, the removal of social barriers and social capital designed to help the poor. Thus the language of alternative development seems to have triumphed – participation and empowerment are increasingly seen as the solution to world poverty and the search for development.

The question remains – does this widespread adoption of the language of participation and empowerment mean that the differences between alternative and mainstream development have collapsed? If the discourse is the same, is the meaning and practice the same as well? What does this mean for gender, empowerment and participation? At the level of discourse, close attention to the language of the *World Development Report* (2000/2001) reveals an assumption that empowerment requires leadership from the top, that poverty is an individual matter and that poverty alleviation does not require serious alterations to the current global capitalist world (Braathen 2001). At the same time, while alternative development practitioners generally claim to support societal transformation through empowerment (Friedmann 1992; Craig and Mayo 1995; Mayoux 1995), their documents sometimes reveal a rather top-down approach to empowerment (Parpart 1995). Thus, even at the level of discourse, contradictions emerge.

Other voices add to the confusion. Critics of post-development have challenged the attack on development discourse, pointing to the many ways in which the language of universal rights has been taken up, redefined and redeployed by peoples in the South to defend their interests and create their own discourses/meanings about modernity and development (Cooper and Packard 1997; Lehmann 1997). While recognizing the contributions of post-development thinking, Corbridge (1998) warns against assuming that development discourse and practice can control the messy business of running development projects. Alternatively, political economists are less impressed with the power of discourse, pointing to the crucial role played by states, markets and institutions in the current global (dis)order (Payne 2001). Some warn that conflicts and the apparent anarchy in the South may have more to do with efforts to position the South in an increasingly competitive, global/local world than a sign of the need for Western development 'solutions' (Duffield 2001).

Thus, divisions and debates within development have never been so vibrant or so complex. How are these various interpretations of empowerment and development to be reconciled? Are we at another impasse, or is this a fertile conjuncture? Since the various theoretical positions seem rather firmly entrenched, perhaps lessons from the field have something to offer. All too often, theorists of development have fought their conceptual battles on paper while development practitioners have gone their own way. Neither seems to believe they have much to learn from the other. I believe there are many lessons to learn from the field, particularly when considering the often yawning gap between discourse and practice as well as the complexities of working and empathizing across cultural and class divisions. To that end, we turn to voices from the field.

Lessons from the Field

PRA is a particularly useful entry point for evaluating lessons from the field. Developed over the last twenty years by Robert Chambers and others, participatory rural appraisal has evolved a set of techniques and practices designed to enhance participation and empowerment among the poorest of the poor (Chambers 1997). It is based on the assumption that indigenous peoples, no matter how uneducated, have the skills and knowledge to define and solve their own development problems. It rejects the role of the development 'expert', arguing that development 'facilitators' should work with the poorest of the poor in ways that empower them to transform their lives and societies (Chambers 1997: 106). PRA has been seen as particularly effective for challenging gender inequality and enhancing women's empowerment. It thus provides a convenient lens for evaluating the possibilities and limits to empowering women, especially among the poor.

Above all, PRA is a methodology that emphasizes experiential innovation rather than theories and abstractions (Chambers 1994b: 1263). It has developed a cluster of very assessable, easily understood techniques such as mapping, walking about and the use of symbols rather than words to overcome the literacy barrier. The onus for discovery and learning is placed on local people rather than the development 'expert', who acts as a facilitator rather than a director (Chambers 1994a; 1994b; 1997). Above all, PRA seeks to include the marginalized by giving them voice and bringing them into the centre of local decision making. Chambers believes this provides a platform for identifying problems and resolving conflicts within communities (Chambers 1994c: 1445).

In the 1990s, projects using PRA and committed to participatory empowerment approaches to development spread around the world. Remarkably, both mainstream and more 'alternative' development agencies have adopted PRA techniques and language. Everyone seems to be doing PRA, but it is not clear what happens on the ground. We now have enough evidence to begin answering this question. Numerous success stories have been recorded (Krishna, Uphoff and Esman 1997). Mapping and transect walks seem to be particularly popular with villagers (Kelly and Armstrong 1996; Tiessen 1997). Indeed, maps can reveal the gendered character of daily life. For example, Allison Goebel discovered that map-making in Zimbabwean resettlement areas highlighted women's concerns with home and neighbourhood in contrast to male preference for roads, fields and pastures. The maps provided a talking point for discussions of gendered environmental use (Goebel 1998). Group activities are also quite popular, although women's attendance is often affected by their heavy workloads (Mayoux 1995; Wieringa 1994).

However, certain problems keep surfacing in reports from the field. They raise some difficult questions about some of the methods and assumptions of this approach, particularly for women, as well as larger questions about post-development and gender. One of the most significant limitations facing PRA practitioners and the participatory empowerment approach comes from its emphasis on the local and its tendency to either ignore or underplay the impact of national and global power structures, discourses and practices. Yet, even the smallest village has links with people and countries beyond its borders (Cleaver 1999: 603–4). Even small community-based projects have to deal with government structures and officials at one point or another and these dealings are often problematic. Many government officials neither understand nor empathize with PRA techniques, nor do they tend to believe that the poor (especially women) should contribute to policy making or programme development (Thompson 1995). This bias surfaces in many places. In Senegal, for example, Jesse Ribot discovered that political administrative laws systematically disabled local representation, despite official 'support' for a community forestry project (1999: 26). Moreover, even sympathetic bureaucrats are frequently constrained by political and economic factors, such as structural adjustment programmes (SAPs) or male-dominated political and economic structures. Official support for a project means little when the budgetary constraints of SAPs and economic malaise eliminate promised fiscal support (Mayoux 1998: 192–3; Botchway 2001).

The participatory 'solution' – more broad-based representation of marginalized groups on government boards and committees – has done little to challenge national and regional power structures. An Oxfam project in Burkina Faso, for example, placed members of peasant organizations on a government/NGO participatory planning board, but discovered this had no observable impact on the board's planning agendas (Ashby and Sperling 1995: 757). Even élite women in male-dominated parliaments find it difficult to ensure they are taken seriously (Rai 2002). It should come as no surprise that representatives from marginalized groups often require intervention by donors who can insist that participatory methods and processes be followed.[3] This is particularly true when the representatives are women, as government officials often operate within a cultural context that undervalues women's opinions and contributions to public discussions (Mosse 1994: 498–9). Unless these rather intractable and often unrecognized practices are recognized and challenged, participation will do little to alter the gendered imbalance in most bureaucratic structures (Mayoux 1995). Indeed, 'the complex nature of gender subordination means that increasing women's participation may exacerbate rather than reconcile contradictions in the position of individual women' (Mayoux 1998: 181).

Moreover, development practitioners often have deeply held, sometimes unconscious, reservations about the knowledge and capacities of the poor, especially women. For example, the evaluation of a Zambian participatory agricultural extension programme revealed male-biased project leaders and difficulties dealing with gender issues (Frischmuth 1998). Many PRA 'experts' use the language and methods of PRA 'without adequately acknowledging the complexity of social realities, or properly absorbing or practising the intended notions of "participation"' (Goebel 1998: 279). Additionally, some development practitioners believe in participatory development methods, but find it difficult to give up their authority over the poor. They want to empower the poor, but on their terms. This heavy-handed approach is particularly common with women, as most development practitioners come from cultures where women's subordination and need for direction is taken for granted (Rahnema 1990: 206–7). As Heather Crawley cautions, the language of empowerment and participation 'creates an aura of moral superiority', which can protect practitioners of PRA from criticism and 'critical self-reflection about the truth of their claims' (1998: 25).

Power structures exist at the local level as well. Indeed, even the smallest village has its own power brokers. Chambers's belief that inequities can be transcended through the powers of persuasion, discussion and inclusion is frequently contradicted by reports from the field. Jesse Ribot, for example, discovered that local élites involved in participatory forestry projects in French West Africa had neither support from villagers nor an interest in participatory practices (1996). Local officials, like their national counterparts, often reflect and support a gendered social context that dismisses women's contributions to public discussions. Once again, simply placing women on local project committees can do little to make them heard or bring them into committee activities in a meaningful way (White 1996). Mayoux points out that 'statistics on cooperative and peasant movements indicate a continuing marginalization of women in mixed-sex participatory organizations' (1995: 240). In Zimbabwe, for example, Goebel discovered that in general village meetings, 'women constantly had to be invited and reinvited for their views, while men regained control each time a woman had spoken' (1998: 284). Moreover, women committee members sometimes support the *status quo*, because it legitimates their superior position *vis-à-vis* other women. A Zimbabwean participatory ecology project, operating through Zimbabwe's Campfire programme,[4] for example, was initially captured by the local élites, including women. When the team leader disbanded the committee and set up a more representative one, the project stalled for lack of support from the more powerful members in the community (Robinson 1996).

This example raises the issue of the relationship between the PRA team and the villages/region they work in. Lack of familiarity with the community's power structure and cultural context may lead to problems such as those described above, particularly in the early stages of a project. But even when such fault lines are discovered, they may be very difficult to deal with (Robinson 1996). The specific historical experiences of communities may influence relations as well. In India, David Mosse discovered deeply entrenched suspicion towards development practitioners, which participatory methods did little to allay (1994: 505). The informal and public nature of PRA techniques can alienate people accustomed to more formal behaviour. Moreover, non-directive, consultative approaches may be misconstrued, especially mapping, transect walks and wealth measurements, when they suggest all too familiar interventions by government officials. When combined with ignorance of the local and national power structures, these practices can undermine the effectiveness of participatory methods (Mosse 1994: 506–7).

The collection of local knowledge and the fostering of local analytical and planning skills are also a rather more complicated process than anticipated by PRA specialists. Knowledge is not something that just exists out there, ready to be discovered and used. It is embedded in social contexts, exerted in relations of power and attached to different power positions (Scoones and Thompson 1993: 2). Control over knowledge is often an essential element of local power relations and structures. It reinforces local hierarchies, and is often highly gendered. As we have seen, women often have difficulty speaking and being heard (Jackson 1997; Rasavi 1998). Yet the consequences of this tendency are not easy to evaluate. Cleaver discovered that while few women attended meetings in a Tanzanian water use project, those who attended spoke for all the women while the men spoke only for themselves (1999: 602). However, most women have to struggle to be taken seriously in public meetings. Moreover, communities accustomed to dealing with development agencies have discovered the importance of presenting the 'right' kind of information to development specialists and government bureaucrats. These presentations are often very public, and offer an opportunity to silence and marginalize the poor, particularly women (Mosse 1994: 508–9).

Ironically, giving people voice does not always empower the poor, especially women. Control over knowledge, even through silence, can sometimes be an empowering survival strategy for the marginalized (Mahoney 1996; Suski 1997).

For example, members of secret societies gain power through their ability to decide when to speak, to whom and about what. The power associated with gossip and information, the ability to decide when, where and with whom it will be shared, reminds us that giving voice to women (or men), especially in public, is not always empowering (Gal 1991). Among the Bedouin, for example, self-control and careful speech are seen as a sign of honour and power (Abu-Lughod 1999: 90–3). In Java, women's ability to control their speech and public behaviour is equated with empowerment (Brenner 1998). Consequently, the public discussions so popular with PRA may sometimes be disempowering, in fact, for the more marginalized members of a community – particularly women. Moreover, seeking the 'voices' of Third World women has too often become a means for building the careers of development 'experts' rather than an empathetic attempt to bridge cultural and material divides (see Chapter 6).

PRA activities also do not always fit women's schedules or agendas. Mosse discovered that projects in India often conflicted with women's work schedules or took place in male space, yet their lack of participation was often explained as 'natural' and their absence went unnoticed (1994: 512). Mapping and transect walks are often seen as men's work. In Sierra Leone, for example, women criticized a spatial mapping exercise because 'the changes we need cannot be drawn'. Gender issues such as relations between men and women and violence against women did not surface on maps (Welbourn 1996). Many women are reluctant to discuss sensitive issues like domestic violence or quarrels in public, even with other women. Moreover, social and economic hierarchies often divide women and may inhibit open discussions as well (Mayoux 1995: 242–5). Sharing thoughts and dreams will not necessarily overcome these divisions, despite the best hopes of PRA supporters.

The need for specific skills training is also rarely discussed in the PRA literature. Yet we know women, especially poor women, often need specific skills in order to challenge existing stereotypes about their inability to plan and monitor activities. Participatory approaches call for full participation in development projects, but they often underestimate the skills needed for such participation, especially report writing and evaluation – skills which poor women rarely have. Participatory projects, like all development projects, must submit frequent reports and budgets. These requirements have become all the more daunting with the current emphasis on results-based management (RBM) (Wieringa 1994). While intended to ensure project effectiveness, RBM creates obstacles to grassroots participation in PRA projects, and forces project managers to employ highly numerate and literate specialists in base line data and measurements (Duffield 2001). Thus, just as participation and empowerment have triumphed at the level of discourse, the rules and regulations of development seem to be moving in the opposite direction. Poor people are left outside the discussions; measurement and evaluations are once again the purview of development 'experts' rather than local people, and women, with their lack of skills, are left outside the loop.

Other experiences and insights from the field highlight the difficulties encountered in trying to integrate cultural practices with empowerment strategies. Mejai Avoseh, for example, blames the many failures of adult education using participatory methods in Africa on their lack of attention to culture and tradition. While agreeing that adult education should try to 'empower the people to think for themselves, to show them how to be the architects of their own collective liberation' (2000: 571), he warns that to do so it must 'wear an African face'. It must recognize 'the people's religious and cultural roots, and value systems' (2000: 575–6). Bonny Ibhowah makes a similar point when discussing human rights in Africa. He does not deny the importance of human rights, but questions the utility of universal definitions grounded in Western experiences and perceptions. A human rights discourse with meaning for Africa will have to 'articulate ... an African sense of human rights or dignity, which flows from the African perspective', particularly 'the African sense of community obligation that goes beyond charity' (2001: 61).

While the position of these authors resonates with post-development attacks on Western universalism, neither of them calls for a total abandonment of Western notions of rights, progress and development. They do, however, argue against the assumption that the West/North sets the parameters for discussion and practice, arguing instead for a mix of Western and 'traditional' values – recognizing that neither are fixed, unchanging conventions. Instead they posit a process, a continuing dialogue, with possibilities for growth on both sides. As Ibhowah points out, the more communal orientations to rights issues coming out of Africa, Asia and other parts of the world may have much to offer Western notions of individual human rights, and vice versa (2001: 61–2). Avoseh says much the same thing (2000: 57). Both call for a process of negotiation, empathy and openness. The argument is not against Western notions of development discourse and practice, but rather against the assumption that the West/North has all the answers.

This more eclectic, interactive and truly participatory approach to the Enlightenment assumptions embedded in development discourse is reflected in much of the activism around gender issues in the South (and North) as well. Rather than simply reject 'universal' Western norms, many Third World gender activists have based their challenges to patriarchal systems in their own societies on appeals to human and women's rights. Maria Nzomo (1995), for example, points out that the women's movement in Kenya has used universalist Western-based claims about human rights and women's rights to legitimize their own demands. Activists in Southern Africa have legitimated their call to address gender violence on the basis that it is an issue 'where international human rights standards, practices and implementation can be enforced.... Governments must implement international conventions that protect women's rights by translating the same into domestic law and policy' (Ndungu 1999: 9). The Declaration of the African Women's Anti-War Coalition bases its claims on the objectives and principles of the UN Charter, the Universal Declaration of Human Rights and recommendations of various United Nations world meetings (West African Workshop 1999). Thus, feminist efforts to empower women in the South often involve syntheses of Western discourses on development and rights with various local understandings and goals. They also raise larger questions of the impact of gendered political and economic institutions in an increasingly unequal world.

Rethinking empowerment, gender and development: melding theory and praxis

Clearly empowerment is the word of the moment for an impressive variety of development theorists and practitioners. It is a slippery word, a chimera that lets everyone feel comfortable – a 'motherhood' term with a warm, cuddly feeling. However, our survey of both theoretical debates and experiences in the field raises some doubts about the empowerment approach to development. How can a word be so comfortable for such disparate players? Should we abandon it because we cannot bring it under control?

Anti-development thinkers such as Rahnema (1990) suggest this might be a good idea. He argues that participatory empowerment approaches to development actually do little to challenge established power structures. Yet others argue that the very flexibility of empowerment and participation can provide a cover for more radical thoughts and actions. This may seem naïve, but the fact that the leading architect of the *World Development Report* (2000/2001), Professor Ravi Kanbur, resigned when the higher Bank authorities insisted on reducing the report's emphasis on empowerment suggests that the term may have subversive potential (Braathen 2000: 333). His resignation alone throws doubt on an easy dismissal of either empowerment or participation.

Indeed, this overview of development debates and field experiences (which are intertwined and from the South and North) reveals some impressive contributions by participatory empowerment approaches to development in the field. Bringing the marginalized and the poor into discussions, encouraging and facilitating local knowledge and analytical skills is crucial to development as an economic activity and as a personal and societal goal. However, the above research also demonstrates the limitations of the participatory empowerment approach. Clearly, gender inequalities do not disappear simply through giving voice to women or including them in development activities. Nor do many other inequalities. The challenge is to draw on current development debates as well as lessons from the field in order to rethink participation and empowerment, particularly for women. We need to meld theory with praxis in ways that address fundamental impediments to participation and empowerment while maintaining the accessibility and practicality of PRA and other empowerment interventions. This requires a more sophisticated, nuanced analysis of power and empowerment, one that pays attention to material and institutional forces, cultural and discursive factors, and the strategies people use as they seek to survive and even flourish in a rapidly changing world.

Participatory empowerment as a development practice cannot rely on the assumption that giving people voice and increasing participation will solve developmental problems. It will have to pay more attention to the way national and global power structures constrain and define the possibilities for change at the local level. Structural adjustment programmes, for example, have often hampered local and national development efforts, as have corrupt governments and hostile laws. The analytical tools of political economy have much to offer this endeavour. Attention to institutions, states and markets as well as global financial and trade flows are essential. Interviews with key élites are often necessary, but rarely open to participatory methods. Recent scholarship on international conflicts and crime also raises some important issues. It warns us against simple-minded arguments for imposing Western 'solutions' on a chaotic world, reminding us that current conflicts often reveal the many ways different political economies are responding to the challenges of global change (Duffield 2001). Thus globalization requires specific analysis (Mittelman 1997), but only if it incorporates difference, including attention to the gendered character of political and economic structures, and their differential impact on women and men (Peterson and Runyan 1993; Staudt, 1990). This will require incorporation of critical political economy, particularly by feminists, and a move beyond the local.

Local power structures need more explicit analysis as well. One of the strengths of the participatory empowerment approach to development has been its focus on the local and its belief that even the poorest communities can understand and solve their own developmental problems. This approach assumes divisions in society can be overcome by full and frank discussion by all parties. This rather liberal belief in democratic processes underestimates the intractable nature of many local economic and political structures. Moreover, sensitivity to existing social arrangements has often led to the uncritical acceptance of traditional inequities, especially those based on gender, which is regarded as private, and thus outside the realm of economic development and challenges to the status quo (Fals-Borda and Rahman, 1991). PRA exercises can uncover the differential access to power and resources of men and women, but offer little explanation for how these differences come about. To understand the forces in play, we need to know how women and men participate in local political and economic structures, whether (and why) some women are able to use them to their advantage, while others are silenced and marginalized. The conceptual tools of materialist feminists (Hennessy, 1993) and gender and development scholars (Kabeer 1994; Moser 1993), offer some insights for this endeavour, as do the struggles of activists dealing with the material and institutional impediments to achieving gender equality.

A focus on the material and institutional elements of power is not sufficient by itself, however. We need to understand the way belief systems, cultural practices and discursive patterns legitimize and reinforce material structures. The link between language/knowledge and power is increasingly recognized as a central factor in development activities, particularly the power of development practitioners to define developmental 'problems' and 'solutions' (Crush 1995; Marchand and Parpart 1995; Escobar 1995). PRA techniques pick up on this critique with their rejection of top-down development practices and their desire to bring the marginalized into development discussions and plans. This is an important first step, but it is based on an overvaluation of the power of development discourse and an underestimation of the various often unexpected ways discourses have been used for personal and group liberation. Indeed, as we have seen, people in the South, including women, have used Western discourses of rights to legitimate their demands for change. The alternative/post-development critique has urged development practioners to abandon Western notions of modernity and development, and to embrace the local and traditional. This romantic, uncritical evaluation of development discourse ignores the complexity of social change in the South (and North). It overestimates the power of the North, underestimates the resilience of the South, and fails to see the need for a more interactive, grounded approach to development.

Moreover, the romantic assumption that giving voice to the poor, especially women, will solve gendered power inequities is questionable. We know that the marginalized, especially women, can speak but not be heard. Moreover, speaking is not always a source of power. Speaking can disempower a person if it removes the ability to control the dissemination of knowledge. To address these issues, PRA techniques need a much more sophisticated analysis of voice, language/knowledge and power. This is particularly true in matters of gender, which are deeply embedded in the unconscious, and often presented as natural, unchanging cultural practices.

Finally, the current interest in identity politics and shifting and multiple subjectivities offers some insights into the analysis of individual behaviour, and thus to empowerment. PRA techniques are sensitive to the complexity of local conditions and the need to bring the marginalized into the centre. But they fail to theorize the subject (Hennessy 1993). Individuals are generally assumed to play a particular role in the community, when, in fact, they may play several, sometimes conflicting roles. These conflicts can offer entry points for otherwise unexpected alliances. For example, women from the wealthier groups in a community may align more with their class than their sex, thus having little empathy with their poorer sisters. However, some gendered practices may cross class lines and thus provide an issue for mobilizing women from different class backgrounds. PRA techniques, with their attention to local voices, have the potential to reveal such complexities, but to do so they must move beyond description to analysis – something that requires attention to theory as well as technique.

These ruminations on debates and practices over empowerment, gender and development reveal both the promise and the limitation of present practice. Clearly, PRA and participatory empowerment as practice are undertheorized, especially in relation to power. The emphasis has been on *doing* development rather than analyzing it. While the development of assessable, participatory techniques has contributed much to our understanding of the daily lives of the poor, especially women, the transformatory potential of this approach remains in question. The challenge is to develop techniques that retain the accessibility and practicality of PRA and other participatory empowerment practices, yet incorporate the insights of current thinking on the material and discursive nature of power. This requires moving beyond the glib assumptions of alternative post-development thinking, with its anti-modernist stance, its inattention to structures and its underestimation of the ability of the poor to create their own discursive understandings and arguments. Such a project will take time, effort and considerable experimentation. Some important efforts in this direction have been taking place (Fals-Borda and Rahman, 1991; Jackson, 1997; Goetz, 1995). More are needed. But one thing is clear. If PRA and participatory empowerment approaches do manage to meld theory and practice in ways that successfully destabilize established power structures, and reinforce the need for more open, consultative and empathetic South–North theory building, they will certainly no longer be the darling of *all* participants in the development enterprise.

Notes

1 I use the term alternative development agencies to include the variety of NGOs involved in development work. These vary both in size and approach, but are distinguished by their separation from governments and their commitment (at least at the level of rhetoric) to a more participatory form of development.

2 Some scholars (particularly Pieterse 1998, 2000) equate post-development with the anti-development school characterized by Escobar (1995) and Rahnema (1997). Others, most

notably Ronaldo Munck (1999) posit two wings to post-development. One is anti-development and the other is alternative development, with an emphasis on a people-first, populist, participatory approach. See more below.

3 Interview, Canadian International Development Agency (CIDA) consultant, Masakar, Indonesia, 20 September 1997.

4 The Campfire (Communal Areas Management Programme for Indigenous Resources) programme in Zimbabwe focuses on conservation, with a focus on community-based resource management, decentralization, institution building, ethnicity and gender. Originally focused on wildlife, Campfire projects now involve forestry and mining resources as well. Robinson was involved in the Sunungukai Tourism Project in Mashonaland Central, which was designed to enhance the community's ability to use its natural resources through tourism. The project adopted a PRA approach. The programme was Campfire's first attempt to develop non-consumptive tourism, with cultural interaction as a central focus.

2

Dismantling the Master's House with the Master's Tools?

Gender Work in and with Powerful Bureaucracies

Kathleen Staudt

Audre Lorde eloquently warned those who hope to reform and transform wretched and obscene inequalities. To her, such tools would *never* dismantle the house.[1] The image reminds us of slavery in the first half of the history of the United States, but the image also offers insights to those who confront overwhelming global inequalities, the deep institutionalization of male privilege, and savage capitalisms in which wage slavery characterizes the lives of many.

What are the master's houses? To contrast the local and the global, is the slave plantation analogous to the World Bank and the World Trade Organization? Many critics of this thing called international 'development' would probably agree. Yet between those obscene polarities – plantation and WTO – lay many other institutions (houses?) that the masters designed and sustained. In these institutions – families, workplaces, universities, national women's bureaus, and seemingly progressive NGOs – we live and work on day-to-day bases with some degree of agency. Women and other 'non-masters' develop their own words, skills, and strategies in these houses, but master-free houses are few and far between. Should the non-masters, then, disengage, or marginally engage with their own tools, such as language, skills, and knowledge? If the answer is yes, and all non-masters would disengage, then the masters' schemes in those multiple houses would be ever so much easier. Victimhood would be complete, and all hope would be lost. If the answer is no, and non-masters would engage instead, then the challenge would be to choose battles carefully and engage in struggle on different fronts. One of these fronts is inside development institutions, whether NGO or official. To challenge, change, and transform the institutions, people must act strategically on the inside *and* outside in broad-based transformative coalitions.

Horrors, say the purists. This strategy is nothing less than being suckered into cooptation that, in the end, sustains the institutions. How pure are the purists? Those who study and work in higher education institutions are complicit. We perpetuate language tools and discourses to groom and socialize new generations in the 'production' of knowledge. We write articles for journals, most of which have master-like gatekeepers, in language sometimes so obscure that few want to read it, or in journals that few readers consult. The process of obtaining graduate degrees disables broad-based communication skills. Our traditional undergraduate teaching tools are often based on the expert-lecture format, a format that future teachers in our classes might replicate to the next generation. Of learning styles, we prize the read–write–listen style, as opposed to others. Many scholars utilize the 'banking style' approach with students that Paulo Freire so criticized: we deposit knowledge and expect to document those deposits with assessment tools.[2] Academics are working in the master's house where narratives and discourses, distant from action, can offer deep critiques about development institutions, but often from the privileged tools and spaces of word processors in air-conditioned rooms.

Multiple discourses operate simultaneously in the multi-hierarchical world. The discourses that dominate the movement of capital and trade dominate one sphere, clearly a powerful hegemonic sphere, while the critical discourses of human rights dominate in others. Among critical academics, the discourses of 'women' and 'gender' operate in yet others. And in development studies, the discourse in the English language is yet another hegemonic force, pushing its language and meaning forward with little regard for significance and meaning in translation. The master's house of the university, and of academics in dominant-English language universities, illustrates the multiple discourses that swirl for possible collaborative compromises toward gender equality or cooptation to stall or disguise action. Who's coopting whom? At bottom line, what difference does this make for gender relations or for women acquiring more power? Development institutions operate with sacred discourses, but discourses always change in response to political and economic forces. We must be wary of changes that are merely rhetorical and symbolic, meant to appease critics; we must actively work for changes that produce change of some significance for social justice.

In this essay, I argue that engagement *in* the master's house is one among many valid political strategies in contemporary development enterprises. I'll call this the 'politics of the inside'. It complements those strategies *outside* masters' houses. Those who privilege outsider strategies may be privileging yet another master's house with its own compromising perils. How quickly those in the contemporary era have forgotten the hierarchy and male privilege in leftist and civil rights organizations of recent decades! 'Take her off the stage and ____ her';

'the only position of women in the ____ is prone.'[3] And the ultimate goal of transformative institutions, the 'revolutions' of the twentieth century, had too few 'insiders' putting revolutionary policies (including gender equality) into practice. A real challenge is for insiders and outsiders to work together, whether in mastered development or university institutions, for the multiple contradictions that prevail: insiders may perpetuate hierarchies and inequalities in the name of *collaborative models*; outsiders may draw polarizing lines which acknowledge no inside change in the name of *conflict models*.

There's more to the analysis than political style, collaborative or conflictive. At bottom line, the substance and content of institutional action represent accountability and responsiveness to people. Institutional discourse supposedly reflects that substance, but language is one of the master's tools. The 'politics of the inside' requires mastery of multiple discourses in order to forge compromises that acknowledge institutional failure, legitimize critiques, and advance the transformative agenda. But outsiders and insiders must also be vigilant about institutional cooptation of critical language. The language of 'gender' as a case is examined herein. In this essay, I draw both on literature about international institutions, including my own research over twenty years, and on my own experiences in development and university activism, drawing in part on participant observation. I close with a call for academic community activism in a global–local world.

Many masters' houses: official and NGO

In the world of development institutions, most houses could be called masters' houses. Whether bilateral technical assistance agencies (one government to another), or multilateral agencies (many governments through United Nations or global conduits to many governments), men founded and staffed these organizations as part of established national agencies, 'foreign' policy, and global *status quo* relations. Among bilateral technical assistance agencies we would include the Canadian International Development Agency (CIDA) and the US Agency for International Development (USAID), among many others. Among multilateral agencies we would include the World Bank, the IMF, the United Nations Development Programme (UNDP), the Food and Agricultural Organization (FAO), and the International Labour Organization (ILO), among many others.

Dare we use the phrase masters' houses to refer to national governments, the state generally, and individual departments, ministries, and agencies within governments? Of course. Within those masters' houses, spaces and niches have been created to form what the United Nations calls 'women's machinery', such as women's bureaus, ministries of women, women's departments, and ministries of equal rights or of families. Sometimes those spaces are the sole high-level decision-making positions that women hold in national governments. Usually, those spaces are underfunded and understaffed. Their mandates and jurisdictions may be limited, even as expectations rise about visionary missions to 'mainstream gender' throughout government and hold it accountable to women.[4] Few masters respect national women's bureaus with their meagre resources, although 'gender mainstreaming' strategies are the resolution talk of the United Nations international women's conferences, from Nairobi in 1985 to Beijing in 1995.

Let's go back to the international agencies for a moment. In unusual and rare circumstances, technical assistance agencies challenged the *status quo.* One example is the Swedish International Development Authority (SIDA), which developed partnerships with democratic socialist nations (like Tanzania and Mozambique, which were shunned by other agencies) in the 1960s and 1970s, and paid early (late 1960s) attention to women. The United Nations Children's Fund (UNICEF) represented a rare multilateral organization with an early commitment to mothers and children, though the early rationales for UNICEF's work evoked welfare for the weak and vulnerable. More recently, UNICEF has used the strong language of 'gender apartheid' as a rationale for its work.[5]

Rising political forces of the early 1970s prompted other agencies to open opportunities to redistribute minuscule amounts of funds to women, initially on the grounds of welfare and poverty, but increasingly with the rationales of equity and administrative effectiveness.[6] Women and some progressive men took this discourse into their governments, or to departments and ministries within their governments, to facilitate change, but it has hardly been transformative, given the strength of the masters' houses in which they work. Outsiders and activists also organized around the United Nations conferences on women (the first in Mexico City, 1975), and lobbied governments within national politics to the extent that free and open organizing could exist in nations called democracies.

On the inside, women and some progressive men brokered the leverage of these outside forces to promote changes in procedures, budgetary allocations, and compromise language to nudge institutions toward change. They did this brokering through inside units with various names, the earliest of which was 'Women in Development,' or WID. Agencies continually hire staff, or contract tasks with NGOs, supposedly 'non-profit organizations', not all of which shared an interest in or commitment to women or changing gender relations. Non-profit organizations are not the same as independent people's organizations, with democratic accountability mechanisms operable from within. Those bilateral agencies that made a commitment to hire more female staff included several in Scandinavian countries, the Netherlands and Canada.[7]

In the 'politics of the inside', women advocates struggled at the frontlines, learning, using, and manipulating the dominant discourses. At the FAO, women struggled not only to twin the words women and farmer, but also to transform a traditional home economics unit. Many agencies doubled, tripled, or quadrupled the budgetary amounts directed to women, but of course the base line from which they multiplied was a drop in the budgetary bucket. Women built alliances inside agencies in order to promote simultaneous changes and spread responsibility among a variety of inside units, not just the separate women's unit. As one phrase summarized it, 'getting institutions right' was the agenda, clever for the way it coopted the mantra of economists in the 1980s for whom 'getting prices right' was the agenda.[8]

Some of these women's units involved cosmetic change: they symbolized change, but the change was not deep. Cosmetic changes continued beyond the women's unit. Advocates successfully pushed for 'gender' units, a name that symbolized change, but change not necessarily deep or grounded in practice.

The case of gender language

The earliest of insider and outsider advocates used the word women in their scholarship, activism and politics, both in and outside the bureaucracy. The word 'women' translates well into most languages. Some texts, however, interrogate even that word for its social constructionism; it is disconcerting to see the word in quotes throughout a whole book, though such narratives make the point well that this word can be socially constructed as biological, social relational, or both.[9]

The word 'development' does not translate well into different languages. In fact, even in the English language, the meaning of development is contested and fuzzy. Is development about economic growth, real estate deals, housing contractors, and the exploitation of green areas around cities? This is an English-language meaning grounded in US local politics. Or is development a semi-sacred term that stands for (pick your 'development' era): increasing people's choices, reducing inequalities, growing *per capita* incomes and employment, addressing basic human needs, or whatever? Critics, including feminist critics, have contested these semi-sacred definitions hotly for the last two decades.

Some critics attacked the phrase Women in Development (WID) to promote instead the phrase Gender and Development (GAD). WID, as insider work, made the language complicit. By definition, they were inside, sleeping with the enemy. For insiders, sleeping with the enemy was far from the practice. They were often treated with disdain, experiencing the crude and insulting everyday sexism of people who wanted them ousted. In WID language, the word 'in' (between Women, Development) seemed integrationist; it did not confront the contested terminology of gender. The word 'and' (between Gender, Development) was preferred. WID change was surely undramatic (as initial work in any master's house would be), but if WID was a long-term strategy for incremental change without questioning paradigms, then it was time to change course (and discourse). Gender, critics said, was about social construction and power relations between men and women (or 'men' and 'women').[10] In the hierarchy among English–speaking critics, most of them excluded from national and international development institutions, gender discourse was privileged and pure; the word women was passé. Never mind that gender was obscure terminology from sociology and linguistics, disciplinary narrative and by definition élitist in activist terms. Never mind also that gender did not translate well into many languages.[11]

For some outsider activists, the move away from women toward gender was not about ideological purity. It was about a retreat from politics, power, and struggle for women. And they were sceptical when some of the biggest international agencies like the World Bank and UNDP were so quick to jump on the gender bandwagon. In the minds of many outsiders and insiders, the World Bank was and is no friend to women, gender, the environment, or other critical paradigms that question mainstream and orthodox economic growth models.

For those practising the 'politics of the inside', gender was very convenient. It offered compromise language that undercut the sort of patriarchal critique of WID that became the butt of bureaucratic jokes: Why not Men in Development? Let's be fair! Gender language also sounded very technical in a world dominated by capitalists and economists – even in bureaucracy. It sounded like the neutral, rational language that women's advocates had long been searching for. And men felt more comfortable.

By the mid-1980s, as change advocates longed for quick fixes, 'gender training' became the be-all solution. And training advocates, from none less than Harvard University, packaged gender-training modules that international agencies could purchase cheaply to show they responded to the critics and acknowledged their historical failures.[12] Agencies began to recognize and focus on victimized men or 'at-risk boys'. (US universities, too, once women became a slight majority at 53 per cent, worried about at-risk men. Never mind the centuries of female exclusion and marginality.) Some of the early advocates wondered: What about women? Mastery is deep and historical, not addressed in a few years (or in a two-day gender-training workshop).

Not surprisingly, some of the most virulent bureaucracies, hostile to women and to budgetary redistribution more inclusive of women, adopted the gender terminology. Again, early adopters included the World Bank and UNDP, two very different agencies – centralized versus decentralized and responsive to sovereign 'masters' – but both masters' houses, to be sure. Other agencies, more responsive to the women/gender critique, also adopted gender in a corporate-management-type strategy that sought to mainstream accountability to women and men. NGOs with progressive track records also adopted gender language, as addressed below with Oxfam, confounding many on the language issue. Whether investing in honest or manipulative symbolic responses to the critique, many bureaucracies developed their gender teams and their gender units.

Gender advocates, many of them ex-WID, pushed evaluation and data-collection units to disaggregate results by gender, by male and female. The class inequality critique, while compatible with gender scholarship, was more difficult to incorporate in big bureaucracies that found it hard enough to categorize 'beneficiaries' by male and female, much less other categories.

How different are things with a gender rather than women's unit? We may never know the answer to such questions, for insider advocates keep plugging away with whatever language seems to move the institutions. Meanwhile, though, some women wonder if the critical political edge has been lost in bureaucracies so comfortable with gender language.

The inside struggles continue (and women *have* gained a bit more ground)

The WID and GAD critiques have been around for about a third of a century. And advocates have pursued the 'politics of the inside' for just as long. Have bureaucracies budged? Have paradigms shifted? Did it make any difference to have insiders pursuing gender politics? The answer to all three questions is a tentative yes. Insiders aligned themselves with outsiders, opening spaces that ought to have been free in contexts that call themselves democratic. Paradigm pathways swayed, although in the minds of some they regressed with the 'triumph of capitalism' and the multitude of free trade agreements and deals behind closed doors. But the polar shift produced its own backlash against free trade (for 'fair trade') and the capitalist–bureaucratic collusion in the World Trade Organization. The technological tools that facilitate capital movement also facilitate transnational mobilization.

Yet the nudges forward toward modest gains in gender equality are perhaps best illustrated in the seemingly progressive non-government organizations. Let us take the case of Oxfam, a critical NGO that symbolizes challenges to the idea that money should rule. Oxfam organizations span the globe, but it is Oxfam Great Britain on which we will focus primarily. It is a tribute to the organization and its staff that the politics of the inside got exposed – that dirty linen, once aired, has the potential to cleanse other organizations with lessons about the way things were and now are.

In *Gender Works*, 36 insiders discuss the organization over a two-decade period through the century's end in 1999. The contributors write frankly about this seemingly idealistic organization, purer than most, one might have thought. The personal was (and always is) political, and the grinding everyday sexism made work as difficult as in international agencies. (The 'enemy' seems less clear with a progressive veneer.) Consider the following:

> Then [in 1980], overtly sexist behavior was not only tolerated but openly exhibited by some, but by no means all, of the almost exclusively male managers.[13]

> We could be discussing the provision of wells and the need to look at women's role in water collection, and then be asked, 'Well, my wife looks after our children while you are here lecturing us. What about your children?'… 'Is it true you are all dykes in the room?'… 'What are the ladies plotting today?'[14]

Such language seems tame compared to the taunts women faced in outsider leftist organizations during the US anti-war and civil rights eras (see note 3). Yet it illustrates the depth of resistance – a resistance most organizations, including Oxfam, have now moved beyond.

As in many organizations, Oxfam insiders used different tools (gender units, gender teams); these tools were sometimes foisted upon them. But the tools resulted in policies and programmes that spread throughout the organization, into, and with the everyday lives of women in various parts of the world. Still, one finds no gender-disaggregated budgets in Oxfam (likely never to emerge in international agencies). At the Beijing Women's Conference in 1995, Oxfam advocates and others instigated a campaign called 'Women's Eyes on the World Bank' in Washington to amplify the voices of Southern civil-society groups. Since then, similar organizations have opened in countries where the World Bank lends money, strengthening the watch from many sides.[15]

Yet progressive organizations and movements have their priorities, and women/gender are rarely central. During the mobilizations against the World Trade Organization and World Bank/IMF meetings of 1999 and 2000, feminist critiques virtually fell through the cracks of public and virtual discourse, including global mobilization web sites.[16] The mobilizations pushed for new paradigms, but there was a *déjà vu* sense in the language: 'and women' was added here and there, just as it was in the old days with the challenges to the discourse and practice of 'development'. Will women (or gender equality advocates) have to start all over again, even with progressive paradigms?

Dinosaur masters' houses like the World Bank don't change with a few critics, but from many. At its fiftieth anniversary, as it congratulated itself for a half century of 'development' work that many considered destructive and inequality-enhancing, other groups organized around the theme '50 Years is Enough!' The damage done over fifty years will take a great deal to overcome, including damage that in many cases *deepened* gender inequalities and strengthened male privilege. The World Bank continues and grows, but budgetary priorities have shifted somewhat – a shift that results from inside and outside political struggle. Although budgetary numbers say nothing about how money is spent or who is empowered with such expenditure, the shift is noteworthy.

Table 2.1
World Bank percentage of lending[17]

	1980 (%)	1999 (%)
Education, health, nutrition, social	5	25
Economic policy and reform	6	23
Administrative and regulatory reform	0	4
Transportation and telecommunications	14	11
Water and urban development	8	4
Industry, oil, gas, mining	10	4
Electric power and energy	21	2
Agriculture and environment	32	12

These changes seem historically progressive (although, again, it is impossible to understand gendered benefits and damages from these numbers). I applaud changes in budgetary priorities, such as education and social funding increasing fivefold while heavy industry and energy diminished. How do outsiders view this change? Here is where the conflict model may be relevant, yet it is a model with consequences for insiders who toil at their struggle in those masters' houses.

A conflict model draws lines and polarizes friends and enemies. Its advocates keep pressing, painting historic images of horrific masters' houses. Its advocates are reluctant to acknowledge change, for that change would diminish their critique. For insiders, for whom mainstream staff members rarely acknowledge their presence, the continuing polarization is disheartening.

The World Bank, Oxfam and other organizations, official and non-governmental, now have policies, procedures, budgets, and leverage that insider and outsider women/gender critics can use to push change. Space has opened for action on gender equality where none once existed. Careful studies suggest the changes are sometimes meagre. However, policy and budgetary changes have the potential to affect large numbers of people. Gender gaps in power and resources are still large, but women's increased longevity and larger proportions of girls in schools are historically progressive. Struggles over budgets are in order, not futile dreams to be dismissed, especially by writers in comfortable rooms of their own.

Yet how comfortable can we be with these tensions between insiders and outsiders and the obscene inequalities that continue? The *collaborative model* also presents problems. Insider brokers seek resources to fund NGOs and seeming non-profits in both Southern and Northern countries. The packages they develop emerge from masters' houses, complete with RFPs (requests for proposals), funded projects, and franchise development models plunked down in diverse contexts. Project funding caps may be minuscule compared with the overall institutional portfolio. Is three million dollars for women better than nothing? How about 50 million? What about a billion? Who decides? Accountability issues behind the often-closed doors of bureaucracy are almost always problematic. Outsiders have little or no voice in the big-picture questions, decisions and judgments, undermining the potential collaboration from their viewpoint.

Insiders massage RFPs that ultimately sustain inequalities in funding and labour contributions, except in extraordinary circumstances. Take salaries for a moment: if working toward a world of more justice, how can one countenance salaries paid to Northerners that are double or triple those of Southerners? How does one rationalize the overvaluation of 'thinking' work compared to 'activist' work? Even supposed 'non-profits' that generate funds from international agencies set up projects that sometimes fund the NGO and its staff with overhead expenses and salaries many times the resources and salaries of those funded – those who complete the labour for the projects. Higher education brokers, in institutions that exist solely as money conduits, trickle minimal funds to the universities where the work is done at no or low cost to the broker. Foundations have foisted franchise models on NGOs seeking funds; the model operates the same way, no matter the context or place in Africa, the Americas, or Asia. As a community activist, I have been on the receiving end with the *pobrecitas* for this bounty. In one case, our leadership said with some practicality: let's just get the money and then contextualize it for our community. In a more recent case, the strict, control-oriented assessment criteria locked us into marching steps to the tune of the funding organization.

When insiders perpetrate these activities in the name of collaboration, or when the politics of the inside controls in a way that undermines community responsiveness, the collaborative model strays far from genuine partnership.

It's about more than writing: toward action

To dismantle the master's house, we must do more than write to and for each other. The exchange and critique are essential, but will do little to change institutions and paradigms unless we widen the pool to mainstream writers *and* to mainstream organizations. In the mainstream, policies and budgets proceed with a vengeance without realistic and practical challenges. Even more important, we must act inside and outside these institutions.

If positionality and vantage points are meaningful concepts for understanding, contextualizing and interpreting the geographic spaces and cultural groups in which we are situated, so also are they meaningful for other spatial situations: the writer–observer and the analytic activist, including activism 'on the inside'. It would do abstract thinkers well to experience a dose – even an immersion experience – of activism to enlighten their work, just as activists would do well with thinking time and space.

It is incumbent upon us to understand and diagnose organizations and to act politically within and outside of organizations. Transformations are not made from air-conditioned offices, behind word processors alone. They occur through relationships with people, acting in alliances and coalitions that produce results with meaningful resource changes. The relationships are sometimes murky and compromised, and often require multiple discourses and languages (even disciplinary languages) to forge and advance collaborations that move policies, institutions, budgets, and ultimately power relations. The relationships may lean toward conflict or toward collaboration, but in a world still run by the masters, gender and women activists – whether inside or outside – need to understand their common ground.

If the common ground is difficult to reach on women and gender, consider the huge gulf between the larger paradigms: the savage capitalism of the master's grand house versus the critics who call for social justice and environmental sustainability from outside the house, on the lawn, in the outhouse, or in the sky. This is the language that distinguishes development from post-development, suggesting some linear movement. This was the same parallel language that distinguished the *status quo* from its revolutionary critics in numerous geographic settings and historic eras. Post-revolutionary worlds rarely lived up to their promises, especially for women, whether a result of antithesis creeping in, Thermidor, masters' tools, or masters themselves calling the shots. (Thus, we might even call into question assumptions about linear versus non-linear change models.) Few masters in the post-development set seem to have shed their gender blinders, as is painfully clear among the anti-globalization protesters. Few non-masters with a gender lens exercise and engage power in this post-development set. Scholarly edited collections make ever-so-little a dent. If and when post-development thinking takes hold in institutional houses (past our lifetimes, in all likelihood), I wonder whether women will have sufficient action experiences to prepare them for continued engagement and, most certainly, struggle. Struggles do not end, but re-emerge in new guises and languages; non-masters must be positioned to engage, then and now. Experience is a great teacher, and that kind of learning means we must do more than write.

This essay is a passionate plea for engagement within and outside the international institutions, NGOs, universities, and/or governments. It is also a plea for insiders and outsiders not only to work together, but also to challenge the perpetuation of inequality in the name of collaboration and to avoid the polarization of conflict that responds to the strings with which masters try to push and pull us. No matter where we live and work, academic–community activism is imperative in a global–local world.

Notes

1 Audre Lorde (1984: 110–13).

2 Paulo Freire (1970), especially Chapter 2. Learning styles are multiple, from the read/write (common to the small percentage of the population who identify as 'academics') to the visual, interactive, and kinesthetic. Howard Gardner (1993) is usually credited with identifying at least eight intelligences, most of which are not readily assessed through standardized tests and few of which can be evaluated through analytic essays.

3 Jo Freeman (1975) documented the male stridency of late 1960s leftism to feminism, as have many others writing about the United States. The 'only position' phrase comes from male stridency in US civil rights movements of the same era.

4 Accountability became a buzzword in Beijing, following mainstreaming in Nairobi, and NGOs like the Women's Environmental and Development Organization (www.wedo.org) make it prominent in their newsletters and monographs. See UNIFEM (the United Nations Women's Fund) (www.unifem.org) on mainstreaming. See also the introductory theoretical chapter and the comparable bureaucratic accountability chapters in Kathleen Staudt, ed. (1997, second edition).

5 On the institutional–political analysis of bilateral and multilateral agencies, see Kathleen Staudt (1998).

6 Rationales have been analyzed in Mayra Buvinic (1983) and Caroline Moser (1989).

7 See Rounaq Jahan (1995) on the relatively progressive Norwegian and Canadian experiences, including larger female staff numbers.

8 Anne Marie Goetz, ed. (1997).

9 Christine Sylvester (1994) puts women in quotes throughout!

10 Eva Rathgeber (1990: 489–502).

11 See Jahan (1995) on translation. Also see Ines Smyth (1999: 139) who discusses the interpretation of gender as an 'anti-feminist ploy' among women in Oxfam's Middle East office.

12 Staudt (1998: 200–1) analyzes the gender training literature and practice.

13 Dianna Melrose (1999: 109).

14 Tina Wallace (1999: 188).

15 Lydia Williams, (1999: 234–42). In November 1999, at the Association for Women in Development (AWID) conference in Washington, DC, a field trip took scores of international women to 'the' Bank, under Eyes sponsorship (while, ironically, some participants eagerly sought consulting opportunities at the overall conference event). In late 2000 visits to the Oxfam web site, Women's Eyes on the Bank was not evident, raising questions about its priority to Oxfam's webmaster. (www.oxfam.org)

16 Kathleen Staudt, Shirin Rai and Jane Parpart (2001).

17 World Bank figures in 'Global Loan Agencies Buckle Up for Washington Turbulence', *New York Times*, 16 April 2000, p. 6.

3

Trails of Turquoise

Feminist Enquiry and Counter-Development in Ladakh, India

Ravina Aggarwal

There is a saying in the Himalayan region of Ladakh, high on the northern front of India, that *mi tshes sang gtam tshe ring* ('longer than peoples lives is the talk about them'). In Leh town, Ladakh's capital, there is much talk about a new woman who has appeared in the marketplace. Dressed in wedding finery with velvet robes brocaded at the edges, silver and pearls gleaming on her body, this woman overlooks the busy street from her wooden frame by the signboard for Ladakh Arts Palace, the biggest jewellery and antiques shop in the region. A turquoise headdress (*pad rag*, pronounced *perag*) rests on her head. When the fitful spells of electricity permit, she raises her hand to her forehead as if to say '*Juley*,' greeting and welcoming wayfarers, inviting them to sample the cultural artefacts that the store offers.[1]

More than twenty years before the coming of this virtual woman, there sat in the marketplace another unusual woman called Docha Ringmo, also decked in turquoise *perag*, with long strings of shells dangling on her thigh. At one time, there was a lot of talk surrounding this woman too, but, unlike the mannequin perched above, Docha Ringmo occupied an everyday space, the ground of the sidewalk. In this chapter, I explore the biographical details of Docha Ringmo's life to understand how women's place in the market features in development and post-development discourses prevalent in Ladakh. My presentation strives to illuminate the social and spatial frames through which gendered identity is expressed and remembered as women's movements become increasingly transnationalized.

Ladakh is the largest and northernmost district of India, located at a politically strategic juncture in the state of Jammu and Kashmir, bordering Pakistan to the west and Occupied Tibet to the east. In the last decade or so, it has received worldwide attention as a glaring contradiction to modernity's promise of emancipation. Development policies that are extensions of colonial programmes have ushered in an expanded market sector and altered concepts of land use and methods of revenue collection drastically. These policies continue to sanction the disenfranchisement of women's labour because they are based on the assumption that the region is backward and local practices and religious customs are ineffectual and ornamental.

Critical of development and market agendas, some transnational women's networks have expressed the need to tap into the troves of Ladakhi tradition and pre-modern spaces to salvage evidence of women's collective power and indigenous knowledge. But post-development strategies also constrain women when they control the definition of what it means to be indigenous. Policies that support or oppose modernization in Ladakh both decree a fixed and authentic subjectivity for Ladakhi women so that they are viewed as either victims of backwardness or else as spiritual and maternal environmentalists. 'The validation of indigenity erases the complex nature of contemporary tribal-based movements, and undermines their struggles for democracy and social justice,' argues Sangeeta Kamat (2001: 31) in her article on the politics of representing tribals in the Indian state of Maharashtra. Other postcolonial writers have also taken issue with feminist agendas that luxuriate in nostalgia or submerge difference under a universalizing mission of assimilation.[2] Sangari and Vaid (1989: 17) have cautioned against mistaking 'desired continuity' between past and present as 'actual continuity' in defining women's roles. According to them, 'both tradition and modernity have been, in India, carriers of patriarchal ideologies. As such neither is available to us in a value free or unproblematic sense, nor is either, as they are usually conceptualized, necessarily the solution.'

Through Docha Ringmo's biography, I am interested in addressing the sites of power and the ambiguous and contradictory subject positions within which the agency of women is mediated and authorized.[3] The story of Docha Ringmo that I shall relate in this essay portrays the colonial and postcolonial contexts in which transnational organizing efforts reconstruct categories of the indigenous as a basis for their struggle. Her story points to the dilemmas and contradictions that lie in identifying the past as indigenous and women as repositories of tradition.

Trailing the story

I first came across a reference to Docha Ringmo in an essay on the marketplace of Leh written by the Ladakhi historian, Sonam Phuntsog (1993: 38–40). Docha Ringmo was listed in a paragraph that alluded to storytellers, jokers, and vendors who had inhabited the sidewalks of Leh bazaar during the 1940s.

Sonam Phuntsog remembered that she was an alcoholic, sold *chang* (beer brewed from barley grains), and had a huge *perag*.[4]

The *perag* is a type of headgear worn by Buddhist women, often an heirloom passed from mother to oldest daughter.[5] It is made of a piece of dark fabric adorned with turquoise, corals and silver ornaments. Smaller and newer *perags* are made for younger daughters and existing ones extended by adding pieces of turquoise. According to some scholars (Kaplanian 1981; Tashi Tshomo 1992), the *perag* is meant to give a woman's head the shape of a serpentine *klu*. The pleated skirt of women's garments and the long, creased pyjamas they wear represent the scaly body of the *klu*. The *klu* are subterranean guardian deities who live in the earth and water, infecting those who accidentally or intentionally injure them with sores, boils, leprosy, and sterility. In wedding and love songs, a woman's hair, *perag*-adorned, braided, and covering her back, is often called *rgyal lcang* ('the willow tree of the world') with turquoise leaves that cover the world of humans and white shell roots that spread underground. As this willow tree links the three sectors of the cosmos, hair, housed in a *perag*, becomes an interconnecting channel between worlds.

In the past, married women were required to wear a *perag* during all public occasions. They were prohibited from crossing springs and streams without a *perag* or a hat because loose and exposed hair was a sign of unchecked sexuality. The *perag* was also intricately related to power and status. A *perag* with seven or more lines of turquoise was looked upon as a status symbol. During precolonial times, queens wore nine-lined *perags* with a golden brooch in the middle as a distinguishing mark, whereas ordinary people had *perags* of three, five or seven lines (Tashi Tshomo 1992: 79–89).[6] *Perags* were a crucial means of financial support for women as they adjusted to life away from their birthplace in the patrilocal dwelling of their husband's family. Thus, they were 'frequently changing households, representing the status of the matrilineal line of kinship' (Reis 1983: 221).

It was a *perag* of five or seven lines that Docha Ringmo wore while selling beer in Leh bazaar. Born in 1894, with the formal name Phuntsog Dolma, she had been raised as a Buddhist in the Dopa Gongma household in the village of Kharu. While visiting Leh bazaar for the annual Dosmoche festival parade, she met her husband, a hospital peon called Paljor. Paljor did not have much money so, after marriage, Docha Ringmo found herself working in the fields of the noble Kalon family for wages. She was famous for her proclivity to dress in full finery even as she toiled in the fields, and that is why the Kalon's wife named her *ldo ca ring mo*, 'the one with the long thigh-ornament'. Docha Ringmo didn't have any children and eventually she and Paljor divorced. She then took Stanzin Nyima, a peon in the District Commissioner's office, for her husband. Their relationship was stormy and they were often embroiled in drunken brawls. She began selling alcohol because she needed money desperately and because she was quite a consumer herself.

A barber called Mohammed Khalil who now owns a salon in the old section of the market remembered Docha Ringmo sitting in the Red Square to sell beer, not far from the spot that his father once occupied to cut hair. The Red Square had been the stage for upright speeches by powerful men. From here drums alerted citizens that important declarations were to be announced. In this marketplace, Docha Ringmo became notorious for yelling obscenities, particularly against people who had aroused her displeasure. One of the targets of her inebriated slander was Sonam Wangyal, a powerful politician, who had married her niece and then divorced her. In despair, the niece had cut off her hair and become a nun. Docha Ringmo abhorred Sonam Wangyal and wouldn't let him near the main square. She called him such appalling names that he would slink away in shame. So strong was Docha Ringmo, legend has it, that Sonam Wangyal once threw her from the balcony of the top floor, but she bounced back, unhurt. The king of Ladakh, Kunzang Namgyal, was watching this incident and admonished Sonam Wangyal for getting physical with a defenceless woman. When her second husband, Stanzin Nyima, was fired from his job one day, she was convinced that Sonam Wangyal had a major hand in his dismissal. After that, Docha Ringmo declared war. She called Wangyal and his kin abusive words and made it difficult for him to walk in the bazaar. Wangyal was the right-hand man of Kushok Bakula, a high-ranked abbot of the Gelugpa order and the first Ladakhi to be appointed Minister of State for Ladakh Affairs in 1953. Kushok Bakula was contesting the State Legislative Assembly elections, a move not acceptable to those who were patrons of Hemis monastery, belonging to the rival Kargyudpa order. These opponents from Hemis, often landed aristocrats, formed a party called the Democratic National Conference (DNC) in 1962 to protest against what they saw as the Kushok's ineffective leadership (Bertelsen 1996). Some of the people who remembered Docha Ringmo alleged that her disruptive behaviour in the market threatened to sabotage Kushok Bakula's campaign. Others attributed her words to madness caused by alcoholism and dismissed them as futile, obscene, or amusing. When her husband died, Docha Ringmo moved into the housing shelter (*lha brang*) owned by Chemre monastery, an affiliate of Hemis, the largest and most powerful religious institution in Ladakh. Chemre monastery was also patronized by Docha Ringmo's natal village, Kharu.

According to Tshering Phuntsog Shunu (Shunu Meme), the DNC candidate of 1962, now an octogenarian famous for his memory of the past, and Nawang Choldan, a member of Docha Ringmo's patri-fraternity (*pha spun*) and a monk in the Chemre monastery who cared for her in her dying days, she had once met Rimpoche Stagtshang Raspa Nawang Jampal (the fifth incarnate abbot of

Hemis) and had expressed the desire to bequeath her *perag* and wealth (*nor ca lags*) to Chemre monastery because she had no children. On her request, the Stagtshang Rimpoche had issued an edict (*bka'shog*) in which it was written that after Docha Ringmo died, the monastery would honour her with a Copper Mask funeral (*zangs-'bag*). A Copper Mask funeral is rather extraordinary, reserved for only the royalty, select houses of the nobility, incarnate monks, and special members of the clergy. Of the different classes of funeral processions held for Buddhist Ladakhis, it is the most prestigious.[7] The service is led by sixteen monks wearing bronze masks painted with gold who assist the deceased person's consciousness in its journey to an auspicious rebirth.

Shunu Meme attested that he was one of the three witnesses to the promissory document. Nawang Choldan, too, testified that he had witnessed this edict that Docha Ringmo kept secured in a chest. But monks at Chemre monastery were equally insistent that such a promise of a Copper Mask funeral could not have been made. In our conversation, they maintained that Docha Ringmo had indeed been felicitated by the Katinchan funeral for donors, but there was no remnant of any other commitment. It was illogical, they argued, to assume that a laywoman could have inspired such a distinguished ceremony.

Later that year, Phuntsog Ladakhi, a Ladakhi friend whose father was once a supporter of Kushok Bakula and whose mother, like Docha Ringmo, was from the village of Kharu, provided information that further complicated matters. His mother had wanted me to know that the promise about the Copper Mask funeral had indeed been made but it had not been carried through. Like the world of the living, the world of the dead is dependent on the prayers and patronage of those who are left behind. Without children, there was no one to stake this claim for Docha Ringmo after her death.

That the promise was not fulfilled was also a position maintained by Docha Ringmo's nephew, Nawang Choldan, although the reasons he proffered were different. In 1976, when death came upon her after an illness that lasted three days, the political environment and the administration of Chemre monastery had changed. More than twenty years had passed since the promise had been made. The fortunes of Hemis monastery had undergone much turmoil, with the sixth abbot being exiled in Tibet after leaving Ladakh in 1956 and a new incarnation, Drugpa Rimpoche, taking over its affairs in 1975. In these new climes, the storekeeper (*phyag mdzod*) of Chemre refused to grant Docha Ringmo a Copper Mask funeral. Her *choga* (a ceremony in which the possessions of the deceased are disposed of) was held in the Jo Khang temple in Leh and all the monks from Chemre were present, but when her relatives came forward to claim her property, three respected and affluent elders, including Shunu Meme, were summoned to bear witness to her will. The relatives were stalled by police intervention.

Such clashes between the interests of household and monastery are not uncommon when childless women die without willing their *perag* explicitly to their kin. Ordinarily, funerary rites are sponsored by those who expect to inherit the name or wealth of the deceased. Monks accrue proceeds from auctions of the dead person's personal possessions. In this case, the monastery of Chemre was awarded the property and Docha Ringmo's corpse was led in a Katinchan procession through Leh bazaar. It was a sight that astonished people. On the streets was frequently heard the refrain, '*ldo ca ring mo so de can*' ('Docha Ringmo is a fortunate one') because it was the first time in a hundred years that a body was carried so ceremoniously through the marketplace. In 1977–8, dismantled turquoise (*gyu*) pieces from the *perag* were used for the interior and exterior ornamentation (*phra rgyan*) of seven statues of Buddhist deities that were commissioned for Chemre monastery. The rest of the turquoise was sold to buyers in the bazaar of Leh.

Women and labour in the modern marketplace

The marketplace of Leh where Docha Ringmo spent a considerable part of her life is popularly called Bazaar Soma, 'the New Market'. The bazaar features in almost all the memoirs of travellers who passed through this region during colonial times. For example, the British artist Arthur McCormick (1895) describes it as a cosmopolitan place where traders from beyond the Karakorams sat with their wares in the month of September, selling carpets and furs and telling stories of their travels. Correspondingly, the memoir of Moravian missionary doctors Adolf and Kathleen Heber (1926: 140) concludes that 'no description of Ladak could be complete which did not consider the merchants who meet here from the four points of the compass'. Commenting on the bazaar's contemporary importance to the display of status and self, Abdul Ghani Sheikh, a prominent historian of Ladakh, has this to say:

> When one political faction won an election or a team championship, they demonstrated their trophies through the bazaar. It was here that women greeted VIPs and dignitaries with pitchers of consecrated beer. In the Red Square, or Indira Gandhi Square as it was later named, some were honoured with prayer scarves of white silk while others were denuded of their ceremonial attire. Boasts, praises, grievances were all aired here. Blood has stained this market, bullets have been fired, stones have been thrown, and hearts have been laid bare under the influence of alcohol.[8]

In addition to its role as a political stage, the bazaar is an architectural testimony to the colonial conflation of commerce and administration. Although it had been a bustling hub in precolonial times, it was vastly expanded and systematized after Ladakh was annexed by the Dogras in1834. The Dogra king reached a settlement with the British government through the Treaty of Amritsar in 1846 whereby he was able to buy the region of Kashmir for a sum of 7.5 million rupees and an annual indemnity that included three pairs of *pashmina* shawls. The British, however, held on to their control over regional trade through a commercial treaty that they signed with the Dogra Maharaja in 1870. This accord facilitated their access to lucrative raw *pashmina* and allowed them to establish the post of a British Joint Commissioner to be stationed in Leh for three months for the purpose of monitoring trade. The marketplace was extended and a court, treasury, police station, *charas* (cannabis) warehouses and tax checkpoints were erected within its parameters. The British even renamed it 'Victoria bazaar' in 1901.[9] Under Dogra/British colonial rule, a new mercantile capitalism arose, built upon earlier feudal systems of trade around the luxury commodity, *pashmina.* Much emphasis was placed on regulating trans-Himalayan trade and finding new ways to generate profits from it. Agriculture was overhauled through land surveys in such a way that the ownership rights and hereditary privileges of aristocratic families (*sku-drag*) were consolidated as they were put in charge of revenue collection from the villages. The system of *begar* labour obligated villagers to provide human services as porters, herders and workers on royal and monastic estates (Grist 1985: 91–102). Consequently, subsistence cultivation and ideals of self-sufficiency received a considerable setback. As the reliance on trade goods increased, the marketplace and its male-centred activities rose in importance. At the same time, a shadow economy of prostitutes and beer sellers like Docha Ringmo grew in response to the new migrants and traders.

The accomplishments of male merchants and their caravans laden with wool, silk, salt, tea and turquoise have been relatively well documented. As far as women's productivity is concerned, colonial travellers and officials frequently contrasted the freedom enjoyed by Ladakhi women with veiling and other restrictive customs that constrained Kashmiri and Indian women.[10] For example, in his descriptions of the summer caravan traffic, Marco Pallis (1939), a member of an English mountaineering expedition, mentions traders from Turkestan who were accompanied by women wearing embroidered dresses and veils 'as opposed to their Ladakhi sisters who moved about freely'. Frederick Drew (1875: 248), who served as Governor of Ladakh, refers to the hardiness of Ladakhi men and women who functioned as coolies, carrying as much as 60 pounds for distances as far as 24 miles and coming in singing at the end. Yet despite comments on their mobility and freedom, English travel descriptions compared the labour of Ladakhi women to the industrious yet backward character of peasants at home.

After the collapse of the *pashmina* trade due to shrinking markets in Europe,

Ladakh's thriving economy was severely affected (Rizvi 1999). It continued to be a significant locus in British imperial designs, no longer as a place for potential profit but as a buffer state and frontier zone against Russian advances in the great game of political dominance over Asia. These interests kept the colonial investment in development alive. As part of the colonial endeavour, missionary wives stoically combated physical hardships, frequent illnesses and separation from their families with philanthropic initiatives, including classes for knitting socks, pullovers and girdles. Moravian missionaries started an industrial school in Leh in 1939 in which women learned to weave carpets and blankets that were subsequently sent to British soldiers stationed in the Northwest Frontier province and to the Indian Red Cross Society.[11] In addition to a civil dispensary in the bazaar, a Rescue Centre was opened for destitute women where they were instructed in knitting and Christian prayers. Missionary wives gave lessons on bible stories, hygiene and secular education to modernize the locals (Bray 1985).

Toward the mid-twentieth century, development became the mission of the nationalist and postcolonial government as well (Chakravarti 1989: 259–87). During the period following Indian independence in 1947, there were demands by local interests in Ladakh that a substantial budget be allocated for development projects such as the construction of roads and canals, agriculture and horticulture, small-scale industrialization, education and health (Kaul and Kaul 1992). After the Sino-Indian war of 1961–2, large numbers of troops were stationed in Ladakh and concerted improvements were made in transport and communication links. A Development Committee was constituted in 1965 to intensify work on electrical power, education and irrigation, and to rectify regional imbalances within the state. Forms of indentured labour were abolished. As Ladakh's significance as a border area increased, subsidized foods flooded in, making local agriculture less viable and generating a culture of dependency. The district became targeted for large-scale development.

But if the region's developmental potential was recognized in government reports and five-year plans, it was centred on male-dominated marketing and import transactions. Economic activities in which women prevailed, especially selling local foods during the chaos of Partition and then fruits and vegetables that were essential sources of survival for the army from 1961 until the late 1970s, were usually small-scale and seasonal and therefore were overlooked or treated as domestic pastimes. Even today, government considerations about integrating women in the development process are channelled mainly through welfare schemes undertaken by the Social Welfare Department – providing training and credit for handicrafts, immunization, soup kitchens for children, and enhancing school enrolment. These programmes have had limited success, alleges Spalzes Angmo (1999: 383–8), the councillor nominated to represent women in the Ladakh Autonomous Hill Development Council of Leh, because they are patterned according to national frameworks that fail to recognize the distinct cultural and geographical conditions of Ladakh. According to her, women do not have a greater say in decision making around the family budget because they are not financially stable and lack cooperative societies for marketing their products. The government's failure to consider women's labour seriously is indicated in a paragraph from the *Economic Review of the District of Leh (1990–1991)*, used as a guideline for drafting the annual budget, which states that 'the arts and crafts of Leh are as peculiar as the people themselves.... Pretty women sell vegetables, fruits and typical Ladakhi handicraft in the bazaar.'

While postcolonial trends reinforce late colonial practices of relegating Ladakhi women's subsistence and economic strategies to a primitive past that must be modernized, *perag*-clad women have made a comeback as icons of tradition. They adorn national commercials, first-day covers, and even the gates of military sites, symbolizing the quaint and diverse heritage of border zones that the state supposedly protects. Despite their growing presence, real women find little recognition as economic actors in the marketplace.

Indigenous pasts and transnational agendas

The year that Docha Ringmo died marked a major transformation in market relations. The Leh–Srinagar highway was completed and the improvement of transport fostered a new wave of tourists, often interested in 'green travel' – alternative tourism and sustainable development. Ladakh's topography and cultural landscape captured the imagination of travellers inspired by the harmonious balance between environment and humanity prescribed in Buddhist teachings.[12] Visitors to the region now included students earning school credit or work experience from volunteering in one or more of the numerous non-governmental organizations. Tourist brochures, documentary films, and even advertisement campaigns for products like Rolex watches played on the image of Ladakh as a pristine site inhabited by endangered species of antelopes, snow leopards, ibex and ecologically responsible, serene natives.

Perhaps no other work directed as much attention to Ladakh as Helena Norberg-Hodge's book *Ancient Futures: Learning from Ladakh* (1991), making the region famous in international circles as a haven of sustainable development. This book has seen several reprints and has been translated into more than 25 languages. The 1993 video that accompanies it is popular viewing in classrooms around the world. Norberg-Hodge produces a passionate argument against 'the development hoax' by showing how the rampant pursuit of Western-styled 'monocultural consumerism' has led to environmental degradation, fragmented social relations, and loss of self- sufficiency. In her model, Ladakh represented a precolonial economy organized on the principles of cooperative agriculture.[13] It was a place for strong women whose contributions to field and hearth were tremendous and whose control over resources was substantial. Development policies have now tilted the balance of power towards an economic structure of trade controlled by men. Therefore, according to Norberg-Hodge's argument, Ladakh's sustainability depends on 'ancient futures' where counter-developmental efforts must incorporate traditional modes of agricultural and labour practices. Funded largely by Danish and Swedish sources, Norberg-Hodge's NGO, the International Society for Ecology and Culture (ISEC) established the Ladakh Ecological Development Project (LEDeG) in 1983, with the objective of promoting alternative technologies in the areas of energy, agriculture and handicrafts, and programmes for education and information (Bertelsen 1996).

In the early 1990s, Norberg-Hodge launched the Women's Alliance of Ladakh (WAL) under the umbrella of ISEC for the preservation of cultural pride and dissemination of indigenous women's knowledge. This Alliance claims to have a constituency of over 4,000 women from 82 villages in the Leh district. WAL inaugurated its own centre in Leh in 1999. Its Ladakhi name, *la-dwags a ma'i tshogs pa*, translates as 'Ladakh Mother's Alliance'. A stalk of barley is the organization's emblem. Barley is the staple subsistence crop of the countryside that is facing stiff competition from government subsidies of rice and wheat, and rapidly losing popularity in locations where urban tastes are setting in. WAL serves as a platform for farming women who have otherwise been relegated to the background by patriarchy and by educated groups. In recent years, the more prominent assignments that it has undertaken include the Farm Stay Project, placing Western youth in homesteads in Leh to acquire practical training in farm work, and taking Ladakhi women on 'reality tours' of the West and other parts of India to demystify the glamour of modernity. WAL encourages traditional agricultural methods that avoid the use of chemical fertilizers and pesticides. Many of its members are skilful horticulturalists who sell surplus vegetables in the market. They often place signs in English to advertise their organically grown products. The group also holds annual fairs where women demonstrate their skills in spinning and cooking, and display their agricultural products.[14] Such programmes support the key assumption promoted by WAL that women historically have been guardians of the earth, of the family and community, and that social development (*yar gyas*) can only be achieved by paying heed to Ladakh's feminine heritage.

WAL attempts to reclaim neglected voices and give credence to women's words by speaking out against social injustice so that women can take pride in their knowledge and defend their rights. This organization has initiated campaigns in Leh and in the countryside, urging women to assert their cultural heritage by wearing the *perag* and clothes spun of local wool for festivals and ceremonial gatherings. It prescribes fining women who are not traditionally dressed. In its earlier phase, WAL members from Leh also went on tours to rural areas to urge peasants to continue eating barley-based foods. These measures were not too popular with rural women who felt they were being lectured to by urban women. It has been difficult for WAL to retain momentum among its rural members, despite its desire to be seen as a decentralized and pan-Ladakhi movement inspired by 'the ethical and spiritual values on which Ladakhi culture is based'. Where WAL has been more successful is in its practical measures such as relief for flood victims, the revival of anti-polythene campaigns to restrict trash in urban areas, and the annual fair in which group action seems more spontaneous. WAL remains a Leh-based project so far, managed by efficient and knowledgeable women.

As the primary fund raiser for WAL, Norberg-Hodge's ISEC has come under criticism for promoting a selective interpretation of indigenous knowledge where indigenous has meant Buddhist, even though half of Ladakh's population is Muslim (Bertelsen 1996). The main drawback of its orientation is a lack of historical and class analysis, so that Ladakhis are depoliticized and their demand to make development work for them misrepresented (van Beek 2000: 250–66). Although Norberg-Hodge's approach formulates insightful associations between globalization and the marginalization of local economies, it is based on the assumption that an authentic Ladakhi past can be recuperated, and that when this recovery takes place it will result in a society more egalitarian in terms of gender. But if we have learned anything from critiques of ecofeminist readings of the Chipko movement in the Himalayan foothills, it is that we cannot take for granted that agricultural initiatives by Southern women have a naturalized spirit of collectivity, when legitimate means of community participation are not available to all women.

Aggrandizing female reproduction and agricultural fertility as a local solution to the problems of capitalism assumes that control over land is neutral and equal. Dislocation and migration, however, are not only realities for men attracted to the market economy, they are also generated by systems of marriage and inheritance, which make it difficult for women to derive permanent connections with land. Women derive respectability from the upkeep of fields and hearth where they play a vital role in cultivation, but the Ladakhi system of descent is largely patrilineal and land is generally transmitted through the male line. The eldest son customarily inherited the house and the fields, but since polyandry was legally prohibited in 1941 and primogeniture in 1943, all brothers are equally entitled to the land. Instead of fixed property, daughters, especially the eldest ones, receive kitchen vessels and livestock as well as their mother's *perag* over which they retain control if the marriage fails. Under modified inheritance laws, daughters are now entitled to shares of paternal land but they seldom feel free to claim it.[15]

It must also be remembered that, even though Ladakhis regard motherhood as an avenue of strength and empowerment for women (Reis 1983: 217–29; Ahmed 1996), the consequences of childlessness are severe. Childless women are pitied and are often subject to allegations of witchcraft, promiscuity and evil. Because female fertility is the way most women secure their future, to be without children is to know the desolate possibility of being without name, without status, without family, and of dying without leaving any memory. Bearing children is therefore one of the primary ways through which women can stake a claim in familial, religious and national heritage. Women without children can select spiritual renunciation or modify their childless situation by adopting offspring. Motherhood is celebrated and encouraged in lay households where the entrance of a child into the monastic order will bring prestige to the family (Grimshaw 1994). The production of devoted citizens who become members of monasteries results in the regulation of the sexual and reproductive powers of women. Monasteries, the biggest land-owning institutions besides the state, rely on the labour of household women for the bulk of farm work on their lands. Women also contribute to religious efforts by sponsoring prayer ceremonies and household rituals and giving donations for the construction of shrines and places of worship. In their capacity as oracles, enlightened saints or Tantric teachers (Shaw 1994; Klein 1995), divinities (Gyatso 1987) and nuns, women are considered an integral part of Buddhism. But while there are means for them to attain enlightenment, they are prevented from realizing spiritual self-worth by systems of social and ecclesiastical hierarchy (Klein 1995). Nuns, for instance, serve as mediators between profane and sacred domains, performing practical chores but rarely rising to positions of power such as teachers or supervisors of liturgical services (Grimshaw 1994; Havnevik 1994: 259–66). As a result, they cannot accumulate the same land endowments as monks and are subject to censorship and surveillance by monastic authorities (Gutschow 1998). Most nuns reside in their homes and assist in domestic chores; only a small percentage are sent to nunneries, where they are seldom given opportunities for learning the scriptures.[16]

A celibate path of nunhood is what the niece of Docha Ringmo who had been divorced by Sonam Wangyal opted for, but for this she had to leave Ladakh and reside in Dharamsala. Docha Ringmo eked out a living in the marketplace as a migrant instead, away from customary networks of her family and village community. Like most married women in this largely patrilocal society, she had made the journey to the abode of her husband in Leh, where she was propelled into a public sphere in which the terms of trade were generally controlled by men. The commodity that she sold, home-brewed beer (*chang*), had become increasingly 'criminalized', to use David Hardiman's term (1986: 165–228), because both colonial and postcolonial governments in Ladakh made attempts to prevent its sale on the grounds that liquor consumption promoted indolence and immorality.[17] *Chang*, brewed in virtually every Buddhist house in rural areas, was a crucial commodity in their social exchange and cultural life. For the land-owning classes, *chang* was a symbol of prosperity and surplus when food is plentiful. In Leh, the conversion of agricultural land into hotels and guesthouses for tourism and administrative purposes, and the increased migration from rural areas, altered the traditional production and cultural significance of alcohol.[18] Selling alcohol on market streets was eventually banned in the early 1970s by a series of official directives.[19] Although prohibited on the streets of the market, this business continued to be practised in private houses or domestic pubs. Local pubs came to be concentrated around an alley called Chang Gali. Their clientèle largely comprised rural migrants, working-class locals and soldiers. Whereas serving beer in agricultural households was considered appropriate and honourable for women, its commodification has meant that women like Docha Ringmo, who provided such services for remuneration in urban areas, were associated with landless destitution or prostitution.[20]

These days, migrant *chang* sellers have been pushed out from the front of the market into its back alleys, but vegetable and fruit sellers, who mostly hail from landowning households in Leh, have thwarted recurrent threats of eviction by town planners and mercantile cooperatives.[21] Other migrants and landless women who hawk a variety of petty commodities – hand-knitted woollen clothing, roasted potatoes, buttermilk, inexpensive fabrics, household utensils – have also been made to conduct their business on pavements further away from the main strip. Migrant workers still find it difficult to find hostel accommodation in Leh that is safe and free from sexual harassment.

The problems of migrants and sex workers have been taken up by women-centred NGOs that were often started as philanthropic efforts by educated women in Leh. The Leh Mahila Mandal, begun in 1986 under the Social Welfare Department, has among its objectives schemes to uplift destitute women and provide social and economic opportunities for them. Two of the organizations started in the 1990s, the Women Welfare Society, registered in 1994, and the Ladakh Pume Yarketh Tsokpa (LPYT) or Ladakh Women's Development Society, founded in 1992, aim to assist uneducated, single and economically deprived women by educating them and providing employment skills so that they can rise out of poverty or prostitution. But to be effective these organizations need to heed critiques of structural inequalities in the modern market sector rather than merely looking upon modernity as the answer to impoverishment.

Groups such as ISEC and WAL could also re-examine their assumption that indigenous Ladakhi femininity is uniformly Buddhist, landed and maternal. For Docha Ringmo's case reminds us that retrieving and identifying indigenous women only on the basis of their religious, agricultural and maternal roles runs the risk of precluding a collective space for those like her who are neither householders nor learned nuns, who possess a legacy of neither land nor progeny. While recognizing the constraints placed on women by the marketplace, one must ask what are the experiential aspects of their lives that would propel them to service a male world.[22] Even within the shadow economy of sex work and alcohol sales, Docha Ringmo led a visible life in the market with several lines of turquoise flowing from her head.[23] She stood up to what she perceived to be an injustice to her niece and husband by taking on powerful political figures. But she also went against the imperatives of her family and bargained for her own meritorious rebirth and place in history. Such a paradoxical life demands a complex response and careful attention of transnational feminist networks, not simple classifications of Ladakhi women as exemplary, *perag*-wearing ecologists resisting modernity or downtrodden victims of market economies deserving occasional charitable intervention.

Ornamental histories

Histories and legacies of women have left their traces in the marketplace of Leh. Two of its main edifices, the mosque that stands near the palace at one end of the bazaar and the sacred *mani* wall built of consecrated rocks at the other end, were constructed under the aegis of Queen Gyal Khatoun in the seventeenth century and Zilzom, wife of an eighteenth-century prime minister, respectively. Aristocratic ladies can sometimes inspire ancestral walls and shrines that live on in public memory. The tragic and heroic aspects of the lives of such queens and noble women are aired on radio and performed on stage. Not having the means for religious patronage or spiritual rank, ordinary women have fewer opportunities to command grand funerals, much less Copper Mask ones. Their histories can lapse into collective amnesia without folk genres of telling and retelling to keep them alive.

Docha Ringmo's life blurs lines between legend and history, story and information. Replete with elements that fuse spiritual, heroic, and tragic motifs, it finds resonance with tales of courtly intrigue and descriptions of sacred quests for a virtuous and transcendent afterlife. As a narrative that emerges from the market, it can be classified as *ba zar ri dpe ra* ('market talk'), both to connote 'the latest in the market' or else 'just market talk', indicating the slippery nature of the market, a locus for the dissemination of information but also for the generation and distribution of rumours and gossip. Her story reflects the struggle between familial priorities and spiritual obligations that are a vital component of the biographies of female saints (Allione 1984). Unlike the teachings of these saints which are retold as crucial lessons, however, several middle-class women I interviewed perceived the words of Docha Ringmo as dangerous or absurd, partly out of sympathy for her plight but also because they exposed areas of women's anxieties: homelessness, childlessness, gossip. Docha Ringmo had put on her *perag* and jewellery, ornaments suggesting landed status, in a place and for a profession not subject to the norms of the class they were meant to represent. 'It's not that her *perag* was so big but that she wore it all the time, ridiculously. Sitting on the street – day in and day out,' commented a government clerk who lives in the neighbourhood behind the bazaar. If it was men who could substantially narrate details of Docha Ringmo's life to me, it is because she lived and died in domains they were familiar with. Doubly outcast by her childless status and her slippage into a lower class category, Docha Ringmo lives on as a dubious ancestor for women, an uncomfortable reminder of the real misfortunes that can befall even the wealthiest of them. Her infamous speech is still subject to silencing mechanisms. When children utter unacceptable words, mothers in Leh warn them not to talk like that outrageous old woman. It is the older generation of women, who have risen from poverty by selling *chang* and working in the fields of landholders, who speak compassionately of Docha Ringmo. For instance, a woman called Abhi Lhazom, who was also from Kharu and had once sold *chang* too, sympathized with her suffering, her work and her resilience, and marvelled at the funeral she was given.

As Ladakhi women are directly affected by the world of market capitalism, Docha Ringmo's biography can lend itself to pragmatic agendas and public policies so that initiatives on sustainability and collective action are modelled not on virtual women, essentialized through tradition or modernity, but on the multiple positions of class and caste that women identify with. Biographical information on the lives of women reveals that subjects are not fixed in bounded categories of class or place and that the realms of identity are constantly being contested. Such histories are pertinent, not for the absolute retrieval of an authentic subjectivity, but 'as an intervention in the historical present' (Sinha 1994: 499), opening possibilities for redressing structural inequalities in the marketplace and in the home, and for reinforcing efforts that enhance women's agency.

In Ladakhi poetry, metaphors are considered ornaments that adorn the bare body of words, enabling the articulation of ideas more expressively and truthfully. Similarly, turquoise tales told through local contexts can prove to be valuable jewels for understanding the multiple constructions of womanhood in Ladakh. By pointing to the common dilemmas which Ladakhi women face and also to the differences between women from different classes, the story of Docha Ringmo can blaze trails on which more realistic coalitions between transnational groups can be formed.

Notes

1 It is ironic that this mannequin's movements are so dependent on electrical power, given that the biggest development scandal in Ladakh has been the much-publicized and expensive Stakna dam project which electrifies Leh, plagued as it is by endless delays, corruption, and design flaws, operating sporadically and at a level of efficiency far below the expected rate.

2 For example, Spivak (1988: 271–313). See Basu (2000: 68–84) for a critical analysis of transnational networks.

3 Abu-Lughod (1990a: 41–55), Enslin (1998: 269–300), and Visweswaran (1996: 83–129) also discuss women's subjectivity in this manner.

4 After reading about her in 1996, I have continued to investigate the story of Docha Ringmo's life but even though virtually every Ladakhi adult above the age of thirty-five that I have interviewed knows about her, there are gaps and contradictions in their accounts that are still difficult to resolve.

5 One exception to this system of transmission is the royal family of Leh, in which it is the new queen, usually the daughter-in-law, who inherits the royal *perag*.

6 Similarly, in her autobiography, *House of the Turquoise Roof*, Dorje Yudon Yuthok (1990: 185), says that 'In Tibet the jewelry, dress, and make-up of ladies differed according to their station in life and according to the region.' She reports that in 1929 the thirteenth Dalai Lama, believing that women's obsession with jewellery was driving households into debt and hardship, decreed restrictions on the monetary value of jewellery that women could own or wear, stipulating differential amounts for women of the noble and lower classes. With the Dalai Lama's death in 1933, this limit was abolished.

7 The eminent Sonam Norbu was one of the only men outside the aristocratic and ecclesiastical order to receive a Copper Mask funeral from Hemis.

8 With the writer's permission, I have translated this quote from a commentary given by him on All India Radio, Leh.

9 I obtained this information from the Political Department files of the Jammu and Kashmir State Archives, record number 72–B–59.

10 The seclusion and alleged barbaric treatment of Indian women became the justification for the civilizing mission of British imperialism. The British used 'the woman question' to argue that Indian society was incapable of self-rule (Mani 1989: 88–126; Sinha 1995: 477–504).

11 From the 'Annual Report of the West Himalaya Mission' (1940–1), *Periodical Accounts of the Work of the Moravian Missions* 150, 3–9.

12 See Tony Huber (1997: 103–19) for discussion of how political and environmental ideologies of the 1980s shaped the perception of Tibetan Buddhist cultures as 'green'.

13 In several interviews (for example, Asia Source 2001 at http://198.31.4.183/news/special_reports/hodge.cfm), Helena Norberg-Hodge has erroneously stated that Ladakh provides a vision of an economy that has not been colonized. Additional information on the philosophy and programmes of ISEC can be found on their website, http://www.isec.org.uk.

14 These objectives are spelled out in a flyer distributed by WAL.

15 In the absence of a brother, women can bring in a spouse (*mag-pa*) and pass on the family's land to her children. Reforms in Buddhist civil law come under the Hindu Civil Code in India. Changes in the legal status of Indian women's property rights have been documented by Agarwal (1994). In Ladakh, the Ladakh Autonomous Hill Development Council is now making new land allotments in Leh town jointly in the name of husband and wife (van Beek 2000).

16 The welfare of nuns has now been taken up by NGOs such as the Ladakh Nuns Association, established in 1996 by the Venerable Tshering Palmo.

17 Excise duties on *chang* produced at home, however, were exempted by Maharaja Ranbir Singh; this was upheld in later years by the Dogra and British administrators (Political Department files of the Jammu and Kashmir State Archives, 6/H–34, 1901).

18 During the last two decades, numerous bars and restaurants have opened with licences to

sell bottled liquor imported from outside Ladakh. These Western-styled bar enterprises primarily employ men.

19 In recent 'social reform' movements by Buddhist youth organizations, the curtailment of *chang* has been the target of intense campaigning.

20 For a description of women hosts serving *chang* in the rural Himalayas, see also Kathryn March (1987: 351–87).

21 To an extent, exiled Tibetan women from other parts of India who move to Ladakh in the summer with the flow of tourists, selling jewellery (including ready-made *perags*), souvenirs and art objects, have also formed alliances through which they press their claims for space in the market.

22 Recent studies on gender and labour (Babb 1989; Clark 1994; Kapchan 1996; Watkins 1996) have revealed that the market is a domain where women face exploitation but it is also a location in which they can recontextualize histories of labour and exchange through new social and expressive forms. The presence of Tibetan women in the public space of the Leh bazaar, for example, enables them to feed their families, patronize Buddhist institutions, especially liturgical services to the goddess Tara, and also to cope with conditions of exile (Aggarwal 1995: 33–8).

23 As Oldenburg (1990: 259–87) has demonstrated, women can select sex work as a means to accumulate wealth and subvert oppressive bonds of family and marriage.

I am indebted to Aba Sonam Phuntsog and all those who shared their knowledge about Docha Ringmo with me. I owe many thanks also to Frédérique Apffel-Marglin, Piya Chatterjee, Carol Greenhouse, Martijn van Beek, Kamala Visweswaran, Christopher Wheeler and Suzanne Zhang-Gottschang for their support and comments, and to discussions at the Anthropology seminar at Harvard University, the Five College Women's Studies Center at Mount Holyoke College, and the Annenberg School of Communication at the University of Pennsylvania, where different versions of this chapter were presented.

Part II

The Feminization of the Global Economy

4

Counter-geographies of Globalization

Feminization of Survival[1]

Saskia Sassen

The last decade has seen a growing presence of women in a variety of cross-border circuits. These circuits are enormously diverse but share one feature: they are profit- or revenue-making circuits developed on the backs of the truly disadvantaged. They include the illegal trafficking in people for the sex industry and for various types of formal and informal labour markets. And they include cross-border migrations, both documented and not, which have become an important source of hard currency for governments in home countries. The employment and/or use of foreign-born women covers an increasingly broad range of economic sectors, some illegal and illicit, such as prostitution, and some in highly regulated industries like nursing. The key actors giving shape to these processes are the women themselves in search of work, but also, and increasingly so, illegal traffickers and contractors as well as governments of home countries.

The evidence for any of these conditions is incomplete and partial, yet there is a growing consensus among experts that they are expanding and that women are often a majority, including in situations that used to be mostly male. All of these conditions have emerged as factors in the lives of a growing number of women from developing or struggling economies. These are, in many ways, old conditions. What is different today is their rapid growth and their rapid internationalization. This article maps some of the key features of these counter-geographies, particularly as they involve foreign-born women. The logic organizing the effort is the possibility of systemic links between, on one hand, the growth of these alternative circuits for survival, for profit making, and for hard-currency earning, and, on the other, major conditions in developing countries that are associated with so-called 'development', particularly through economic globalization. Among these conditions are a growth in unemployment, the closure of a large number of typically small and medium-sized enterprises oriented to national rather than export markets, and large, often increasing government debt. While these economies are frequently grouped under the label developing, they are in some cases struggling or stagnant and even shrinking. For the sake of brevity I will use 'developing' as shorthand for this variety of situations.

Mapping a new conceptual landscape

The variety of global circuits that are incorporating growing numbers of women have strengthened at a time when major dynamics linked to economic globalization have had significant impacts on developing economies. The latter have had to implement a bundle of new policies and accommodate new conditions associated with globalization: structural adjustment programmes, the opening up of these economies to foreign firms, the elimination of multiple state subsidies, and, it would seem almost inevitably, financial crises and the prevailing types of programmatic solutions put forth by the IMF. It is now clear that in most of the countries involved, these conditions have created enormous costs for certain sectors of the economy and of the population without fundamentally reducing government debt.

Among these costs are, prominently, the growth in unemployment, the closure of a large number of firms in often fairly traditional sectors oriented to the local or national market as a result of growing foreign investment and lifting of import barriers, the promotion of export-oriented cash crops which have increasingly replaced survival agriculture and food production for local or national markets, and, finally, the ongoing heavy burden of government debt in most of these economies resulting partly from the massive increase in public and private loans extended to these countries in the 1980s and 1990s.

Are there systemic links between these two sets of developments – the growing presence of women from developing economies in the variety of global circuits described above and the rise in unemployment and debt in those same economies? One way of articulating this in substantive terms is to posit that (1) the shrinking opportunities for male employment in many of these countries, (2) the shrinking opportunities for more traditional forms of profit making in these same countries as they increasingly accept foreign firms in a widening range of economic sectors and are pressured to develop export industries, and (3) the fall in revenues for the governments in many of these countries, partly linked to these conditions and to the burden of debt servicing, have (4) all contributed to raising the importance of alternative ways of making a living, making a profit, and securing government revenue.

Prostitution and labour migration are growing in importance as ways of making a living; illegal trafficking – in women and children for the sex industry and in labourers – is growing in importance as a way of making a profit; and the remittances sent by emigrants, as well as the organized export of workers, are increasingly important sources of revenues for some of these governments. Women are by far the majority group in prostitution and in trafficking for the sex industry, and they are becoming a majority group in migration for labour.

These alternative circuits, which I call counter-geographies, are deeply imbricated with some of the major dynamics constitutive of globalization: the formation of global markets, the intensifying of transnational and translocal networks, the development of communication technologies which easily escape conventional surveillance practices. The strengthening and, in some of these cases, the formation of new global circuits is embedded or made possible by the existence of a global economic system and its associated development of various institutional supports for cross-border money flows and markets. These counter-geographies are dynamic and changing in their locational features: to some extent they are part of the shadow economy, but it is also clear that they use some of the institutional infrastructure of the regular economy.

These circuits can be thought of as indicating the (albeit partial) feminization of survival, because it is increasingly on the backs of women that these forms of making a living, making a profit and securing government revenue are realized. Thus in using the notion of feminization of survival I am not only referring to the fact that households and indeed whole communities are increasingly dependent on women for their survival. I want to emphasize the fact that *governments* are also dependent on women's earnings in these various circuits, and so are types of enterprises whose ways of profit making exist at the margins of the 'licit' economy. The main effort, analytically, is to uncover the systemic connections between, on one hand, women who are considered as poor, low-earning and in that regard low value-adding individuals, often represented as a burden rather than a resource, and, on the other hand, what are emerging as significant sources for profit making, especially in the shadow economy, and for government revenue enhancement.

What I have described above is indeed a conceptual landscape. The data are inadequate to prove the argument as such. There are, however, partial bodies of data to document some of these developments. Further, it is possible to juxtapose several data sets, albeit independently gathered, to document some of the interconnections presented above. There is, also, an older literature on women and the debt, focused on the implementation of a first generation of structural adjustment programmes in several developing countries linked to the growing debt of governments in the 1980s; this literature has documented the disproportionate burden these programmes put on women. And now there is a new literature on a second generation of such programmes, one more directly linked to the implementation of the global economy in the 1990s, some of which is cited later on in this chapter. But all these various sources of information do not amount to a full empirical specification of the actual dynamics hypothesized here. They do, however, allow us to document parts of it.

Strategic instantiations of gendering in the global economy

There is by now a fairly long-standing research and theorization effort engaged in recovering the role of women in international economic processes. The central effort in much of this earlier research literature was to balance the excessive focus, typically unexplicated, on men in international economic development research. In the mainstream development literature, these processes have often, perhaps unwittingly, been represented as neutral when it comes to gender. In my reading, globalization has produced yet another set of dynamics in which women are playing a critical role. And, once again, the new economic literature on current globalization processes proceeds as if this new economic phase is gender-neutral. These gender dynamics have been rendered invisible in terms of their articulation with the mainstream global economy. This set of dynamics can be found in the alternative cross-border circuits described above in which the role of women, and especially the condition of being a foreign woman, is crucial. These dynamics can also be found in key features of the mainstream global economy, but this is not the place to discuss these. I think we need to see these current developments as part of this longer-standing history that has made visible women's role in crucial economic processes.

We can identify two older phases in the study of gendering in the recent history of economic internationalization, both concerned with processes that continue today, and a third phase focused on more recent transformations, often involving an elaboration of the categories and findings of the previous two phases. A first phase is the development literature about the implantation of cash crops and wage labour generally, typically by foreign firms, and its partial dependence on a dynamic whereby women subsidized the waged labour of men through their household production and subsistence farming. Boserup (1970), Deere (1976), and many others produced an enormously rich and nuanced literature showing the variants of this dynamic. Far from being unconnected, the subsistence sector and the modern capitalist enterprise were shown to be articulated through a gender dynamic; this gender dynamic, furthermore, was shown to have the effect of veiling this articulation. It was the 'invisible' work of women producing food and other necessities in the subsistence economy that contributed to maintaining extremely low wages on plantations and mines, and thereby supported the 'modernization' of this type of economic activity. The subsistence sector was seen, if at all, as a drag on the modern sector by standard economic analyses. Feminist analyses showed the actual dynamics of this process of modernization and its dependence on the subsistence sector.

A second phase was the scholarship on the internationalization of manufacturing production and the feminization of the proletariat that came with it. The key analytic element in this scholarship was that off-shoring manufacturing jobs under pressure of low-cost imports mobilized a disproportionately female workforce in poorer countries which had hitherto largely remained outside the industrial economy. In this regard it is an analysis that also intersects with national issues, such as why women predominate in certain industries, notably garment and electronics assembly, no matter what the level of development of a country (Benería and Feldman 1992).

Together these two analytics have produced an enormous literature, impressive in its detail and its capacity to illuminate. (For some collections and lengthy bibliographies see Ward 1991; Tinker 1990; Bose and Acosta-Belen 1995; Nash and Safa 1976). It is impossible to do full justice here to these two bodies of scholarship and their contribution to new frameworks for empirical analysis and theorization. The quality of the empirical studies and theoretical formulations they produced helps us understand how much work we need to do in order to theorize the current phase, which contains both these two longer-standing dynamics and a whole new one.

A third phase of scholarship on women and the global economy is emerging around processes that underline transformations in gendering, in women's subjectivities and in women's notions of membership. These represent many different literatures. Among the richest and most promising is the feminist scholarship on women immigrants, which focuses, for example, on how international migration alters gender patterns and how the formation of transnational households can empower women (for example, Chaney and Castro 1987; Grasmuck and Pessar 1991; Boyd 1989; Morokvasic 1984; Hondagneu-Sotelo 1994). There is also an important new scholarship which focuses on the household as a key analytic category to understand global economic processes (for example, Smith and Wallerstein 1992) and on new forms of cross-border solidarity, experiences of membership and identity formation that represent new subjectivities, including feminist subjectivities (for example, Basch *et al.* 1994; Soysal 1994; Eisenstein 1996; but see also Ong 1996).

One important methodological question is what are the strategic sites where current processes of globalization can be studied from a feminist perspective. In export-oriented agriculture it is the nexus between subsistence economies and capitalist enterprise. And in the internationalization of manufacturing production it is the nexus between the dismantling of an established, largely male 'labour aristocracy' in major industries with shadow effects on an increasing sector of developed economies and the formation of an off-shore, largely female proletariat in new and old growth sectors. Off-shoring and feminizing this proletariat (which is, after all, employed in what are growth industries) has kept it from becoming an empowered 'labour aristocracy' with actual union power, and prevents existing largely male 'labour aristocracies' from becoming stronger. Introducing a gendered understanding of economic processes lays bare these connections – the existence of the nexus as an operational reality and an analytic strategy.

What are the strategic sites in today's leading processes of globalization? Elsewhere I have examined this issue from the perspective of key features of the current global economic system (Sassen 1998: Chapter 5). There I emphasized global cities – strategic sites for the specialized servicing, financing and management of global economic processes. These cities are also a site for the incorporation of large numbers of women and immigrants in activities that service the strategic sectors; but this is a mode of incorporation that renders these workers invisible, therewith breaking the connection between being workers in leading industries and the opportunity to become – as had been historically the case in industrialized economies – a 'labour aristocracy' or its contemporary equivalent. In this sense 'women and immigrants' emerge as the systemic equivalent of the off-shore proletariat. Further, the demands placed on the top-level professional and managerial workforce in global cities are such that the usual modes of handling household tasks and lifestyle are inadequate. As a consequence we are seeing the return of the so-called 'serving classes' in all the global cities around the world, made up largely of immigrant and migrant women.

The alternative global circuits that concern me here are yet another instantiation of these dynamics of globalization, but from the perspective of developing economies rather than from the perspective of global cities. Economic globalization needs to be understood in its multiple localizations, many of which do not generally get coded as having anything to do with the global economy. In the next section I give a first empirical specification of some of the localizations of these alternative global circuits, these counter-geographies of globalization. Because the data are inadequate, this is a partial specification. Yet it should serve to illustrate some of the key dimensions.

Government debt

Debt and debt servicing problems have become a systemic feature of the developing world since the 1980s. They are, in my reading, also a systemic feature inducing the formation of the new counter-geographies of globalization.

The impact on women and on the feminization of survival is mediated through the particular features of this debt rather than the fact of debt *per se*. It is with this logic in mind that this section examines various features of government debt in developing economies. There is considerable research showing the detrimental effects of such debt on government programmes for women and children, notably education and health care – clearly investments necessary to ensure a better future.

Further, the increased unemployment typically associated with the austerity and adjustment programmes implemented by international agencies to address government debt have also been found to have adverse effects on women. Unemployment, of women themselves but also more generally of the men in their households, has added to the pressure on women to find ways to ensure household survival. Subsistence food production, informal work, emigration and prostitution have all grown as survival options for women. Heavy government debt and high unemployment have brought with them the need to search for survival alternatives; and a shrinking of regular economic opportunities has brought with it a widened use of illegal profit making by enterprises and organizations. In this regard, heavy debt burdens play an important role in the formation of counter-geographies of survival, of profit making and of government revenue enhancement. Economic globalization has to some extent added to the rapid increase in certain components of this debt and it has provided an institutional infrastructure for cross-border flows and global markets. We can see economic globalization as facilitating the operation of these counter-geographies on a global scale.

Generally, most countries which became deeply indebted in the 1980s have not been able to solve this problem. And in the 1990s we have seen a whole new set of countries become deeply indebted. Over these two decades many innovations were launched, most importantly by the IMF and the World Bank through their structural adjustment programmes and structural adjustment loans, respectively. The latter were tied to economic policy reform rather than the funding of a particular project. The purpose of such programmes is to make states more 'competitive', which typically means sharp cuts in various social programmes. By 1990 there were almost 200 such loans in place. During the 1980s, too, the Reagan administration put enormous pressure on many countries to implement neoliberal policies which resembled the SAPs.

SAPs became a new norm for the World Bank and the IMF on grounds that they were one promising way to secure long-term growth and sound government policy. Yet all of these countries have remained deeply indebted, with 41 of them now considered as Highly Indebted Poor Countries. Furthermore, the actual structure of these debts, their servicing and how they fit into debtor-country economies, suggest that it is not likely that most of these countries will, under

Table 4.1 *Budget allocation to basic social services and debt service in selected countries*

	Country	Year	Total basic social services (%)	Debt service (%)
Asia	Nepal	1997	13.6	14.9
	Philippines	1992	7.7	30.7
	Sri Lanka	1996	12.7	21.5
	Thailand	1997	14.6	1.3
Africa	Benin	1997	9.5	10.8
	Burkina Faso	1997	19.5	10.2
	Cameroon	1996–7	4.0	36.0
	Cote d'Ivoire	1994–6	11.4	35.0
	Kenya	1995	12.6	40.0
	Namibia	1996–7	19.1	3.0
	Niger	1995	20.4	33.0
	South Africa	1996–7	14.0	8.0
	Tanzania (mainland)	1994–5	15.0	46.0
	Uganda	1994–5	21.0	9.4
	Zambia	1997	6.7	40.0
Latin America and the Caribbean	Belize	1996	20.3	5.7
	Bolivia	1997	16.7	9.8
	Brazil	1995	8.9	20.0
	Chile	1996	10.6	2.7
	Colombia	1997	16.8	7.9
	Costa Rica	1996	13.1	13.0
	Dominican Republic	1997	8.7	10.0
	El Salvador	1996	13.0	27.0
	Honduras	1992	12.5	21.0
	Jamaica	1996	10.2	31.2
	Nicaragua	1996	9.2	14.1
	Peru	1997	19.3	30.0

Sources: UNICEF and UNDP 1998.

Table 4.2 *Public expenditure on health, malnutrition, and life expectancy in selected highly indebted countries*

	Public expenditure on health % GDP 1990–8	Prevalence of malnutrition % children under age 5 1992–7	Life expectancy at birth, % change 1990–7
Angola	3.9	35	1.0
Botswana	2.7	27	n/a
Côte d' Ivoire	1.4	24	–3.1
Ethiopia	1.7	48	–1.7
Haiti	1.3	28	n/a
Kenya	2.2	23	–5.0
Mozambique	2.1	26	n/a
Nigeria	0.2	39	1.5
Tanzania	1.3	31	–2.1
Uganda	1.8	26	–4.3
Vietnam	0.4	n/a	1.6
Zambia	2.3	n/a	–6.0
Zimbabwe	3.1	16	n/a

* n/a = not available

Sources: *World Development Report 1999/2000*, World Development Indicators 1999.

current conditions, be able to pay this debt in full. SAPs seem to have made this even more likely by demanding economic reforms that have added to unemployment and the bankruptcy of many smaller firms with national markets.

Even before the economic crisis of the 1990s, the debt of poor countries in the South grew from US$507 billion in 1980 to US$1.4 trillion by 1992. Debt service payments alone had increased to US$1.6 trillion, more than the actual debt. Further, as has been widely recognized now, the South had already paid its debt several times over, and yet its debt grew by 250 per cent. According to Toussaint (1999: 1), from 1982 to 1998 indebted countries paid four times their original debts, and at the same time their debt stocks went up four times.

Yet these countries have been paying a significant share of their total revenues to service their debt. Thirty-three of the 41 Highly Indebted Countries paid US$3 in debt service payments to the North for every US$1 in development assistance. Many of these countries pay over 50 per cent of their government revenues toward debt service or 20–25 per cent of their export earnings (Ambrogi 1999).

This debt burden inevitably has large repercussions on state spending composition. It is well illustrated in the cases of Zambia, Ghana and Uganda, three countries which have been seen as cooperative and responsible by the World Bank as well as effective in implementing SAPs. In Zambia, for example, the government paid US$1.3 billion in debt but only US$37 million for primary education; Ghana's social expenses, at US$75 million, represented 20 per cent of its debt service; and Uganda paid US$9 *per capita* on its debt and only US$1 for health care (Ismi 1998). In 1994 alone these three countries remitted US$2.7 billion to bankers in the North. Africa's payments reached US$5 billion in 1998, which means that for every US$1 in aid, African countries paid US$1.4 in debt service in 1998.

Debt service ratios to GNP in many of the HIPC countries exceed sustainable limits (Oxfam 1999a); many are far more extreme than what were considered unmanageable levels in the Latin American debt crisis of the 1980s. Debt to GNP ratios are especially high in Africa, where they stood at 123 per cent, compared with 42 per cent in Latin America and 28 per cent in Asia (Cheru 1999).

It is these features of the current situation which suggest that most of these countries will not get out of their indebtedness through such current strategies as SAPs. Indeed it would seem that the latter have in many cases had the effect of raising the debt dependence of countries. Further, together with various other dynamics, SAPs have contributed to increases in unemployment and poverty.

In this regard the financial crisis in Southeast Asia at the end of the 1990s is illuminating. These were and remain, indeed, highly dynamic economies. Yet they have been thrown into high levels of indebtedness and economic failure among a broad range of enterprises. The financial crisis – both its architecture and its consequences – has meant the imposition of structural adjustment policies and a growth in unemployment and poverty due to widespread bankruptcies of small and medium-sized firms catering to both national and export markets. The US$120 billion rescue package that allowed for the introduction of SAP provisions, thereby reducing the autonomy of these governments and raising unemployment, went to institutional investors from the outside, rather than to solve the poverty and unemployment of a large number of the people. The management of the crisis through IMF policies has been seen by some as worsening the situation for the unemployed and poor.

Alternative circuits for survival

It is in this context of what I would consider a systemic condition marked by high unemployment, poverty, bankruptcies of large numbers of firms, and shrinking resources in the state to meet social needs, that alternative circuits of survival emerge and can be seen as articulated with those conditions. Here I want to focus on some of the data on the trafficking of women for sex industries and for work; the growing weight of this trafficking as a profit-making option; and the growing weight of remittances sent by migrants in the account balance of many of the sending states.

Trafficking in women

Trafficking involves the forced recruitment and/or transportation of people within and across states for work or services through a variety of forms, all involving coercion. Trafficking is a violation of several distinct types of rights: human, civil, political. Trafficking is related to the sex market, to labour markets, to illegal migration. Much legislative work has been done to address trafficking: international treaties and charters, UN resolutions, and various bodies and commissions (Dayan 2000). NGOs are also playing an increasingly important role.

Trafficking in women for the sex industry is highly profitable for those running the trade. The United Nations estimates that 4 million people were trafficked in 1998, producing a profit of US$7 billion to criminal groups. These funds include remittances from prostitutes' earnings and payments to organizers and facilitators in these countries. In Japan, profits in the sex industry averaged ¥4.2 trillion in recent years. In Poland, police estimate that for each Polish woman delivered, the trafficker receives about US$700. In Australia, the Federal Police estimate that the cash flow from 200 prostitutes is up to A$900,000 a week. (STV–GAATW report). Ukrainian and Russian women, highly prized in the sex market, earn the criminal gangs involved about US$500–1000 per woman delivered. These women can be expected to service on average 15 clients a day, and each can be expected to make about US$15,000 per month for the gang (IOM 1996).

It is estimated that in recent years several million women and girls have been trafficked within and out of Asia and the former Soviet Union, two major trafficking areas. Growth in both these areas can be linked to women being pushed into poverty or sold to brokers owing to the poverty of their households or parents. High unemployment in the former Soviet republics has been one factor promoting growth of both criminal gangs and trafficking in women. Unemployment rates among women in Armenia, Russia, Bulgaria and Croatia reached 70 per cent, and in the Ukraine 80 per cent, with the implementation of market policies. There is some research indicating that economic need is the bottom line for entry into prostitution.

Trafficking in migrants is also a profitable business. According to a UN report, criminal organizations in the 1990s generated an estimated US$3.5 billion per year in profits from trafficking migrants generally (not just women) (IOM 1996). The entry of organized crime is a recent development. Before, migrant trafficking was mainly in the hands of petty criminals. There are also reports that organized crime groups are creating intercontinental strategic alliances through networks of co-ethnics throughout several countries; this facilitates transport, local contact and distribution, provision of false documents, etcetera. The Global Survival Network reported on these practices after a two-year investigation, using the establishment of a dummy company to enter the illegal trade (1997). Such networks also facilitate the organized circulation of trafficked women among third countries – not only from sending to receiving countries. Traffickers may move women from Burma, Laos, Vietnam and China to Thailand, while Thai women may have been moved to Japan and the US.

Some of the features of immigration policy and enforcement may well contribute to make women who are victims of trafficking even more vulnerable and to give them little recourse to the law. If they are undocumented, which they are likely to be, they will not be treated as victims of abuse but as violators of the law insofar as they have violated entry, residence and work laws. The attempt to address undocumented immigration and trafficking through greater border controls over entry raises the likelihood that women will use traffickers to cross the border, and some of these may turn out to belong to criminal organizations linked to the sex industry.

Further, in many countries prostitution is forbidden for foreign women, which further enhances the role of criminal gangs in prostitution. It also diminishes one of the survival options of foreign women, who may have limited access to jobs generally. Prostitution is tolerated for foreign women in other countries while regular labour market jobs are less available to them – this is the case, for instance, in the Netherlands and in Switzerland. According to IOM data, the number of migrant women prostitutes in many EU countries is far higher than that for nationals: 75 per cent in Germany, for instance, or 80 per cent in the case of Milan in Italy.

While some women know that they are being trafficked for prostitution, for many the conditions of their recruitment and the extent of abuse and bondage only become evident after they arrive in the receiving country. The conditions of confinement are often extreme, akin to slavery, and so are the conditions of abuse, including rape and other forms of sexual violence, and physical punishments. They are severely underpaid, and wages are often withheld. They are prevented from using protection methods to prevent against HIV–Aids, and typically have no right to medical treatment. If they seek police help they may be taken into detention because they are in violation of immigration laws; if they have been provided with false documents there are criminal charges.

As tourism has grown sharply over the last decade and become a major development strategy for cities, regions and whole countries, the entertainment sector has seen a parallel growth and recognition as a key development strategy (Wonders and Michalowski 2000; Judd and Fainstein 1999). In many places, the sex trade is part of the entertainment industry and has kept pace with its growth. At some point it becomes clear that the sex trade itself can become a development strategy in areas with high unemployment and poverty and governments desperate for revenue and foreign exchange reserves. When local manufacturing and agriculture can no longer function as sources of employment, of profits and of government revenue, what was once a marginal source of earnings, profits and revenues now becomes a far more important one. This increased importance of these sectors in development generates growing tie-ins. For instance, when the IMF and the World Bank see tourism as a solution to the development impasse in many poor countries and provide loans for its development, they may well be contributing to developing a broader institutional setting for the expansion of the entertainment industry and indirectly of the sex trade. This tie-in with development strategies signals that trafficking in women may well see a sharp expansion.

The entry of organized crime in the sex trades, the formation of cross-border ethnic networks, and the growing transnationalization in so many aspects of tourism, suggests that we are likely to see a further development of a global sex industry. This could mean greater attempts to enter into more and more 'markets' and a general expansion of the industry. It is a worrying possibility, especially in the context of growing numbers of women with few if any employment options. And such growing numbers are to be expected given high unemployment and poverty, the shrinking of a world of work opportunities that were embedded in the more traditional sectors of these economies, and the growing debt burden of governments rendering them incapable of providing social services and support to the poor.

Women in the sex industry become – in certain kinds of economies – a crucial link supporting the expansion of the entertainment industry. That industry in turn is crucial to tourism as a development strategy and a main source of government revenue. These tie-ins are structural, not a function of conspiracies. Their weight in an economy will be raised by the absence of or limitations on other sources for securing a livelihood, profits and revenues for (respectively) workers, enterprises and governments.

Remittances

Women, and migrants generally, enter the macro-level of development strategies through yet another channel: the flow of remittances which in many countries represent a major source of foreign exchange reserves for the government. While these flows may be minor compared to the massive daily capital flows in various financial markets, they are often very significant for developing or struggling economies.

In 1998 global remittances from immigrants to their home countries reached over US$70 billion. To understand the significance of this figure, it should be related to the GDP and foreign currency reserves in the specific countries involved, rather than compared to the global flow of capital. For instance, in the Philippines, a key sender of migrants generally and of women for the entertainment industry in several countries, remittances have represented the third-largest source of foreign exchange over the last several years. In Bangladesh, another country with significant numbers of its workers in the Middle East, Japan, and several European countries, remittances represent about a third of foreign exchange.

Exporting workers and receiving remittances are means for governments to cope with unemployment and foreign debt. There are two ways in which governments have secured benefits through these strategies. One of these is highly formalized and the other is simply a by-product of the migration process itself. Among the strongest examples of the formalized mode are South Korea and the Philippines (Sassen 1988). In the 1970s, South Korea developed extensive programmes to promote the export of workers as an integral part of its growing overseas construction industry, initially to the Middle Eastern OPEC countries and then worldwide. As South Korea entered its own economic boom, exporting workers became a less necessary and attractive option. In contrast, the Philippine government, if anything, expanded and diversified the concept of exporting its citizens as a way of dealing with unemployment and securing needed foreign exchange reserves through their remittances. It is to this case that I turn now as it illuminates a whole series of issues at the heart of this chapter.

The Philippines government has played an important role in the emigration of Filipino women to the US, the Middle East and Japan, through the Philippines Overseas Employment Administration (POEA). Established in 1982, it organized and oversaw the export of nurses and maids to high-demand areas in the world. High foreign debt and high unemployment combined to make this an attractive policy. Filipino overseas workers have sent home an anuual average of almost US$1 billion over the last few years. On the other side, the various labour-importing countries welcomed this policy for their own specific reasons. OPEC countries of the Middle East saw the demand for domestic workers grow sharply after the 1973 oil boom. Confronted with a sharp shortage of nurses, a profession that demanded years of training yet garnered rather low wages and little prestige or recognition, the US passed the Immigration Nursing Relief Act of 1989 which allowed for the import of nurses. And Japan passed legislation which permitted the entry of 'entertainment workers' into its booming economy in the 1980s, marked by rising expendable incomes and strong labour shortages.

The Philippines government also passed regulations that permitted mail-order bride agencies to recruit young Filipinas to marry foreign men as a matter of contractual agreement. The rapid increase in this trade was centrally due to the organized effort by the government. Among the major clients were the US and Japan. Japan's agricultural communities were a key destination for these brides, given enormous shortages of people and especially young women in the Japanese countryside when the economy was booming and the demand for labour in the large metropolitan areas was extremely high. Municipal governments made it a policy to accept Filipino brides.

The largest number of Filipinas going through these channels work overseas as maids, particularly in other Asian countries. The second-largest and fastest-growing group is entertainers, largely to Japan (Sassen 2000: Chapter 9). The rapid increase in the numbers of migrants going as entertainers is largely due to the over five hundred 'entertainment brokers' in the Philippines operating outside the state umbrella – even though the government may still benefit from the remittances of these workers. These brokers work to provide women for the sex industry in Japan, where it is basically supported or controlled by organized gangs rather than going through the government-controlled programme for the entry of entertainers. These women are recruited for singing and entertaining, but frequently, perhaps mostly, they are forced into prostitution as well.

The Philippines government approved most mail-order bride organizations until 1989 when, under Corazon Aquino, stories of abuse by foreign husbands led to the banning of the mail-order bride business. But it is almost impossible to eliminate these organizations and they continue to operate in violation of the law. In the US the Immigration and Naturalization Service (INS) has recently reported that domestic violence towards mail-order wives has become acute

(INS 1999). Again, the law operates against these women seeking recourse, as they are liable to be detained if they do so before two years of marriage. In Japan, the foreign mail-order wife is not granted full equal legal status (Takahashi 1996) and there is considerable evidence showing that many are subject to abuse not only by the husband but by the extended family as well.

Philippines, while perhaps having the most-developed programme, is not the only country to have explored these strategies. Thailand started a campaign in 1998 after the 1997–8 financial crisis to promote migration for work and recruitment by firms overseas of Thai workers. The government sought to export workers to the Middle East, the US, Great Britain, Germany, Australia and Greece. Sri Lanka's government has tried to export another 200,000 workers in addition to the one million it already has overseas; Sri Lankan women remitted US$880 million in 1998, mostly from their earnings as maids in the Middle East and Far East (Anon 1999). Bangladesh organized extensive labour export programmes to the OPEC countries of the Middle East as early as the 1970s. This has continued and, along with individual migration to these and various other countries, notably the US and Great Britain, is a significant source of foreign exchange. Its workers have remitted US$1.4 billion in each of the last few years (David 1999).

Conclusion

We are seeing the growth of a variety of alternative global circuits for making a living, making a profit and securing government revenue. These circuits incorporate increasing numbers of women. Among the most important of these global circuits are the illegal trafficking in women for prostitution as well as for regular work, organized exports of women as brides, nurses and domestic servants, and the remittances sent back to their home countries by an increasingly female emigrant workforce. Some of these circuits operate partly or wholly in the shadow economy.

This chapter has mapped some of the main features of these circuits and argued that their emergence and/or strengthening is linked to major dynamics of economic globalization which have had significant impacts on developing economies. Key indicators of such impacts are the heavy and rising burden of government debt, the growth in unemployment, sharp cuts in government social expenditures, the closure of a large number of firms in often fairly traditional sectors oriented to the local or national market, and the promotion of export-oriented growth. Further, the growth of a global economy has brought with it an institutional infrastructure that facilitates cross-border flows and represents, in that regard, an enabling environment for these alternative circuits.

I call these circuits counter-geographies of globalization because they are (1) directly or indirectly associated with some of the key programmes and conditions that are at the heart of the global economy, but (2) are circuits not typically represented or seen as connected to globalization, and often actually operate outside and in violation of laws and treaties, without being exclusively embedded in criminal operations as is the case with the illegal drugs trade. Linking these counter-geographies to programmes and conditions at the heart of the global economy also helps us understand how gendering enters into their formation and viability.

It is increasingly on the backs of women that these forms of survival, profit making and government revenue enhancement operate. To this we can add the additional government revenue garnered through savings due to severe cuts in health care and education. These cuts are often part of the effort of making the state more competitive as demanded by structural adjustment programmes and other policies linked to the current phase of globalization. These types of cuts are generally recognized as hitting women particularly hard, in so far as women are responsible for the health and education of household members.

These counter-geographies lay bare the systemic connections between, on one hand, the mostly poor and low-waged women often represented as a burden rather than a resource, and, on the other hand, what are emerging as significant sources for illegal profit making and for governments in search of hard currency.

Note

1 This is a revised version of the article originally published as 'Women's burden: counter-geographies of globalization and the feminization of survival', *Journal of International Affairs* (Spring) 2000, 53, No. 2: 503–24.

5

Engendering Globalization in an Era of Transnational Capital

New Cross-Border Alliances and Strategies of Resistance in a post-NAFTA Mexico

Marianne H. Marchand

For a while now it appears that we have been living in a 'post-world' – the era of 'post-nationalism', of 'post-development', of 'postmodernism', of the 'post-Cold War' and, as some suggest, of 'post-feminism' (although the editors of this collection are clearly distancing themselves from the latter notion). Much ado about these developments in talk shows, magazines and the opinion pages in national newspapers has led to a popularization of such debates. And, in turn, these discussions have stirred a wave of reactions by advocates of the *plus ça change* camp. Interestingly enough, the best-known of these claims, Fukuyama's post-ideology/history thesis, is grounded in the continuation of the two most prevalent ideologies and organizing structures of our times: liberalism and capitalism. One thing is clear, though: these debates, and recent events since the demonstrations against the third ministerial meeting of the World Trade Organization (WTO) in Seattle, are indicative of the fact that we are going through a period of important shifts and changes, both materially and ideationally. The question that most of the participants in these debates and demonstrations are trying to grapple with is how we are going to make sense of all of these changes.

In this chapter, I will try to unpack some elements of the dominant discourse(s) on globalization and show that current transformations are multidimensional and mediated through mechanisms and structures of inequality based on gender, ethnicity and class (to name just a few). At the same time, the chapter will try to show that within the context of these transformations new mechanisms of exclusion are emerging as well as new opportunities for certain subgroups. The emergence of new inequalities, mixed with or superimposed on old ones, and of new opportunities – much heralded in dominant discourse on globalization and also adopted by international organizations such as the World Bank and the United Nations – is very much tied to the rearticulation of identities and attendant constructions of space and spatiality. In order to unpack the multi-dimensionality and gendered underpinnings of globalization (discourse) this chapter will rely on the feminist approach of relational thinking. Relational thinking is based on the idea that 'gender operates in at least three distinct, yet interconnected ways: (1) ideologically, especially in terms of gendered representations and valorizations of social processes and practices; (2) at the level of social relations; (3) physically through the social construction of male and female bodies' (Marchand and Runyan 2000: 8).

Using insights gleaned from the author's recent research on the Mexican maquiladora sector and the Latin American horticultural sector[1] as illustration, this chapter will attempt to show the contingent nature of identity rearticulation and the reconceptualization of (gendered) bodies in the workplace as embedded in broad(er) global political and economic transformations. In so doing the chapter will raise more questions than it will be able to answer, especially in terms of the broader implications: how do we have to rethink work and labour relations? What kinds of resistance (strategies) can be formulated? What does this mean for feminist (post-) development thinking?

In the first section of the chapter I will outline the main tenets of globalization, showing in particular the multidimensionality of its processes and how these are being mediated through various structures of (power) inequality. Needless to say, the discussions around globalization are a tricky swamp into which one gets easily drawn. It should be noted from the outset, therefore, that it is not my intention to engage in another exercise on such questions as: what is globalization? Does it exist or not? And who are the major actors?[2] Rather I will show the complex nature of globalization or global restructuring. In the next section I deal specifically with gender and globalization. Here relational thinking will be used to show the gendered and interlocking nature of transformations in the global political economy. The third section will further develop these ideas by looking in particular at the transformations in Mexico's maquiladora industry. It is argued that a triple feminization has taken place in Mexico's political economy. Finally, it will be argued that these transformations in the global political economy also involve rearticulations of space and attendant identities which is partially reflected in the emergence of a regionally based, transnational politics of resistance.

Global restructuring: an overview

As was indicated in the introduction, major transformations in the global political economy are taking place. Often these changes are captured under the umbrella term of globalization. For reasons I have argued elsewhere, I prefer to use the term global restructuring instead of globalization (Marchand 1995; see also Marchand and Runyan 2000).[3] Global restructuring refers to a complex set of processes and transformations which are multidimensional, occur at differing speeds and involve a rearticulation of boundaries: public–private, global–local, national–international, as well as state–market–civil society (Marchand and Runyan 2000). As such, it encompasses economic, political, social and cultural dimensions (Castells 1996–8; Held *et al.* 1999; Scholte 2000). Global restructuring involves changes in a wide range of areas: trade liberalization; the emergence of a global financial system; changes in the process of production; a rapid diffusion of products, technologies, information and consumption patterns; and a growing tendency toward individualism and individualized lifestyles in certain parts of the world. Politically, we have also seen changes in response to or as part of the previously described transformations. For instance, states have altered their relations with the market and civil society. In the last two decades states have withdrawn themselves increasingly from the market through, for instance, the privatization of state-owned enterprises. Instead they have taken on much more of a managing and balancing role, trying to stimulate economic development through indirect measures and balancing demands from the local to the regional and global levels. Manuel Castells has referred to this as the emergence of the network state, in conjunction with the network society (Castells 1996–8). It is often forgotten, however, that these processes and transformations are being mediated through unequal power relations, including those informed by gender, class and ethnicity, and tend to result in the social exclusion of particular groups such as minorities, the aged and women with minimum levels of education (Marchand and Runyan 2000).

As the definition of global restructuring provided above is rather sketchy and abstract in an attempt to capture the complexities of the ongoing changes, it may be helpful to describe some of the major areas in which these changes have occurred or are still under way. Economically, global restructuring is associated with changes in the social organization of production, the liberalization of trade and the emergence of global finance. The introduction of new information and communication technologies has significantly changed production methods and organization. In particular transnational companies (TNCs) have developed so-called global commodity chains (GCCs), integrating production from start to finish at a regional, or sometimes even global, scale (Gereffi 1997; Held *et al.* 1999). The organization of these GCCs involves changes in the organization of production often captured by the term post-Fordism. In order to increase or regain their competitiveness many TNCs restructured and refocused on core activities during the late 1970s and 1980s. As a result they introduced flexible production strategies which tend to be demand-oriented. This flexibilization involved significant changes in labour relations, creating on one hand a group of core workers who became part of quality control teams, and on the other people employed on a variety of flexible and thus less secure contracts. At the same time TNCs started to outsource large parts of their production process, relying on just-in-time delivery (by themselves to clients and by their suppliers to themselves). This, of course, involved yet a further flexibilization of both the suppliers and the labour force employed by these suppliers. As Lourdes Benería and Martha Roldán have demonstrated in their seminal work *The Crossroads of Class and Gender* (1987), the further down the contracting (or commodity) chain one goes, the more casualized and feminized the labour force becomes, as these chains often reach into the informal sector and home work.

The changes in the organization and methods of production did not take place in isolation: economic globalization also involved the liberalization of trade and the emergence of a global financial system. Together with deregulation and privatization, trade liberalization has been pursued as one of the main objectives of the neoliberal economic agenda, which became the dominant platform for economic policy makers during the 1980s and 1990s. For most of the Latin American and African developmental states, this meant that their role in the domestic economy was altered significantly, with the introduction of structural adjustment policies as well as ongoing reform policies since the early 1980s. In various sub-Saharan countries this led to a severe crisis of the state and, under certain conditions, has even indirectly contributed to outbreaks of civil war (Reno 1998; Braathen, Bøås and Sæther 2000; Hodges 2001; Sæther 2001). During the same period in Latin America the state became less responsive to the needs of one of its main constituencies, the urban middle classes. In Asia the financial crisis of 1997 has triggered similar changes. States in the former socialist countries have arguably undergone the most significant transformations and many policy makers in these countries are still trying to get to grips with the magnitude of change their societies are facing. Although less dramatic, states in the Organization for Economic Cooperation and Development (OECD) have also undergone a restructuring, shifting away from their post-war welfare state regimes.

Overall, it is clear that there has been a rearticulation of the public–private and state–market boundaries whereby the latter (respective) domains are being favoured. Recently, however, a backlash against the rule of the market and globalization has emerged. For one thing, failures of deregulation and privatization (for example, the power failures in California and rail accidents in Britain) have resulted in an increased wariness and scepticism among a growing segment of the general public, in particular in Western Europe. In addition, the demonstrations in Seattle during the 1999 WTO ministerial meeting and in Prague during the IMF gathering, as well as the summer 2001 meetings in Gothenburg

(European Union) and Genoa (G–8) are indicative of increased opposition against unbridled globalization (Rupert 2000). Ironically, the increased activism of civil society groups has in part been stimulated by neoliberalism's discourse on reducing the state and strengthening civil society. The question, of course, is whether NGOs and other grassroots organizations will become permanently involved in policy making and implementation, as is already happening to a significant extent, and what this entails for issues concerning accountability, representation, participatory decision making and formulating policy recommendations in any specific policy area.

Gendering global restructuring: representations, bodies and social relations

As has been argued above, global restructuring is not a neutral set of processes but is mediated through gender, ethnicity, class and other social factors, thus producing and reproducing inequalities, but also providing new opportunities (Marchand and Runyan 2000). Within the context of global restructuring we are witnessing the emergence of new (gendered) notions concerning the qualities needed to perform well in this changing environment. One example is the interest by the business community in incorporating and promoting a more 'feminine' management style which tends to be more team-oriented, flexible and less hierarchical (Hooper 2000). This change in perception has provided new opportunities to women in finding management jobs, although it appears that women's initial advantage is already levelling off (Hooper 2000). In terms of social relations we can observe some positive and negative developments. On one hand, women's contributions to society in terms of both paid and unpaid work are increasingly recognized. The activities of the UN and regional bodies, as well as women's groups around the world, have significantly contributed to this. On the other hand, emerging religious fundamentalisms have also negatively affected women's position and empowerment in certain countries. Finally, bodies of men and women are socially constructed and social actors (including employers) tap into these constructions to justify certain social and employment practices. The 'manual dexterity' argument often used to employ women in export processing zones (EPZs) or for the peeling of shrimps is an example of this. As we will see below, the three dimensions of relational thinking combine to explain and understand the differential ways in which men and women relate to (global) transformations and the extent to which such changes may provide new opportunities or limitations to improve their situations.

Women and men enter the labour market as gendered beings. In other words, they are being considered for certain jobs at least in part on the basis of assumed gender characteristics. As has been well documented for the export processing industry (Fernandez-Kelly 1983; Mitter 1986; Ong 1987) women became the preferred labour force because of gender stereotyping which depicted them as docile, nimble-fingered and only working for some pocket money, as they were not seen as breadwinners. Interestingly, employers in agro-industry have also tapped into existing gender ideology and contracted many female employees on the basis of their assumed 'gender' qualities (Barrientos *et al.* 1999). In the fruit export industry, which now has a highly specialized division of labour, this means that women tend to perform tasks that require a high level of concentration and manual dexterity. They are mostly involved in cleaning, selecting and packing the fruit, a task associated with women's traditional roles in food preparation and presentation. In contrast, men are found in the fields or perform tasks which are seen as more masculine and requiring less finesse and concentration, such as transferring boxes (Barrientos *et al.* 1999).

Although the similarities between EPZs and the fruit and vegetable export industry are striking, local variations remain and may sometimes benefit women to some degree. For instance, in Chile employers don't seem to prefer young unmarried women as part of the labour force (Barrientos *et al.* 1999), while Kirstin Appendini found that for the Mexican fruit and vegetable industry this is the case (1995: 14). Although women often receive lower wages than men (as is the situation in EPZs), Appendini as well as Barrientos *et al.* found that this is reversed for specific jobs in the fruit and vegetable export industry, where women tend to receive the highly desirable, and sometimes better-paying jobs in the packing area (Appendini 1995; Barrientos *et al.* 1999).

Another example of the manipulation of gender ideology by employers is the case of the sugar cane plantations in Guatemala. Over the last 20 years the Guatemalan sugar plantations have tripled their productivity (Oglesby 2001). According to Elizabeth Oglesby, this was possible because the sugar plantations 'are now devising alternative means to achieve labour discipline, by combining new technologies with wage incentives, human capital investments and a refashioning of workers' identities' (2001: 16). In addition to providing heavier machetes, and mechanizing certain parts of the production process, the employers engaged in a masculinization of the labour force by feeding the cane cutters high energy diets of 3,700 calories daily (high in protein and carbohydrates) and by tapping into the cutters' machismo by organizing competitions (with prizes) for production quotas. Competition among cutters has become so fierce that quite a few of them inject themselves with vitamin B, which is supposed to enhance their endurance, and some have even resorted to amphetamines (Oglesby 2001).

In the remainder of the chapter I will use the example of the Mexican maquila industry and its predominantly female workforce to explore some of the connections between structural transformations, discursive constructs and representations of gendered bodies. The main argument put forth is that a triple feminization is taking place, namely a feminization of the labour force, a feminization of the Mexican political economy and a symbolic feminization. This in turn is reflected in the rearticulation of space and identities.

Triple feminization in/of Mexico: some connections

The regionalization or continentalization of the North American political economy, in conjunction with the institutional framework of the Canadian–United States Free Trade Agreement (CUFTA) and the North American Free Trade Agreement (NAFTA), has been leading to a deepening of the regional division of labour in line with neoliberal principles. Various metaphors have been employed to describe this, including the hub-and-spoke model or the core–periphery model. While supporters of NAFTA have interpreted this regional division of labour as something positive, opponents have focused, in particular, on the social and economic costs of this neoliberal restructuring for ordinary people. For Mexico, in particular, the impact of the further deepening of the regional division of labour has been enormous. After the implementation of NAFTA its exports to the US market have improved considerably, although this has been somewhat offset by increased levels of imports (*Mexico and NAFTA Report*, 12 January 1999).

Yet this supposedly positive picture alters when it appears that much of the exports have been a consequence of the exponential growth of the maquiladora or export processing industry. As feminist analysis has repeatedly pointed out, women are often targeted for jobs which have been created in the context of a global/regional economy organized around services and just-in-time production processes. The representation of women as being physically better suited for repetitive and often tedious tasks, as being more submissive and hence less likely to join a labour union than men, and their association with reproductive (often non-paid) labour have been the main rationale for this (see, for example, Fernandez-Kelly 1983).

With the creation of the maquiladora sector in the late 1960s and its post-NAFTA boom Mexican women have been employed in great numbers in the maquiladoras and are also performing subcontracted sweatshop labour and home work (see, for example, Fernandez-Kelly 1983; Herrero 1991; Gonzalez *et al.* 1995; Kopinak 1995; González *et al.* 1997). Moreover, the employment of women and, increasingly, men in the maquiladora industry[4] involves the manipulation of gender and gender relations in various ways. This is illustrated by the following passage taken from an article by Debbie Nathan, 'Work, Sex and Danger in Ciudad Juárez':[5]

> But they [young male assembly workers] often are deliberately segregated from their female counterparts: by job classification (women do 'light' work, such as soldering circuit boards, while men put together bigger and heavier television cabinets); by the color of their work smocks (at one factory, men's are dark blue and women's light blue); and by physical placement in separate sections of the plant. Thus, men are marked different from women. Yet they are also derisively equated with women. For one, they earn the same wage as women: one that has always been recognized as a pittance, but which has for long been justified for females .... Male maquila workers also feel devalued by management disregard for their masculinity. 'Manliness' in male workers ... is ignored or even deprecated. At best, male operatives are invisible. At worst, those who misbehave or do bad work are disciplined by being moved to the female-only assembly sections. The ultimate humiliation for Juárez's young male workers is thus to be symbolically turned into women. (1999: 27)

It is clear from this passage that Mexican male maquila workers find their masculinity under attack. Interestingly, the increased transnationalization and dependency of the Mexican economy (of which the maquiladora industry is the clearest expression) is often perceived by critics in gendered terms as well. One example is the gendered metaphor used by former finance minister Jesus Silva Herzog in his reaction to President Salinas de Gortari's proposal for NAFTA: 'Mexico should have waited to be caressed first, before dropping its pants.'[6] This statement alludes to one of the recurring images of Mexico as a young 'maiden', who needs to be (romantically) wooed before any sexual advances can be made.[7] At the same time, Silva Herzog's words reflect what Debbie Nathan (1999: 29) describes as Mexico's historical obsession with 'open female bodies' which symbolically 'signify the openness of the border to the needs of the "other" [the USA]'.[8] The second example invokes the perceived threat of the USA or transnational capital to Mexico's manliness – as is illustrated in the rather explicit caricature by *El Fisgón*, which depicts Uncle Sam holding Mexico, balancing on the edge of a cliff, literally by the testicles. In this caricature the cliff represents the financial abyss, created by the 1995 Mexican financial crisis, and the only way for Mexico to be 'rescued' is being bailed out by the American government and private as well as multilateral financial institutions – but with severe conditionalities attached (*El Fisgón* 1996: 82).

In general terms critics have assailed the maquiladora industry, now not only present at the border but throughout much of Mexico, for not providing a balanced long-term development as it locks Mexico into a primarily low-productivity, low-tech and highly labour-intensive strategy. Although conditions seem to be improving somewhat, much of the attention from anti-NAFTA groups has been directed at the maquiladoras for their bad labour conditions, sexual discrimination and unsound environmental practices. As a result, various complaints have been filed under the labour side agreement.[9]

The increased maquiladorization of the Mexican economy has resulted in a situation where, despite its export growth to the US and the growth rates of its economy as a whole, wages have been falling in real terms since 1993 (in addition to their steady decline in the 1980s). The unequal growth, both in terms of wages and in terms of the increased differentiation among subregions in Mexico, has even prompted the World Bank to caution against too much optimism. Apparently, the Mexican public is also not very optimistic, as a poll of January 1999 revealed: two thirds believed that NAFTA had not brought anything positive to the country (*Mexico and NAFTA Report*, 12 January 1999).

Thus, the feminization of labour in the context of global restructuring involves, on one hand, an enormous increase in the numbers of women workers in the formal (and informal) labour force. On the other hand it involves 'the "flexibilization" and "casualization" of (especially women's) labour to keep labour costs down and productivity up in the name of free trade, global competitiveness and economic efficiency' (Marchand and Runyan 2000: 17). Finally, the examples discussed above illustrate in addition the *symbolic feminization* of the Mexican economy through gendered and sexualized representations and discursive constructs at the level of both the workplace and the state.

Another feature of the gendered impact of global restructuring is the rearticulation of the public–private divide (Marchand and Runyan 2000). For instance, the economic problems since the mid-1980s have forced Mexican women to engage in a variety of household survival strategies resulting, among other things, in an increasing number of Mexican women migrating across the US border to earn an income and provide foreign exchange for their families, and by extension their government. Moreover, the North American continentalization of the late 1980s and 1990s has been superimposed on the structural adjustment programmes that the Mexican state was required to implement under the auspices of the IMF and World Bank. As is well documented, this has led to cutbacks in social services and subsidies on food and transportation provided by the public sector, and women have been disproportionally affected by these cutbacks because of their specific assigned (and expected) reproductive tasks as well as the types of productive labour (working in the public sector or performing contract or part-time work) in which they are engaged (see for example, Harrington 1992; Dahlerup 1994; WIDE *et al.* 1994; Sen 1997). In other words, economic privatization and deregulation are effectively creating a triple burden for women: engaging in productive labour to contribute to the household income, facing an increasing burden in terms of reproductive labour because the state has been reducing its responsiblilty in terms of social welfare, as well as participating in community level organizing in order to improve immediate living conditions. As some feminist scholars have reported, this often leads to renegotiation of gender relations in households (see, for example, Benería 1992; Kromhout 2000; Moghadam 2000). Whereas such renegotiation can and sometimes has resulted in an increase in women's empowerment, it can also lead to quite the opposite, such as a high incidence of alcoholism among male household members, domestic violence and sexual abuse in both the workplace and the home (Nathan 1999).

Finally, the restructuring brought about by the deepening of the regional division of labour has also affected communities, industries (in particular, forestry and fishing) and regional economies in Canada as well as parts of the manufacturing sector in the US (Public Citizens' Global Trade Watch 1998; Canadian Labor Congress 1999). It can be argued, then, that the continentalization or regionalization of the North American political economy is creating new social, political and economic inequalities along the lines of class, race, gender and ethnicity (for more details see Marchand 1999).

Space and spatialization of the North American political economy: implications for resistance strategies

The continentalization of the North American political economy has important consequences in terms of the ways in which regionalization processes are creating new social, economic and political spaces. In other words, a fundamental transformation of Mexico's political economy involves, as we have discussed in the previous section, a maquiladorization which is being accompanied by a reorganization and reordering of space. The creation of these new spaces is leading to and exacerbating forms of exclusion along the lines of class, gender and ethnicity. This involves the emergence of multiple, interlocking and reinforcing inequalities that are being perpetuated because they reflect stratified access to global spaces, a decline of the redistributive (developmental) state, the establishment of social hierarchies in global regimes of governance (such as the WTO or NAFTA) and the flexibilization of labour and labour markets (Scholte 2000).

At the same time the reordering of spaces is creating new opportunities for some women and men. As I have argued elsewhere, the contestation over and rearticulation of space also involve a production of meaning concerning the North American region (Marchand 2000; 2002). As such it is foregrounding questions of identity and identity construction. Much of this meaning production has focused on Mexico's most transnationalized space, Mexamerica, and its relation to subaltern spaces. More specifically, it involves a renewed concern with modernity and modernization centred around a reinterpretation, or even rejection, of the images, narratives and symbols of the Mexican revolution (Marchand, 2000; 2002).

Against this background an interesting issue emerges on the connections between the rearticulation of space, with attendant identity construction, and emerging transnational strategies and practices of resistance. As we have suggested in the introduction, the emergence of anti-globalist groups in the last few years has engendered a keen academic as well as policy interest in the activities of transnational 'protest groups'. Often analyses about such groups are framed in terms of an emerging global civil society. However, such discussions have devoted very little if any attention to the spatial articulation of this development – by focusing, for instance, on the possible emergence of a regional civil society. Instead, most discussions about a global civil society have centred around definitional problems, the role of social movements and NGOs, and its connections to the state. One of the most interesting readings of global civil society has been provided by neo-Gramscians, who argue that a global civil society has emerged in relation to global capitalist accumulation. Yet a paradox emerges if we compare this reading with Michel Albert's suggestion that there are different (regional) types of capitalist accumulation. The question which presents itself is whether we can still speak of a global civil society, or whether we should interpret the emergence of a regional civil society as contingent upon regional regimes of accumulation as well as spatial articulations of global civil society. An additional feature which may contribute to the idea of an emerging regional civil society is the ongoing creation of regional institutional frameworks such as NAFTA, Mercosur, the EU or the Asia–Pacific Economic Cooperation forum (APEC). As we have seen in the last few years, these institutional frameworks often provide focal points for social movements to rally around and can thus further engender a regional politics of resistance. This is not to say, of course, that a transnational politics of resistance takes place exclusively within a regional context or space.

It would go beyond the scope of this chapter to elaborate fully the previous suggestions about the emergence of regionally/spatially articulated transnational practices and strategies of resistance. However, I wish to illustrate the rudimentary points raised through some brief examples. These examples illustrate that the politics of resistance is not only transnationalized but also involves spatial (re-)articulations and constructions of identity.

Focusing in particular on the transnationalized politics of resistance in Mexico, we see that much of this is being concentrated at two opposing poles of the political economy's spatial hierarchy. On one hand we see how many groups are opposing 'neoliberal globalization' from the locality of 'Mexamerica'. Red Mexicana de Acción Frente al Libre Comercio (RMALC) and its activities around NAFTA, the Mexico–EU Agreement, the Free Trade for the Americas

(FTAA), APEC and other issues is a good example. The organization has many ties to groups in Canada and the US and forms part of the Hemispheric Social Alliance. Yet RMALC is not exclusively directed at events in Mexico and the Western Hemisphere. It has ties to social movements and NGOs in Asia and Europe as well, illustrating clearly that one cannot assume an exclusive arena called regional civil society.

Although often less visible, women's groups have been very active in organizing within the transnational space of the Mexican as well as the wider North American political economy. Although they share certain commonalities with other (non-feminist or women's) groups they often employ different resistance practices, foregrounding in particular issues of positionality and identity. For instance, during the discussions about the creation of NAFTA an interesting practice of resistance emerged which has been labelled 'feminist internationality' by Gabriel and MacDonald (1994). This feminist internationality entailed an explicit recognition of different subject positions and structural realities of the various Canadian and Mexican women's groups. Implicitly this practice of feminist internationality entailed a rejection of an imposed homogeneous identity under NAFTA. After the implementation of NAFTA, during its consolidation phase, the focus of resistance of these women's groups has shifted. There is now less attention to questions of identity construction; moreover, attention is also directed less at the legislative process around NAFTA and the more general issues concerning free trade regimes. Instead, the focus of these groups, most of them united in the Coalition for Justice for the Maquiladoras, has shifted to see how far NAFTA rules (especially the labour and environmental side agreements) allow local groups to challenge labour and environmental practices. The primary focus of their attention has been on challenging a variety of practices by the subsidiaries of major TNCs, the so-called maquiladoras. In fact, we can see something of a bifurcation in this respect: RMALC is much more involved in a politics of resistance concentrated on challenging various (regional) free trade and investment agreements, while the Coalition for Justice in the Maquiladoras is more interested in focusing on concrete border issues as they relate to labour conditions, environmental issues and human rights concerns. In line with this divergence, the latter also deals more specifically with women's issues. This bifurcation does not entail an unbridgeable gap, however, as both RMALC and the Coalition for Justice in the Maquiladoras are participating in the Hemispheric Social Alliance.

In contrast to these examples of groups active in Mexamerica, we find at the bottom of the spatial hierarchy the Zapatistas. Much has been written about the Zapatistas and I will not reiterate here the arguments made elsewhere concerning the uniqueness of this movement (cf. Castells 1998). The immediate context within which the Zapatistas are active is, of course, the subaltern space of Chiapas. According to the Zapatistas, the combination of the historic legacy of large landholdings, recent land reforms in Mexico allowing for privatization, and the implementation of NAFTA have further paved the way for the production of cash crops (and the importation of staple goods), thus seriously affecting already marginalized indigenous communities. Although the Zapatistas are primarily active within a local and national context, this does not mean that their politics of resistance is not transnationalized. From the outset, the group has used advanced communication technology (e-mail, internet, etcetera) to reach beyond the boundaries of the immediate struggle. It explicitly located its struggle spatially within a wider national, regional and global context, using the cosmopolitan argument that we are all living on the same planet, even in the same galaxy, and share our humanity. As a result it has fostered and has been supported by a widespread transnational activist network consisting of solidarity groups (especially in the rest of Latin America, the US and Europe). This widespread support has been further strengthened by the two *encuentros* (meetings) organized in part by the Zapatistas – one in Mexico and one in Spain.

What can we learn from these examples? All three show that spatial articulations of issues and resistance practices are interwoven with identity constructions and that the regional context does play an important, albeit not exclusive, role. As I have argued elsewhere (Marchand 2000; 2002) these resistance practices involve a redefinition of Mexico's project of modernity based on a reinterpretation of the symbols, narratives and images of the Mexican Revolution in a regional/global context. They aim at a grounded, socially inclusive ethical cosmopolitanism which has as its primary referent the (North American) region.

Conclusion

What I have tried to address in this chapter is that from a (postcolonial) feminist perspective globalization/global restructuring is a complex and contingent set of processes which needs to be historicized and contextualized. Most important, in this respect, is to understand and challenge the ways in which gendered, racialized and sexualized representations and discursive constructs dovetail with material inequalities. This may result in a situation in which inequalities are actually legitimated and sustained through such representations and discourses. As the example of North American continentalization and the maquiladorization of the Mexican political economy illustrates, the conditions (and processes) under which inequalities occur are not only multilayered and contingent, but also lead to a rearticulation of space and identities. It is in the context of these rearticulations that opportunities are being created to resist dominant representations and discursive constructs and thus challenge the (discursive) mechanisms that help to sustain inequalities. The transnational organizing which has emerged in the context of NAFTA is indicative of how alternative, more inclusive spaces and identities are being created.

At this point it is too early to say what the outcome of such resistances and reformulations will be. All that is clear now is that different regionalism projects pursued by different actors are coexisting, and that this coexistence already undermines the representation or discursive construct that North American continentalization can only lead to one outcome. Instead, these different projects reflect different expressions of regional identity. For instance, the North American, élite-led regionalism project based on neoliberal principles is connected to an emerging regional identity based on notions of exclusive cosmopolitanism (see Marchand 2000; 2002). On the other hand, opposition groups have formulated an alternative ethics-based regional identity or more inclusive cosmopolitanism around notions of social and environmental sustainability and social justice. These different projects and associated partial identities are also tied to different positions and policies towards those who may be excluded from the overall process of global/regional restructuring. The élite-driven neoliberal regionalism project is primarily focused on a minimalist institutional framework for trade and investment. The broad coalition of opposition forces is clearly supportive of a much more inclusive, socially driven regionalism project. As such it is challenging the gendered, sexualized and racialized discursive constructs and dominant representations which help to legitimate and perpetuate a whole complex of inequalities on which the North American continentalization project is being constructed. The practices of resistance developed by a range of groups are important in a variety of ways – not only because they involve concrete examples of a transnational politics of resistance and because they represent an alternative project and attendant (regional) identity, but also because through their practices they are actually constructing a regional civil society.

Notes

1 See 'Competing Regionalisms in North America: Contestation, Spatiality and the Emergence of Cross-Border Identities', various versions of this chapter as presented at international workshops and conferences during 2000 and 2001; and 'Engendering Globalization: from Subsistence Farming to Rural Industrialization and Agribusiness', paper prepared for the Expert Group Meeting on 'The Situation of Rural Women within the Context of Globalization', organized by the Division for the Advancement of Women (DAW) and the United Nations Development Fund for Women (UNIFEM), 4–8 June 2001, Ulaanbaatar, Mongolia (available under UN document classification EGM/RW/2001/BP.1).

2 For some of these discussions I refer to the introduction and early chapters in Marchand and Runyan (2000).

3 I also recognize that it is difficult to go against the flow and stick to a different terminology to the now widely popularized term of globalization. In this chapter I will try to be as consistent as

possible and use the term global restructuring when dealing analytically with processes of globalization. I will use the term globalization when it is in line with dominant or popular discourse, as a way to represent the terminology employed in such discourse.

4 This is because of a shortage of women workers. See Kopinak (1995) for an analysis of the changing make-up of the maquiladora workforce and her arguments on why gender continues to be an important 'vehicle' for the subordination of women.

5 This article appeared in the special issue 'Contested Terrain: the US–Mexico Borderlands', *NACLA Report on the Americas*, 33, 3 (November/December 1999).

6 Quoted in R.. A.. Pastor, 'Post-Revolutionary Mexico: the Salinas Opening', *Journal of Inter-american Studies and World Affairs*, 32, 3 (1990), p. 17.

7 See, for a more detailed explanation of the use of gendered (and racial) images (sometimes literally in the form of caricatures) to depict Mexico and other Latin American countries: Slater 1997; Johnson 1980.

8 Nathan is basing her discussion on the work by Pablo Vila ('Border Identities: Narratives in Gender, Class and Religion on the US–Mexico Border', unpublished manuscript) and Norma Alarcon's influential work on the uses of images of the Virgin of Guadalupe and la Malinche as good versus bad woman in Mexican nationalist myth.

9 For detailed information see the publications and/or web sites of such organizations as: American Friends Service Committee, Canadian Labour Council, Committee for Justice in the Maquiladoras, Common Frontiers (Canada), Human Rights Watch, Labornet, Public Citizen, Red Mexicana de Acción Frente al Libre Comercio (RMALC).

Part III
More Worldly Feminisms

6

Development: Feminist Theory's Cul-de-sac

Marnia Lazreg

This chapter is a reflection on the limitations of postmodernist feminist theory when it seeks to transcend its national, cultural and political boundaries and address the issue of 'development'. It treats postmodernist feminist theory as a subset of feminist theory which it deliberately assumes to be a more or less homogeneous *body* of knowledge, notwithstanding claims to the contrary. This posture is grounded in the very nature of the concept of 'development', the phenomenological referent of which – women in 'other', non-European/North American places – has been both a major stumbling block for feminist theorizing and the test of its ultimate validity. Accounting for these women's forms of life and 'liberating' them (from themselves, their men, their cultures, their former colonizers) to be more or less like 'us' has always been the dream of feminists in their symbolic conquest of the world of Otherness. I will refrain from systematically reviewing the various shades of thinking women/gender in/and development. Although possibly rewarding from a purely academic standpoint, I find this task tedious and redundant. My objective is to explicate the meanings of the incursion of feminist postmodernist thought in the 'field' of development. I borrow and adapt the concept of 'field' from Pierre Bourdieu's theoretical vocabulary to emphasize the fact that ideas and theories of development belong to a system of relations between individuals and groups representing 'forces' that position themselves for a struggle over their relevance, legitimacy, and/or practical applications.[1] This means that whoever engages the field of development from the perspective of gender must also critically engage their own interests as part of the forces that sustain it and reproduce it. Women in this field are as much its agents as they are its objects. My ultimate interest is in development-in-practice, which still bewilders me with its complexity, and which I have witnessed first-hand, through my peregrinations across continents, in search of ways of adjusting it, ever so slightly, to accommodate women. I must acknowledge, however, that, at times, I felt that it was women who were adjusted to it.

Two questions guide my approach:

1 Has the encounter between development and postmodernist feminism changed the nature of the debate about the inclusion of women in development policies/programmes/projects?

2 Is the postmodernist trend in development, feminist or feminizing,[2] the answer to the impact of globalization on women (I am not concerned here with men, although they are implied despite my reluctance to use the concept of 'gender')? Or is it a new adaptation to the phenomenon of globalization in its latest incarnation since the collapse of socialism in 1989?[3] Is it possible at this historical conjuncture to talk about 'post-development', as Arturo Escobar seems to think?[4]

Postmodernism/feminism and development

Academic feminists dealing with the relevance of postmodernist theory to understanding and refocusing development theory and practice trace the inadequacy, if not irrelevance, of previous notions of development to the lingering legacy of the Enlightenment. Questioned is the notion of 'progress' as the ultimate goal of humanity in its quest for control over its environment through the combined forces of reason and science. By contrast, postmodernist feminism is touted as holding the promise of transforming development-as-usual by uncovering its complicity with a totalizing, evolutionary and patronizing view of people of the 'Third World'.[5] Likewise, postmodernist theorists of development who do not profess feminism, but recognize its import, also ground their views in theoretical critiques of the Enlightenment. Harnessing the insights yielded by studies of orientalism, Africanism and post-colonialism, Escobar engages in a Foucauldian critique of the category of development expressed in specific practices recounted as 'tales'. He defines development in broad terms as 'a historically singular experience, the creation of a domain of thought and action', that expresses itself in 'forms of knowledge … the system of power that regulates its practice, and the forms of subjectivity fostered by this discourse, those through which development people come to recognize themselves as developed or underdeveloped'.[6] The comprehensiveness of this definition transforms the concreteness of the issue of development, which varies from country to country, into an implicitly homogeneous system of knowledge/power articulated by ideal-typical international organizations such as the World Bank, and exercised *against* poor peasants and women in Latin America.[7] Subsuming the concrete under the abstract, practice under theory, results in the blurring, if not the obliteration of the difference, or the often noted lack of fit between theories and practices of development. It further assumes a homogeneity in the field of ideas of development that is not borne out by the facts. For example, the field of development economics alone is a 'hodgepodge of theoretical and empirical work'.[8] Moreover, theories of development run the political gamut from conservative to 'radical'. To dismiss all of them as being bankrupt, and focus on the presumably ascendant 'neoclassical' economic theory, also obscures the haphazard and inconsistent ways in which development is *negotiated* by various local and international forces that face one another in the international field.

The postmodernist rediscovery of the 'West' and its 'development' meta-narratives mobilizes the language of deconstruction to dismantle the oldest approach to the inclusion of women in development, or WID.[9] Yet, prior to the emergence of postmodernist feminism, it was the debate among international organizations over women (and, subsequently, gender) which *by implication* questioned the rationality of development practices that ignored a significant part, if not the majority, of the population involved in agricultural production. The first advocates of women-in-development programmes were women working in international organizations. Although WID deserves to be subjected to close scrutiny, it has been unfairly dismissed without due consideration to its historical origins, or its significance in drawing attention to the marginalization, if not exclusion, of women by development policy makers and funders. To label this approach 'neocolonial' presumes that subsequent views, including the postmodernist, have in fact broken with the theoretical/empirical problematic of development, of 'modernity' – with or without women.

Advocates of postmodernist development further argue that GAD, the successor to WID, fell short of questioning the (Enlightenment-tainted) premises of development and, consequently, cannot help to transform the theory and practice of development. Postmodernist feminism is counterposed to previous *approaches* (not theories), and held to bring about the 'empowerment' of women from formerly colonized societies, or countries of the 'South'.[10] The term 'empowerment' is identified with giving women 'voice', a feminist romantic act of creationism. A postmodernist analysis of this act of giving social birth to women, engendering their being, imbuing them with self-presence through the act of speaking, re-encodes confession, a 'Western' act of soul-cleansing, as a form of *normalization* of power over those who had previously been silenced. Giving women voice presumes that these women were/are mute. Implicitly, it is the emergence of postmodernist feminism as the interpreter of the new holy bible of globalization that will literally call/speak Third World women into being. Yet, these women have always spoken about their misery or happiness. If they did not speak them to postmodernist feminists who have just discovered their 'voices', and they have not been listened to, it was not because of WID, WAD or GAD. Many of those who did not listen were academic feminists whose profession was to translate these women's reality, and construct their subjectivity to fit theoretical models now about to fall under the axe of deconstruction.

The advocacy of postmodernist development theory rests on a number of unexamined issues:

1 The uncritical rejection of the legacy of the Enlightenment perceived as homogeneous in its treatment of the 'Other'. As Melvin Richter points out, among European societies there was little agreement about what the eighteenth-century Enlightenment was, to what it should apply, and whether it happened at all.[11] The dismissal of development as the product of a homogenizing Western thought overlooks the fact that there are theoretical systems that partake in the heritage of the Enlightenment but seek the liberation of people from the logic of the market and inequality. Marxism did just that, but Escobar disposes of it in half a sentence as implicitly not being able, as postmodernism is, 'to explore more fruitfully the conditions of possibility and the most pervasive effects of development'.[12] My intention is not to dictate what theory a scholar should select, but to point out that the discursive analysis of development is not the same as the historical analysis of the ways in which societies achieve or cannot achieve self-sufficiency in producing and reproducing their material and social lives. Imbuing discourse with an ontological existence that essentially determines people's lives and thoughts is another form of objectifying them. Individual women and men in countries of the Third World do not live their lives in terms of the category of development.

2 The reduction of the structural complexity of development to individuals' feelings and opinions. This confessional mode of empowerment is elliptically meant to increase women's participation in the identification of their needs so that development policies/programmes/projects are better targeted, a requirement that had already been emphasized by the GAD approach.

3 That women in the Third World are not aware of the power of national and international forces in their lives. Postmodernist development is meant to lay bare the exercise of power for these women. The implication is that women's awareness of power will transform development practice. Presumably, funding institutions will somehow learn from having their power analyzed and will rethink their conceptions of what development is.

Empowerment through speech

The assumption of empowerment through speech (a throwback to the psychoanalytical cure) merits a closer inspection. It extends the postmodernist concern with narrative ethnography which retrieves personal (often biographical) accounts from the complexity of individual entanglement in socio-economic and political structures while appropriating them as so many pieces of documentary evidence of a social system gone awry. In so doing, it lingers on the subjective assessment of this and that development experience, and claims to prove or disprove a given view of development. A good example is provided by Marianne Marchand in her analysis of 'witness' accounts provided by women from Latin America concerning their feelings about development. Although aware of the pitfalls of using life histories as ethnographies, and the latter as a substitute for a holistic approach to the relationship between the individual and society, she resolves to utilize such accounts to 'contextualize gender and development issues'.[13] The author strenuously argues for the use of witness accounts without demonstrating the theoretical or empirical imperatives (as far as development is concerned) that would make such accounts necessary. And this is so '[i]n order to challenge the Western feminist discourse on non-Western women'.[14] The implication being that Third World women speak so that 'Western' women-qua-'developed' may speak to one another about 'them'. The issue is not so much that women's speech is valuable. Naturally it is. The point is that Third World women are solicited, cajoled, encouraged to speak as a result of a 'need to create discursive spaces which will allow Latin American women and other Third World women to be heard'. From a postmodernist perspective, this view evinces a desire for power, a 'will to power', the power to carve out spaces for others, convene them to talk about themselves under the fiction of polyphony and multiple-authorships which are meant to aid local women to acquire 'voice'. Postmodern feminist development eschews the linkage between power, desire and interest. Although advocates of this approach may sincerely wish to see Third World women evolve their own development discourse, and perhaps even reach the promised land of development, their desire to frame these women's 'discourse' and their advocacy of the use of life histories as ethnographies reflect their interest in women as a field and an object of study.

If Foucault's contribution has been to point out the 'indignity of speaking for others', postmodernist feminism seems to be unaware of the indignity of making others speak about themselves to 'us', purportedly to help us to build a post-development theory.[15] More importantly, inserted in this conception of what postmodernist feminism can do for development is an unmistakable desire to *do knowledge.*[16] Women's life stories are an occasion to engage in the 'production of knowledge about development'.[17] At an abstract level, there is nothing ominous about collecting witness accounts about development. However, since a feminist development theory must necessarily result in improving development practices or else it is no improvement over previous perspectives, it is legitimate to ask whether this approach distinguishes between problems that are related to weak, failed or insufficient development, and those that cut across all societies, 'developing' as well as industrial. The accounts referred to by Marchand run the gamut, from domestic violence (a perennial issue everywhere) to poverty. It might be argued that development is multi-pronged and thus involves all facets of life. Ultimately this is true, but development practice requires focus if it is to be helpful to women and postmodernist feminist development often appears to be less interested in 'development' than in ascertaining the contours of its own discourse in the wake of 'globalization', as will be discussed below.

It is noteworthy that the role assigned to ethnographies by postmodernist feminism leaves open the question of which women are worth opening a 'discursive space' for. Marchand quotes from women who ascended to notoriety, who could articulate their views and hold their own on the international circuit of global feminism. The poor women who were allowed to speak appear to give their voices rather than being given one. They are said to provide 'a gold mine of information, ideas and knowledge about Gender and Development'.[18] The 'G' and 'D' are capitalized in the text to signal the generality of the information provided by local, specific women. This information/knowledge is claimed to be 'contextualized', undoubtedly by the researcher. What if women refuse to be given a voice, or have discordant voices?[19] When proposing to carve out a 'space' for others, one is implicitly locating oneself outside of that space, arranging it, and furnishing it to suit one's own desire and interests.

In 1988, I suggested that feminist theory which claimed to account for the different lives of women in the Middle East fell short of the mark, primarily because it did not comprehend their 'lived reality'.[20] Life histories treated as documentary evidence of a discourse on development do not capture women's unmediated 'reality', lived or re-lived for the interviewer. In fact, they may even be a form of silencing, in the sense that they make women from the Third World complicitous with an international development establishment (which includes academic institutions) that calls for their guided opinions in order to make its own aid more 'efficient'. In one country where native women have not been saturated with development experts and programmes, when a farm woman was asked how she would like an international organization to assist her, she responded that giving her husband a job in the area would help her to get him back to his family from one of the Gulf countries where he had emigrated in search for work. As for herself, better hand tools would have been welcome in order to make her work easier. But she was gratified to have a tractor which she drove herself to within a couple of miles from her village before turning the wheel over to a male relative in deference to the normative order by which her neighbours lived. Turning the conversation I had with this woman (who also happened to be illiterate) into a discourse on development would distort her feelings and expressed needs by fitting them into a particular conception of what development means to her (or ought to mean) when her existential concerns were for daily survival without her husband. That emigration is a sign of lack of, or insufficient, economic development goes without saying. However, what is meant by development is indeterminate and fluid when one is confronted with the struggle for survival. The woman farmer was not discoursing about development, she lived specific circumstances just as 'we' do. 'We' do not ask ourselves whether the molestation of children, the rape of college women, the murder of estranged wives are terms of a discourse of development in America. Rather, we see them as expressions of the resilience of misogyny, gender inequality, the commodification of women's sexuality, etcetera. The 'development' of America is not questioned. The transformation of women's lives into a discourse relinks with the early feminist tradition of focusing on other women's victimization by their culture, 'patriarchy' or religion. For women's life histories are seen as valuable not so much for their intrinsic value to the women themselves as for what they tell us about this amorphous entity called 'development'. Hence, in postmodernist terms, neither the signifier nor the signified have changed, only their relationship *for the researcher* has been rearranged. Development, whatever this means, has become the marker that separates 'them' from 'us'.

Perhaps metaphorically, 'development' is seen as the functional equivalent of Foucault's conception of prison. Prisoners' opinions constitute a counter-discourse that expresses a counter-power. But the prisoner's speech is radically different from the woman farmer's in Kenya, Syria, Egypt or Turkey. The researcher may not have contributed to the jailing of the inmate, or, most of all, benefited from it. This is not so for development theorists, feminists or not, for they partake, directly or indirectly, in the very reproduction and maintenance of the notion of 'development'. At any rate, the discursivization (to use an unwieldy neologism) of women's lives represents a *normalization* rather than a transformation of their daily existence, of development-as-usual. They continue to be there for 'us', for 'our' understanding of 'development'. And 'we' *recuperate* their experiences, mould them, channel them, conceptualize them.[21] The concept of recuperation conveys two meanings, appropriation and deception: appropriation of speech through the deception of liberation/voice. In the end, it is 'our' notion of 'development' (even if we single-handedly decide that it should now be preceded by the particle 'post-') that gives Third World women's lives meaning. They are subsumed under a category of 'our' thought. The possessive pronoun 'our' denotes a reality, an intellectual tradition tied to imperial ventures to which 'we' belong, which 'we' have not relinquished, and which sustain 'our' professional livelihoods no matter how 'we' formally denounce it. If applicable at all, the prison analogy signifies the imprisonment of women in the discourse of development turned into the perfect alibi for the practice of a purportedly 'objective', value-free, sister-friendly, study of women from the Third World.

The intrusion of postmodernist feminism into the field of development took place just as more and more women from the Third World began to examine critically not only feminist theory and its imperial claim to liberation, but also development practices. They infused debates with new ideas. They were/are quoted in academia and in international organizations.[22] Women from Europe and North America seem to have heeded their call for rethinking Otherness/difference in theory. But they managed to include these critical ideas in their work in ways that neutralize them. Postmodernist theory is an ideal framework of containment because of its inherent critical bent, and its call for vigilance against the complex and insidious ways in which power can present itself. But postmodernist theory is a double-edged weapon that can also be turned against those who use it in a positivistic fashion. There is a tendency to reify this theory's critical core (as is exemplified by 'taking' speech, even when constrained, as empowerment), and smother its reflexive nature by turning its indeterminate conception of power – its hesitations, its open-endedness – into a closed theoretical system the truth of which lies in its blind application. Where Foucault, Deleuze, Lyotard and Derrida had questions, their epigones have prescriptions. Containment through inclusion transcends the bounds of intellectuals' desire to retain the power to name, classify, interpret, translate others' experiences into a theoretical language. It is part and parcel of an international trend, in this post-Cold War era, where 'ideological' differences between nations are presumed to have disappeared, and, by implication, the world has become a safer place for intellectuals to operate. They can freely denounce old systems of government, liberation movements and different cultures. Postmodernist feminists can indict societies for customs that 'mutilate' women, call for the 'rule of law' and the establishment of 'rights', and, most of all, feel more than ever before empowered to use the world of women as a field of study, a playground for voyeurism.

A competition of sorts has appeared between female researchers from the globalizing countries to search for and reveal more and more aspects of Third World women's lives. This empowerment is partially made possible by the critical scholarship of Third World women in industrial countries, the so-called 'transnationals'. Globalization has meant a flattening out of ideas with a critical edge, a normalization of the study of other women wherever they are. In a sense, the issue is not the nationality or the ethnicity of a woman. After all, in the field of development, it is a Scandinavian woman, Ester Boserup, who blew the whistle on international aid organizations for their gender blindness.[23] Rather, it is the pretence to theorize other women's lives while using other women intellectuals' ideas, stripping them of their original meaning and bending them to fit conceptual schemes that sustain unequal power relations between countries. In so doing, serious differences between women scholars from different sides of the 'development' divide are obscured. More importantly, feminist postmodernist development as practised does little to problematize researchers'/theorists' own investment in the venture of development, or lay bare the reasons behind their continued desire to fashion other women in their own image.

Recuperation

The labour of recuperation under the banner of empowerment is best studied through academic feminists' entanglement with international organizations, especially in the field of 'gender-and-development training'. The professionalization of gender-and-development has created a merger of interests between academic women, whether professed feminists or not, and professional women working for various international organizations who do development work in Third World countries. Beginning in the 1980s the rapprochement between these groups of women was facilitated by the United Nations Decade for Women, which brought together women from various fields and walks of life at its international conferences; a greater receptivity to women's issues worldwide; and the involvement of academic women in consultancies on gender-and-development. Thus each group of women sought the other out for helping it in its own work. Academic women got to know how international organizations functioned and dealt with the issue of gender; officers of these organizations were able to catch up on academic debates and concepts of gender/development, and (more importantly) felt the need to hire academic women to help with training their organizations' staff in gender-and-development. It was only a question of time before a number of women unattached to academic institutions began to offer their skills as 'trainers', setting up consultancy firms focused solely on gender-and-development.[24]

The professionalization of gender resulted in two related outcomes: a transformation of women from the Third World into objects of technical knowledge; and a greater difficulty including women in development policies/programmes. This is not to say that training worsened a bad situation. Rather, in seeking to present the understanding of women/gender as requiring the acquisition of specialized knowledge, it activated a latent resistance among male development practitioners in international organizations that made the need for gender 'experts' an even greater necessity. Where experts are not readily available, or there is no funding for them, programme officers can justify a lack of attention to gender issues on grounds that they do not possess the required skills. Each organization has its own training manual and favourite team of trainers. Theorists of training rise and fall, and with them the methods they advocate. Often manuals are so dense that staff in the field cannot read them without help.

The discourse of gender training may have resulted in empowering individual trainers, possibly at the expense of the women they intend to help. In this sense, the logic of training turns a practical activity into a discourse. It lends itself to the postmodernist feminist search for development knowledge. Knowledge stands in the way of practice, abstract notions of women/gender hamper the unmediated understanding of real, concrete women farmers who get turned into 'target populations', 'beneficiaries', or 'resources'. It bears noting that a number of women who avail themselves of the postmodernist feminist approach also engage in gender training. Whether training helps women in the field is an empirical question that is beyond the scope of this discussion. It goes without saying that training is an important tool of skill acquisition. However, it is the manner in which it has been constructed, manualized and packaged that is at issue. The packaging of training in gender-and-development represents another link in the chain of the normalization of the development enterprise in the global era through a convergence of academic feminism and organizational interests. If anything, it sheds light on the nature of the relationship between interest, desire and power.

The fact that the language of training seeped into debates among local women is attested to by Marianne Marchand's report that operationalization of the distinction made by Caroline Moser (a former trainer and author of a training treatise) between 'practical' and 'strategic needs' fed into a secondary distinction that women make between 'feminine' and 'feminist' groups.[25] Mired in this semantic enterprise, Marchand argues that when used 'to legitimize one's political mobilization it [the distinction] is emancipatory in nature.'[26] This conclusion fails to question the power of 'training' to shape local political identities, and define the terms of the debates over development.

Perhaps it was inevitable that gender training and the inclusion of gender in development programmes/projects would become highly specialized knowledge, and thus more amenable to discoursing about it than being translatable into practical help to women.[27] Indeed, training had to achieve two goals at once: raise the consciousness of trainees (men as well as women) that women are invisible in development-as-usual, and impart to them the skills necessary to make women visible by integrating them effectively in programmes/projects. The inevitable tension between gender 'expertise', the domain of individuals who tend to be outsiders to the organizations for which they consult, and the logic of development aid, which generally focuses on the technical rather than the human side of its work, accounts for a greater specialization of gender, and shapes the selection of concepts. Thus, the shift from 'women' to gender-and-development came about not so much because of the discovery of the concept of gender, which predates the emergence of academic feminism, but because officers in international organizations found it more palatable than 'women'.[28]

All sorts of rationalizations have surrounded the currency given to the concept of gender, some of which are more plausible than others. The most common centres on the relational character of gender that connotes both women and men. However, in practical terms, operationalizing a relationship between roles when what is needed is giving women the means necessary to access aid, shifts the focus of aid from the economics of development to its politics. Experts find themselves having to argue *against* improving the material life of rural women for fear of upsetting the 'balance' between men and women and thus arousing the anger of men. Experts also find themselves having to recommend actions to be taken in favour of men in order to prepare them for improvement in women's lives. What this all means is that gender experts have been transformed into the surrogate micro-managers and distributors of dwindling aid, who recommend who should get what in the name of social stability, family harmony, gradual change, 'empowerment', 'mainstreaming', etcetera.[29] Thus, in a country of the Middle East that shall remain nameless, a gender 'expert' recommended that an international organization set up sewing cooperatives in a rural area where most of the workers were females, and in need of better equipment as well as transportation to ease their agricultural work. That at times such recommendations also play in favour of women is beyond doubt. Nevertheless, gender expertise is now part and parcel of an international order of things, the arrangement of which it sustains rather than upsets.

The postmodernist feminist approach feeds into this trend by inscribing the life histories and ethnographies of women into the larger international script. International organization studies of gender often feature, in prominent boxes, statements made by local women about their life circumstances. These accounts adorn reports but their import is left indeterminate, as if the structures and processes that caused the featured miseries and struggles were anonymous, out of anyone's (including the development agencies') control. The normalization of women's accounts (no matter what they reveal in intensity of suffering or heroism) rests on an ever-increasing search for such accounts, since they serve the double function of illustrating how bad life can be on the underside of development, and how it can be improved microscopically. Without the confessions of misery and heroism, there is nothing to justify development work in human terms. The choreography and design of the postmodern management and packaging of gender and development adds faces and colour to women's accounts by displaying them on posters: old and young, rural and urban, in shiny attire or happily ploughing their fields. That this process fits perfectly into the global trend of poverty 'alleviation' (not eradication) and discoursing about development hardly needs pointing out.

Evidence indicates that gender training has become a discursive formation with its own language, foundational concepts, relations of power and ambitions of total liberation. As such, it expands the field of postmodernist feminist conception of development. Development is not theorized, it is a given, a field of knowledge acquisition helped tremendously by the unhindered migrations of concepts from 'North' to 'South' with a few relays represented by the 'Southern' intellectuals in the North, reluctant or willing helpers. Development as speech and the postmodernist feminist assumption that women's speech is empowering render women *interchangeable.* The language of development is implicitly assumed to be universal, just like the capacity to speak. Consequently, it does not matter who speaks, whether it is a Latin American, African, Asian or Middle Eastern woman. *Interchangeability* need only be 'contextualized' by the gender expert to be meaningful. Finally, the utopia of North American feminists has been realized: other women are truly the same in their different modes of existence! Even those others among 'us' who have been marginalized because of their race, colour, ethnicity or class are the same as those on the other side of 'our' borders. But 'we' have escaped the homogenization that only *under*- 'development' can cause. Meanwhile, gender as a substantive issue in development practice is losing ground before the advance made by 'poverty' in the globalized economy.

'Globalization' and 'post-isms'

The preceding discussion calls for an exploration of the international context (globalization, for example) that legitimizes the academic feminists' insertion of postmodernist thought into development practice. The collapse of communism in the former Soviet Union and its satellites signalled the emergence of the market as the steering mechanism for social formations not only in the former Soviet Union, but also in the Third World. These countries are now seen as in transition towards a social system in which the logic of free exchange of equivalents informs political and social decisions. The general acceptance of the market as the mediator between state and society refocuses the concept and practices of development. In the years immediately following the independence of formerly colonized societies development centred on infrastructure projects to help expand and facilitate economic exchange. In the post-Cold War era, development has shifted away from aiding component parts of existing economies to overhauling local economies. Development today means the establishment of capitalist economies. The focus of aid rests on the privatization of the means of production, and the restructuring of local financial and legal institutions. The state is tolerated as an institution but its role is confined to making the environment safe for the operation and expansion of the private sector.

Of significance is the erosion of the sovereignty of the state as the protector of the economic and social rights of its citizens.[30] On one hand, existing transitional governments may welcome the shield that the market provides by hiding behind the anonymous twin principles of supply and demand as justifications for leaving unattended the social consequences of contractions, lay-offs and restructuring. On the other hand, the state's (forced or all too willing) withdrawal from the social sphere which it supported through subsidies for food, education and health care creates a responsibility vacuum: now, more than ever before, women are left to their own devices in a new economic era filled with promises that have yet to be realized. The freer movement of capital, the selectivity of investments, the socio-economic disruptions caused by the incipient market economies all combine to make women, whether in the Third World or the former Soviet Union, more rather than less vulnerable to international systemic change. The academic postmodernist response has been to reify globalization by presenting it as if it were a natural environment, and/or hailing it as an irreversible situation that simply needs to be managed.[31] Gender emerges as the secret weapon of this discursive accommodation. As Saskia Sassen indicates, gender can reveal the 'nexus' between international capital, law and the transformation of national sovereignty in the 'global city'.[32]

However, postmodernist/post-development practitioners are not engaged in delineating globalization's contours and historicizing its evolution. The use of gender as a tool of conceptual management dovetails with the needs felt by international aid organizations to manage international capital. Managing globalization through gender requires canvassing the world made closer by the electronic revolution, jets, and availability of funding for gender and development, in search of organizations that might help make the penetration of international capital more targeted or efficient. Non-governmental organizations, the rising stars of the global era, fulfil this need. Many of these are formed and led by local women who compete with one another for funding from international donor agencies. Many of these institutions play an important role at the community level. However, they are assigned structural functions in the global reshaping of local economies. They are perceived as more reliable relays in the distribution of ideas and practices pertaining to a capitalist socio-political *culture.* Some are 'trained' in gender and development, others in how to advocate for (directed) political and legal change. The support they receive is made in the name of 'civil society'. Thus a second shift has occurred in the use of women in development, from beneficiaries of development, to 'participants', to agents of civil society. It is easy to see this shift as an auspicious one that might lead to women's active involvement in structural change. But many NGOs cannot survive without donors' financial help, let alone technical assistance. Their goals as institutions cannot be assumed, by definition, to coincide with those of the people they are expected or claim to serve. They may represent another stage in a conception of development that seeks to evade the task of systemic change. This appears to be an endless process of ostensibly turning over to local women and men living under development/globalization the task of helping to decide what is good for them without giving them the means to control the material conditions under which they live, or comprehend and redefine their (and their countries') inscribed location in the global economy. Postmodernist feminist discourse on gender adjusts 'gender' to this new order by hailing as empowerment speeches of misery and glory, speeches of 'resistance' to a process largely left blissfully anonymous because 'global'. Anonymity fosters surrogate targets such as migrations, marginality, identity, (tired or tireless) patriarchy, customs, corrupt states or democratization.

The shift of focus to civil society as a tool of development results in the identification of any organized body other than the local state as comprising civil society. Women who have organized themselves into NGOs often claim in international fora that they represent civil society. This organizational view of society leaves out the majority of the illiterate women as a mass to channel according to the requirements of 'democratization', 'poverty alleviation', 'social development', 'governance', etcetera. The prospects of the rewards that a market economy can bring about, the availability of coveted goods on the local markets and the extolling of easy wealth on television conjure up a tantalizing image of globalization. Enduring the ills of lack or insufficient (capitalist) development[33] is made both more and less bearable: *more*, because individual women and men can try out their newly discovered business acumen and throw their hats into the market ring; *less*, because the spectacular rise of the newly rich and speculators of all stripes makes the efforts of those who play by the rules seem trivial, if not doomed to failure. The difficulties encountered by women entrepreneurs in the former Soviet Union, many of whom entered the market with starry eyes, are just the most noteworthy examples of a condition told many times over throughout the countries in transition.[34] It might be argued that these difficulties are transitory, and that in the long run women in Russia or Kenya will be better off. But what is under consideration here is not so much the future of the women and men (not gender) of these countries, as the *labelling* of what is happening to them. Development is not the issue, or may never have been. The issue concerns the conceptual schemes elaborated to arrange it, harness it, distribute it, withhold it, tantalize with it. Individual women and men do not blame 'development' for their problems. They live their lives just as 'we' do, taking care of their problems with the means available to them, not according to the criteria theorists use to define their societies for them.

The inscription of women's (and men's) life histories as 'contexts' of development effects another semantic shift in the linguistic chess game of development. The multiple changes (often in the form of deterioration of an already bad situation) that have affected women's lives acquire value *for* academic women from industrial societies who compete with one another as neocolonial, postcolonial or above the fray altogether by locating themselves in a postmodernist thought assumed to be beyond ideological reproach. Development exists in the personal accounts of poor women/people. As Marchand puts it, 'development is personal'. This replay of the original motto of second-wave feminism – that 'the personal is political' – signals an ominous trend. It pushes further the old feminist desire to penetrate other/different women's private selves, explore their nooks and crannies, lay bare their inner workings, and reshape them in the interest of knowledge. The unleashing of 'subjugated' women's voices when well 'contextualized' will yield a 'subject status', for 'Ultimately, testimonies construct the subject as well.'[35]

From this perspective, the personal holds the key to an entity (development/ globalization) that exists only in accounts given about it in everyday life. This would be fine, were it not for the fact that what is identified as 'development' in a personalized form is what is usually defined as the lack of it. Why is there a need to use a term with a problematical historical and intellectual baggage? Why not simply address women's accounts of poverty and struggles to survive? Could it be that poverty as a concept does not lend itself to a postmodernist analysis? This is the cul-de-sac of the postmodernist theorizing of 'other' women, living under different material conditions in which 'we' also partake. The antinomy between the postmodernist claim that development is a discourse and the modernist view that female *subjectivity* is socially constructed is left unresolved. It bears reiterating that Foucault had difficulty connecting 'epistemes' or 'discursive formations' with subjectivity, for which he did not have a theory. In his defence, he did not address subjectivity *per se*; rather, he traced the genealogical itinerary of *categories* such as madness, sexuality and reason. Without the help of psychoanalysis, the antinomy remains. It will be an unhappy day when the 'subjectivity' of 'other' women is constructed by postmodernist development experts. The personal is not development, just as development is not a purely personal matter. The 'subject status' that postmodernist feminism claims to bestow upon the Third World is vitiated by the assumption of a self constituted by structures of development (it should be called pre-development, or insufficient development or just dependent economies) that are assumed but never spelled out. This use of the concept of 'development' as a sign with no signified is a bizarre ploy in which we use women themselves as signs of our new virtuosity in understanding the concrete reality of development. The issue for development feminists should be to figure out how the insertion of the local into the international will reproduce the inequities of development-as-usual for women as well as men, while making it possible for some groups to enter the global market primarily as needed subsidiaries. For women these processes signify a double jeopardy in that the poverty and inequality they endured before is compounded by a more direct and palpable exploitation in the name of restructuring local economies, and/or doing away with the state as a mitigator of the impact of the harsh logic of the market on people's lives.[36]

Passing the post[37]

The shift from postmodernist development to a post-development approach requires examination. The beginning as well as the end of the 'tales' of development recounted by Arturo Escobar provide an excellent illustration of the convergence of postmodernist/feminist and globalization studies. He views globalization as an environment of the discourse of development, which is endowed with the power of constituting subjectvities/identities of an 'underdeveloped' nature.[38] In so doing, he displaces the locus of development from structure to the private domain of subjectivity/identity. Escobar does not provide any empirical evidence of the existence of such 'underdeveloped' identities. This point is not trivial since it questions the facile use of postmodern concepts, thereby revealing their unwarranted application to the private domain of primarily illiterate people. The lack of reflexivity inherent in this view is similar to that of postmodern feminists doing development. In explaining the relevance of his theoretical choice, the author argues that it 'gives us the possibility of singling out "development" as an encompassing cultural space and at the same time *separating ourselves from it* by perceiving it in a totally new form [italics added]'[39] In other words, the discursive study of development is a matter of individual perception and not the objective (a non-postmodernist term) analysis of objective structures of knowledge and practices. Why would Escobar's *discourse* of development be more acceptable to those who live on the *under*side of development than that offered by UNDP, USAID or SIDA, especially if he acknowledges that some good was done by the ongoing development practices?[40] On what grounds can he justify separating himself from the 'developed' space from which he writes about the 'underdeveloped' reality of others?

Although there is not much in Escobar's critique of the intended or unintended consequences of development-from-above that one would disagree with, his conclusions are problematic.[41] His post-development view implicitly conflates structural change at the local level, in formerly colonized societies, with international political phenomena such as the collapse of the former Soviet Union. Admittedly, post-development can only be understood as another moment in the history of Third World societies. However, since *no* empirical evidence is given to justify the use of this concept, except that development practices failed to achieve their goals, the only marker of the emergence of the 'post-development era' is the collapse of socialism. This neutralization of globalization as an unspoken environment bespeaks an assumption of a closure of history.[42] This brings the postmodernist stance, feminist or feminizing, dangerously close to social conservatism.

The notion of post-development also assumes a superficial view of formerly colonized societies as somehow having crossed the divide that separates them economically and politically from industrialized nations. The claim to post-development made by Escobar and supported by feminists doing development is based on a contradictory and flimsy foundation. The emergence of ecology-minded groups in many countries of the South, and the concern for preserving biodiversity in the face of the corporatization of seed production are hailed as reflecting an incipient new mode of thinking development at the grassroots level. This is so only if one had bought into the notion that people in formerly colonized societies are passive and/or unaware of the preservation of their natural habitat. Naturally, it is good that such movements exist. However, these groups do not necessarily oppose development, if we understand by this concept employment, regular income or access to health and education.

Perhaps the most problematical aspect of 'post-development' in Escobar's version is social-psychological: the alleged emergence of 'hybrid' forms of knowledge and identities produced by individuals in Third World societies, who borrow elements from their own traditions and those of the 'West'. Respect for and strengthening of cultures that have been eroded and weakened by colonial policies is one thing, but the celebration of 'hybridity', a term with a biological baggage, is another. All cultures (including those of industrial nations) are hybrids in one sense or another: they have borrowed from one another and continue to do so. However, what is advocated through this concept has all the trappings of a rearguard action to stem cultural change, the direction of which is predefined as necessarily 'Western'.

The obsession with Western culture seen as a monolithic entity is the functional equivalent of the Luddites' movement that rejected all forms of technology. Perhaps it should be remembered that the West did not blink before incorporating Chinese, Indian, Middle Eastern and African contributions to science, technology, philosophy and the arts. This has not made the West Asian or African, but it did make it more complex. Escobar's justified concern is the defence of 'minority subjectivities'.[43] Considering the excesses that have been committed in the name of cultural identity in countries such as Algeria, Egypt, India and sub-Saharan Africa, it is unfortunate that hybridity is proposed as a new way of thinking culture and development. Isn't one of the criticisms of development agencies that they did not respect the cultural integrity of the peoples of the South? One cannot have it both ways: arguing for the preservation of local cultures from the ills of development *and* claiming that poor rural people hold the key to development because they allegedly borrow freely and integrate different cultural elements at will.[44] The concept of hybridity does not belong in the language of synthesis and coherence. Rather it belongs in the language of 'colour', 'underdevelopment/development', 'Third World/First

World', 'us and them' – the language of Otherness which postmodernist theory was meant to deconstruct.

The proposed 'alternative' is no alternative at all. It is a flight, not forward but backward, a retreat to identity politics as a cure for structural problems. The discursive retrieval of some (partial) ontological identity that has been pushed down in the recesses of the women's and men's beings in formerly colonized societies occults the very practices of the poorest among them. They are interested in buying goods such as TV sets, dish antennas, clothes, foodstuffs, education for their children – all items that make 'their' lives, like 'ours', easier. One only has to observe what travellers and expatriate labourers take back home with them from Western countries to realize that being a consumer may take precedence over being a Nigerian Yoruba, an Algerian Kabyle or a native Colombian. An 'alternative' theory of development, if there is need for one, must take into consideration the fact that people living on the *under* side of development are 'our' contemporaries, and that to romanticize their circumstances is to do them violence. To what extent frustrated desires for the tangible, material signs of development contribute to the essentializing of identities, or the imposition of collective identities, on individuals living in the same geographical or ethnic space is an empirical question that the postmodernist approach fails to raise. It is worth noting that this concern for the grounding of identity is another expression of social conservatism. In fact, globalization has room for the preservation of indigenous peoples' cultures, judging by the policies that some international organizations have formulated in this respect. The emphasis on cultural preservation, whether as a living museum, or as a 'hybrid', denotes a diffuse nostalgia for a passive order, and a view of development as destruction instead of transformation.

Unlike Escobar, Aihwa Ong and Donald Nonini, among other postmodernist development writers, have opted for a normalization of globalization, which they refer to as 'late capitalism', by asserting that its has created a cultural environment that is transforming 'transnational subjectivities' in ways that point to a modernity that differs from its Western counterpart.[45] The much-touted new subjectivities/identities are *derived* from interviews with transnationals or poor people living in the Third World. The unavoidable question is how, on the basis of interviews or questionnaires, a writer can find and delineate the contents of subjectivities and identities. Likewise, how and why, when considering essays about women's attitudes towards globalization, do they conclude that they reveal 'new forms of feminism, which do not necessarily use the label "feminism" or terms and categories associated with Western feminism, but nevertheless entail self-conscious analyses of women's oppression'.[46] Even when the documentary evidence points to the contrary, the authors insist on a feminist subjectivity that would extend, by confirming it, its Western counterpart. Foucault warned against the changed role of the intellectual in bourgeois societies, which is 'no longer to place himself "somewhat ahead and to the side" in order to express the stifled truth of the collectivity: rather it is *to struggle* against the form of power that transforms him into its objects and instrument in the sphere of "knowledge", "truth", "consciousness" and "discourse"'.[47] It is the women and men of the Third World who must take on the role that Foucault felt should be assigned to intellectuals, for *their* consciousness, subjectivity, identity are at stake. They are moulded, bartered, auctioned off in the name of the 'posts'. As with the postmodernist feminist development discourse, its male version also deals with peoples of the formerly colonized societies as *interchangeable* units. Thus Escobar discusses the practices of development prevalent in Latin America as if they were the same as those in other parts of the world. Even within Latin America, Colombia is used as an ideal type of sorts. What is good or true for one country is presumed to be good or true for another. In this, Escobar follows in the footsteps of the postcolonial theorists who Sanskritize colonialism by making the case of India an iconic figure. By reducing different development experiences to those of one country, postmodernists relinquish their advocacy of multiplicity of experiences of reality, and, most of all, of 'voices'. Most contradictory is Escobar's assertion that the retrieval of 'minority identities' will somehow help 'the valorization of economic needs and opportunities in terms that are not strictly those of profit and the market'.[48] In other words, what he identifies as a post-development space which somehow skips development is based on a non-capitalist economy. He wants these minorities to be different from those who are reaping the fruit of development. Their world will run 'parallel' to those who live in 'cyber culture', thus ushering in an era where both will 'learn to live humanly in a posthumanist (postman and postmodern) landscape'.[49] Such a conclusion clearly indicates the confusing outcomes of the postmodernist approach which, after exhausting the limits of the discourse of knowledge/power, finds itself compelled to appeal to principles it has attempted to bury. In a final contradictory moment, Escobar appeals to the 'reconstruction of the connection between *truth* and reality' (emphasis added).[50] Truth, the nemesis of postmodern theory, returns by the back door. This concept, inserted as an afterthought, dismantles the whole conception of development as a constituted and constitutive discourse. Development is dead, long live development! A postmodernist would want to know whose and what truth is appealed to? If there is any truth, it is that development is more than a concept, or a discourse. It is a state that societies, groups, cultures, individuals partake in, in one form or another. 'We' are all engaged in it, in 'our' various occupations. It expresses aspirations for a better life. This accounts for the resilience of its appeal. Aspiring to it should not mean, as it has, mimicking those who have been engaged in it longer than others. There are many paths to development, even within its capitalist modality, as Japan has shown. It is the lack of self-confidence on the part of local leaders who approached advanced technology with a mixture of awe and excitement that may account for their love/hate relationship with development.[51] Such an attitude was/is expressed in the fetishization of local customs and practices, often seen as repositories of an unrecognized science. It is a thin line between accepting one's culture as valuable but understanding that it is susceptible to change, and stifling it by fearing for its absorption by industrial cultures. It is worth noting that 'development' also means cultural change in directions that are not always controllable. After all, people in industrial nations have seen their cultures change as the material and political conditions under which they live have changed.[52]

It is not enough simply to pass the 'post' to the next writer, who will pass it to the next, as in a relay contest. It is better to pass the post as horses do in race tracks, by leaving it behind. Development theorists, be they postmodern feminists or postmodern males dabbling in feminism, should do away with all posts as so many crutches or batons. To go back to the title of this essay, 'posted' feminist development theory has crossed the divide between women-centred studies and conventional theories. That this turn is a mark of the social conservatism of our age is what I have tried to reveal. The retreat into the study of the selves of Third World women, now seen as the expressions of the workings of a system of relations between nations defined as globalization or late capitalism, attempts to accomplish what non-posted feminist theory could not: the theoretical elimination of difference. It remains to be seen whether, in practical/real terms, the endeavour will be successful. Seeking refuge in subjectivism by proxy can be very appealing. But, as with all subjectivism, reaching the 'real' Third World woman might be an ever-receding illusion. It may very well be that posted feminism's will to knowledge has finally reached the point of no return, in a postmodern cul-de-sac. As Foucault put it:

> The historical analysis of this rancorous will to knowledge reveals that all knowledge rests upon injustice (that there is no right, not even in the act of knowing, to truth or a foundation for truth) and that the instinct for knowledge is malicious (something murderous, opposed to the happiness of mankind).

Who is next on the block?

Notes

1 Pierre Bourdieu (1990: chapters 1, 5 and 9).

2 I use this term to refer to postmodernist males who incorporate feminist thought in their writings to achieve greater critical comprehensiveness.

3 'Globalization' in this chapter is defined as the incorporation of local (Third World) economies

into a capitalist world economy *and culture* characterized by a rapid movement across nations of capital and labour made possible by the electronic/information revolution.

4 Arturo Escobar (1995: Chapter 6).

5 In this post-Cold War era, the term 'Third World' has lost its original meaning and is, therefore, inadequate. I will use it for the sake of coherence, however, since it is used by some of the theorists I address in this chapter.

6 Arturo Escobar (1995: 10).

7 *Ibid.*: 10.

8 See M. Shamsul Haque (1999: 44).

9 The term 'inclusion' is used here more to denote 'insertion' than substantive integration of women in development policies/programmes/projects. It simply refers to attempts made by women to call attention to the necessity to address women in development practice.

10 Among international organizations, the concept of empowerment was first used by the International Labour Organization (ILO) with reference to the social category of 'workers'. In the 1990s the United Nations Development Programme started using it within the context of its annual human development reports as part of the Gender Empowerment Index, which seeks to measure the extent to which a country has sought to redress the gender balance in access to parliamentary, managerial, professional and technical positions.

11 Melvin Richter (1997: 25–47). Voltaire, a major figure of the French Enlightenment, did not theorize the category of the Other, and held some Others' political practices to be superior to his country's. This did not mean, however, that he was above cultural prejudice.

12 Escobar (1995: 6). Samir Amin, among others, has demonstrated that the 'Green' movements that seek to oppose the nature-unfriendly logic of the market share similar concerns with Marxists, but by ignoring their own embeddedness in the global processes they oppose, end up espousing views and strategies that turn them into the functional equivalents of religious fundamentalists. See 'A Propos the Green Revolution', in Herb Addo *et al.*, eds. (1985: 271–81).

13 Marianne H. Marchand, 'Latin American Women Speak on Development', in Marianne H. Marchand and Jane Parpart, eds. (1995: 64).

14 *Ibid.*

15 This expression was used by Gilles Deleuze. See Donald Bouchard, ed., *Language, Counter-Memory, Practice. Selected Essays and Interviews by Michel Foucault*, p. 209.

16 Just like 'doing sociology', 'doing postmodernist feminist development' is a task fraught with unspoken assumptions, and in need of a reflexive methodology that constructs itself as it constructs its subject matter. See Harold Garfinkel (1967), especially Chapter 1.

17 I*bid.*: 68.

18 Marchand and Parpart (1995: 70).

19 I am keenly aware that I am given a space from which to 'speak' in this book in a section entitled 'More Worldly Feminisms', a title I do not care for. I find cover in my desire to be a counter-point, an anti-voice.

20 See Marnia Lazreg (1988: 81–107).

21 The Latin root of recuperation is *capere,* meaning to catch, to seize. *Per* by derivation means to appropriate. The Latin form of this word also combines with the suffix *kap* (or take) to signify deception. See the *American Heritage Dictionary of the English Language.*

22 Women such as Peggy Antrobus, Noeleen Heyzer, Naila Kabeer, Chandra Mohanty, Aihwa Ong (in her early work), Gita Sen, to name only a few, either documented inequities deriving from development practices in the field, or attempted to theorize them.

23 See Ester Boserup's first book (1970). Boserup's work confined itself to women's specific work in farming. Her forays into the customs that shed light on the type and intensity of the work undertaken by women lacked the ambitions and the conceptual distortions of later treatments of women in developing societies.

24 Escobar (1995: Chapter 5) and Parpart (Marchand and Parpart 1995: Chapter 12) raise the issue of professionalization of development/gender, but do not address training.

25 The training vocabulary provides a good illustration of the intriguing, albeit unavoidable, transformation that takes place when the technology of development dictates the terms of inclusion of women in development aid. The expression 'gender planning' is a case in point. See Caroline Moser (1993).
26 Marchand and Parpart (1995: 71).
27 I am not implying that women are not sometimes helped by gender expertise. However, small rural projects relying on community participation have generally been carried out without any specific gender expertise resting on complicated 'gender planning' charts.
28 On the positive side, the difficulty of mainstreaming gender has sometimes led organizations, such as UNDP, to make gender balance in staffing within the organization one of the dimensions of mainstreaming.
29 Mainstreaming gender in development work is the latest phase in the gender-and-development saga. Broadly speaking, it means the incorporation of gender in all development activities.
30 Saskia Sassen, one the most lucid observers of global economic trends and their social significance, rightly points out that 'the globalization of the economy has reconfigured the fundamental properties of the nation-state, notably territoriality and sovereignty' (Sassen 1998: 81).
31 Aihwa Ong and Donald H. Nonini study 'transnationalism', a function of globalization as an enduring phenomenon that has created 'alternative modernities' (Ong and Nonini, eds. 1997). In their 1995 anthology, Marchand and Parpart do not engage globalization. Marchand and Anne Sisson Runyan (2000) correct this oversight in a book devoted to global restructuring, but focus on the effects at the expense of the causes of globalization – deemed too economistic.
32 Sassen (1998: 86).
33 It is important to note that the former communist countries were not underdeveloped. Socialism followed a different path to development.
34 See, among others, Marnia Lazreg, ed. (2000).
35 Marchand and Parpart (1995: 68 and 70).
36 This analysis does not rest on an idealistic view of local states. However, it does point to the importance of the state as a tangible force on which citizens may make demands. Where the state becomes a mere relay in the unhindered penetration of international capital in search of cheap labour, it ensures the anonymity of the sources of exploitation, thus depriving citizens of recourse. The rise of NGOs is meant to create an intermediary between the people and international capital, not so much between the latter and the local state.
37 I thank Dr Melvin Richter for bringing this expression to my attention.
38 Escobar (1995: 10).
39 *Ibid.*: 6.
40 *Ibid.* See Chapter 5, especially the section on 'The Struggle for Visibility and Empowerment,' pp. 182–92.
41 Algeria provided the best example of the problems inherent in development from above designed by a French economist, Gerard Destannes de Bernis who, in spite of high unemployment inherited from the colonial era, managed to convince the government to adopt a development policy based on labour-saving technology that bypassed agricultural development altogether.
42 This trend in thought has already been expressed in the conservative scholarship of Francis Fukuyama, especially *The End of History and the Last Man.*
43 Escobar (1995: 225).
44 *Ibid.*: 216–26.
45 A. Ong and D. Nonini (1997). Non-postmodernist development writers also bemoan the 'loss of culture'. See S. Haque (1999: 153–7).
46 Marchand and Runyan (2000: 227).
47 Michel Foucault, 'Intellectuals and Power', in D. Bouchard (1977: 207–8, emphasis added).
48 Escobar (1995: 226).
49 *Ibid.*

50 *Ibid.*: 223.

51 The first generation of Third World leaders such as Boumedienne in Algeria, Nasser in Egypt, Nehru in India, Kwame Nkrumah in Ghana and Sukarno in Indonesia approached development from a nationalist perspective that is much maligned today. They tried without much success to control the multidimensionality of development politically by limiting its scope. What they failed to do was to *adapt* the tools of development to their cultures as lived by the majority of their citizens. Implicitly they perceived industrialization as a mere technical problem.

52 Escobar dismisses Habermas's view that Third World societies are shot through by processes of change that are similar to those experienced by industrial societies as just another expression of the Enlightenment philosophy. Yet, in many countries of the Third World, changes in family size and structure, perceptions of self and attitudes towards money are changing in ways that do not support a 'post' view of development.

7

Picture More at Variance: Of Desire and Development in the People's Republic of China[1]

Tani Barlow

There is almost no equation in the formulas for sustainable development and peace in which China will not be an important factor. The world has entered a period in which China's and the planet's fates are linked, and this period promises to be long and dangerous.

Peter C. Goldmark, Jr, 'The President's Letter', The Rockefeller Foundation Annual Report, 1997

As in other societies which underwent a socialist revolution, the 1949 Communist Revolution in China transformed women's lives through the 'top-down' liberation of women, overturning traditional gender notions and restrictive feudal practices. During the Socialist era China adopted a number of policies and programmes to redefine women's roles and grant them equal status with men. Women were drawn into the mainstream of the economy during this period. Women also gained from an extensive health network and the government's emphasis on universal basic education.

'China: Country Gender Profile: Gender Context', World Bank, 'Gender Net', webpage, http//www. worldbank.com.

[T]he relationship between global capitalism ... and nation-state alliances ... is so macrological that it cannot account for the micrological texture of power. To move toward such an accounting one must move toward theories of ideology – of subject formations that micrologically and often erratically operate the interests that congeal the macrologies. Such theories cannot afford to overlook the category of representation....

Gayatri C. Spivak, 'Can the Subaltern Speak? in *Marxism and the Interpretation of Culture* (1988: 279, 306)

> It is a mistake to assume that a critique of teleology stands in for a critique of macrological explanations.... [R]esistances and contestations at various sites make the direction taken by macrological processes such as capitalism and postcoloniality uncertain.
>
> Akhil Gupta, *Postcolonial Developments: Agriculture in the Making of Modern India* (1998: 12).

China in development is already a preoccupation in policy circles and is likely to absorb the attention of planners and budget officials for the arduous period Peter Goldmark anticipates in the statement quoted above.[2] China in development is consequently, necessarily, this essay's geopolitical horizon. The organizers of this book on rethinking development discourse asked me to consider whether or not development dreams like the ones sketched out in the programmatic notes of the Rockefeller Foundation and the World Bank have forgotten to ask what it is that female subjects of development want. In my thinking this is actually a political question of access to the subject of concern and an analytic problem about the place of desire in politics: that being so, I take up three points. First, I revisit Professor Spivak's initial formula regarding the question of the gendered subaltern: it was her suggestion that in the absence of ideological mediation there is no express desire. Second, I consider the question of access through the articulated texts of a national feminism, because historically feminisms pursue politically adequate subject forms for women within constraints of citizenship. I supply three twentieth-century feminist formations in which the theoretical subject 'Chinese women' was differently constituted – woman as a biogenetic agent, as a revolutionary subject, and as an eroticized consumer – in various ways. Third, I conclude this short essay with two questions: 'What does it mean to ask, "Can the subaltern desire?" in the context of a very old, socialist, revolutionary tradition?' and 'What does it mean when some state agencies in the PRC generate and collaborate with globalized commercial capitalist development discourses and practices?'

Desire and ideology

It is useful to reiterate Gayatri Chakravorty Spivak's core criticisms of poststructuralist theory in 'Can the Subaltern Speak?' First, she pointed out that poststructuralists had rewritten history and theory without acknowledging imperialism; consequently they had blindly resituated Europe in the position of the centre, discounting theory and history in other places. Second, since these so-called poststructuralist theorists had carelessly substituted 'power' and 'desire' for what, as Spivak argues, is really the problem of ideology or ideological mediation, they ended up 'valoriz[ing] the concrete experience of the oppressed, while being ... uncritical about the historical role of the intellectual'. Third, because 'power' and 'desire' are unitary concepts they smuggle back into analysis agents that resemble nothing less than the old-fashioned 'sovereign subject'. 'Subjects of desire or power' (or, indeed, subjects of 'development') are always the same as the force – desire or power – that fields the subject itself. That is why poststructuralism admits few counter-hegemonic possibilities.

When they impute to the Other (the masses, the oppressed, the 'women') a false concreteness rooted in 'desire' or 'power' and invite the oppressed to 'speak for itself' (that is, act politically, represent itself), theorists can do so only because they presume that their own positioning as intellectuals is neither invested nor contradictory. European intellectuals like Deleuze and Foucault are confused about representation: they envision subjects lying outside themselves while disavowing their own involvement in the processes of 'subject predication'. Refusing the view that they 'speak for the masses' puts European intellectuals in bad faith. They cannot see how intellectuals are implicated in thinking or that their representation of the masses is oppressive because it is ideological. Such self-abdicating intellectuals compel the oppressed to speak for itself while robbing it of the very tools – critique or deconstruction of ideological formation – that might enable 'speech' to occur. As is well known, the test case for Spivak was the gendered or sexed or female oppressed.

Spivak's understanding of ideology is thus necessarily complex. She distinguishes two senses of representation, the semiotic and the classical liberal-political, a fine point that allows critical access to the tiny strictures and injunctions that a-systematically fix larger oppressive forces in the everyday lives of people demarcated in relations with one another.[3] She argues further that mediate or ideological formations situate subaltern, élite, and intellectual relationally and in hailing distance to each other, but never in transparent immediacy – which is why there is no 'true subaltern' who can 'know and speak of itself'.[4] Ideological formations consist of vested, silenced, unacknowledged spots that throw the visible world into relief, according to this argument. So for Spivak counterhegemonic intellectuals must focus on exposing the political interests that solidify the mechanics of oppression. Her broader point rests on the insight that the historical, legal abolition of widow burning during the colonial era precluded all representable feminine subjects other than, except for, the good wife, who either steps up to the plate (nativists) or is rescued at the last moment (imperialists). That is why the figure of woman disappears into the 'violent shuttling' between tradition and modernization and why, in the end 'There is no space from which the sexed subaltern subject can speak.' Yet, nonetheless, oppressed or subaltern women do resist or 'speak', as Spivak demonstrates in her interpretation of the chaste political suicide of a young girl, Bhuvaneswari Bhaduri.

The question is, what happens to desire here? Not only is subaltern desire always mediated through complex ideological formations; its counter-hegemonic expressions are also difficult to read. The oppressed may desire things that are not germane to development or to non-development, since the desires of the oppressed may be a picture more at variance than dreamed of in development discourse.[5] These are important points since macrological discourses also come in many shapes other than historical or colonial discourses. The point I'd raise here is that social revolution is itself a macrology in the sense that Aihwa Ong and Akhil Gupta have demonstrated. Macrologies are mediated through bodies, and these are gendered, raced and sexed (subaltern female Malaysian or rural Indian subjects of development) whose resistance and contestations make up the direction of macrological processes. My point is simply that what Miss Bhaduri addressed through her careful, chaste, orderly suicide was a desire for an adequate political subjectivity, sufficient to the political ends she could only halfway dream.

As I consider a revolutionary tradition where the ideological asymmetries of gendered oppression were in fact raised to the level of outright counter-hegemony – and I am talking here about the Maoist tradition of women's liberation theory and practice – I adopt some of Spivak's main admonitions: (1) no unmediated access to the other woman's desires; (2) no point in commanding that the other woman speak; and (3) a recognition that the mediations of difference that constitute subaltern and intellectual, élite and non-élite, urban and rural are inextricably ideological, and that the first line of consideration must always be how counter-ideology is being positioned through critique.

Three desiring subjects in the history of revolutionary Chinese feminism

Ideally I should begin by making visible the 'self-conscious centre of a critical practice' that is the singular, century-old itinerary of Chinese feminist thinking.[6] Second, I should trace out the ways that theoretical stream has concerned itself with gendered oppression. Third, I should illustrate the long-term preoccupation of Chinese feminisms with partial, incomplete or constitutionally deficient female subjects. All this is impossible here, though the project is viable.[7] This chapter sketches out three historical-ideological feminist discourses in which the subject 'Chinese women' was differently constituted and consequently desired different things. Reviewing these moments retrieves their emancipatory possibilities, while not overlooking their embeddedness in 'congealing macrology,' to borrow Spivak's vivid language again. Let me be utterly clear: I am not suggesting that the Revolution liberated Chinese women, or that to understand Chinese women as a social collectivity you must know Chinese feminism, or that only Chinese people can understand Chinese women's liberation, or even that only a better revolution will liberate Chinese women.

Rather, my point is finite and simple. The praxological theories (actually policies for globalized social investments, as Goldmark notes) that we are now forced to reconsider in our scholarly politics – this so-called development theory and its institutional practices – will not, indeed cannot, encounter the desire of a subaltern Chinese woman without first engaging the mediated and 'sedimented' (to use a term from 1980s Chinese neo-Marxism) female subjects of what are complex, situated, revolutionary historical formations. Feminism is one avenue into reconsideration of this history because it rests on accepting that the 'other is not just a "voice"' but that, like me, others 'produce articulated texts, even as they, like us, are written in and by a text not of our own making'.[8] It is simply impossible to know what 'the subaltern' desires because subjects are neither abstract nor theoretical. What sort of development projects are at hand conditions what sort of subjects of development appear; yet the subject in question is never cut of whole cloth, can never be 'theorized' in the absence of a consideration, for instance, of what desires may lie outside development.

Biogenetic agency[9]

Progressive thinkers in the 1920s took a series of geopolitical claims to modern citizenship inherited from mid-nineteenth-century semi-colonialism and grafted onto notions of women's universal humanity and integrity as a natural community a newer, just globalized theory of evolutionary sexuality. Eugenics legitimated the call to liberate women because it justified women's autonomy in evolutionary terms. Briefly, in order to compete in the global struggle of the fittest nations Chinese women had to be freed from a hyperstable Chinese culture back into nature so that they could reassume the task nature gave females of the species – sex selection – and thus accelerate national evolution through individual biogenetic agency.[10]

One example is Gao Xian, who argued that because sexual intercourse is the secret of human life it should lie at the centre of national efforts to improve the race and accelerate national evolution. Another is the social scientist Mei Sheng, whose enormous edited compendium *Zhongguo funü wenti taolun* (Discussion of the Chinese Woman Question, 1929–34) collated fifteen years of Chinese feminism. Mei created an ideological object out of a superabundant theoretical archive, using editorial techniques of taxonomy and framing, and drawing on the silent presumption that a uniform social field vested in natural processes where women ought to appear could be established in revolution. Though many contributors to Chinese feminism were male, female feminists and the female 'subaltern' participated in this form of speech, no less convinced of the revolutionary import of these claims than male theorists. Qian Yu, an élite, female academic writer, argued for the need to abolish the buying and selling of women because it damaged the subjectivity of Chinese women, ruining them as US slavery had ruined the Africans; women's emancipation would thus improve the national biological matrix. A feminist calling herself Three-Four, and noting widespread female dependency in all classes of Chinese women, advocated economic independence as the antidote to slave marriage and forced reproduction. Japanese feminist theorist Yosano Akiko, whose inclusion here reminds us that Chinese feminism of this era was foundationally heterogeneous and internationalized, argued that marriage custom enshrining chastity made Asian women prostitutes, commodities and slaves.[11] Theory and colloquial language representations of the subalternized woman – poor women, working women, wives, daughters, foreign women, slave women, Indian women, etcetera – echoed and endorsed a primary theoretical framework: (1) healthy civilization rests on unfettering procreative males and females to choose each other; (2) recognition of the biogenetic agency of women among women and men would liberate women; (3) women's liberation is an event in nature as much as a historical overthrow of feudalism.

The point is not that female feminists were rare (they were) or that they had a difficult time (they did), but rather that when women produced articulated texts on these matters their texts either illustrated the truths of the new theory or contributed to reinforcing the presuppositions – for example, that until women choose the father of their children women will continue to be prostituted, bought and sold like cattle in cultural marriage practices that degrade the people and the nation – that structured progressive feminist eugenics.[12] Women were not silenced in these texts; they were incited to the speech of women. The question is how that sanctioned speech was symptomatic. What representational styles, areas of unsaidness, what system of politically engineered, invested prohibitions cathected in what ways to the positions male and female progressive feminists advocated? What got lost or undone in the incitement to liberatory, revolutionary speech?

Revolutionary agency

In his monumental *Shehui wenti cidian* (Dictionary of Social Problems, 1929) social scientist Chen Shousun encapsulated prevailing assumptions among élites:

> The two most significant social problems of the contemporary era are the labour problem and the women problem.... The women problem is not simply concerned with Woman, but broadly speaking with the lives of men and women so it has an intimate relation to social life generally. What is most important in regard to this problem is reforming current male-centred civilization and abolishing the slave status of women, reestablishing a society

> with the objective of equal rights for women and men. To date, the social status of nüxing [women] has not only been under the conquest of men, it has become virtually a class subordinated to men, seeming almost to constitute a second world to that of men. (589)

That was true but not accurate. One thing that got lost in the predication of the biogenetic agent of Chinese feminism was history. From inception this subject of *nüxing* had its detractors, like the female theorists Yang Zhihua, Xiao Chunnü, Xiang Jingyu and Ho Xiangning, who laid the earliest ground of institutionalized, communist, theoretical feminism and bridged the gap between the women and labour movements. The theoretical agent they predicated was capacious and the desire that allegedly drew all potential social elements into a revolutionary female agent was historical, according to Xiang Jingyu. In fact, she argued, the labour and female questions always occurred together historically and were characteristic configurations not only in Europe but also in all Europe's colonies and semi-colonies. The epochal, epistemic moment facing Chinese women was the stage of national revolution which meant, according to Xiang and Deng Yingchao, that the Chinese movement resembled movements in India or Soviet Russia. Core notions such as universal human rights, women's rights and critiques of inequality were all positive, desirable contributions to China's political history because they are the central objects in all women's movements, whether in metropole, colony or semi-colony. In their self-positioning these pioneering theorists encountered a problem not so different from ours: how to understand access to the oppressed and how to analyze the desire of subalternized women in or for political liberation. As Ho Xiangning noted, in Chinese conditions of semi-colonial-semi-feudalism (unequal treaties and economic imperialism on one side, Chinese custom and bound feet on the other), women are naturally systematically underdeveloped: it is unreasonable to blame them for misconstruing their own interests. The question was how politics could make the constraints visible to them and offer a way out.

The predication of woman as revolutionary agent was and has continued to be accompanied by great analytic anxiety. The problem that Chen Shousun encapsulated in his remark that women appear to have become a second class of humanity shows how much revolutionary communist writing encodes the presumption that oppression diminished the oppressed woman. Ding Ling's presumptuous and anxious 1928 story 'Ah Mao Guniang' draws a portrait of an oppressed rural girl whose longing to exceed her world is characterized as foolish because it takes shape as the desire to be bourgeois, like a cheap movie star. Yet a decade later, in 'When I was in Xia Village', an urban woman revolutionary listens as a preternaturally intelligent rural woman, raped, delirious with syphilis, tells an ambiguous tale of the ruinous effect of feudal patriarchal social relations on her desire to marry for love. She would rather prostitute as a spy for the future nation that refuses to treat her disease than return to the arms of a loving patriarchal family. The tension of a revolutionary agent suspended between the fantasy of the semi-colonial movie stars and the loving treachery of feudalism keeps the revolutionary female subject off balance. In one regard, then, the work of Ding Ling, a communist writer, exemplifies the double movement which Meng Yue and Lingzhen Wang note as a characteristic of communist women policy: the emergent state transmits its objectives in the offer of subject forms it makes to subaltern women, but in the action of extracting them from domestic oppressions it transforms these women into the agents it requires to politicize privacy.[13] But the point I wish to draw out is rather the degree to which this off-balance agent of revolution was also a liberatory matrix. It enabled collective action not obtainable elsewhere. It also held open invention of the personal in the sense of predication of an individual. The possibilities for subaltern women of this tremulous agent is suggested in Ding Ling's final 1984 short story in which an orphan girl, sold into marriage and thus classified as a dependent, spending her life as a despised, illiterate rural cadre, takes hold of the revolutionary agency of communist propaganda to enact her own (albeit circumscribed) self-predication.[14]

Now Ding Ling, like so many of her cohort, was to settle eventually for a nationalist and post-feminine communist feminism. Analytic sexualization of social relations, as Xiao Chunnü argued in the late 1920s, was deleterious because the promotion of binaried sex made it appear 'as though women were some other kind of animal' than men. And in the years between the late 1920s and the mid-1980s what emerged in theoretical pronouncements and mobilization tactics was, Lin Chun says, 'extensive and often also voluntary female participation in public activities – productive, social, and political – under [a] communism' that was 'intrinsically feminist in the explicit sense that it fought simultaneously against interdependent powers (as recapitulated by Mao): semi-colonial state, superstition, clan authority, and the husband-turned-master'[15] but rejected the primacy in emancipation theory of reproductive (and therefore 'personal') agency. The question of whether the disenfranchised actually ever desired this political mobilization, this national liberation, inaugurated the current debate of feminists in China over access and desire.

Eroticized consumers

An exemplary case for contemporary mainstream feminism is Li Xiaojiang. The complex Li seems to have worn out her welcome at the government Women's Federation, but she retains lines of communication to the Ford Foundation and other donors. Also, Li has been eclipsed academically and politically; the women's movement in China is big and contentious, and Li is now one of a crowd.

However, in the late 1980s she became prominent for staking out positions that have hardened into foundation stones. The female Chinese revolutionary agent who had sacrificed feminine difference needed to find a means of mobilizing that discredited element of personhood, and Li felt that the procreative drive embodied feminine difference. She sought to link her rediscovery of the universal foundation of human difference (the sex gap in nature and in history) to a historical teleology, familiar in Mao, Bebel, Marx and Engels. Her polemic, *Sex Gap*, argued that male history progressed through stages of productive labour, because masculinity-humanity-history coincide and overlap. But that was only because male history rests on the necessarily compliant, unpredicated female body which provides a material base. History for women lies in the infinite particularization within the regimes of social gender (*shehui xingbie*) where history/men necessarily impose immobilizing and particularizing reproductive work through patriarchal kinship relations. Woman as a subject does not yet exist for herself in theoretical terms, since the social conditions for that emergence are not yet in place.[16]

Li Xiaojiang's question was when and how that subject form would emerge. Li has attempted various resolutions over the years. Two stand out. First, she has made an argument that the category 'Women' is legible in global mythology; thus, to establish a women's legible counter-history requires the collation/ dissemination of world myths about eternal femininity in pre-patriarchal times. Second, she has written popular self-help guides directed at ordinary urban women encouraging them to establish their femininity. To that end she questions the Engelsian dogma that the measure of liberation is workplace, productive labour. When women make the collective decision that their historical and thus personal objectives are undercut in dead-end, barely compensated labour, their most progressive option is housekeeping. Li Xiaojiang wrote popular essays on domestic science which gave detailed instruction on discriminating consumption practices, petty investment strategies, enhancing domestic life and sexual science.[17]

However, not only is Li's style of representation indebted to the Maoist education she received, but her target reader is also, particularly in her domestic science publications, the plebian, female reader. Her mobilization style is heavily indebted to the past, as well. Li included in her publication project *Funü yanjiu congshu* a dozen or so major works in the New Feminism, including a 1988 volume by the plebian historian Du Fangqin. This meditation on aporia in women's history is titled *The Great Transformation.*[18] Du's book aims to substantiate historically some of the theoretical points that most Chinese feminists of the 1980s appeared to hold in common. The history of the concept of women from matriarchal through feudal eras excoriates superstructural, ethical discourses, Confucianism particularly, because by 'replacing human nature (*renxing*) with human relations (*renlun*)' it situated women as lesser than men and consequently made them socially despicable.[19] The point, however, in her volume *Collected Poems of He Xuangqing* and in the oral history project funded by the Ford Foundation that involved Du Fangqin and Li Xiaojiang among other Chinese feminists, was the ordinary woman. Du's primary interest is the subaltern rural woman of genius, who, despite being born in a nameless village, goes on to rise out of obscurity and inscribe her name in history.[20]

The theoretical work of Li Xiaojiang, Du Fangqin and many others has unfolded in a great macrologic transformation. PRC economic state planners must negotiate the shoals of episodic and catastrophic meltdowns of neoliberal 'development', which in the light of the so-called Asian finance crisis of 1997 threaten the entire globalized, neoliberal or neocolonial financial edifice. Now, as domestic neoliberalism in China has won the day for the PRC's entry into the World Trade Organization, hot money may overwhelm what in the late 1990s served as a bulwark against further hot money panic.[21] Will PRC authorities be able to announce, as they did in 1998, their willingness to expend vast amounts of domestic capital reserves in improvement schemes, or strengthen legal bars to capital flight, maintain internal consumption levels, and slow integration into the disintegrating world economy?[22] And, yes, consumers are absolutely necessary in the economic transformation: Li has an important point when she advocates that women specialize in consumption. Yet we truly have to ask – along with Li's critics in the PRC and its diasporic community – whether or not a collusive, effeminate, female consumer really is an acceptable agent of liberation.[23]

'Development' and historical specificity

One of the burdens of this essay has been to suggest why it is impossible to clarify the mediated desire of oppressed women directly through the prism of development stories. Subjects of development will be seen to desire only development unless, as Gupta argues, one is willing to see how such a macrology is mediated through bodies whose resistance and contestations shape the direction of macrological process. In India decades of development have made legible the mediation and its direction. In the PRC decades of revolution have done an analogous job. I have argued in this essay that although there are other ways to gauge the subject 'Chinese women' (demographically, propagandistically, as a labour market, as niche consumers, and so on) one way is through theoretical practice. So rather than focus on the metaleptic extension of distinctive terms – worker, peasant, etc. – I have engaged the desire of those who articulate the categories that they and we make ideologically accessible in a subaltern revolution. These articulate theorists can themselves be subject to ongoing, deconstructive criticism. It is the condition, after all, of our thinking through one another. But my point is that in the context of the present preoccupation of development with the extension of its domain into the political economy of the PRC, it is prudent to map out the 'Chinese' position that 'despite its ambiguous implication in Western discourse', has sought to 'emerge and establish itself as the self-conscious centre of a critical practice'.[24] This is not to say that I wish to adopt native categories (if such are even conceivable in something as spectral as feminism), salute the Chinese flag, or any such nonsense. It is prudent because, for better and for worse, a long record exists already and because any negotiation with the forces of development will unfold through that deep archive.

But there are heroes in my story. There is desire that must not only be recognized, but will prove useful in other places. The heroes are critics and feminists. Despite a history of failure, complicity, collusion and myopia (and in this they are not different from national feminists in the US), they keep open space for the still unpredicated female subject. Film and film criticism provide one such arena. Xie Fei's formula film, 'Women of the Lake of Scented Souls' (*Xiang hun nü*) relies on communist feminism's commitment to women's emancipation through development or productive labour while calling that very thesis into question. There narrative brilliantly knits up the tremendous complications facing women who cannot put into speech, as they have no common language, a desire to be done with male dominance. Huang Shuqin's 'Woman, Demon, Human' (*Ren, gui, qing*), which feminist critic Dai Jinhua praised for being the only contemporary feminist film in China, is another. The plot again focuses attention on the economically productive, emancipated, self-aware woman subject whose unspeakable longing for a means to be woman outside the damaging codes of masculine gender performativity takes the foreground. These and other films and cultural spaces kept open through seemingly endless bruising struggles feed desires for things beyond our present damaging conditions of gendered power.

The desire that all of the women, caught up in economic development, express wordlessly in these films is actually a desire for emancipation from the pall of male dominance. My ultimate point is that the desire for an end to the conditions of injustice that blight their lives is mediated through the often failed but still extraordinarily potent vision of social revolution in which gender is a vector of power and injustice. The revolution – socialist development – did not wholly succeed, but it also did not wholly fail. One alternative, commercial capitalist development, seems now to be threatening us all.[25] However, what is so moving is quite simply that my desire for liberation – encoded through the historical sedimentation of my national history, the experiences of international and transnational commitments, and personal history – is reflected in the equally difficult subjects represented in these Chinese films. There is always the possibility of contestation and moreover, as I have tried to show, there is always the history of the effort to contest the mandated or legalized asymmetries of power.

Notes

1 This title is taken from Myung Mi Kim, 'Anna O Addendum', published in *The Bounty* (Kim 1996). The verse is: 'When fury/To full sum/Summon deluge/Come now and hear/Picture more at variance.' My gratitude to Donald M. Lowe, who patiently read the drafts. This essay owes more to him than anyone.

2 Peter Goldmark's remarks on resigning as president of the Rockefeller Foundation after a decade of service put 'the question of China' among five weaknesses in Foundation policy. He exemplifies enlightened thinking on the China question now that development policy is seeking a new 'fit' with the People's Republic of China (PRC). A report in the *Women's Review of Books* suggests that 'international feminism' already means 'China' in mainstream women studies programmes. This is due partly to the UN's Beijing meetings, but is as much a consequence of a ten-year Ford Foundation initiative to finance the NGO women studies movement in the PRC, replete with centres, scholarly publications, international seminars in feminist theory, a rural oral history project, and so on. See Deborah Rosenfelt (1998: 28–9). The Canadian International Developmental Agency is supporting a special university linkage project with women studies educators in Xian. I wish to thank Professor Ping-Chun Hsiung of the Department of Sociology, University of Toronto at Scarborough for sending me her report (Ping-Chun Hsiung 1998) and for keeping me informed about her project.

The Luce Foundation has funded a multi-year project, 'A Cultural History of Women and Work in 20th Century China,' that includes a theory school for Chinese scholars and a book project mapping the recent Chinese women's movement.

In the Spring of 1998 I served on the selection committee for a major history conference suddenly in need of China experts. Against my repeated arguments, the committee saw no problem in accepting five panels on prostitution in Eastern Asia to the exclusion of virtually all other representations of Chinese women. In the same month I read a major history of prostitution in China and the vitriolic attacks on it by yet another historian, himself the author of a history of prostitution. I was also asked to review a manuscript, submitted to a major press, that purported to be the translated, subaltern speech of a Chinese prostitute. Nick Kristof's *New York Times* front-page article, 'With Asia's Economies Shrinking, Women are Being Squeezed Out' spectacularizes prostituted female labour in East Asia (Kristof 1998). (Below the fold, one finds Fred Stevenson's article 'Fed Chief Calls the Economy One of the Best He Has Seen', but that is 'another story'!) As the PRC is moved into the orbit of development discourse its familiars are already prosaic – the prostituted Chinese woman, her dangerous fertility, her doomed female infant.

3 In 'Can the Subaltern Speak?' the citation is: 'of subject formations that micrologically and often erratically operate the interests that congeal the macrologies' (Spivak 1988: 279).

4 The oppressed are defined by their difference from others and evidence of their presence is difficult to read because context – who it addressed, how it was fashioned, whether the wrong person has gotten hold of it – is hard to establish.

5 This is closer to the position that Arturo Escobar takes in his *Encountering Development: The Making and Unmaking of the Third World* (Escobar 1995).

6 Jing Wang, cited in Nick Kaldis (1999: 421).

7 See Tani E. Barlow, *The Question of Woman in Chinese Feminism* (forthcoming, Duke University Press).

8 Spivak (1997: 483).

9 Some of this text is adapted from 'Foundations of Progressive Chinese Feminism', Chapter 3 of *The Question of Woman in Chinese Feminism* (Barlow, forthcoming (a)).

10 See my forthcoming essay in Japanese, 'The Question of Women in Chinese Feminism of the

Twenties and Thirties' (Barlow, forthcoming (b)).

11 They appear in Mei Sheng, I:1, pp. 94–6, 34–52, and Vol. V:13, pp. 87–93.

12 Lest anyone make any mistake about how difficult this project was for female feminists, a look at the progressive fiction of women, particularly autobiographical fiction, is recommended.

13 Meng Yue (1993); Lingzhen Wang (1999).

14 Kimberley Manning has shown empirically how inextricable and enabling the revolutionary agent has been to female predication and the women's movement in recent years. See her unpublished manuscript (Manning, no date).

15 Lin Chun (1996: 279). One of Lin Chun's extremely interesting insights is that in general Chinese women are 'less liberated and more backward as citizens than as wives and daughters as measured by individual and associational freedom, independence, and consciousness of self-determination. While the so-called private sphere appears to be socialized or publicized as such, what Chinese women lack the most may not be dignity before normative male dominance but rather individual fulfilment and full citizenship in a condescending and repressive system.... [F]eminism, by reclaiming and constructing genuine citizenship through gender politics, may have the potential to lead the way in China's general political reform' (1996: 284).

16 This paragraph is adapted from my essay 'Spheres of Debt and Feminist Ghosts in Area Studies of Women in China' (Barlow 2000).

17 Li Xiaojiang (1989).

18 Du Fangqin (1988). Du Fangqin has written other books and a flood of articles from her centre for Women Studies at Tianjin University. Du is a great collaborator and colleague of Li Xiaojiang. In raising her name here I mean only to point out that what metrotheorists in the PRC now call the new 'uprising of women' involves a great many differently positioned, feminist, female writers.

19 Mei Yue, 'Review of Du Fangqin', in Du Fangqin (1996), appendix.

20 See Du's introduction to her edited volume *He Xuangqing ji* (1993). In my 1997 meeting with Du at Tianjin University she described the Ford project at length.

21 This argument is paraphrased from my draft paper (Barlow 1997b).

22 See *New York Times*, 'China Applies Brakes on Move Toward Market Economy' (30 September 1998).

23 See my 'Woman at the Close of the Maoist Era in the Polemics of Li Xiaojiang and her Associates' (Barlow 1997a) for citations and a very long exposition of Li Xiaojiang's work.

24 Cited in Nick Kaldis (1999: 421–57).

25 Peter Gowan (1999).

8

Developmentalist Feminism and Neocolonialism in Andean Communities

Frédérique Apffel-Marglin and Loyda Sanchez

Bolivia began neoliberal reforms in 1985. As part of these structural changes and also as part of a new emphasis on 'sustainable development' the Bolivian State eventually established the Junior Ministry of Gender, Generations and Family Affairs.[1] This institution is responsible for integrating as well as fostering a gender focus in all development plans, programmes and projects. In this framework gender is a category of analysis for the planning of sustainable development. In the latter, the focus on women – now called gender – is one of the most important. In this, Bolivia is typical of what has been happening in the other Andean countries and indeed in most of the so-called Third World. In this essay we will question the unexamined cultural and epistemological assumptions underlying the focus on gender which a contrast with native views puts in sharp relief. We will also offer our views as to the hidden agenda of the state, and with it of international development organizations, in their firm embrace of a particular version of gender which we are here calling 'developmentalist feminism'.

The coupling of concerns with women and/or gender[2] and development is a phenomenon whose widespread implementation in Southern countries was intensified by the publication of the United Nations' World Commission on Environment and Development known as the Brundtland Report, entitled *Our Common Future*, published in 1987. The Brundtland Report, as is well known, proposes 'sustainable development' as a solution to its own diagnostic of the situation of the environment globally. After several decades of unchecked industrial development the report gives a picture of the environmental effects resulting from reckless growth. Among the most serious environmental effects, one can highlight a dramatic decrease in genetic and cultural diversity, an increase of the ozone hole over Antarctica, the progressive heating of the atmosphere, the steady growth of desertification, the steady loss of forests, population growth and the growth of a disparity between rich and poor both within as well as across nation states.

The Report is concerned with the fact that the rate of development in the North, translating into increased consumption – a goal also pursued by élites in the South – seems to be incompatible with nature's ability to regenerate itself. However, the solution it offers does not fundamentally call into question these trends. For reversing the environmental damage, the report relies essentially on more efficient managing of resources as well as on lowering fertility rates through human resource development. What happened at the UNCED Rio conference in 1992, which took up the concerns of the Brundtland Report, fully confirms that the latter had correctly reflected the mood of governments both North and South. Although envoys from the South did point out that the North's rate of consumption puts a much greater burden on the environment and tried, unsuccessfully, to put this on the agenda, this did not mean advocating a radical rethinking of the whole enterprise of industrialization and development. Southern governments stood for the 'right to development' and President Bush simply asserted that 'the lifestyle of the US would not be up for discussion at Rio' (Sachs 1993: 3). The problem was conceived in terms of managing the environmental crisis globally. However, as Sachs states it so clearly,

> [For] the task of global ecology can be understood in two ways: it is either a technocratic effort to keep development afloat against the drift of plunder and pollution; or it is a cultural effort to shake off the hegemony of aging Western values and gradually retire from the development race. (1993: 11)

In this essay we will focus on one set of aging Western values that are being institutionalized widely in the South, taking the example of Bolivia. These values come wrapped up in a discourse of gender and development, promising women's emancipation viewed as a necessary correlate to sustainable development. This emancipatory discourse means to extend to women the rights of the citizen. We will attempt to make visible the dark side of this discourse and its link to colonial mindsets when it is deployed in native Andean communities.

Developmentalist feminism in Bolivia

The Brundtland Report focuses on the role of women in development mostly in its chapter on population and human resources. The Report points out that by attaining the basic right of self-determination women will then be in a position to control the number of children they will have and thus contribute to re-establishing the right equilibrium between resources and population. Women's ability to have at their disposal the means to exercise a choice is by itself viewed as an index of the level of development in the nation. Emphasis is placed on the development of the human potential which both furthers development as well as the right of all to a full life with dignity. The Report links sustainable development and equity with lowering population growth in the following manner:

> [S]ustainable economic growth and equitable access to resources are two of the more certain routes toward lower fertility rates.
>
> Giving people the means to choose the size of their families is not just a method of keeping population in balance with resources; it is a way of assuring – especially for women – the basic human right of self-determination. (Brundtland Report: 96)

Thus the Brundtland Report makes a tight connection between sustainable development, equitable access to resources, women's right to self-determination and the lowering of fertility rates. In implementing this vision in the *campesino* communities, the Junior Ministry of Gender in Bolivia has emphasized women's right to self-determination and their equity with men in terms of access to resources. It has established agreements with various international cooperation agencies in order to receive support – financial as well as methodological – to carry out its plans.

The platform of the Junior Ministry of Gender is as follows:

- To respect the organizational, political, physical, and economic autonomy of all the forms of organization adopted by women, especially those relating to the equality of opportunity in the implementation of the Law of Popular Participation.
- To strengthen the self-esteem, negotiating capacity, decision-making capacity, and self-determination of women by creating juridico-legal conditions for the exercise of citizenship.
- Respect women's decisions concerning their sexuality and fertility and democratize roles both within the family and the society at large.
- Consolidate women's right to education and to their own cultural identity.
- Strengthen and value the productive role of women by consolidating their right to dispose of property as well as equity in their usufruct of goods and income. (SNDR: 1995)

In order to implement this platform, the Junior Ministry has formulated a strategy to train the personnel of all organizations in charge of development programmes in *campesino* communities. These training programmes focus on the deployment of gender equity. They have also been established in the Junior Ministry of Popular Participation and Municipal Support, in city halls and prefectures throughout the country. In 1994 the Junior Ministry of Gender signed an inter-institutional agreement with the National Secretariat of Agriculture, Cattle Ranching and Fisheries to implement a strategy of education in gender and rural development with the general objective to facilitate and strengthen the participation of women in the processes and benefits of rural development as a dimension of the equity of such development. This agreement focuses on three strategic goals:

- The participation of women in local management and decision making.
- Women's access to and control of productive resources.
- Women's access to services to achieve an improvement in the quality of life of the female population.

The goal of development itself is, of course, taken for granted. What these programmes are meant to ensure is gender equity within development programmes and their consequences.

The world for which women are being prepared is emphatically not that of their *campesino* native communities. They are being prepared to be individuals and citizens, with their own autonomous access to 'resources', decision making, services, education, their bodies, etcetera – in other words, to relate autonomously to the market, to commodities, to productive resources, to reproductive resources (mainly their bodies), and the like. The state uses a developmentalist feminist discourse to create individual female citizens. Such a discursive move is at once creative and destructive; the female individual citizen emerges from the destruction of the *comunera* (female member of a native community) and of her world.

The wisdom of such a path can be questioned on many grounds. One obvious one is the fact that concerns with gender equity in matters of access to economic and other resources in *campesino* rural communities must be placed in the larger context of the Bolivian economy. An education no longer assures one of a job, unemployment rates being extremely high. One cannot but wonder what the state's agenda is when such emphasis is placed on gender inequity in access to productive resources within *campesino* communities while these communities collectively own only 10 per cent of cultivable land although they form 80 per cent of the agricultural population. *That* glaring inequity is not focused upon with the same enthusiasm. There is, however, one area in which the state's programmes to transform *comuneras* into individual citizens has more direct returns in terms of the state's development goals, and that is women's ability to control their fertility.

The state's campaigns among rural *campesino* communities to foster reduced rates of fertility must also be placed in a wider context. The glaring inequity as to access to agricultural land is the historical legacy of a 500-year history in which the European conquerors, and later their descendants, expropriated the indigenous inhabitants. The Andes region has experienced a severe demographic collapse as a consequence of such a history. It is only in the last half a century that the indigenous population has begun to rise and is now approaching its original size.[3] Given such a history, it would be surprising if *campesinos* perceived efforts to curb the growth of their population with equanimity. They have displayed a very remarkable ability to survive and even thrive under the most difficult of conditions. They are not likely to envisage population control in the way the state does. It must also be borne in mind that the population density of Bolivia is quite low, standing at seven persons per square kilometre.

We need to question the unspoken assumptions of the state's developmentalist feminist discourse that the creation of the autonomous woman who has control over her body and access to economic and political resources represents progress. We need to question the unspoken assumption that the body should become an entity to be possessed and controlled. We need to question the unspoken assumption that gender arrangements in *campesino* communities are *a priori* to the detriment of women. We need to question the unspoken assumption that the transformation of the non-human world into 'resources' is an improvement over campesinos' ways of being in the world.

We will begin with the emergence of the biological body since it is foundational for the emergence of the autonomous self. We will attempt to make visible the reasons for its being an indispensable prop in developmentalist feminist discourse and the state's purposes.

The emergence of the biological body

In Andean peasant communities the basic scientific assumption of the unicity of the body as the object enclosed by the skin, is not found. The following dialogue between an Aymara grandmother and her granddaughter (from a peasant community in the region of the Altiplano), recorded and translated from Aymara into Spanish by Greta Jiménez Sardón (1995: 60)[4] makes this clear:

> – Blood is sacred as well, you have always seen, surely, how you *ch'alla* [to spill a liquid offering] with the blood of the llama, or with the blood of the alpaca, when you raise a house, that also is used to nourish the house....
>
> – So quiet was I, listening hard to hold on to each word, all of my bodies were sweating, everything went puth, puth, puth in my bodies.

This passage goes on to recount, in the granddaughter's words, how her grandmother instructed her about the 'white waters' and the 'red waters' in men and women's bodies and how those waters are also in the rain, the rivers, the springs, etcetera. The granddaughter retells her first union with the man who became the father of her children and her lifelong companion, and how all the beings of the *pacha* (the time/place) were participants in this first sexual encounter, protecting and blessing the couple. After their first union in a carefully selected spot near where she grazed her alpacas, the couple, having made a circle of stones, knelt and spoke with Pachamama, the earth deity, as follows:

> Holy earth Pachamama, receive us then, nurture us then, protect us then, as we are your children we want your protection, we need your care.... Holy earth Pachamama may our waters from inside (us) also nourish your body.... These waters that before birth already ran in our body, these waters which we kept for you, we offer to you.... May our waters be good, to have strong children, good children.... (*Ibid.*: 65)

The red and white waters that run inside as well as outside the body, those waters which existed before birth in 'our' body, conjure up a world where the unitary materiality of the biological body makes no sense at all. Pachamama is the womb in which the seeds of all life reside and generate/regenerate from. So before birth these waters already ran in this couple's 'body', namely Pachamama.

Such utterances by Aymara peasant women are variously interpreted by different modern disciplines – whether belonging to the social sciences such as anthropology or the natural sciences such as biology – as being either a belief, a symbolic or metaphorical statement, or, less generously, a superstition.

However, as historian Barbara Duden (1991) has shown, the 'real', 'biological' body is in fact a unique historical creation of the past 300 years or so in the West. The modern, biological, universal body is a creation of a certain time and place, specifically Western Europe beginning in the seventeenth century. This biological body was created as a new kind of object, the discrete, isolated, objectified and material body, one of the many consequences of the seventeenth-century Cartesian separation between *res extensa* and *res cogitans.* It is also a consequence of the separation between the realms of nature and the realm of the semiotic, which includes the realm of the sacred, established in mid-seventeenth-century Europe with the scientific revolution.

Women's bodies were experienced quite differently in pre-modern Europe. Particularly in popular peasant experience, women's bodies were the vessels of life and death. Old women could divert a thunderstorm by baring their buttocks and virgins could influence the weather by opening their bleeding vulvas to heaven. Women's periodicity and fertility were the wellsprings of many village rituals of life and death. The body was not a discrete entity, enclosed by the skin and separate from the outside, the larger cosmos, both human and non-human. It was open and fluid (Duden, 1991: 8–10; Ginzburg 1985).

By the seventeenth century, the work of the Inquisition had essentially succeeded in severing the connections between the body and the cosmos. During the centuries of witch hunting and the burning of hundreds of thousands of women (perhaps millions, see Merchant 1980), the body as an embodiment of local community vitality was destroyed. Although the Inquisition and the witch hunt was exported to South America with the Conquistadores (Silverblatt 1987: 159), it was unable to eradicate native practices there. In Europe, however, on the ashes of the witches' and other heretics' scaffolds, the new centralized state gained power. The enclosing of the body by the skin, which made it a discrete object, enabled a relationship of property between the discrete body and the self. This new self, anchored in a discrete and separate body, became the individual economic and political actor as well as the civic individual, the citizen. In the late eighteenth century the French philosopher Volney considered the body to be the most elementary form of property (Duden 1991: 13). This was the culmination of a process during the eighteenth century which created the bourgeois body – that is, the human being as an economic factor in its physicality, with its closed, clean and restrained body (Elias 1978). However, peasants and women of all classes did not fully participate in this new biological body and the new individual self. The act of transforming all bodies into biological bodies and all people into individuals, progressively albeit unevenly, deployed itself in the West throughout the nineteenth and twentieth centuries. This same movement continues today beyond the West, not only in the Andes, but indeed globally.

What is particularly interesting in Duden's work is her discovery that the notion of 'health' was foreign to her eighteenth-century German doctor's women patients. This was a difficult realization to come by for Duden, since the idea that all people strive for good health has become self-evident for academics today. This led her to investigate the historicity of this category. The German author Krunitz's *Economic Encyclopedia* (1788; cited in Duden 1991: 18) speaks thus of health:

> Whoever neglects the precious treasure of health offends all of society, of which he is a member. Society rightly demands of him that he sacrifice a part of his energies and time to her needs and for her benefit, who every day contributes so much to his needs and benefit.

Such exhortation was needed, since the lower classes resisted the medical concept of the body. A quite precise parallel can be made with the native *campesino* communities in the Andes. Such behaviour reveals a resistance to the interests of the new political and economic authorities in the objectification of the body and the individualization of persons for the purpose of increased productivity and the increased power of the centralized state. Medically defined health did not correspond to how people experienced their lives and what they felt they could put up with in early modern Europe as well as in contemporary Andean *campesino* communities. The biologization of the body and the medicalization of health created norms and therefore deviance from those norms, or pathologies. As Duden articulates it: 'By attributing this desire [for a healthy body] to humankind and grounding it in human nature, the human right to the "pursuit of happiness" (as laid down in the Constitution of the US) took on concrete form as a right to health, and a new dependence on unrealizable professional promises was born' (Duden 1991: 19).

The biologization of the body and the medicalization of health hides the political and economic agenda embedded in these practices. Biology and medicine were practices of science by the seventeenth century, during which Robert Boyle – the inventor of experimental science – and Thomas Hobbes may be said to have invented the two halves of our modern world (Schapin and Schaffer 1988; Latour 1993: 27) – in which the representation of things in the laboratory and the representation of citizens through the social contract are separated from each other. The effectiveness of this arrangement depends on rendering invisible the dependence of the state on science and the dependence of science on a strict separation between the realms of politics (society), of religion (God), and of nature (science). These separations are of course arbitrary and, at the time of their creation, the subject of vigorous debate. After about a century, they took root and are now assumed to be self-evident in the North and by élites in the South. With these separations nature became totally separated from the semiotic realm. Nature was transformed into an inert mechanical object, endlessly open to man's exploration, manipulation and exploitation – while society, Hobbes's Leviathan, was seen as depending solely on the calculation of human atoms totally separate from the larger cosmos. These deeds of the founding fathers of modernity instantly created a superstitious and obscurantist pre-modernity in Europe and in the rest of the contemporary non-Western world. Being modern means being enlightened, advanced, scientific, developed. The pre-scientific wrongheaded notions of the non-Western world, in which semiotics is not clearly separated from material causality, are then perceived as being in need of the modern world's enlightenment and help.

The concept of the modern body as 'real' and 'biological' arose in the context of the political establishment of the bourgeoisie, the creation of the centralized state and the deployment of capitalism.[5] René Descartes' dualism divided the mind from the external world and the body. Thus the body became a mechanical object of scrutiny to be dissected, internally explored and defined.

This biological concept of the body was deployed through education and public propaganda as well as through the professionalization of medicine.

The term 'biology' when applied to the human body assumes a given or natural boundary between the human and the non-human world. This boundary corresponds to the boundary between the biological and the cultural. Thus the Aymara vision of a woman and a man's white and red waters flowing in their bodies before their birth completely muddles the human/non-human boundary the term 'biology' (when referring to the human body) implies.[6] Thus the speech of the Aymara woman quoted above evokes a continuity and boundlessness between bodily fluids moving from the earth to human bodies and back to the earth when she speaks of offering these 'waters' of intercourse to the earth. In fact, the body as well as its waters are spoken of as continuous and flowing out of and into the earth's body and back again in a human body. The Aymara woman's words also confound the biological/cultural divide in making Pachamama a mother, their mother as well as their child's mother. Pachamama has agency in a way similar to that of the couple.

What is at stake here is the divide between the human and the non-human and its implication for agency. Karen Barad – a theoretical physicist doing feminist science studies – uses Monica Casper's work to make the following point:

> In a special issue of the journal A*merican Behavioral Scientist*, devoted to the 'Humans and Others: the Concept of "Agency" and Its Attribution', Monica Casper offers a politically astute critique of the debates on non-human agency within science studies. She argues, for example, that they have failed to consider how the very notion of non-human agency is premised on a 'dichotomous ontological positioning in which [non-human] is opposed to human' (840). She points out that these approaches to non-human agency exclude a crucial factor from analysis since 'the *attribution* of human and non-human to heterogeneous entities' is always already the consequence of particular political practices. (1998: 113)

Our brief notes on the historical emergence of the biological body in Western Europe try to make evident some of the political practices that went into the making of the biological body.

As Sarah Franklin has pointed out in her work on assisted reproduction, the modern biological model of the 'facts of life' can no longer be taken as a universalist absolute. It 'expresses a particular view of the power to know.... It is no longer possible to assume this particular view of the power to know unproblematically...' (1997: 211). The term 'biology' refers both to the phenomenon of life and to the study of it, thus betraying an implied perfect transparency between the two. Such transparency can no longer be innocently held.

More generally, the transparency between reality and the scientific study of the phenomenon of life (what is called 'biology') can no longer be innocently held. The famous delayed choice and Einstein–Podolsky-Rosen (EPR) quantum experiments in physics force us to reconsider such transparency between things-in-themselves and their scientific explanations and representations. In the context of her study of the philosophical/physical writings of the Danish physicist Niels Bohr, Barad affirms that reality is things-in-phenomena rather than things-in-themselves. According to Barad, phenomena 'constitute a non-dualistic whole so that it literally makes no sense to talk about independently existing things as somehow behind or as the causes of phenomena ... what is being described is our participation *within* nature, what I term "agential reality"' (1996: 176).[7]

Moving from things-in-themselves to phenomena makes it impossible to separate the cultural from the natural, the semiotic from the material. Donna Haraway (1991) uses the expression 'material-semiotic actors' to capture the same thing. The difference between the world of the Aymara woman quoted above and the industrialized world seems suddenly to begin to evaporate – so much so that anthropologist and philosopher Bruno Latour's science studies lead him to proclaim that 'we have never been modern' (1993).[8]

The unicity of the biological body is taken by developmentalist feminism as a universal given, thus holding constant the correlation between an unchangeable biological body and a variable socio/cultural 'gender' (the sex/gender differentiation). Although 'gender' is recognized as variable across time and place, what is not variable is gender's anchoring in a universally given biological body, and with it the notion that gender is something that characterizes *individual* human men and women. This entire construction presents insuperable difficulties in the post-quantum, post-modern West, as we have seen. When deployed by developmentalist feminism in an Andean context it becomes a (neo)colonialist move.

In the Andean world a person can be under certain circumstances a plant, a seed, an animal, a mountain, water, etcetera. The notion of the person is radically non-essentialist. Within the person nest numberless other forms of life, it being understood that everything in the *pacha* is alive, not just humans, animals and plants. (Rengifo 1998: Chapter 3) These other forms of life – let's say a seed, a constellation, an animal – can manifest themselves under the proper ritual circumstances. One such is the festival of the Ispallas celebrated by Aymara communities on the shores of Lake Titicaca in the Andean altiplano. During this ritual women become seeds (of root crops, cf. Chuyma 1998: 17). Such fluidity extends to one's gender. Under certain circumstances a woman can be a man and vice versa.

Another important Andean notion – that of *uj* or *juk* in Quechua and *maya* in Aymara – further helps to dissolve the modern unicity of the biological body as well as its exclusive relationship to one gender. *Uj* (or *juk* or *maya*) literally means 'one' or a 'unit'; however it is a unit made up of two, of a pair, and in the Andean world everything goes by such dual units (Gomel Apaza 1998: 9). The words of one Aymara peasant capture this dual unicity:

> In life all goes in two, male and female, there is no one alone; you well know that it is thus with plants ... not to speak of animals and humans. It is just the same with the mountains, they all have their pair (or opposite); there are male *Qullus* (protector mountains) and female *Qullus*; with the rivers, lakes and ocean, they are male and female; the *warawara* (constellations), the wind, the clouds also live like that. The departed also have to be accompanied by their pair; you do know that when they are alone, so that they do not suffer from (the lack of their) pair, one has to find one for them. (Jiménez Sardón 1995: 129)

While both partners in a couple are alive, the unit is made up of both male and female. However, upon becoming single through death of one of the partners, or through separation, that one remaining 'gender' becomes the dual male/female unit. It is thus clear that the developmentalist notion of gender does not correspond to Andean reality. This is further compounded by the fact that neither the Aymara nor Quechua language have grammatical gender.

The term 'gender' (*género* in Spanish) has forced itself on many Andean peasant communities since the establishment in Bolivia of the Junior Ministry of Gender (and in Peru of a corresponding Ministry of Women's Affairs) in the last decade or so. In these countries developmentalist feminism has become officially institutionalized feminism. The official notion of gender cannot be mapped onto Andeans' notions of what is male and female. Even though the official notion of gender is meant to emphasize the sociocultural variability of the content of gender, what creates the difficulty is its invariable anchoring in a universal unitary biological body, re-establishing thereby the whole of Western modernist dualist ontology. This became evident in the several workshops that the authors organized (with others) to discuss these issues with members of the Junior Ministry of Gender in Bolivia (between 1995 and 1997). We were not able to open the official notion of gender. The official notion of gender, institutionalized into laws by the government of Bolivia, remains anthropocentric as well as Eurocentric.

Developmentalist feminism and individualism

The Junior Ministry of Gender has commissioned many institutions to carry out basic research on the theme of gender to guide its programmes. In this chapter we will take a look at one such study carried out in a community where one of us has been doing work for several years. The study commissioned by the Junior Ministry of Gender was carried out in 1993 by researchers in the Programme of Training and Research in Andean Irrigation, a part of the Universidad Mayor de San Simon in Cochabamba, Bolivia. When the results of this investigation on gender and irrigation reached the community members, they did not recognize themselves in it and requested an explanation. This incident led the National Programme for Irrigation (PRONAR), which had been working in that same region, to commission its own research. Loyda Sanchez has been the person charged with explaining the first study to the *comuneros/as*. Along with Marina Arratia, Loyda Sanchez was commissioned by PRONAR to do the second study (see Sanchez and Arratia 1996).

The first study, which we will call the 'official gender study', takes as a basic unit of the community the nuclear family. Within this nuclear family, it has endeavoured to establish the roles of men and women through a documentation of their activities, the time spent by each gender in these activities; the differential access to and control of resources by men and women; and their differential participation in decision making.

The assumptions underlying this methodology are several. One we have already noted is the boundary drawn between the human and the non-human world. Another is the assumption that the non-human has no agency and exists for the use of humans. This is particularly vividly conveyed by the expression 'access to and control over resources'. Such an expression also indicates a utilitarian, anthropocentric relationship between humans and the non-human world. Another assumption is that of linear measurable time, reflected in the use of a chronometer to measure the time spent in each activity by men and women. Yet another assumption is the applicability of the separation between a public and a domestic domain in these peasant communities. Finally, we find the assumption that the relevant unit of analysis is the nuclear human family. Underlying all these is the assumption of 'individualism', namely, that agents are individual human beings and action is taken on the basis of their decision-making powers.

What Sanchez and Arratia found in their own research in this community is that agency, in all affairs involving irrigation, could only be located in the relationship between several entities: a source of water, a human community, a community of deities, a network of irrigation channels and the fields to be irrigated, that is the *chacras*. In other words, agency is held not only by humans but also by the several other entities involved. And, very importantly, they found that agency could only be located in the orchestrated activity of all of these entities together. They have reached this conclusion not only on the basis of what peasants say, but on the basis of what they themselves observed (Sanchez and Arratia 1996).

However, it is not easy to render verbally this reality so profoundly at odds with what we moderns are used to calling reality. The problem in formulating it in this way is that these five entities are not always or even necessarily discrete ones. Rather, they often flow and leak into each other. Furthermore, in all irrigation activities, the leadership that shapes activities, teaches how things are done, and organizes the human community, is the water. The relationship of the human community with the water is according to the form in which the water presents itself. The conversation that takes place with the water is different according to the type and source of the water. These intra-actions (the term is Barad's) are what gives rise to what Sanchez and Arratia call the 'community of waters', referring to the intra-actions between all the participants listed above.

To give the flavour of these ritual conversations or intra-actions, let us listen to the voice of the peasants themselves. The following quote is taken from a publication by one of our colleagues in the Altiplano, Jorge Apaza. Apaza here quotes a *campesino* who uses the term 'community of waters'. The *campesino* here is referring to the building of irrigation channels:

> To build a *jich'a* (the path where the water will travel), we do not use a tape measure or a level. To build a channel the first thing we do is to make offerings (*t'inkha* and *ch'illt'a)* to Pachamama and then to the *Awichas* (the sources of water, the springs). After that we commence the work; the water all by itself leads us, we only follow it, that's all. (Apaza 1998: 28)

The next quote refers to the 'leaking' between these entities, referred to above. In this case it is between the human community and the water:

> To go and bring the water, the *paqo* (Andean healer-priest) designates the persons that have been accepted by the *Achachilas* (grandparent mountains). They go two by two, in pairs, and they carry clay jars for the water. We well know how to bring *tollqa* (the son-in-law) from this particular spring, in order to marry him with a young virgin girl of our community. The water is a person, and he marries a girl here. When the *tollqa* (the water son-in-law) arrives to participate in the ceremony, we do it exactly like a wedding between a human couple. The *comuneros* must not know who the daughter-in-law or the bride of the water is going to be. If they knew, she could die. That is why all the participants in the ceremony, we address each other as *aukch'is* and *taych'is*. We are all mothers-in-law and fathers-in-law to each other because the water is marrying the community. That is how we address each other. (*Ibid.*: 29–30)

It is clear that the boundary between the human and non-human world is drawn very differently, that the notion of agency is completely different and that it would be doing a fair amount of violence to the *comuneros*' world to speak of a unilateral instrumental relationship between individual human beings, males or females, and non-human 'resources'.

The authors, along with Marina Arriata, have held workshops, conferences and meetings trying to make the government aware of the difficulties of using its methodology and theoretical framework in the context of Andean peasant communities. We have pointed out that the categories used in the interview protocols are based on notions inapplicable in peasant communities, notions that violently affront such communities. Such notions as the division between a productive and reproductive domain, the notion of the sexual division of work, the notion of access to resources, the notion of decision making, of the empowerment and autonomy of women, the notion of linear measurable time among others, we find to be non-viable in *campesino* communities. We have endeavoured to make visible the anthropocentric and Eurocentric character of these notions, as well as their individualistic assumptions.

Sanchez and Arratia in their study make it clear that one of the central assumptions underlying the official gender research is that women are oppressed by being treated as walking wombs marginalized in a feminized reproductive domain. Access to power and autonomy is valorized and sought through participation in the public domain of production and economic as well as political decision making. Developmentalist feminism in Bolivia rejects the modern construction of women as 'two-legged wombs', defined solely by their reproductive capacity, but it does not reject the other assumptions we have mentioned in this chapter. What the official gender critique focuses upon is the construction of women as mindless wombs, destined by their biology to the sole role of motherhood in the now isolated nuclear family.

The division between a public domain of production and a private domain of reproduction cannot be found in Andean peasant communities, or at least those that are only marginally integrated in a national or international market economy (Apffel-Marglin 1996; Tilly and Scott 1987). In the Andean peasant communities all the members that make up the *pacha* – both human and others – collectively act to generate and regenerate the *pacha*, the place/time, with both its human and more-than-human participants. Through ritual action they take collective moral responsibility for the outcome of their actions. In such a context all activities can be said to be at once 'productive and reproductive', whether carried out by men, women or the other beings of the *pacha*. Human regeneration does not happen without the concurrence of the more-than-human participants and the reverse also holds true. The notions of individuality, rationality or autonomy are profoundly alien to that world.

Developmentalist feminism asserts women's rationality and individuality, qualities denied them by professionalized bio-medicine and the new bourgeois order, institutionalized with the eighteenth-century revolutions in Europe and the US. As historian Elizabeth Fox-Genovese states, 'Feminism as an ideology developed in interaction with the development of individualism and cannot be understood apart from it' (1991: 138).

The eighteenth-century bourgeois revolutions in the US and in France marked the consolidation of capitalism and the triumph of bourgeois individualism. The sovereign individual was the atom that made up the political and economic public order. This supposedly universal 'man', representative of all 'mankind', was in fact – if not in rhetoric – a propertied white male. This fact was pointed out somewhat later by non-white males as well as by women. The United States declaration of independence uses the universal 'man': 'We hold these truths to be self-evident, that all men are created equal, that they are endowed by their Creator with certain inalienable rights, that among these are life, liberty and the pursuit of happiness.' This is the public man and accountable voting citizen. Non-propertied white males, as well as most non-white males and all women, were excluded from this category, could not vote and thus had no public role. Women were cast as men's appendages, restricted to the domestic sphere and the role of the mothers of individuals.

The bourgeois sovereign individual is constructed in universalistic terms and this creates the contradiction that has fuelled most modern emancipatory movements, including the feminist movement. Since the enlightenment the individual has been imagined as the basic atom of the economy, of the polity and of civil society, preceding all collectivities. The modern liberal state and the modern market economy are both based on this individual. The sovereign individual is stripped of all relationships, all particularity of time and place, and all specificity. It is also, of course, radically separated from the more-than-human world. The modern bourgeois individual is an abstraction.

The bourgeois democratic revolutions of the eighteenth century created 'man' as free of bonds to community and to place and as prior to such bonds. It is precisely because this new individual is an abstraction that the rhetoric of the new bourgeois state did not, and indeed could not, give it specificity as a propertied white male. Abstraction, along with the construction of a radical separation between the realm of the semiotic and that of materiality, enables the construction of a universal discourse. Such a universal discourse was a keystone of the new bourgeois order and the new modern science, since it made certainty and, with it, social order possible at a time when Europe was engulfed in an interminable and irresolvable armed conflict between two equally dogmatic Christian religious factions (Toulmin 1990). In the case of the more-than-human world, science has redefined it on its own terms, excluding from it all evidence for a non-material reality, all non-repeatable and non-measurable phenomena, as well as all evidence for the impossibility of separating the observing subject from the observed object.[9] Only by redefining reality in such a manner could modern bourgeois man secure universality and hence certainty and social order. The effect of such a discursive move is that by presenting what in fact is the white propertied male as the abstract universal 'man', that is 'everyman' – and by that is meant every human being – a standard or norm is created. 'Universal man' as an abstraction does not really exist; what really exists under its guise is the white propertied male who becomes the norm, the standard, making all persons who do not fit the mould into an 'Other'. White Western feminists in particular have made the 'Othering' of woman (de Beauvoir 1961) visible. But, as much feminist writing since then has pointed out, this universal 'woman' turned out to be, in Audre Lord's unforgettable words, 'white, christian, middle-class, thin, heterosexual and financially secure' (Lorde 1984). This universal 'woman' nested within herself the othering of different kinds of women. Needless to say, this othering pertains to all those who do not fit the mould, not just women.

Similarly, the creation of the autonomous sovereign individual simultaneously casts those who do not fit its mould into the devalued 'Other'. This 'Otherness' has often been cast in biological terms. For a long time, women's biology was seen to make them incapable of being rational and autonomous (Martin 1987; Hubbard 1990, Ehrenreich and English 1979; Moreau 1982; Jordanova 1989; Scheibinger 1989).[10] Non-European races' imputed inferiority has been seen as grounded in their biological or more recently in their genetic make-up. In such a perspective, the universality of biology guarantees the universality of the autonomous individual.[11]

The autonomous individual's thoughts and actions are unilateral; he is an independent agent with the power to act. This subject is constituted on the premise of its independence, the denial of its inter-existence with others, both human and more-than-human. This subject can maintain the illusion of autonomy and self-originating thought and action solely by concealing and denying that reality emerges from intra-actions. Self-originating action means unilateral action. The discrete, separate individual bounded by his skin perceives and defines all difference as Otherness. This 'Other' becomes the objectified Other upon whom this modern subject acts. The Other's object status is grounded in objective biology. The subject/object or knower/known dichotomy of science becomes a self/Other dichotomy in society.

Bourgeois political individualism established the rights of citizens as a parcel of sovereignty. Thus this subject is constituted by power, and the idea of the individual is conflated with the concept of a self. The construct of the self as essentially containing power constitutes the ideal of autonomy (Fox-Genovese 1991: 116; Addelson 1994: 108). The ability of this individual to establish a set of norms that are considered ultimate or beyond question is a way of disguising as well as extending its own power through recourse to universality

(Butler 1992: 7). The universal individual's sense of self renders other ways of being in the world invisible or illegitimate, thus establishing itself as a universal norm. This universal concept of the individual is violent by nature, as evidenced in the ravages of colonialism, imperialism, sexism and the violence unleashed on the more-than-human world. Although developmentalist feminism has rejected the status of 'Other' for women, it seems to have done so by grafting women onto the autonomous individual while denying that individual an exclusively masculine essence. Such developmentalist feminism, implemented by state institutions in the Andes, is neocolonialist.

In the US it is precisely the universality of the language of individualism that enabled white women (as well as black people) to conceive of themselves as individuals, similar and equal to white propertied men. Liberal feminist criticism has focused from the beginning on the masculinity of this universal subject. Early nineteenth-century liberal feminists like Mary Wollstonecraft and John Stuart Mill pursued what seemed to be the obvious answer to the masculine subject: they appropriated it in order to open up the category to include women. They believed, as did socialist feminists, that the 'belief in a rational, agentic subject is crucial to the argument for women's equality' (Hekman 1995: 195). They posited a universal 'woman' to match the universal 'man', focusing intently on the de-masculinization of the modern individual. Given the political and legal structures of the US, this may have been necessary for the purpose of access to public life. The difficulty arises from extending such a politico-legal notion of the person to all other areas of life. This has been the path followed by most emancipatory struggles in the USA, be it the women's suffrage movement of the late nineteenth century or the civil rights movements in the early 1960s (which focused on the 'de-whiting' – as it were – of the universal individual), or the liberal women's movement of the same period.

The French philosopher Simone de Beauvoir is at the centre of this approach. Her widely read and highly influential book *The Second Sex* discusses the ways the subject of modernity is defined in masculine terms, and how it thereby makes woman into the 'Other'. She argues that this subject is incidentally rather than inherently masculine, and that purged of its masculine elements it would truly become universal and include women. While de Beauvoir is generally highly aware of racism, classism, and imperialism, her analytical strategy of attempting to isolate sexism led her to focus on white, middle-class Christian women. She argued that this group of women – being free of class, race, religious or imperialist oppression – would allow her to focus on the nature of oppression solely based on sex. While de Beauvoir acknowledges the differences between women, she dismisses these as 'irrelevant to understanding the condition of "woman", insofar as she takes the story of "woman" to be that provided by the examination of the lives of women not subject to racism, classism, imperialism, and so forth' (Spelman 1988: 71). De Beauvoir essentially took what was the modern masculine individual subject and grafted woman onto it. The following quote from *The Second Sex* reveals de Beauvoir's motivation in her choice of analytical strategy:

> On the biological level a species is maintained only by creating itself anew; but this creation results only in repeating the same Life in more individuals. But man assures the repetition of Life while transcending Life through Existence [i.e. goal-oriented, meaningful action]; by this transcendence he creates values that deprive pure repetition of all value. In the animal, the freedom and variety of male activities are vain because no project is involved. Except for his services to the species, what he does is immaterial. Whereas in serving the species, the human male also remodels the face of the earth, he creates new instruments, he invents, he shapes the future. (1961: 59)

De Beauvoir wants women to be like white bourgeois men, to exercise their power to remodel the face of the earth and shape the future. In her separation of a biological level from a mental/cultural level, all value goes to the latter and the former is demoted to mere mindless repetition. The power to create and change the world, so admired by de Beauvoir, is the same unilateral power nesting in the very notion of the autonomous sovereign individual, which necessarily makes of that individual one who dominates both the more-than-human world and those people that do not fit its mould. In de Beauvoir's reality there is no room for intra-action between humans and more-than-humans and the diversity of peoples and places it creates.

Many brands of feminism – liberal, socialists, and Marxist in particular – have since de Beauvoir's foundational book appropriated the rational transcendental subject and focused on sexism and male dominance. In so doing they have reproduced the very domination that they sought to escape, erasing non-white women by such expressions as 'women and blacks'. Black feminists and other non-white or non-Western women have pointed out how this generic, universal 'woman' is in fact white, middle-class and Christian. This is the inevitable consequence of the appropriation of the transcendental, autonomous, independent, rational agentic subject (hooks 1981; Lorde 1984; Spelman 1988; Amadiume 1987; Ahmed 1992; Mohanty 1991; Marcos 1994; Fox-Genovese 1991; Addelson 1994; Butler 1992; Hekman 1995; Apffel-Marglin 1995).

Liberal feminists have sometimes argued that by jettisoning the transcendental subject they would lose what women have wanted, namely the power to act, the power of their own voices – in a word, agency. Some feminists see the critique of the autonomous individual as a conspiracy against the gains that women have made in this century. It would seem that, in the very struggle towards emancipation, liberal feminism, and its offshoot developmentalist feminism, have reproduced the very domination by which they saw women being oppressed. Developmentalist feminism in Andean countries seems unaware that domination also works through the construction of a particular type of person and a particular epistemology and ontology.

Conclusion: gender and the hidden agenda of the state

Family planning is a goal congruent with developmentalist feminism's notion of the autonomous individual. It is indispensable to bringing about women's control over their fertility. Such an individual woman voluntaristically and autonomously makes a life plan. The work of Kathryn Pyne Addelson indicates that in the world of the autonomous agent, family planning transcends the community by becoming an individual act to control the course of one's fertility. Her example is based on the national organization Planned Parenthood in the US and the epistemology of family planning. She illustrates that the white middle-class value of planned fertility is rooted in the ideology of individualism and in rational choice. Individuals are able to and should choose the number and timing of the births of their children. This individualistic outlook assumes that the same planning outlook should be espoused by all persons and that they should all plan ahead and orient themselves towards a goal presumed to be universal. She recounts how poor black teenage mothers whose communities welcome the new baby are publicly stigmatized as deviant by school, medical and other professionals. The strategy that Planned Parenthood wanted was one of educating the 'they', these poor black 'others', up to the individualistic planning ethics of the 'we', the normative white middle-class individual. These poor black others are morally condemned for their lack of 'responsibility' as the liberal writer Theodore White's remark about the 'black pattern of mating and breeding without responsibility' makes clear (White 1961, quoted in Addelson 1994: 114). International Planned Parenthood exports this internal colonizing dynamic worldwide. Planned Parenthood – whether nationally or internationally – understands the common good to be achieved by aggregation, with each family or each woman individually deciding how many children they can afford. The common good is achieved by each acting in its own self-interest, thereby adhering to the basic paradigm of bourgeois economics and society (Addelson 1994: 104, 112).

The autonomous individual who controls her fertility acts with carefully planned intent. She determines the world according to her own needs. The modern bourgeois epistemology of individualism and its value of self-control transmutes all those who do not live their lives in that fashion into deviant 'others' who need either to be educated or, failing that, coerced into the proper, normative behaviour. Professionals – therapists, educators, doctors, and so on – construct rational and individualistic models to be applied universally. Universality is inextricably linked to the idea of normalcy, for it imposes a singular sense of self on a wide variety of people. The universality of this contextless subject accounts for its unilateral determination of the world, for it does not change its views according to circumstances. If things do not go its way, it must change the world, violently if need be. Removed from context, it is untouched, and hence portrays a false reality in its removal from daily relationships of mutuality, from intra-actions. The idea that the individual has absolute control over itself, its body and its life establishes a unilateral vision and action as well as a barrier between it and the world of different humans and of more-than-humans.

Given the economic and political situation in countries such as Bolivia and Peru, the state's investment in creating autonomous female individuals can hardly be motivated by its desire to give *campesina* women access to education or jobs. Education no longer guarantees one a job since jobs are extremely scarce. Access to the most important 'productive resource' – to use the state idiom – namely land, is in any case overwhelmingly in non-*campesino* hands since, as we have seen, they own only 10 per cent of the agricultural land while constituting more than 80 per cent of the agricultural population. The state's gender agenda is clearly not designed to lead *campesina* women to have more control over land outside their communities. It is difficult to avoid the impression that the state's gender discourse is mostly functional to its family planning agenda. The language of the Junior Ministry of Gender in Bolivia wraps its agenda of fostering women's autonomous decision-making power over their fertility and their sexuality in a seductive language of 'respecting women's decisions and women's rights' as well as respecting their right to their own cultural identity. However, the discourse of developmentalist feminism does create the object desired, namely the woman receptive and pliable to the state's family planning agenda.

This would be problematic in any context, but in the Andean context, given its history of demographic collapse and low population density, followed by the *campesino* communities' remarkable resilience and ability to survive and thrive, it is simply unacceptable. Furthermore, abuses in population control programmes carried out either by states or international agencies, or by a combination of these, seem to be endemic in the Andes and elsewhere (Hartmann 1995; Bandarage 1997). Whether intended or not, too often such developmentalist gender agendas have not only led to abuses but inevitably also to the erasure of other realities and other lives.

Developmentalist feminism in Bolivia and Peru thus reproduces the internal colonizing dynamics in such countries as the US by implementing its family planning programmes as well as its development projects. Family planning can be seen as diametrically opposed to the manner in which the human collectivity in Andean communities lives its own regeneration as part of the regeneration of the whole *pacha* with all its inhabitants, humans and more-than-humans. In such a world, there is no pre-existing socio-political-economic order within which autonomous individuals make choices. The Andean world is continuously generated and regenerated through intra-actions among all its participants, both humans and more-than-humans.

Notes

1 This junior ministry was originally entitled the Subsecretariat of Ethnic, Gender and Generations Affairs (Subsecretaria de asuntos étnicos, de género y generacionales).

2 In Peru the corresponding state institution is called the Ministry of Women's Affairs (El Ministerio de la Mujer).

3 The demographic loss is of the order of 9 out of 10 people. The demographic curve for the indigenous population began an upward move only in the 1940s. According to PRATEC, the Peruvian NGO, it has only in the last few years reached its estimated pre-conquest level.

4 Greta Jiménez Sardón's book was first written as a thesis for the PRATEC course in which she participated in 1992 .

5 Here most of the corpus of Foucault's work is relevant, but especially *Discipline and Punish*, 1977.

6 It also completely muddles the modernist notion of linear time and the beginning of a person's life.

7 On this point see also the work of quantum physicist Arthur Zajonc (1993).

8 This is not to imply that Barad, Franklin, Haraway and Latour's views are isomorphic. They are not, but on this crucial point they do seem to agree.

9 As mentioned earlier, in quantum physics such experiments as the EPR and the 'delayed choice experiment' have shown experimentally the impossibility of separating the knower from the known. Other experiments have also shown the materialist assumption underlying classical science to be false.

10 The French nineteenth-century historian Michelet (1842: 174) gives expression to a widely held view at the time, namely that rationality is a 'manly' power.

11 Two fairly recent books are instances of this attitude: Herrnstein and Murray, *The Bell Curve* (1994); and Itzkoff, *The Decline of Intelligence in America* (1994).

Part IV
The Science Question in Development

9

Mad Cows and Sacred Cows

Vandana Shiva

When I gave a speech at the Dalai Lama' s sixtieth birthday celebration, he wrote me two beautiful lines of compassion: 'All sentient beings, including the small insects, cherish themselves. All have the right to overcome suffering and achieve happiness. I therefore pray that we show love and compassion to all.'[1]

What is our responsibility to other species? Do the boundaries between species have integrity? Or are these boundaries mere constructs that should be broken for human convenience? The call to 'transgress boundaries' advocated by both patriarchal capitalists and postmodern feminists cannot be so simple. It needs to be based on a sophisticated and complex discrimination between different kinds of boundaries, an understanding of who is protected by what boundaries and whose freedom is achieved by what transgressions.

In India, cows have been treated as sacred – as Lakshmi, the goddess of wealth, and as the cosmos in which all gods and goddesses reside – for centuries. Ecologically, the cow has been central to Indian civilization. Both materially and conceptually the world of Indian agriculture has built its sustainability on the integrity of the cow, considering her inviolable and sacred, seeing her as the mother of the prosperity of food systems.

According to K. M. Munshi, India's first agriculture minister after independence from the British, cows are not worshipped in vain. They are the primeval agents who enrich the soil – nature's great land transformers who supply organic matter which, after treatment, becomes nutrient matter of the greatest importance. In India, tradition, religious sentiment, and economic needs have tried to maintain a cattle population large enough to maintain the cycle.[2]

By using crop wastes and uncultivated land, indigenous cattle do not compete with humans for food; rather, they provide organic fertilizer for fields and thus enhance food productivity. Within the sacredness of the cow lie this ecological rationale and conservation imperative. The cow is a source of cow-dung energy, nutrition and leather, and its contribution is linked to the work of women in feeding and milking cows, collecting cow dung, and nurturing sick cows to health. Along with being the primary experts in animal husbandry, women are also the food processors in the traditional dairy industry, making curds, butter, ghee and buttermilk.

Indian cattle provide more food than they consume, in contrast to those of the US cattle industry, in which cattle consume six times more food than they provide.[3] In addition, every year, Indian cattle excrete 700 million tons of recoverable manure: half of this is used as fuel, liberating the thermal equivalent of 27 million tons of kerosene, 35 million tons of coal, or 68 million tons of wood, all of which are scarce resources in India. The remaining half is used as fertilizer.

Two-thirds of the power requirements of Indian villages are met by cattle-dung fuel from some 80 million cattle. (Seventy million of these cattle are the male progeny of what industrial developers term 'useless' low-milk-yielding cows.) To replace animal power in agriculture, India would have to spend about $l billion annually on gas. As for other livestock produce, it may be sufficient to mention that the export of hides, skins and other products brings in $150 million annually.[4]

Yet this highly efficient food system, based on multiple uses of cattle, has been dismantled in the name of efficiency and development. The Green Revolution shifted agriculture's fertilizer base from renewable organic inputs to non-renewable chemical ones, making both cattle and women' s work with cattle dispensable in the production of food grain. The White Revolution, aping the West's wasteful animal husbandry and dairying practices, is destroying the world's most evolved dairy culture and displacing women from their role in the dairy-processing industry.

The Green Revolution has emerged as an enemy to the White, as the high-yielding crop varieties have reduced straw production, and their by-products are unpalatable to livestock and thus useless as fodder. Further, hybrid crops deprive the soil of nutrients, creating deficiencies in fodder and disease in livestock. The White Revolution, in turn, instead of viewing livestock as ecologically integrated with crops, has reduced the cow to a mere milk machine. As Shanti George observes,

> The trouble is that when dairy planners look at the cow, they see just her udder; though there is much more to her. The equate cattle only with milk,

and do not consider other livestock produce – draught power, dung for fertilizer and fuel, hides, skins, horn, and hooves.[5]

In India, cow's milk is but one of the many by-products of the interdependence between agriculture and animal husbandry. There, cattle are considered agents of production in the food system; only secondarily are they viewed as producing consumable items. But the White Revolution makes milk production primary and exclusive – and, according to the Royal Commission and the Indian Council of Agricultural Research, if milk production is unduly pushed up, it may indirectly affect the entire basis of Indian agriculture.[6]

Worse, trade liberalization policies in India are leading to the slaughter of cattle for meat exports, threatening diverse, disease-resistant breeds and small farmers' integrated livestock–crop production systems with extinction. In the United Kingdom, giant slaughterhouses and the factory farming of cattle are being called into question by the spread of 'mad cow disease' (BSE – bovine spongiform encephalopathy), which has infected over 1.5 million cows in Britain. While this disease is sounding the death knell of the non-sustainable livestock economy in Britain, India's 'sacred cows' are being sent to slaughterhouses to 'catch up' with the beef exports and beef consumption figures of 'advanced' countries. This globalization of non-sustainable and hazardous systems of food production is symptomatic of a deeper madness than that infecting UK cows.

Ratcheting up the milk machine

As the idea of the cow-as-milk-machine runs into trouble worldwide, multinational biotech industries are promoting new miracles of genetic engineering to increase milk production, further threatening the livelihoods of small producers. Multinational corporations such as Elanco (a subsidiary of Eli Lilly), Cynamic, Monsanto and Upjohn are all rushing to put bovine somatrophin (BST), a growth hormone commercially produced by genetic engineering, on the market, in spite of controversy about its ecological impact.[7]

When injected daily into cows, BST diverts energy to milk production. Cows may get emaciated if too much energy is diverted to produce milk. And, as in all other 'miracles' of modern agricultural science, the gain in milk production is contingent upon a number of other factors, such as use of industrial feed and a computerized feeding programme.[8] Finally, women' s traditional role in caring for cows and processing milk falls into the hands of men and machines.

The use of genetically engineered BST, or bovine growth hormone (BGH), is leading to major consumer resistance and a demand for the labelling of milk, which the biotechnology industry actively opposes. The European Union has voted against the labelling of genetically engineered products, and Monsanto has sued US farmers who label their milk 'BGH-free'. Democracy is thus stifled by 'free trade'.

The inherent violence of the White Revolution lies in its treatment of the needs of small farmers and of living resources as dispensable if they produce the wrong thing in the wrong quantity. The same global commoditization processes that render Indian cattle 'unproductive' (even when, considered holistically, they are highly productive) simultaneously dispense with European cattle for being overproductive. Annihilating diverse livestock destroys knowledge on how to protect and conserve living resources as sources of life. This protection is replaced by the protection of the profits of rich farmers and the control of agribusiness.

Crops as food for all

In ecological agricultural cultures, technologies and economies are based on an integration between crops and animal husbandry. The wastes of one provide nutrition for the other, in mutual and reciprocal ways. Crop by-products feed cattle, and cattle waste feeds the soils that nourish the crops. Crops do not just yield grain, they also yield straw, which provides fodder and organic matter. Crops are thus food for humans, animals and the many organisms in the soil. These organically fed soils are home to millions of micro-organisms that work to improve the soil's fertility. Bacteria feed on the cellulose fibres of straw that farmers return to the soil. In each hectare, between 100 and 300 kilogrammes of amoebas feed on these bacteria, making the lignite fibres available for uptake by plants. In each gramme of soil, 100,000 algae provide organic matter and serve as vital nitrogen fixers. In each hectare are one to two tons of fungi and macrofauna such as anthropods, molluscs and field mice. Rodents that bore under the fields aerate the soil and improve its water-holding capacity. Spiders, centipedes, and insects grind organic matter from the surface of the soil and leave behind enriching droppings.[9]

Soils treated with farmyard manure have from 2 to 2.5 times as many earthworms as untreated soils. These earthworms contribute to soil fertility by maintaining soil structure, aeration, and drainage, and by breaking down organic matter and incorporating it into the soil. According to Charles Darwin, 'It maybe doubted whether there are many other animals which have played so important a part in the history of creatures.'[10] The little earthworm working invisibly in the soil is actually a tractor, fertilizer factory and dam combined. Worm-worked soils are more water-stable than unworked soils, and worm-inhabited soils have considerably more organic carbons and nitrogen. By their continuous movement through soils, earthworms aerate the soil, increasing the air volume in soil by up to 30 per cent. Soils with earthworms drain four to ten times faster than soils without earthworms, and their water-holding capacity is 20 per cent higher. Earthworm casts, or droppings, which can consist of up to 36 tons per acre per year, contain carbon, nitrogen, calcium, magnesium, potassium, sodium and phosphorus, promoting the microbial activity essential to soil fertility.

Industrial farming techniques would deprive these diverse species of food sources and instead assault them with chemicals, destroying the rich biodiversity in the soil and with it the basis for the renewal of soil fertility.

The intensive livestock economy

Europe's intensive livestock economy requires seven times the area of Europe in other countries for the production of cattle feed.[11] These 'shadow acres' necessary for feed production are in fact an extensive use of resources. While this feed production system does not conserve acres, the concentration of animals in unlivable spaces does save space. The efficiency question that the intensive livestock industry is always asking is, 'How many animals can be crammed into the smallest space for the least cost and the greatest profit?'[12]

In a complementary system of agriculture, the cattle eat what the humans cannot. They eat straw from the crops and grass from pastures and field boundaries. In a competitive model such as the livestock industry, grain is diverted from human consumption to intensive feed for livestock. It takes two kilogrammes of grain to produce one kilogramme of poultry, four kilogrammes of grain to produce one kilogramme of pork, and eight kilogrammes of grain to produce one kilogramme of beef.

Cows are basically herbivores. The biomass they eat is digested in the rumen, the huge first chamber of the four stomachs of the cow. The livestock industry has increased cows' milk and meat production by giving them intensive, high-protein feed concentrate, an inappropriate diet since cows need roughage. One of the methods developed by the livestock industry to circumvent this need for roughage is to feed them plastic pot-scrubbing pads. The scrubbing pads remain in the rumen for life.[13]

Robbing cattle of the roughage they need does not merely treat them unethically; it also does not reduce the acreage needed to feed the cows, since the concentrate comes from grain that could have fed people. The shift from a cooperative, integrated system to a competitive, fragmented one creates additional pressures on scarce land and grain resources. This in turn leads to non-sustainability, violence to animals, and lower productivity when all systems are assessed.

Breaking boundaries: transforming herbivores into cannibals

As food for animals from farms disappears, animal feed is based increasingly on other sources, including the carcasses of dead animals. This is how the conditions for the mad cow disease epidemic were created. BSE infection, known as 'scrapie' in sheep, typically bores into the brain and the nervous system and does not show itself as a disease until the infected animals are adults. Infected cows are nervous and shaky, and rapidly descend into dementia and death. Dissection of affected cows shows that their brains have disintegrated and are full of holes. In humans, this disease is called Creutzfeldt-Jakob disease, named after two German doctors.

The first case of BSE in the United Kingdom was confirmed in November 1986. By 1988 more than 2,000 cases of BSE had been confirmed. By August 1994 there were 137,000 confirmed cases, more than six times the number predicted by the government in their 'worst case scenario'. The epidemic spread by feeding healthy cattle the remains of infected cattle. In 1987 1.3 million tons of animal carcasses were processed into animal feed by 'rendering plants'. The largest portion of the animal material processed, 45 per cent, came from cows. Pigs contributed 21 per cent, poultry 19 per cent, and sheep 15 per cent. This created 350,000 tons of meat and bone meal and 230,000 tons of tallow.[14] Sheep infected with scrapie were thus fed to cows, which contracted BSE, and their carcasses were again fed to cattle. By 1996 more than 1.6 million cattle had become victims of BSE.

British farmers, increasingly dependent on industrial cattle feed, demanded that the sources of cattle feed be labelled, but the feed industry has denied farmers' and consumers' 'right to know'. Instead, the feed industry has been labelling its feed on the basis of its chemical constitution, thus camouflaging its biological sources.

The BSE epidemic: crossing species barriers

When the BSE epidemic broke out, scientists started to warn that if the disease had jumped from sheep to cows, there was every possibility that it could shift from cows to humans. The government continued to state this was impossible.

But in January 1996 a degenerative brain disorder in ten children was linked to the consumption of beef infected with BSE. Ten thousand schools stopped serving beef in their meals. Many countries in Europe and as far away as New Zealand and Singapore have stopped importing UK beef. In April 1996 the European Union announced that it would help fund the mass slaughter of 4.7 million British cattle.[15]

By repeatedly denying the method of BSE transmission, by refusing to call for the biological labelling of animal feed, and by other evasions, both the government and official scientists colluded in exacerbating the BSE epidemic. In an economy in which trade is not subjected to ethical, ecological and health imperatives, 'science' that serves commerce will systematically mislead citizens. Even as new diseases threaten the lives and health of farm animals and consumers, official scientific agencies keep repeating the mantra of 'no hard scientific evidence'. In the meantime, consumers are making their own decisions, voting against hazardous factory farming by boycotting beef.

European consumption of UK beef and beef products dropped by 40 per cent, and the European Union was forced to ban the export of UK beef and beef products.

The new apartheid: contaminated beef for the south

In 1991 the chief economist of the World Bank suggested that, because people are poorer and life is cheaper in the Third World, exporting toxins there made economic sense. In an internal memo, Lawrence Summers wrote,

> Just between you and me, shouldn't the World Bank be encouraging more migration of the dirty industries to the LDCs [less developed countries]?... The economic logic behind dumping a load of toxic waste in the lowest wage country is impeccable, and we should face up to that.... Under-populated countries in Africa are vastly under-polluted; their air quality is probably vastly inefficiently low compared to Los Angeles or Mexico City.... The concern over an agent that causes a one-in-a-million change in the odds of prostate cancer is obviously going to be much higher in a country where people survive to get prostate cancer than in a country where under-five mortality is 200 per thousand.[16]

In these economics of genocide, the largely white, male élite of the North creates class, race and gender boundaries to exclude other social groups from the fundamental human rights to life and safety. This blatant disregard for the rights of Third World people was reinforced in 1996, when the European Union lifted its ban on the export of possibly BSE-infected UK beef and bovine products to Third World countries.

There is a difference between ecological boundaries and socially constructed boundaries. The difference between herbivores and carnivores is an ecological boundary. It needs to be respected for the sake of both cows and humans The difference between the value of human life in the North and South is a politically constructed boundary. It needs to be broken for the sake of human dignity.

Transforming vegetarians into beef-eaters

At a time when meat consumption is declining in Western countries, India's trade liberalization programme is trying to convert a predominantly vegetarian society into a beef-eating one. This programme is based on the false equation that the only source of protein is animal protein, and that higher animal consumption equals a higher quality of life. According to Dr Panya Chotiawan, chairperson of a Thai poultry producer, 'protein ... provides both strength and brain structure. Therefore, consuming sufficient protein will generate a healthier body and promote intelligence.'[17] However, it is not the case that higher animal-protein consumption makes for a better quality of life or higher intelligence. The trend is that people seeking a genuinely high quality of life are shifting to vegetarianism. In the United States, animal protein consumption has dropped, and the mad cow disease epidemic has also encouraged people to move to vegetarianism.

Indians, who are predominantly vegetarian, are not unintelligent. Our source of protein is plant-based. Our diet has a rich variety of legumes, which provide healthy proteins for human consumption and a free enrichment of nitrogen for the soils. Most indigenous farming systems are based on polycultures, which include leguminous crops.

The three most important diseases of the affluent countries – cancer, stroke, and heart disease – are linked conclusively to consumption of beef and other animal products. International studies comparing diets in different countries have shown that diets high in meat result in more deaths from intestinal cancer *per capita*. Japanese people in the United States eating a high-meat diet are three times as likely to contract colon cancer as the those eating the Japanese low-meat diet.[18] Modern, intensive systems of meat production have exacerbated the health hazards posed by meat consumption. Modern meats have seven times more fat than non-industrial meats, as well as drug and antibiotic residues.

Slaughtering india's cattle for export

The cultural attitudes that maintain the widespread vegetarianism in India are seen as obstacles to overcome in order to institute a new meat-eating culture. According to India's 'New Livestock Policy',

> The beef production in India is purely an adjunct to milk and draught power production. The animals slaughtered are the old and the infirm and the sterile, and are in all cases malnourished. There is no organized marketing and no grading system, and beef prices are at a level which makes feeding uneconomic. There is no instance of feedlots or even individual animals being raised for meat. Religious sentiments (particularly in the northern and

western parts of India) against cattle slaughter seem to spill over also on buffaloes and prevent the utilization of a large number of surplus male calves.[19]

The Ministry of Agriculture provides 100 per cent grants and tax incentives to encourage the setting up of slaughterhouses. According to a 1996 Union Ministry of Environment report, at least 32,000 illegal slaughterhouses had been established in the preceding five years. By 1995, the total quantity of meat exports had risen more than twenty-fold, to 137,334 tons.[20] Total meat exports, including beef, veal and buffalo meat, almost doubled between 1990 and 1995. But between 1991 and 1996 cattle, buffalo and other livestock populations have only increased by half that rate. In other words, India is exporting more meat than is being replenished.

Meat exports are leading to a decline not only in livestock numbers, but also in the rich diversity of cattle breeds known for their hardiness, milk production and draught power. According to the United Nations Food and Agriculture Organization, 'the diversity of domestic animal breeds is dwindling rapidly. Each variety that is lost takes with it irreplaceable genetic traits – traits that may hold the key to resisting disease or to productivity and survival under adverse conditions.'[21] If measures to arrest these trends are not taken now, most of us will witness the extinction of livestock within our very lifetimes, and with it the foundation of sustainable agriculture will disappear.

Another significant factor contributing to the decline of cattle is the shortage of fodder, stemming from the emphasis on grains bred for high yields, the planting of monocultures of non-fodder species such as eucalyptus, and the growing scarcity of grazing lands and pastures due to the enclosure of the commons.

The decline of animal wealth is destroying the rural economy and rural livelihoods. This will adversely affect the landless, the lowest castes and women. Women provide nearly 90 per cent of all labour for livestock management. Of the 70 million households that depend on livestock for their livelihoods, two thirds are small and marginal farmers and landless labourers. Because of increased cattle exports, the price of livestock has escalated, and there is less and less dung available for manure and cooking fuel. More fertilizers, fossil fuels, tractors and trucks must be imported to replace the energy and fertility that cattle gave freely to the rural economy. Thus, while animal exports are earning the country Rs10 million, the destruction of animal wealth is costing the country Rs150 million.

A case in point is one of the biggest export-oriented slaughterhouses, Al-Kabeer in Andhra Pradesh. Al-Kabeer slaughters 182,400 buffaloes every year, animals whose dung could have provided for the fuel needs of over 90,000 average Indian families of five. The government's transport of kerosene to replace this fuel costs hundreds of millions of rupees, which means that poor people pay vastly higher fuel expenses. In 1987–8 Rs5.5 billion of kerosene was imported. By 1992–3 this amount had increased almost four-fold.

If livestock were not slaughtered in the state of Andhra Pradesh, farmyard manure would cultivate 384 hectares, producing 530,000 tons of food grain.[22] The state of Andhra Pradesh must now spend Rs9.1 billion to import nitrogen, phosphorus, and potash previously provided by livestock over the duration of their lives. This means that against a projected earning of Rs200 million by Al-Kabeer through the killings, the state could actually save Rs9.1 billion in foreign exchange by not killing.[23]

Al-Kabeer has provided just 300 jobs. In contrast, small-scale slaughtering for local consumption creates livelihoods and allows all parts of an animal to be used. The skin is used for leather, and bones and horns provide material for crafts and fertilizer. In large-scale industrial slaughterhouses, all these by-products are treated as waste and become a source of pollution. The entire area around Al-Kabeer is contaminated with blood, skin and bones from slaughtered cattle. Al-Kabeer has proposed to build a 'rendering' plant to use this animal waste to make cattle feed, yet another symptom of the mad cow culture replacing the sacred cow culture.

In one lawsuit against Al-Kabeer, tbe court ordered a 50 per cent reduction of its capacity in order to save the cattle wealth and the rural economy of Andhra Pradesh. In another case involving a slaughterhouse, the judge ruled that instead of exporting meat, India should export a message of compassion. According to the judgement,

> This fundamental Duty in the Constitution to have compassion for all living creatures thus determines the legal relation between Indian Citizens and animals on Indian soil, whether small ones or large ones....Their place in the Constitutional Law of the land is thus a fountainhead of total rule of law for the protection of animals and provides not only against their ill treatment, but from it also springs a *right to life* in harmony with human beings.
>
> If this enforceable obligation of State is understood, certain results will follow. *First,* the *Indian State cannot export animals for killing;* and *secondly,* cannot become a party to the killing of animals by sanctioning exports in the casings and cans stuffed with dead animals after slaughter. Avoidance of this is preserving the Indian Cultural Heritage.... *India can only export a message of compassion towards all living creatures of the world,* as a beacon to preserve *ecology,* which is the true and common Dharma for all civilizations.[24]

But the Indian constitution's protection of animals and rural livelihoods is being challenged by international trade agreements. In March 1998 the World

Trade Organization announced the initiation of a dispute by the European Union (EU) against India's restriction on the export of raw hides and fur. The EU argues that preventing the free export of furs and hides contravenes Article XI of the General Agreement on Tariffs and Trade (GATT).[25] According to Article XI of GATT, any restriction on imports and exports is illegal, even though such restrictions might be necessary for cultural, ecological, aud economic reasons.[26]

Exporting raw hides and furs would threaten India's cattle wealth as well as the livelihoods of craftspeople, shoemakers, cobblers, farmers and other small producers. In 1993, when India was forced to remove export restrictions on cotton, 2 million weavers lost their livelihoods.

McDonaldization

Globalization has created the McDonaldization of world food, resulting in the destruction of sustainable food systems. It attempts to create a uniform food culture of hamburgers. The mad cow disease epidemic tells us something of the costs hidden in this food culture and food economy.

In 1994, Pepsi Foods Ltd. was given permission to start 60 restaurants in India: 30 each of Kentucky Fried Chicken (KFC) and Pizza Hut. The processed meats and chicken offered at these restaurants have been identified by the US Senate as sources of the cancers that one American contracts every seven seconds. The chicken, which would come from an Indian firm called Venky's, would be fed on a 'modern' diet of antibiotics and other drugs, such as arsenic compounds, sulphur drugs, hormones, dyes, and nitrofurans. Many chickens are nevertheless riddled with disease, in particular chicken cancer (leukosis). They can also carry salmonellosis, which does not die with ordinary cooking.

Both KFC and Pizza Hut have guaranteed that they will generate employment. However, according to studies conducted by the Ministry of Environment on other meat industries, Al-Kabeer has displaced 300,000 people from their jobs, while employing only 300 people at salaries ranging from Rs500 to Rs2,000 per month. Venky's chicken has not employed one extra person after getting the contract for chicken supply from KFC and Pizza Hut. In fact, the company is being encouraged to mechanize further rather than use human labour.

Junk-food chains, including KFC and Pizza Hut, are under attack from major environmental groups in the United States and other developed countries because of their negative environmental impact. Intensive breeding of livestock and poultry for such restaurants leads to deforestation, land degradation, and contamination of water sources and other natural resources. For every pound of red meat, poultry, eggs and milk produced, farm fields lose about five pounds of irreplaceable topsoil. The water necessary for meat breeding comes to about 190 gallons per animal per day, or ten times what a normal Indian family is supposed to use in one day, if it gets water at all.

KFC and Pizza Hut insist that their chickens be fed on maize and soybean. It takes 2.8 kilogrammes of corn to produce half a kilogramme of chicken. Egg layers need a kilogramme of corn and soybean to produce an egg. Over three kilogrammes of corn and soybean are necessary to produce one pound of pork. Overall, animal farms use nearly 40 per cent of the world's total grain production. In the United States, nearly 70 per cent of grain production is fed to livestock.

Maize, though not a major food crop in India, has traditionally been grown for human consumption. Land will be diverted from production of food crops for humans to production of maize for chickens: 37 per cent of the arable land in India will be diverted toward such production. Were all the grain produced consumed directly by humans, it would nourish five times as many people as it does after being converted into meat, milk and eggs, according to the Council for Agricultural Science and Technology.

The food culture of India is as diverse as its ecosystems and its people, who use a variety of cereals, pulses and vegetables as well as cooking methods to suit every need and condition. However, advertising is already having a negative impact on Indians' food and drink patterns. No longer are homemade snacks and lime juice or buttermilk offered to guests; instead, chips and aerated soft drinks are.

Metaphors of ecological culture and industrial culture

The mad cow is a product of 'border crossings' in industrial agriculture. It is a product of the border crossing between herbivores and carnivores. It is a product of the border crossing between ethical treatment of other beings and violent exploitation of animals to maximize profits and human greed.

Cross-breeding programmes meant to 'improve' Indian breeds with 'superior' European breeds are resulting in cross-bred cattle, perceived only as milk machines. During the *Mat tu Pongal* festival in India, villagers decorate, worship, and leave their livestock animals free to roam, but, as far as I have seen, not their cross-bred cows. Meat export programmes are converting the sacred cow into a meat machine, leading to a decline in livestock and eroding cattle diversity.

Species boundaries between humans and cattle are also being crossed to create pharmaceuticals in the milk of factory-farmed animals. This construction of 'mammalian bioreactors' is the ultimate step in the reduction of cows to machines.

These border crossings, promoted by corporate élites for profit, are rationalized by the popular postmodern stances taken by some academics. As technofeminist Donna Haraway writes:

> Transgenic border crossing signifies serious challenges to the 'sanctity of life' for many members of Western cultures, which historically have been obsessed with racial purity, categories authorized by nature, and the well-defined self.... In opposing the production of transgenic organisms, especially opposing their patenting and other forms of private commercial exploitation, committed activists appeal to notions such as the integrity of natural kinds and the natural types or self-defining purpose of all life forms.[27]

This academic rationale for an attack on environmental and Third World movements as they attempt to safeguard their food and livelihoods is based on many false assumptions. The first is that the 'sanctity of life' is merely a Western construct. Diverse cultures, animal rights activists and ecologists all believe in the need for respect for all living things. The sanctity of life is characteristic of the world views of diverse indigenous cultures. As Jerry Mander has indicated, Western industrial civilization has evolved in the absence of the sacred.[28]

The second flawed assumption is to equate 'sanctity of life' with racism and an obsession with racial purity. In fact, racism and life's sanctity are mutually exclusive. The racist obsessed with 'racial purity' indulges in 'ethnic cleansing' and violates the sanctity of life. The existence of diversity and difference in itself does not lead to racism. It is when that diversity is hierarchically ordered on the basis of 'superiority' that we get racism. Anti-racism does not require wiping out the blackness of the black or the brownness of the brown, it requires resisting the view that sees black and brown as inferior to white. In fact, during the apartheid regime of South Africa, 'border crossing' between whites and blacks did not create liberation for the blacks, it created new oppression.[29]

A cow is not merely a milk machine or a meat machine, even if industry treats it in such a way. That is why cows are hurt by the industrial treatment they are subjected to. When forced to become carnivores instead of herbivores, they become infected with BSE. When injected with growth hormones, they become diseased. To deny subjecthood to cows and other animals, to treat them as mere raw material, is to converge with the approach of capitalist patriarchy.

Sacred cows are the symbols and constructions of a culture that sees the entire cosmos in a cow, and hence protects the cow to protect ecological relations as well as the cow as a living being, with its own intelligence and its own self-organizing capacity. Referring to the self-organized nature of animals and other living organisms, Goethe concluded,

> Hence, we conceive of [an] individual animal as a small world, existing for its own sake, by its own means. Every creature has its own reasons to be. All its parts have a direct effect on one another, a relationship to one another, thereby consistently renewing the circle of life.[30]

Mad cows are symbols of a worldview that perceives no difference between machines and living beings, between herbivores and carnivores, or between the Sindhi and Sahiwal and the Jersey and the Holstein. Sacred cows are a metaphor of ecological civilization. Mad cows are a metaphor of an anti-ecological, industrial civilization.

At the threshold of the third millennium, liberation strategies have to ensure that human freedom is not gained at the cost of other species, that freedom for one race or gender is not based on increased subjugation of other races and genders. In each of these strivings for freedom, the challenge is to include the Other.

For more than two centuries, patriarchal, Eurocentric and anthropocentric scientific discourse has treated women, other cultures, and other species as objects. Experts have been treated as the only legitimate knowers. For more than two decades, feminist movements, Third World and indigenous people's movements, and ecological and animal-rights movements have questioned this objectification and denial of subjecthood.

Ecological feminisms recognize the intrinsic worth of all species, the intelligence of all life, and the self-organizational capacity of beings. They also recognize that there is no justification in a hierarchy between knowledge and practice, theory and activism, academic thought and everyday life. Such hierarchies have no epistemological basis, though they do have a political basis. In this perspective, it is not just the Western industrial breeders whose knowledge counts and whose knowledge should displace all other knowers: indigenous cattle breeders, farmers, women, and animals.

Reversing the McDonaldization of the world

'What man does to the web of life, he does to himself.' How we relate to other species will determine whether the third millennium will be an era of disease and devastation, and of exclusion and violence, or – instead – a new era based on peace and non-violence, health and well-being, inclusiveness and compassion.

Unsustainable outcomes are the inevitable result of the deepening of patriarchal domination over ways of knowing and relating non-violently to what have been identified as 'lesser species', including women. But sustainability can be created by an inclusive feminism, an ecological feminism, in which the freedom of every species is linked to the liberation of women, in which the tiniest life form is recognized as having intrinsic worth, integrity and autonomy.

Women of our generation especially have to decide whether to protect the knowledge and wisdom of our grandmothers in the maintenance of life, or allow global corporations to push most species to extinction, mutilate and torture those that are found profitable, and undermine the health and well-being of the earth and its communities.

The mad cow, as a product of border crossings, is a 'cyborg' in Donna Haraway's brand of 'cyborg' feminism.[31] According to Haraway, 'I'd rather be a cyborg than a goddess.'[32] In India, the cow is Lakshmi, the goddess of wealth. Cow dung is worshipped as Lakshmi because it is the source of renewal of the earth's fertility through organic manuring. The cow is sacred because it is at the heart of the sustainability of an agrarian civilization. The cow as goddess and cosmos symbolizes care, compassion, sustainability, and equity. From the point of view of both cows and people, I would rather be a sacred cow than a mad one.

Notes

1 *Quarterly Monitor* (2001) Taken from Shiva, *Stolen Harvest: The Hijacking of the Food Supply* (2001).
2 Munshi (1951).
3 In India, cattle use 29 per cent of the organic matter, 22 per cent of the energy, and 3 per cent of the protein provided to them, in contrast to 9, 7, and 5 per cent respectively in the United States' intensive cattle industry. Shanti George (1985: 31).
4 *Ibid.*: 31.
5 *Ibid.*: 30.
6 *Ibid.*: 59.
7 *Economist* (1987).
8 Kneen (1987).
9 Claude Bourguignon, address at ARISE workshop, Auroville, India, Apri11995.
10 Darwin (1927).
11 Friends of the Earth (International) (1995).
12 Coats (1989: 73).
13 Trials indicated that steers fed 100 per cent concentrate plus pot scrubbers grew at approximately the same rate as cattle fed 85 per cent concentrate with 15 per cent roughage. Loerch (1991: 2321–8).
14 Lacey (1994: 32).
15 'EU agrees to fund slaughter of millions of British cattle', Cable News Network, 3 April 1996.
16 Lawrence Summers, quoted in Shiva (1999).
17 Panya Chotiawan, quoted in Juday (1998).
18 Shiva (1995).
19 India, Government of (1995).
20 www.fao.org,1996.
21 Some of the declining indigenous breeds today are Pangunur, Red Kandhari, Vechur, Bhangnari, Dhenani, Lohani, Rojhan, Bengal, Chittagong Red, Napalees Hill, Kachah, Siri, Tarai, Lulu and Sinhala. *The Hindu* (1996: 115).
22 Calculated on the basis of the average food grain produced per hectare in 1991, 1.382 tons.
23 The annual availability of major nutrients in farmyard manure, from the dung and urine of 1,924,000 buffaloes and 570,000 sheep per year, works out to 11,171.79 tons of nitrogen, which at the current price of Rs20.97 per kg at unsubsidized rates, costs Rs234.2 million to import; 2,164.15 tons of phosphorus, which at the current price of Rs21.25 per kg. at unsubsidized rates, costs Rs46 million; 10,069.29 tons of potash, which at the current price of Rs8.33 per kg at unsubsidized rates, costs Rs83.9 million; for a total import cost of Rs364.1 million. Taking into account an average remaining lifespan of five years, the cost of importing goods previously produced by livestock equals Rs1.8 billion. Following the same argument, if all the animals which are going to be killed during five years of Al-Kabeer's operation live out their natural lifespans, then the state would have to spend Rs9.1 billion on imports. In five

years, Al-Kabeer has killed 920,000 buffaloes and 2,850,000 sheep to earn only Rs200 million a year, according to the company's own projections. It has provided just 300 jobs. See Gandhi (1995).

24 Tis Hazari Court, judgment passed on 23 March 1992, Case No. 267/90, Delhi.

25 Renato Ruggiero, speech given at 'Policing the World Economy' Conference held at Geneva, 23–25 March 1998.

26 World Trade Organization, GATT Agreement, Geneva, 1994.

27 Haraway (1997: 80).

28 Mander (1995).

29 Some go so far as to suggest that gene transfer could 'cure' racist attitudes in society. But, on the contrary, 'gene enhancement' therapy is being requested for changing skin colour (see Rick Weiss, 'Gene Enhancements' Thorny Ethical Traits,' *Washington Post,* 11 October 1997). Genetic engineering is showing every sign of becoming the basis of a new racism, in which the blue-eyed, blonde-haired, white-skinned race becomes the measure for all.

30 Goethe (1988: 121).

31 Haraway (1985: 65–108).

32 *Ibid.*

10

Global Circulations

Nature, Culture and the Possibility of Sustainable Development

Banu Subramaniam, James Bever and Peggy Schultz

> How do you live and think together beneath a light that warms our bodies and models our ideas, but which remains indifferent to their existence? We contemporary philosophers cannot ask this question while ignoring the sciences, which, in their very separation, converge to ask it, even to exacerbate its terms. And when 'the world' means purely and simply the planet Earth … when humanity is finally in solidarity and global in its political existence and in the exercise of science, it discovers that it inhabits a global Earth that is the concern of our global science, global technology, and our global and local behaviours. This is the reason for the necessary synthesis….
>
> Michel Serres
> *Conversations on Science, Culture and Time*[1]

In his book, *We Have Never Been Modern,*[2] Bruno Latour argues for the inextricable interconnectedness of nature and culture, science and society, humanities and the sciences. He marks the impulse to be modern as involving two sets of practices. First, the 'work of purification', whereby we create two entirely distinct ontological zones: that of the non-human/natural world on one hand, and that of the human/cultural world on the other. Thus, the natural and physical sciences can be said to 'discipline' us into the study of non-human 'nature' and its processes, and the social sciences and the humanities into the study of human 'culture' and its processes. However, alongside this work of purification, Latour argues a second set of practices, namely the 'work of translation'. This work of translation, he suggests, creates mixtures between the worlds of nature and culture, or hybrids of nature and culture. Such is the paradox of the moderns – 'the more we forbid ourselves to conceive hybrids, the more possible their interbreeding becomes'. He argues that although we may try to separate (or, perhaps, *because* we try to) the natural and cultural worlds into their discrete categories, hybrids will proliferate. Despite disciplinary impulses to separate the natural and cultural worlds, they are inextricably interconnected. As he puts it, 'In the eyes of our critics the ozone hole above our heads, the moral law in our hearts, the autonomous text, may each be of interest, but only separately. That a delicate shuttle should have woven together the heavens, industry, texts, souls and moral law – that remains uncanny, unthinkable, unseemly.' Such is our legacy of academic disciplinarity, which much interdisciplinary work seeks to overcome and undo.

One field that has grounded its interdisciplinarity in the links between the non-human/natural world and the human/cultural world is feminist science studies.[3] A central focus of much of the social studies of science, especially the feminist studies of science, technology and development, has been about the illumination and elucidation of the interconnections between nature(s) and culture(s). Nature and culture, scholars have argued, are co-constituted, simultaneously semiotic as well as material.[4] Through tracing the networks of power, knowledge, resources and politics, the feminist studies of science and development underscore the centrality of gender, race, class, sexuality and nationality in our understandings of nature and culture.[5] Furthermore, these interconnections and networks are never static, but always dynamic and changing. These dynamic global circulations of power and politics have a profound impact on our study of nature, culture, science, technology and development. As Donna Haraway argues, we must move beyond our binary understandings of nature and culture as separate, non-interacting, non-intersecting realms. Nature is simultaneously material and semiotic and we must find ways to study and understand our world as simultaneously both material and semiotic.[6]

Development is one arena where the natural and cultural worlds implode. Science and technology have been crucial agents in modern development as well as contemporary globalization. Indeed, science is deeply implicated in modernity and the modern state. Among the developed nations and increasingly so in the so-called developing/Third World nations, science is often 'the reason of state'.[7] Therefore, any discussion of development and post-development must necessarily reconcile and grapple with the role of science in such visions. Much of the literature on development, including critiques of development, has focused on the so-called 'underdeveloped' or 'Third' World. The literature has highlighted and documented the ecological, economic, environmental, cultural and political costs of development in 'Third World' countries as well as the increasing reliance and dependence on the 'First World'. While critiques of development in the 'Third World' are essential, our focus in this essay is on the question of 'development' itself. We want to focus on the ideology of development that is at the heart of the modern state, and the central rationale of capitalism, globalization and the rhetoric of 'growth'. This ideology of development has taken hold and continues to sustain economies and public policies in the First World. Our title aims to highlight the global circulations of science in the rhetoric of development. Even within the so-called developed countries, growing inequalities sustain arguments for the need for 'development'. Others suggest that the very ideology of development and growth is at the heart of the growing inequality within and between countries. Recent anti-globalization movements from Seattle to Genoa have begun to highlight, among other issues, the cost of globalization, development and unfettered growth to the environment. It is clear from the reception the protesters received that political and economic power interests continue to nurture and sustain the rhetoric of globalization and development. The globalization of the rhetoric and the ideology of development have pervaded most spaces of political and cultural life. The ideology of development has been so naturalized that it is often difficult to extricate its influences from the larger political, economic and cultural processes.

Often ignoring social studies of science, scientific institutions continue to embrace the notion of objectivity and the possibility of producing unbiased knowledge about the world. In this chapter we explore our growing understanding of how research on the natural world is influenced and shaped by larger political and social issues. In particular, exploring the role of development, we use the case study of 'invasion biology' to illustrate this point. Invasion biology has developed as a field concerned with the increasing presence of exotic and alien plants and animals. We suggest that the problems of development are central to the growing concern about alien plants and animals entering the United States. We argue that critiques of development and the discourse of post-development to which this anthology is a contribution must pay attention to the naturalized ideology of development in addition to the very material consequences of development in the Third World. Invasion biology is also a good case study of the tensions between the global and the local. The global movements of humans, plants and animals as well as consumer products have profound consequences at the local level – of culture, economies and labour as well as nature and its management. As development scholars have already shown, hierarchies such as those based on gender, race, class, nation or sexuality are imbricated in development narratives and ideology, and central to the case of invasion biology as well. These intersections are crucial in any discussion of development.

Locations: scientists and the politics of science

We enter these discussions as three scholars studying questions of ecology, evolution and conservation. The three of us met during graduate school in the biological sciences. While our intellectual and disciplinary academic journeys have varied, we have all been deeply aware of the political nature of science. As fellow graduate students, we initiated and were part of a discussion group on the politics of biology. Early on, we began to recognize that there were deeper questions to be asked beyond the traditional focus on the diversity of the scientific workforce, although we believe this continues to be an extremely important topic. We saw (as well as experienced) that science was not a meritocracy, and that the differing career paths of individuals were embedded in a history of science that was entrenched in certain gender, race, class and national norms and cultures. Our readings and discussions took us deeper as we explored the social and political nature of scientific knowledge production. Science was committed, we came to realize, to certain political economies, geographies, philosophies and histories. While the questions we asked, the methodologies we employed, and the conclusions we drew in our biological research seemed 'obvious' from our disciplinary trainings, we recognized those naturalized impulses as historically and politically embedded. However, these interdisciplinary insights and understandings are not so easy to sustain in the purified world of any discipline. In the sciences, culture and politics are considered irrelevant to scientific pursuits. Within the world of basic scientific research, 'nature' is ontologically real, and separate from the messy world of human entanglements. The scientific researcher is an abstract node, a replaceable investigator in knowledge production, whose personal politics and ideologies are irrelevant to the production of knowledge. Finally, the scientific method is seen as epistemologically pure and the scientist as able to pursue the abstract and intricate workings of the natural world. Biological research can thus produce generalizable and verifiable results separate from the often subjective constructs of the social and cultural worlds. It is virtually impossible to investigate or theorize the interconnections of nature and culture in 'pure' science journals and departments. These are relegated to the applied and social sciences.

Given these realities, developing an interdisciplinary natural science/humanities/social science project, especially one that that engages the ideological and political nature of science, is a difficult academic endeavour, yet one to which we are committed. These are interdisciplinary terrains that we are still discovering and negotiating. To us, each of the disciplines brings something uniquely valuable. We must say at the outset that, from our location as scientists, we are committed to scientific practice and the possibility of understanding and elucidating the mechanisms that sustain biological populations and processes. For us scientific knowledge is crucial in our engagement with the natural world and the possibility of a sustainable planet.

We have read with interest and sympathy many of the critiques of modern science, including those that have called for a total rejection of science, together with its inherently reductionist and violent epistemology and methodology.[8] While we take some of these critiques to heart, we find that many ignore the heterogeneity within science and reduce science to a monolithic caricature with uniform ideology, methodology and epistemology. Scientific practitioners are likewise presented as naïve, apolitical pawns, unaware of or unmoved by their collusion with and in modern capitalism and neocolonialism. Colonialism, similarly, is presented as entirely hegemonic and totalizing in its impact.[9] However, over the last few decades, postcolonial scholars, especially those in Subaltern Studies, have argued and documented the heterogeneity in colonialism's impact as well as local resistances and insurgencies among those colonized. Similarly, scholars in Science Studies have showed the heterogeneity within science and the history of science – not only in its methods but also in its practitioners and their ideologies.

Science has a long history of critics and dissenters; we are inspired and empowered by that history. Like the critics we are often dismayed by the rise of the science/industry/military complex, the patenting of genetic organisms, the prevalence of biological determinism, the uncritical support of the human genome project, the proliferation of genetically modified food and organisms, etcetera. These issues energize and impassion many scientists (as they do us) who have vociferously opposed and have spoken against the scientific merits and ideological commitments of such projects. While the sciences have been used to secure patriarchal, capitalist interests and have been historically linked to them, we do not want to relinquish science to these interests. We embrace science, as others have, for its progressive possibilities that will enable us to build a sustainable world. Furthermore, some critics of science who reject science have postulated the embrace of local 'knowledges' and practices. While we believe local knowledges and practices are crucial to a sustainable world, we do not believe they need be in competition with science as an either/or choice.

While we embrace science and technology, we are always aware of their ethical, political, economic, cultural and ideological connections, often beyond our individual control. While we take issue with those critics who reject science entirely, those who advocate an unquestioned support of science and scientific objectivity equally trouble us. To us the history of science and the current privatization and commodification of science are a testament to the deeply political and ideological nature of science. We are deeply aware of the problematic history of science – of eugenics, Nazi science, Tuskegee syphilis experiments, the atomic bomb – and its role in colonialism and modern capitalist expansions. Science, like any institution, is always embedded in politics and should never be beyond critique. Whether science is advocated by globalists, nationalists or fundamentalists, it should not blind us to the systematic marginalization of certain groups and knowledges in the name of science or development.

Even though we embrace science and scientific practice, 'global' science is not inherently superior to local knowledges and practices.

Vandana Shiva and Meera Nanda are both important and influential voices in the debates around science and local knowledges. Their work and critiques have deeply influenced our own thinking on the subject, although we do not agree with all their positions. We are deeply moved by Vandana Shiva's essay in this collection and share her vision of agricultural practices that pay attention to the complexities of ecological processes. We agree with her vision that we must develop sustainable practices that utilize the vast and complex resources of a diverse array of organisms. However, we would argue that this is not alien to the world of science. Many progressive scientists work with farmers in developing sustainable ways of farming. Such sustainable practices, in our vision of science, are not contradictory.

Second, while Shiva's vision of nature is wonderful, as ecologists we must point out that this 'nature' also includes pathogens, parasites and processes that do not always lead to such an idyllic vision. There are natural toxins in nature, and 'natural' processes by themselves do not necessarily lead to a more sustainable world. For example, Jim Bever's work[10] on the relationship of soil communities and plants shows that ecological interactions are complex. While plants can develop mutualistic and symbiotic relationships with their soil communities, plants also attract pathogens and parasites. These complex ecological processes can result in negative feedback cycles – so that plant communities can contribute to a decrease in the productivity of a plant over time instead of increasing it. Nature is not always harmonious or comforting. We find ourselves between two contrasting visions on the nature of nature – the exploitation of nature by science and capitalism and the idyllic vision of a harmonious and benign nature by ecofeminists. As ecologists, we feel we can embrace neither. The material body of nature is complex and should not be reduced discursively to be either a monster or a friend.

Similarly, Meera Nanda's critiques of the limits of indigenous knowledges are very persuasive. Academic discourse that silence the subaltern only to speak for them are indeed dangerous. We agree with her that local indigenous practices are not always pure and should not necessarily be exalted in the name of pluralism. As she points out, patriarchal and feudal practices are deeply embedded in local practices and should be interrogated and condemned as such.

However, we believe we must extend such critiques to science as well. While post-development should not be top-down, neither should science. The institution of science as it is practised today is deeply hierarchical and top-down. While we cannot accord local knowledges epistemic purity, neither can we do the same for science. We should treat neither as grand theories – both are problematic, embedded in different histories, geographies and politics. While we embrace the possibilities of a progressive science, there is nothing in the history of science *per se* that encourages the hope that science will 'enable the subaltern to see through the mystification of their inherited dialogues'. Western science has been hegemonic and we need to understand the ways in which it has appropriated, dismissed or supplanted other forms of inquiry and practices. Conversely, as Nanda suggests, we need to understand the limitations of local knowledges as well. It seems that such discussions cannot be productive while we continue exalting either science or local knowledges, the primacy of the global or the local; instead, we need to pay more attention to the vast negotiable spaces in between these polarities.

We locate ourselves squarely, rejecting what we see as two unproductive and artificially created binaries – pro-science/anti-science, pro-global/anti-global, pro-local/anti-local. We embrace a contextual combination of both, committed to a reflexive and situated practice of science,[11] one that involves local communities while it embraces the progressive possibilities of a global and local science. Further, while the context in which science is done, and its ethical, historical and political ramifications are all crucial to us, so equally is an understanding of 'nature'. Nature is not entirely semiotic and in the realm of discourse; it is simultaneously deeply material, with its own agency and regulatory practices.

We cannot build dreams or visions of a sustainable world from our armchairs. Science and technology are important. 'Nature' in all its aspects – the flora and fauna that share our planet, the environments, principles and variables that govern their and our lives – are necessary ingredients of any such dreams or visions. We recognize the social embeddedness of such practice and the need and possibility of a reflexive scientific practice that painstakingly examines the context, rhetoric, and conditions under which scientific experimentation takes place. While truth and scientific knowledge may always be partial and situated, the knowledge that science can bring about natural processes is vital.

In this chapter we use a project on invasion biology that we have embarked on collaboratively as a case study to show how we can develop an interdisciplinary research agenda in the sciences – to develop an account of natural and biological processes embedded and enmeshed in cultural and political contexts. To us, such interdisciplinary practices are crucial to any vision of 'post-development' or progressive political action. We begin by elaborating on our conception of 'global circulations', followed by an analysis of our case study of invasion biology. Here, we describe current scientific theories and research on plant invasions followed by an analysis of how deeply cultural the rhetoric of 'nature' is. We conclude with our vision for interdisciplinary work across the humanities, natural and social sciences. At the core of this vision is the imperative that we simultaneously study nature(s) and culture(s).

Global circulations

We entitle our chapter 'Global Circulations' to call attention to the circulations of science, technology and development. None of these are static fields; they are made up of theories, ideas and practices that circulate across time, space and regions. In the contemporary globalized world, these circulations reach the far corners of the globe: decisions in the World Bank in Washington DC, for example, impact on tiny villages across the globe. The title of the chapter is also intended to underscore the profound contemporary impact of globalization, *the* emergent phenomenon of our times, on nations and nationalisms, on the global and the local, and on notions of hybridity and purity. The tensions between globalization and localization, and who is empowered to determine these, are central to the contradictions of our times. On one hand, national boundaries have been transgressed by a world consumerist culture – popular music, McDonalds, Pizza Hut, designer clothes, cosmetics, World Wrestling Federation – that the upper/middle classes across the globe share. Yet, simultaneously, cultural and religious nationalism – the call for the promotion of national and local cultures and values – is also growing. Medical sciences and drugs have dramatically increased life expectancy and the quality of life, yet classes of people in virtually all countries, including the industrial West, do not enjoy these benefits and have virtually no access to these breakthroughs. The World Wide Web connects people from remote corners of the world in common chat rooms and news groups, while others have not heard of a computer. Corporations, free marketers, and the governments of certain countries are developing international treaties and organizations such as NAFTA and WTO to make national boundaries permeable to the free flow of money, goods, people, plants and animals. In response, environmentalists, some farmers, labour unions and activists have lobbied against these stressing the exploitation of workers, the needs of local employment, environmental standards and regulations.

Proponents and opponents of globalization signal the tensions of living in an unequal world with a history of colonialism. 'Development' is one area in which issues of globalization and localization are central. We use the case of invasion biology because we believe issues of development and globalization are central to the story of native and exotic plants. While the panic over exotic species occurs in many countries, our study focuses on the US to highlight the local–global connections, development and environmentalism, globalization and localization.

Invasion biology: a case study

Charles S. Elton's classic book *The Ecology of Invasions* (1958) has led to much interest in studying and cataloguing the establishment and spread of exotic and non-native species in native plant communities and in the landscape in general.[12] Over the last twenty years, ecologists and conservation biologists have chronicled the impact of alien/foreign species on native plants and animals, studying various aspects of the biology of native and exotic plants.[13] While many 'immigrant' species enter new habitats, few survive and only a fraction become naturalized. Some naturalized species, however, become invasive. The field focuses on developing a typology of those species and the conditions that result in invasions in order to develop some predictive power on future invasions. Introduced exotic plant species are believed to impact negatively on managed and unmanaged ecosystems by competing with 'desirable' native species and degrading important ecosystem properties. Invaded ecosystems have been shown to experience dramatic changes in many ecological characteristics such as soil chemistry,[14] fire regimes[15] and local hydrology.[16] These changes in the ecosystem function can then further accelerate the future invasion of these communities. It is believed that virtually all communities can be or have been invaded; communities clearly differ in their susceptibility to invasion by exotic plant species. Several censuses document the increase of exotic and alien plants and the corresponding decrease in native species, often to alarming degrees. Overall, the research in the field characterizes the current status as a national crisis, with the geographic scope and impact alarming. We have seen the development of local and national projects across the country focusing on biological invasions, and the creation of conferences and forums at national meetings devoted to the issue. Local and national restoration projects have also developed, while national and local societies eradicate exotic species and promote the use and establishment of local species.

The rhetoric of invasion

We began this project wanting to explore some of the larger questions the biological literature raised, and in particular to focus on the impact of native and exotic plants on their soils. As we got into the project, we were struck by the rhetoric surrounding plant and animal migrations and the striking parallels with the rhetoric of human immigration. The very term 'invasion' suggests alarm, the influx of a larger volume of undesirable aliens. The terminology of plant and animal migrants – alien, resident and naturalized species – closely parallels that applied to human immigrants. The very terminological distinction between 'native' and 'exotic' species is deeply problematic given the history of migrations over the past centuries. The biological literature, and reports in the popular press in particular, describe the presence of exotics as an 'onslaught'.[17] One article summarizes it as, 'They Came, They Bred, They Conquered'.[18] The rhetoric seems unmistakable and transfers common concerns about alien peoples to alien plants and animals: for example, questions such as hygiene and disease (aliens spreading disease and threatening drinking water); looking different or 'other'; changing familiar landscapes; silently growing in strength and number; surviving under the most extreme conditions with little resources; aggressive predators and pests; hypersexed females and prolific reproducers; parasites on the economy; aliens that consume a lot but contribute little.[19] Nancy Tomes's work on germ panics in the twentieth century suggests that anxieties about immigrants often spill over into our conceptions of nature. She documents how the panic about immigrants spilled over into a panic about germs. The current panic around biological invasions suggests that our anxieties about foreigners are spilling over into a panic about foreign plants and animals.[20]

We find this argument particularly compelling given what gets left out in much of the popular rhetoric surrounding exotic and alien species. For example, the fact that nearly all the US crops are exotic plants, while most of the insects that cause crop damage are native.[21] There is little mention of the tremendous benefits from alien plants and animals (just as in the case of humans). There is virtually no mention of the problematic term 'native'. (Who is native? Who gets to define it?) Finally, and most pertinent to this chapter is that the changing landscape is blamed on aliens and foreigners. There is little focus on the continual degradation of land in the name of development. Rather than focus on the degradation of the quality of land which helps the establishment of weedy species (not just aliens/exotics), current management focuses on policing borders to prevent entry of foreign plants and animals, and on crude efforts to exterminate a few introduced species. For example, President Clinton's 1999 executive order creating the National Invasive Species Management Plan is entirely directed at federal agencies to 'mobilize the federal government to defend against these aggressive predators and pests'. So, rather than rethink growth, which causes the continual deforestation and development of land, we focus instead on policing our borders and boundaries. A study of contemporary discourse suggests that the language of exotic/alien plant and animal invasions reflects a pervasive nativism in conservation biology; a nativism that blames the alien and the foreign for the changing US landscape.[22]

What is striking to us is that rarely is there similar panic around other issues that may contribute to the rise of exotic species and the loss of native biodiversity. Unchecked development, weak environmental controls, and the free flow of agricultural plants and animals across national borders in the name of globalization remain invisible and unproblematized. By identifying the exotic species as the problem, other potential agents of biodiversity loss, such as habitat destruction, are ignored, free of responsibility. The shift of focus onto foreign plants and animals depoliticizes a political problem.

Plants that originate in Eurasia, for example, dominate much of the landscape of Southern California. Many of these plant species were purposely introduced either as crops or as forage for cattle. The preservation and re-establishment of the native flora is the focus of an active movement. While this movement is diverse, a major effort of this movement, and the component of the movement that is endorsed by local, state and federal governments, focuses on the problem of introduced species. However, ecological research has identified that the success of exotic plant species in Southern California is tied to two factors. First, many exotic plant species are more resistant to overgrazing and therefore reached dominance during the long history of profit-driven exploitation of often privately owned land by always privately owned cattle. Second, our own research has identified that many exotic plant species are more successful in disturbed soil, and have therefore increased in response to land use during recent 'development', including the massive disturbances of land for modern agriculture, suburbanization, military exercises and off-road vehicle recreation. Viewed in this way, the dominance of exotic plants in Southern California is a symptom or consequence of past and current development, rather than the cause of the loss of native biodiversity. Problematizing unsustainable land-use practices would quickly focus attention on who made and benefited from these practices – a very political issue of differences in power that government agencies would not endorse. But displacement of blame to 'foreign' plants frees the human agents, the political and economic drivers behind such a problem, from responsibility. Displacement of blame to foreigners, however, does not solve the problem of the extinction of species and the degradation of habitats; indeed, it dilutes our efforts to reverse these trends.

The consequences of unchecked development and growth in the name of globalization remain invisible and unproblematized. What is striking to us about this case study is the global circulation of science and the interconnections between science and politics in contemporary globalization. The inequality of global wealth and opportunities leads to human global migrations; these in turn shape local contexts and issues; and ultimately these local contexts transfer human politics to plants and animals, which in turn demonizes human migrations. What gets little interrogation in the current case are those inequities of wealth and opportunities, and their connections to global capital, globalization and permeable borders.

Intervening in the politics of knowledge

What this project has taught us is the inextricable connection between science and politics. The project leads us into more fundamental questions of the field of ecology. Who/what is native? Who gets to define it? What is considered natural? What models or frameworks surround the use of nature and the natural? What practices and ideas are mobilized in the name of nature? Historically, for example, racism (and in contemporary discourse, heterosexism) and other forms of oppression have been explicitly defended in the name of the 'natural'. These questions are also particularly salient in ecology, where descriptive models of the processes of 'nature' are central to the field. In invasion biology today, foreign plants are eradicated in the name of the natural. How have we evolved around a common rhetoric of the foreign/alien? How have we come to address questions of diversity and difference? It is apparent that ecological research can benefit immensely from such reflexivity – or tracing the interconnecting histories of our theories of plants and animals and those of humans. Language is not the irrelevant, transparent piece of communication that is still taught in graduate programmes in the sciences. It is, instead, potent, central and consequential to the enterprise of science. The reflexivity that an attention to language, history and politics gives us in the present case of invasion biology will help enact better public policy and environmental regulations. It forces us to interrogate the nexus of power in contemporary globalization instead of powerless and poor immigrants.

We realize that our vision of interdisciplinarity does not create an explicit counter-model; that rejecting two binaries does not articulate a new alternative. However, we believe that grand theories have been precisely the problem of development. Our focus is not a new grand practice but rather a call for new processes of negotiations. The grand theories of science must be put to local tests, but not in exporting global practices into local contexts, as in the high-input agriculture that recreate unsustainable practices of agriculture. Instead it is in a contextual science that takes local ecologies, cultures, histories, economies and geographies into consideration. Clearly the nature of the negotiations and solutions will differ in different places. Such negotiated practices must be negotiations of the material and the discursive. Our vision of new processes is one of creating new conditions that will allow certain kinds of knowledge to emerge and flourish.

To us the possibility of such interdisciplinary work is exciting. It brings together the very things modernity divided – the body and the mind; the rational and the emotional; objectivity and subjectivity; ethics, morality and aesthetics with costs and benefits. It allows the possibility of understanding the natural world we live in as participants and co-creators of the same world. The tensions and divisions that emerge in the world are precisely because modernity allows us to separate and reduce what was once whole. Any vision of post-development must bring these parts together again.

Notes

1 Serres and Latour (1995).
2 Latour (1993).
3 We use the term 'feminist science studies' in this essay to include feminist work on technology and development studies. While these fields are in many ways separate, they are interrelated in the inextricable interconnections between science, technology and development. Furthermore, all the fields share a common critique of modernity and its claims.
4 See Haraway (1997) and Goodeve (1999).
5 See for example the works of Ruth Bleier, Evelynn Hammonds, Donna Haraway, Ruth Hubbard, Evelyn Fox Keller, Helen Longino, Anne Fausto Sterling.
6 Haraway (1997).
7 Nandy (1988).
8 See, for example, the works of Vandana Shiva, Ashis Nandy, Claude Alvares.
9 Guha (1997).
10 Bever, Westover and Antonovics (1997: 561–73); Bever (1994: 1965–77).
11 Haraway (1988: 575–99).
12 Elton (1959).
13 For example, see Burke and Grime (1996: 776–90); Groves and Burdon (1986); Mooney and Drake (1986).
14 Vitousek and Walker (1989: 247–65).
15 Mack (1981: 145–65).
16 Walker and Smith (1997: 69–86).
17 Mack *et al.* (2000: 1).
18 Bright (1999: 51).
19 For a discussion on the rhetoric of biological invasions, see Subramaniam (2001: 26–40).
20 Tomes (2000: 191–9).
21 Sagoff (2000, B7).
22 Paretti (1998: 183–92).

11

Do the Marginalized Valorize the Margins?

Exploring the Dangers of Difference

Meera Nanda

I want to begin with a real-life story from Shashi Tharoor's *India: From Midnight to the Millennium*. In the passage quoted below, Shashi, an upper-caste, very liberal-left urbanite from Bombay, is talking to Charlis, a *dalit*[1] from a small village in Kerala. The two men have known each other since they met as boys in Shashi's ancestral village. Shashi had befriended the untouchable boy out of a sense of outrage against his more traditional, caste-bound cousins who would not allow Charlis to play with them. At the time of this conversation, Shashi is attending an élite English-language college in Delhi, which will then bring him to the US and to the UN (where he works as a senior officer in the office of Kofi Annan). Charlis is pulling himself up by his bootstraps: determined to get an education, he has made it to a provincial college near his village – the first in his community to come this far. Here is a part of their conversation:

> From the front pocket of this shirt, he drew out a battered notebook filled with small, tightly packed curlicues of Malayalam writing … interspersed with phrases and sentences in English.... 'Look,' he said, jabbing at a page, 'The miserable hath no other medicine/But only hope. – Shakespeare, *Measure for Measure*, III, 1, 2.' [Some more Shakespeare follows.]
>
> 'Whenever I am reading something that inspires me, I am writing it down in this book,' Charlis said proudly. 'Shakespeare is great man, isn't it?' [Some conversation follows and then Charlis reads out another verse.]
>
> 'For the Colonel's lady and Judy O'Grady,' he declaimed at one point, 'are sisters under their skins.' – 'Rudyard Kipling,' he added. 'Is that how you are pronouncing it?'
>
> 'Rudyard, Roodyard, I haven't a clue,' I confessed. 'But who cares Charlis?

He is just an old imperialist fart. What does anything he wrote have anything to do with any of us today, in independent India?

Charlis looked surprised, then slightly averted his eyes. 'But are we not,' he asked softly, 'are we not brothers under our skins?'

'Of course,' I replied, too quickly. And it was I who could not meet his gaze.

Dead white men's poems: words of 'imperialist farts' for one, and affirmation of an egalitarian idea for another.

This conversation highlights the disjuncture I want to discuss here, namely, the disjuncture between the postcolonial critics of modernity and development and the women on whose behalf they claim to speak.

I will treat Tharoor as a stand-in for the broad class of intellectuals in and from the postcolonial world who are intimately familiar with the West, but who feel compelled to say a 'No' to it, or who, at the very least, feel compelled to approach the West with a presumption of radical difference. Given the limited and uneven reach of development, these intellectuals have come to see their own access to modern scientific learning and modern institutions as a source of their alienation from the lifeworld of the non-modern masses. Not only do these angst-ridden intellectuals desperately wish to speak in a popular idiom derived from symbols and myths shared with the masses, but they also believe that this idiom can provide templates for different sciences, different institutions and, indeed, different ways of being altogether. These differences are valued as seedbeds of alternatives to both capitalism and socialism.

But what of Charlis? Going by his passionate engagement with the words of dead white men, it is clear that he does *not* approach them with a presumption of radical difference. Far from it: he finds in them intellectual resources to combat the difference he has suffered all his life at the hands of upper castes. Contrary to the postcolonial intellectuals who look to 'Third World difference' as a source of salvation, Charlis-the-subaltern is not interested in affirming *any* difference: *he want to put difference out of business altogether.* After all, it is not the Kipling who declared the impossibility of the East meeting the West, but the Kipling who declares 'sisterhood under the skin' who has captured Charlis's imagination.

I want to explore a most peculiar twist in this encounter: the postcolonial intellectual justifies her presumption of radical difference toward the West *in the name of the subaltern* who, if Charlis is our guide, seem to be making a presumption of universalism toward the West. So the question I want to ask is simple: how do discourses of difference actually play out in Third World societies? Can we simply *assume* the consent of the subaltern for embracing 'their own' local knowledge? Can we, to borrow Nancy Fraser's question (1995), assume that a struggle for *recognition* of non-Western, non-modern difference will help bring about a *redistribution* of economic and cultural power within these societies?

Limiting myself to my native India, I will examine three case studies. First the case of Viramma, a remarkable *dalit* woman whose first-person narrative of her life has recently appeared as a book (Viramma and Racine 1997). Here we ask how deep is the difference between Viramma and Western or Westernized Indian women? Is Viramma 'like us, only more so', as Susan Moller Okin (1994) has affirmed? Or does any presumption of shared knowledges and needs between Viramma and the Western women amount to 'discursive colonization' or 'feminist Orientalism' as Chandra Mohanty (1988) and Frédérique Apffel-Marglin (1994), respectively, have charged? For our next two cases, we move from the subaltern to the intellectuals and their acts of commission and omission. The acts of commission take us to the arguments for Third World ecofeminism made most prominently by Vandana Shiva. I ask who exactly is pushing for Shiva's neo-Hindu notions of *prakriti* and *Shakti* – the subaltern women like Viramma or the landed, upper-caste exploiters of these women? I will argue that, far from empowering women like Viramma, ecofeminism has come to serve as a mobilizing ideology of surplus-producing, landowning farmers. Finally, for the acts of omission of difference-oriented theorists, we go to Prem Chowdhry's (1994) study titled *The Veiled Women,* which offers a cautionary tale for all those who denounce modern technology *itself* as fundamentally patriarchal. Chowdhry shows how the pre-existing, religion- and culture-sanctified patriarchal bargains are soaking up the liberatory aspects of the shift from private to public patriarchy made possible by the Green Revolution.

Post-development discourse

But before proceeding with my case studies, I want to define more precisely who my interlocutors are and what exactly concerns me about their critiques of development. Defining postcolonial intellectuals as those who say no to the West is to cast too wide a net. There are those who may say no to particular economic and political policies of the West, and many others who may be troubled by the uneven and exploitative mode of development under capitalism. I have nothing to say about these critics, except that I count myself as one of them.

My concern is limited only to those critics who are postcolonial or post-developmentalist in a strong sense of the word; that is, who bring a post-Enlightenment world view to bear on the problems of development. I include here critics with very different theoretical orientations, including Gandhian communitarians like Ashis Nandy, Vandana Shiva and Claude Alvares;[2] Foucauldians like Arturo Escobar (1992), ethno-sociologists like the Marglins (Apffel-Marglin 1990), and feminist critics like Jane Parpart, Marianne Marchand and their colleagues (Marchand and Parpart 1995) who locate their project in feminist theories of difference. These critics see development as a source of violence, both real and symbolic, towards non-Western people. The violence comes from subjecting non-Western people to a culturally alien, ethnocentric and colonial imaginary of what it means to be developed; forcing them to measure the worth of their lives and their communities by Western norms; and, in the process, silencing their own norms of a good society.

The source of this symbolic violence, or 'the motor of the crisis', as Braidotti and her colleagues (1994) put it, is modern science itself. Scientific rationality, the critics claim, has hidden its Eurocentric and patriarchal interests behind its claims of objective and universally valid knowledge. Riding on the false claims of objectivity and propelled by imperialist interests, modern science has established itself as the norm of what it means to be rational and objective. All other ways of comprehending the world have been delegitimized. Post-developmentalist critics ask not for better implementation of this or that development policy, but for pluralizing the norms of development themselves, for allowing non-Western people to define development in their own culturally grounded conceptual categories to meet these needs through their own local sciences and technologies.

As will become clearer as we proceed, I fully welcome the idea of using local cultural discourses to enable and encourage a more participatory and egalitarian modernization. But the kind of emphasis one finds in post-developmentalist discourse goes far beyond such a strategic use of culture and verges on *culturalism*, which regards the conceptual and imaginary representations of existing cultures in modernizing societies as the ultimate and irreducible force in development.[3] Protestations to the contrary, I will argue that the kind of culturalism one finds in post-developmentalist discourses reifies non-Western cultures by setting them up as the 'Other' of the West and not examining the content and actual practices that give substance – often a highly oppressive and illiberal substance, I may say – to the traditions of these cultures. The post-developmentalist notion of the non-Western cultures is shaped by the ideological needs of *Western* intellectuals (and their 'anti-imperialist' cultural nationalistic allies in the Third World) to invest other cultures with critical force against their own supposedly hyper-rational, one-dimensional scientistic culture. This radical xenophilia of Western intellectuals has minimized the theoretical space for a critical assessment of non-Western cultures.

Let us return, for the moment, to where we started from in our Shashi–Charlis dialogue. *Post-development critics make a presumption of radical difference toward rationality itself*: norms of what is rational, warranted and truthful are '*completely constituted* by the distinctive cultural inheritance of different cultures,' as Sandra Harding (1998) has declared in her recent book, *Is Science Multicultural?* or as Ashis Nandy (1993) put it much earlier in his *Intimate Enemy*. The question before us is: what would Charlis say? Would *he* feel content to rediscover his own definition of what is rational? More importantly, will his own culturally constructed rationality be so different from modern scientific rationality that he will feel violated and silenced by it? Does Charlis see modern scientific rationality and its world view as an enemy or an ally in his fight against his local oppressors?

It will be useful to dwell upon the larger debate about scientific rationality because the culturalism of post-development discourse uses the idea of 'different cultures, different rationalities, different sciences' to legitimate itself. The argument that all of us – and not just Charlis – should prefer Charlis's own standards of rationality in order to get a 'strong objectivity' against the supposedly phoney objectivity of science has been made most forcefully by Sandra Harding, most recently in her *Is Science Multicultural?* where she extends standpoint epistemology into postcolonial concerns. Harding (1998: 44) is emphatic that 'modern science is at an epistemological par with other cultures' traditions of systematic knowledge: they are all equally local knowledge systems, for they are all *completely constituted* by their respective local cultures. Thus there could be many universally valid but culturally distinct sciences.' What is more, Harding insists that the distinct sciences of different cultures are not parts of a puzzle that will all eventually fit together, but they are, as she puts it, 'fundamentally incompatible knowledge claims, encoding different norms shaped by each culture's distinctive discursive inheritance.' Harding is hardly alone: similar claims are the staple of contemporary cultural and social constructivist studies of science.[4]

As this chapter is not about the philosophy of science, I will not go on to refute Harding's claim here.[5] I will only point to what troubles me about this thesis of cultural construction of the very norms of rationality: *treating rationality and knowledge as completely constructed by culture puts culture beyond a reasoned critique.* If at no point in our inquiry can we go beyond, or refute, the cultural categories that we inherit, how can we obtain any critical distance from these categories? Of course, Harding, Donna Haraway and their sympathizers would say that we *can* go beyond inherited cultural assumptions through purposefully adopting the standpoint of the underdog. Underdogs don't need value neutrality, or objectivity, which are Western cultural values anyway. They can legitimately claim the status of science for inquiry based upon their own culturally embedded assumptions – say, of treating nature as sacred, as Shiva argues, or treating the natural and the supernatural as one and the same, as Frédérique Apffel-Marglin argues. Once these local ways of knowing are positively evaluated as sciences and not just folk beliefs, the subaltern and their sympathizers can use them as legitimate norms of rationality against which they measure modern science's assumptions, methods and claims. Well, seeing modern science from the underdog's standpoint *will* reveal differences. But why should it follow that the underdog will reject the difference as alien and undesirable? Moreover, even if adopting a local standpoint can help the underdog see through 'Western science', it still evades the issue of how it can help them see through their own religion – and tradition-sanctified dominant ideologies.

The insistence on local rationalities as progressive standpoints of the oppressed flies in the face of *real* movements of the oppressed, the most radical of which have all been firmly in the Enlightenment mode (Nanda, forthcoming). Take the anti-caste movement of B. R. Ambedkar which, in a sharp contrast to Gandhi's reformist overtures to the untouchables, was a radical attack on the ideology of caste itself. Ambedkar and his *dalit* followers challenged the Brahmanical knowledge about the natural world not in the name of their own dalit caste myths and origin stories but in the name of scientifically obtained objective truth. Unlike their academic sympathizers, the organic intellectuals of *dalits* and women – say an Ambedkar, or a Pandita Rama Bai, people who personally suffered the worst insults and degradations of the traditional Hindu order – were never content to build a counter-hegemony around the standpoint of the *dalits* or women. As Ambedkar repeatedly emphasized, the annihilation of caste would require a challenge to the entire Hindu cosmology that assumes the sacredness of nature and the continuity of the natural and the supernatural – precisely because this kind of 'local knowledge' was used to justify the rationality of Karma and caste. Ambedkar, in other words, linked the liberation of *dalits* to *overturning* the kind of cultural assumptions about sacredness and holism that people like Harding, Apffel-Marglin and Shiva see as the standpoint of oppressed. Ambedkar was convinced that only a secularization of consciousness through a rigorous application of reason and the scientific temper could bring about a transformative change. If Charlis has been influenced in any way by Ambedkar, as most progressive *dalits* are, I am ready to bet that he would any day opt for modern science over Hindu cosmology as his own standpoint.

Viramma

But let us get down to the specifics. Viramma is a Tamil-speaking *dalit* woman in her sixties who narrated the story of her life and the life of her community to two ethnographers who published the entire narrative in her own voice. From the opening sentence ('My paternal grandfather was a serf of the Reddi...') we meet this energetic, life-loving, sharp-witted and sharp-tongued woman who is simultaneously a mother, a wife, a farm worker, a midwife, a devout believer in a whole pantheon of goddesses, a singer of songs, a lead-organizer of religious festivals – all in all, a pillar of her community. Viramma's ability to create a life of love, laughter and meaning is all the more remarkable because she has had more than her share of avoidable misery, losing nine of her 12 children to perfectly curable, ordinary infectious diseases. And she has had more than anyone's share of humiliations at the hands of the upper-caste landlords. No one's fool, Viramma understands perfectly well that the upper castes exploit her labour, and feels perfectly justified in stealing from them. But her everyday resistance is bounded by her internalization of the idea of purity and pollution. She sees caste humiliations as deserved because of the sins in past lives of her entire community.

I want to bring the concerns of the critics of modernity and modern science to bear upon Viramma's life. Is it the case that Viramma experiences modern institutions and knowledge as alien impositions contrary to her own practical and strategic interests? Is it the case that Viramma's local knowledge as a midwife is embedded in a wholly different and more enabling rationality?

Viramma's relationship with modern institutions and ideas is too complex to allow a neat for-or-against classification. She has lived through truly epochal changes, including India's independence, Indira Gandhi, the slow-but-sure loosening of caste hierarchy, the spread of wage labour in place of caste duties, the rising aspirations of her son, the coming of the TV, and so on. While she loves the idea of a woman as prime minister, and values the opportunity to send her son (not her daughters) to school, she finds the new militancy among the younger generation unnerving, and she abhors the TV.

Being a midwife and a healer, her main contact with modern institutions is through public health workers who visit the village for vaccinations, family planning and childbirth. Again, Viramma simultaneously reaches out and avoids: she seems to appreciate the value of timely medical intervention, cooperates with the nurses and seeks modern alternatives for all complicated pregnancies she attends to. But she hates the way the nurses and doctors treat her and others from her community. She finds them arrogant and full of caste prejudice. This love–hate relationship holds even with traditional healing practices that are deeply intertwined with religion. Viramma believes that diseases like smallpox, cholera and hepatitis are caused by the presence of angry goddesses who must be appeased with worship and gifts. She is slow in accepting smallpox vaccination and continues to combine modern treatments with traditional worship.

Modern medicine *is* experienced as different, in part threatening and in part life-saving. The question is *at what level* does the difference operate: at the level of rationality of modern medicine itself, or at the level of institutions? Of course, even an analytical separation between rationality and institutions is unacceptable to critics like Apffel-Marglin, Nandy and their Foucauldian colleagues, who see knowledge and institutional power as co-constructing each other. They explain

Viramma's discomfort with modern medicine as a reflection of her non-logocentric world view in which the natural and the supernatural, health and disease are not separated from each other as polar opposites, but each contains elements of the other: nature is enchanted, and health includes disease and death. What is more, they have claimed that modern hospitals cannot, even in principle, meet Viramma's needs for they incorporate a bipolar, logocentric reasoning (Apffel-Marglin 1990).

But there is very little sign of non-logocentricity in Viramma's local knowledge. She invokes gods and goddesses in order to explain, predict and control disease, just as we moderns invoke the germ theory of disease. There is no sign whatsoever that she offers prayers to the person afflicted with smallpox because she is simultaneously celebrating health, as Marglin has claimed. Whatever the outsiders may read into it, Viramma herself is very clear that her prayers are meant only to cajole the goddess to leave them alone. Absence of the goddess is welcomed as absence of disease. If we take Viramma at her word, we will find that gods and goddesses serve fairly down-to-earth instrumental rationality that seeks freedom from suffering. There is no reason to insist that incommensurability of rationalities will forever make modern medicine alien and oppressive to Viramma. Pitching difference at the level of rationality ignores the possibility of institutional reform, and turns a blind eye to the fact that, after all, Viramma, with all her expert local knowledge and all her mother's love, could not prevent nine of her twelve babies from dying. To conclude: yes, Viramma resists modernization but *not* because of her standpoint epistemology, which actually contains elements of instrumental rationality expressed in a religious idiom.

Ecofeminism

Let us move to the best-known case feminists have made for local knowledges, namely, Vandana Shiva's arguments for Third World ecofeminism. As I have examined Shiva's essentialism and standpoint epistemology in two previous papers (Nanda 1990; 1997) I won't repeat these arguments. Here I want to deal with Shiva's much admired 'politicization' of 'Third World difference': even those who find Shiva's essentialism and romanticism troubling praise her for politicizing the issue of Third World women's subsistence needs and their culturally distinctive uses of nature. But this begs the question: must feminists welcome *all* politicization as progressive? Should we not ask what kind of politicization of difference Shiva's ideas have brought about in India? So I ask a simple question: what has happened to Shiva's idea of the feminine principle in the ten years since her book *Staying Alive* put it on the agenda of new social movements around the world? Which political constituencies have used it and to what end? I want to be clear that the remarks that follow are meant solely to assess the influence of the idea of ecofeminism and not the personal political beliefs of anyone involved.

Gail Omvedt (1993: 316), a sympathetic critic of ecofeminism, provides a fair summary of Shiva's influence in her recent book, *Reinventing Revolution*: 'Shiva's articulation of the feminine principle that sees united action by women and men to transform society in a feminist, ecological and participatory direction finds its echoes in the themes of *stri shakti* [women's power] within the women's movement connected with the Shetkari Sanghathan and other rural organizations.' These are powerful farmers' movements of landowning, surplus-producing commercial farmers who are simultaneously aligned against the state, from whom they demand higher subsidies for modern inputs and higher prices for their crops, and against the mostly *dalit* landless and migrant workers who do not receive even the barest minimum wages.

These farmers' movements differ in their caste, class and ideological orientations. Media reports from India indicate that Shiva is personally involved as an adviser and supporter of the Gandhian, 'anti-imperialist' movement KRRS in Karnataka, and has also lent at least her tactical support to the populist, upper-caste and severely patriarchal Bharatiya Kisan Union (BKU) in Uttar Pradesh, an organization that actively campaigned for Hindu fundamentalists in the 1991 elections. Shiva's idea of *prakriti* and the feminine principle has found a wider women's constituency in the more free-market-oriented, neoliberal Shetkari Sanghathan in Maharashtra. The Sanghathan's 'Laxmi Mukti' (Laxmi-the-goddess liberation) is based upon ecofeminist principles and has won the support of well-known Indian feminists, including Gail Omvedt and Madhu Kishwar. Even Bina Agarwal offers words of praise for the ecofeminist elements of the Shetkari Sanghathan programme in her otherwise remarkable book, *A Field of Her Own*.

But if you place these movements in the larger class structure that prevails in the rural economy (Nanda 1999), it becomes clear that ecofeminism is serving the tactical and ideological interests of landed farmers rather than the strategic interests of either women or nature. KRRS, for instance, has used Gandhian and ecofeminist anti-modernism to cover up class and caste differences among the landowners and landless workers in order to demand concessions and subsidies from the state: the entire modern, urban industrial sector, inside India or outside, is declared to be the enemy of the entire traditional, rural and agricultural 'real India'. While the Gandhian leadership of KRRS mobilizes large numbers of peasants to ransack offices of multinational corporations, it turns a blind eye to the atrocities against *dalit* farm workers that members of KRRS have continued to commit.

Movements like KRRS, BKU, allied new social movements and their anti-modernist intellectual sympathizers end up conferring a seemingly secular, populist and even progressive 'anti-imperialist' gloss on a kind of reactionary nationalism that is no different in substance from the *swadeshi* (self-reliance) platform of the Hindu right. The movements (notably KRRS and BKU) have claimed, following the rhetoric made popular by Shiva and other anti-modernist intellectuals, that Western economic interests represented by multinational corporations and Western culture in general are the major contradiction in Indian society today, and that a fight against the West is in the interest of the ordinary people in India. Western feminists and progressives more or less accept this underlying assumption as well. But such 'anti-imperialism' is hardly warranted by actual economic facts. For much of its postcolonial history, India has been one of the most protected economies in South Asia. The Indian state and Indian businesses have actually invested more abroad than any foreign corporation has been allowed to invest in India (Vinaik 1990: 12–13). Even after the economic liberalization that started in the early 1990s, the total direct foreign investment in the entire South Asian region amounted to a mere 0.5 per cent of GNP in 1996, a figure which compares poorly with 4.2 per cent in East Asia and 1.9 per cent in all other developing countries (World Bank 1997). Clearly, the overheated anti-Western, 'anti-imperialist' rhetoric is serving the ideological need of rural and Hindu nationalistic élites to rally the masses across class and caste divides in support of their own, often shared, agendas.

Let us look at the much-praised Laxmi Mukti programme of Shetkari Sanghathan. Started in 1990 in response to women activists and feminist intellectuals, this programme urges farmers to make a voluntary gift of a portion of their land to their wives on condition that the wives can only use traditional organic farming techniques. The limited usefulness of such a gift can be readily granted: independent ownership does strengthen women's position in the family, although it is not clear if wives can actually sell or mortgage the gifted land if they wish. But I contend that such a programme performs an ideological function by confining women's rights within the traditional framework of family and goddesses. What is worse, it makes the intra-family gift serve as a substitute for land redistribution to those without any assets at all. There are reports that many relatively large farmers are using it as a means to evade the legal land ceiling, which explains their enthusiasm for this programme. Moreover, the restriction of women to organic and subsistence farming reinforces the sexual division of labour. Laxmi Mukti is clearly a middle-peasant programme that serves to absorb women's growing assertion of the right to land within the traditional patriarchal family, and prevents them from making common cause with landless women.

The partly willing and partly inadvertent co-optation of ecofeminism by farmers' movements is a good example of the problems of valorizing symbolic differences over class differences. While it *is* true that the symbolic and the material cannot be separated, it is *not* true that struggles over the terrain of symbols neatly translate into a more equitable redistribution in the terrain of the material. I am not suggesting that *all* struggles over recognition of difference are *necessarily* right-wing or left-wing. All I am saying is that given India's balance of caste and class power, glued together by deeply inegalitarian Hindu norms, critiques pitched at the level of irreducible cultural differences with the West are strengthening the already formidable power of upper-caste, rich rural males, who are the most dubious 'allies' that feminists and other secular democrats could ever want

The veiled women

Let us turn finally, to the acts of omission of Third Worldist intellectuals. Here we turn to Prem Chowdhry's *Veiled Women.* The women in the veil are farm labourers in Haryana who seem to be getting the worst of both worlds: they get neither the freedom from hard labour out on the farm that comes with the veil, nor the relative autonomy that comes with working for wages. Defying all generalizations by South Asian anthropologists and economists, women in Haryana have not experienced any improvement in their social worth, despite the very high levels of wage labour participation encouraged by the Green Revolution. Indeed, the situation seems to be getting worse, with female foeticide on the rise leading to a high sex ratio.

This dismal situation has been cited over and over again by prominent feminist critics of development as an example of the 'violence of science', or as evidence of the *fundamentally* patriarchal nature of modern technology, which supposedly imposes a wholly different, Western capitalist logic on the ecological and moral economy of the peasant. Prem Chowdhry's sensitive field studies show what this meta-level epistemological critique of technology leaves out. The great value of her work is that she never lets you lose track of how 'Western' technology is mediated through traditional 'Eastern' institutions. Let me explain.

The introduction of the Green Revolution (GR) has indeed set in motion social forces that are causally associated with – in Sylvia Walby's (1989) terminology – the transformation of the private patriarchy of a peasant economy into the public patriarchy of the market economy. Because of the adoption of new technology by small and marginal farmers, who now need to earn more cash to buy modern inputs, Haryana has seen a change of cultural norms. Before the GR, women of dominant-caste landowners were not permitted to work anywhere but on family farms, while only lower-caste, landless women worked for wages. In the late 1980s, however, 44 per cent of upper-caste, small and marginal farmers allowed their women to work on other people's farms for hard cash. Important studies of women and work by scholars like Bina Agarwal, Kalpana

Bardhan and Barbara Miller in agriculture, Karin Kapadia in the informal sector, and Naila Kabeer and Swasti Mitter in the garment industry have clearly shown independent income through wage work leads to a slow but steady enlargement of women's freedoms in South Asia. The reason it is not happening in Haryana has everything to do with the culture of female subordination, which has deep historical roots in the desert-like ecology of part of the region, combined with hypergamy, imitation of upper-caste practices and the concept of male *izzat* (honour) which depends upon female propriety. Whatever ecological virtues this peasant culture may have, they were obtained not because of, but at the cost of the equality and autonomy of women. It is these deeply misogynist and illiberal cultural norms that are now acting as shock absorbers to maintain men's *izzat* in the time of rapid changes introduced by Green Revolution.

Conclusion

To conclude, an *enabling* critique of development must engage in a cultural challenge to this inherited discourse of patriarchy, caste and other inequities justified by traditional cosmologies. And that challenge cannot proceed within the confines of local knowledges alone, for these knowledges simultaneously allow everyday resistance but also condition the subaltern to accept their subordination. It is important to acknowledge that, like all cultures, non-Western cultures and traditions have progressive impulses toward autonomy and justice. But if we let traditions define what autonomy and justice are, that is, if we accept that different cultures have different norms of what is true, just and good, we run the risk of easy appropriation by traditional patriarchs who are taking the lead in the rising tide of religious revivalism in many parts of the world. The task of feminism and other progressive social movements ought to be to challenge the terms of the debate. Modern science can assist in this challenge by enabling the subalterns to see through the mystification of their own inherited ideologies. To reduce science to a Western local story is not in the interest of the Virammas and the Charlises of this world, who have everything to gain from it.

Notes

(This is an edited text of the paper read at 'Which Way for Women and Development? Debating Concepts, Strategies and Directions for the Twenty-first Century' a conference organized by the City University of New York, 15–17 October 1998.)

1 *Dalit* is the chosen self-description of the 'untouchable' castes in India. The word *dalit* literally means 'crushed', or 'the oppressed'.
2 For representative writings of this genre, see the entries in Sachs (1992).
3 For a trenchant critique of culturalism, see Al-Azmeh (1993).
4 For recent works, see Hess (1995); Franklin (1995).

Part V

Stories from the Field:

Theorizing Action/Acting on Theory

12

Participatory Research

A Tool in the Production of Knowledge in Development Discourse

Patience Elabor-Idemudia

Grassroots people in developing countries have culturally constructed ways of reflecting on their daily lives. For the most part, they conceptualize 'development' in the sense of belonging to a community and connecting with other people in a way that makes possible the satisfaction of mutual interests. They are able to give their own accounts of what is happening in their lives, what their needs are, what they are doing, what they can do and what they intend to do about their issues. Through this process, their local experiences and indigenous knowledge formulate the cultural environment that informs the social and political life of the community. Yet many well-meaning development programmes have undermined local peoples' ability to control their own lives and have instead made them the targets of exploitative patriarchal economic systems. Most conventional approaches to development implemented by Western 'expert' researchers and their local counterparts in non-Western, 'developing countries' have tended to restrict access to knowledge, especially by the poor, and, at the same time, have neglected to help poor, grassroots peoples to articulate their experiences to the outside world. There is a disturbing failure to recognize that these peoples do theorize in their communities as part of their community life, and that they are not only articulate but also able to interpret their experiences. The end result of this development practice is that 'knowledge becomes mystified, losing sight of the people's needs' (Escobar 1992: 420).

This chapter problematizes the ongoing research method base for constructing knowledge about development. It is argued that development knowledge emanating from certain Western ideological constructs and practices denigrates the indigenous knowledge, expertise and lived experiences of the target groups and excludes their insiders' perspective in formulating development strategies for change. The resulting exclusionary practices not only marginalize the voices of target groups in the development process but serve to objectify them as well. This chapter also explores as an alternative strategy the possibilities and limits of participatory research (also known as participatory rural appraisal) as a catalyst for social change towards equality in development knowledge production. It explores the understanding of community in the production of such knowledge and highlights how this understanding may lead to (un)equal acknowledgment, valuation and inclusion/exclusion of indigenous knowledge and ideological practices from the trenches in the development discourse. This is significant in view of the fact that participatory research is consistent with a social constructionist perspective that suggests that the meanings actors give to their actions and those of others are paramount in understanding social life. As researchers, we are obligated to do whatever we can to 'approximate an understanding of the life-world of social actors as they themselves understand it' (Goodson and Mangan 1996: 43). What better way to achieve this understanding than by inviting people to contribute to the research process itself?

Problematizing knowledge construction in development discourse

Among the many problems with contemporary development practices in developing countries is the failure of the Western-trained experts, researchers and agents who design and implement the programmes to examine critically the 'need' to link research efforts with the 'discursive and material relations that produce [the] multiple subject locations' of the implementers and the targets of the development process in different contexts (Fischer 1996: 1; see also Heron 1996). The development 'experts', including academic researchers, tend to promote development programmes that conform to top-down, core–periphery, centre-outward biases of knowledge that afford no conceptual space for the ideals and perceptions of the poor and disadvantaged. This tendency promotes complicity that does not allow these experts to examine the complex and sometimes problematic relationship between them and the target groups they are addressing. As a result, in the language of Spivak (1988: 308), 'the Subaltern cannot speak'. Developing countries' subalterns or marginalized people are left out, with no subject position from which to be represented.

Although participation has recently come to be recognized as an absolute imperative for the development of both mainstream and alternative development strategies, it has remained an elusive concept. It has, instead, translated into multiple meanings and has been connected to multiple methods of implementation with disappointing results. Moser (1989) in examining the participatory aspects of development projects suggested the need to shift focus from emphasis on participation as a means (efficiency, effectiveness and cost sharing) to participation as an end (empowerment and capacity building). This way, grassroots development efforts can be more effective, especially over the longer term, by moving away from a focus on fixed, externally defined goals towards a more flexible, 'enabling' orientation designed to develop intellectual, moral, managerial and technical capacities of local people (Thomas-Slayter 1992).

Another area of concern in the development process lies in the asymmetrical power relations between researchers and the subjects of study embedded in research methodologies and processes. For example, the parasitic nature of development research and the failure to recognize the epistemic saliency of the subject of subjective knowing have contributed to maintaining relations of domination in the development practice. The role and position of researchers/experts and the targets of development are often contradictory. Despite occupying positions of considerable status, power, privilege and authority in the eyes of local peoples, the roles of (Western) experts 'may seem of dubious value' to marginalized communities (Heron 1996: 4). Hegemonic knowledge that promotes the interest of powerful, élite groups often obscures its value premises by masquerading as totally objective. To create and teach a liberatory and transformative knowledge, we must not only be aware of the knowledge produced, but also understand that the knowledge producer is located within a particular social, economic and political context of society which feminist scholars call 'positionality' (Tereault 1993).

Recognizing the ambiguous consequences of imbalances in power relations between researchers and their subjects is a first step towards altering the manner in which knowledge is perceived. Furthermore, an acceptance of a politics of difference – as opposed to a politics of 'othering' – is, in my opinion, a necessary condition for restructuring the epistemological validity of the knowledge of the 'Other'. In other words, an acceptance of a politics of difference is crucial for the radical changes necessary for the production of knowledge. To reach this stage, researchers – feminists and non-feminists alike – have to go through a process of what bell hooks terms 'meaningful contestation and constructive confrontation' (hooks 1990: 133).

Foucault's (1980) work on power and the formation of subjects is central to this framework. He offers a means of analyzing the contradictory reality of the hierarchical arrangement of power in the research. Foucault sees power as exercised rather than possessed, not primarily repressive but productive and best analyzed from the bottom (Sawicki 1991: 20–1). Also, he sees power as a set of relations dispersed throughout the social formation. He argues that the 'normal' mode of power is how it works at the micro-level of practice. Power relations should be analyzed by looking for strategies, tactics and procedures. Attention should be focused on its effects and not on the intentions of the 'powerful'. In other words, Foucault instructs us to look at what he describes as the 'micro-dynamics of power', that is, the detailed mechanisms of power as they actually work at the lowest level (Foucault 1980).

Knowledge begins with the self and interaction with others. The dynamics of social difference (race/ethnicity, class, gender, and sexuality) significantly implicate how development experts and practitioners come to produce, validate and use 'knowledge' about marginalized communities. The centrality of racialized discourses in the constitution of geopolitical relations allows the West to dominate the discourse about what constitutes 'development' in the non-Western societies (see Comaroff and Comaroff 1988). The failure of development experts and researchers to examine their own subject positions in the development process has become part of the problem of promoting genuine development. Questions about one's identity, culture, history and politics, and the relation of this identity to the development process, can no longer be left unanswered. Researchers have assumed the role of 'others', without questioning the 'right' to go into local communities to conduct social research. Development practitioners have conveniently denied that they have a stake as to which narrative/voice to highlight or privilege.

Code (1991) proposed that knowledge is both subjective and objective and that the knowledge created by the knower reflects both subjective and objective phenomena perceived. Also, she claims that the 'objective/subjective dichotomy is but one of several dichotomies that have structured mainstream Euro-American epistemology' (1991: 28). The attempt to distinguish sharply between two elements of knowing, and to label objective knowledge legitimate and subjective knowledge mere interpretation, is inconsistent with how human beings know.

We should bear in mind that recognizing that knowledge contains both subjective and objective elements does not mean that we must abandon the quest for the construction of knowledge that is as objective as possible. However, if we fail to recognize the ways in which subjective factors – such as race, class and gender – influence the construction of knowledge, we are unlikely to interrogate established knowledge, which contributes to the oppression of marginalized and victimized groups.

If development is truly meant to promote self-reliance and self-sufficiency through a process that is participatory, equitable and sustainable, then it ought to support and build upon the initiatives taken at grassroots level. In many developing countries in Africa, Asia, Latin America and the Caribbean, grass-roots organizations are challenging the conventional model of development and advancing approaches rooted in local knowledge and realities. In view of the limiting and exclusionary nature of the conventional model, the need exists to design initiatives that underwrite social change sustained by the involvement, expertise and commitment of the majority of the people.

Asking new questions

The implication of Western development experts in maintaining global relations of political and economic domination requires that new questions be asked: what are the new politics of 'development research', and what specifically are the implications for developing countries? In terms of the 'ethicality of research inquiry', what is the academic and political project for engaging in development practice? How is it possible to decolonize (social) research in/on the non-Western developing countries to ensure that the people's human condition is not constructed through Western hegemony and ideology? How is it possible to create a climate in which intellectual discursive and political practices are sensitized to the socio-environmental demands and needs of the people in creative, adaptive and productive ways?

Undoubtedly, development takes up local people's time and effort. The benefits of development, however, are not always clear. Development research can simply contribute to a larger 'body of knowledge' for the academic community without necessarily translating to changes in the material conditions of local peoples. Similarly, the vast body of knowledge created from studying marginalized communities in the non-Western societies has not necessarily translated to local control over such knowledge. This may be due to the fact that development discourse in these societies has not sought to portray and value cultural forms of knowledge representation. Many development studies and research in developing countries do not allow marginalized groups, especially women and rural dwellers, to analyze the specific ways in which their marginalization is maintained. Development has merely sought information about the marginalized to enable dominant cultures to continue their domination, rather than shedding light on how social domination is reproduced (Hall 1993). The search for meaningful development practice is long overdue.

The intensification of the neocolonial extractive process through the promotion of the 'magic of the market' holds no future for those of us – the majority of us women – who have no equitable relations to the market. Due to gender inequalities, women are the greatest bearers of the burden of the present models. Their labour is devalued and economists do not consider their skills as valuable skills. They are, therefore, usually low-paid or even unpaid because the myriad caring and nurturing tasks carried out by them in the home and as volunteer labour in social organizations are not recognized as economically valuable work. Women are generally considered to be passive 'vulnerable groups' for whom charity programmes are designed by the managers of the markets. We must realize that the magic is not in the market but in people. There is, therefore, a need for an alternative development model and knowledge base that place human needs, not market needs, at its centre. Two such alternative models are participatory and feminist methodologies of knowledge creation and practice in development.

Participatory research

Participatory research is designed to create social and individual change by altering the role of the relations between people involved in the process. Participants make decisions rather than function as passive objects and the people being studied make decisions about the study format and data analysis. This involves a breakdown of power differences between the 'researched' and 'researcher', the sharing of power, the ownership of information by everyone rather than the researchers, and the rejection of traditional interpretations of 'objectivity'. This rejection of objectivity, so defined, does not mean that basic standards of research are not respected. It simply means adopting a more holist and bias-conscious approach. A consequence of this new role of the researched is that the research results become interpreted with recognition of the interests and concerns of the research subjects. The research insists that the primary recipients and users of this research would be the people who are the subjects rather than the researchers.

Participatory research, to the extent that it involves people, opens up the opportunity for a discussion on access to the production of knowledge and the knowledge derived from a process of engagement. I see participatory research as embodying the praxis of critical theory and as crucial in altering the power–knowledge axis. Supporting the emergence of 'organic intellectuals' (Gramsci 1971), and hence what Foucault (1980) termed 'subjugated knowledges' is an explicit part of engaging in participatory research and hence represents the most direct assault on hegemonic knowledge.

Participatory research requires changing numerous aspects of conventional research including the selection of a sample, the design of instruments, and the use of informed consent. Subject selection, in this case, involves a process of articulating our interest to a number of different groups of local people, including women, and continuing dialogue with those individuals or groups who express interest in the work and want to know more. Such research is communal rather than hierarchical. It develops egalitarian relations among the 'researchers', the 'subjects', and between the two groups. It enables the production of knowledge through democratic, interactive relationships. Through the participatory research process, researchers work with community members to resolve problems identified by the community, with the intention of empowering participants.

The three core aspects of participatory research that require emphasis in development include political action and individual consciousness raising; democratic relationships and equal participation in decision making and skills acquisition; and using the everyday life experiences and feelings of participants as a major source of knowledge (Cancian 1989). Implementation of these core components will ensure empowerment for all in the development process as research has the capacity to emancipate participants when certain approaches are taken. The most emancipatory approaches are the interactive interviews in which researchers demonstrate a range of important skills: they practise self-disclosure; they hold multiple, sequential group interviews; they negotiate their interpretations; and they are able to deal with false consciousness in ways that go beyond dismissing resistance. From this perspective, the subjects of inquiry become active meaning makers who are constantly in the process of constructing, reconstructing and defending the meaning of their lived realities.

Participatory research can be limited to a slight modification of roles or expanded so that all participants have the combined researched/subject role. Here, the feminist participatory research approach becomes relevant as it has the flexibility to be modified. Under this approach, egalitarianism is emphasized, whereby the distinction between the researcher(s) and those on whom the research is done, especially women, disappears. To achieve egalitarian relations, the researcher abandons control and adopts an approach of openness, reciprocity, mutual disclosure and shared risk.[1] Differences in social status and background give way as shared decision making and self-disclosure develop. What this approach calls for is a radical rethinking and reformulation of knowledge forms and social identities that marginalize minorities, often authored and authorized by colonial and Western domination. It involves engaging in giving voice to the resistance of Third World people, particularly women and marginalized others (both past and present), reversing 'orientalist' thoughts, and 'decolonizing' the mind (Hoogvelt 1997). The goal is to undo all the 'binarisms' that are the legacy of colonial ways of thinking and to reveal societies globally in their complex heterogeneity and contingency. In this way, a post-colonial discourse (expanded upon in the next section) is called for because it aims to reconstruct the identities of subordinate people, give them back their pride of place in history and, with it, the confidence to build on the record of their own 'hybrid position of practice and negotiation' (Hoogvelt 1997: 158).

A major concern of participatory research, however, has much in common with what many write about research from a feminist perspective (see Mies 1983; Kirby and McKenna 1989; Mies and Shiva 1993). It has to do with the large absence from the growing literature on participatory research of a consensus on the terminology, its major assumptions and an analysis of the limits and possibilities of the approach. In the following section of this chapter, I question three major elements of this research paradigm – action, transformation, and, in particular, participation.

Unpacking participatory research

The participatory component is the key to both action and transformation. To the extent that the community to be researched is involved in the research process, the likelihood of both effective focus and significant social change is increased. But what does 'participation' actually mean? Two issues are imperative here: First, the matter of who participates: the issue of the representativeness of community members and the participatory researchers/experts needs to be addressed. Second, in what areas of the research process participation should be necessary. Here, I focus on the division of labour between community members and academic researchers in the research process.

Who participates?

The democratizing premise underlying participatory research cannot be assumed. For a start, we must recognize that only a few community members will have the time, means and/or inclination to become involved. In what sense, then, can we claim that the project manifests community participation? One can only claim the extension of the opportunity to participate to the entire community and hope that the few who are involved will pass information to other community members.

The other side of the question focuses on who participates among the academic community, that is, who are these self-described participatory researchers? This question forces a juxtaposition of the ostensibly democratic principles underlying participatory research with the actual backgrounds, motives and practices of participating researchers. Generally, there has been a clear under-representation of non-white, Third World researchers, and those from disadvantaged socio-economic backgrounds. Existing participatory modes of enquiry, therefore, appear to lie within the province of relatively well-established white, middle-class academic researchers. The question becomes: what difference does it make that established scholars are over-represented among participatory researchers? For one thing, given the history of research processes, such scholars are likely to be male, thus possibly reproducing what Maguire (1987) terms the 'androcentric filter' in social science research. More generally, one might hypothesize that the type of community approached as a potential research partner, as well as the dynamics of that partnership, are at least partially a function of the participating academic's social background. Any reflection on the issue of who participates needs to include this dimension.

In what activities?

In order to enable researchers determine what activities are relevant in participatory research to generate balanced knowledge production in the development process, certain questions have to be answered. They might include the following:

- Since participatory research has evolved from critical theory and is part of the emancipatory project of the paradigm, does it imply a restricted range of suitable projects and settings? What, if any, are the limits of this kind of enquiry?
- From what moral theory, if any, can we derive the appropriateness of such external intervention in the life of a community?
- Given the objectives of participatory research, what truth claims are to be evoked to gauge the relative success of the enquiry?
- Should participatory research be subject to the same rules governing any science, social or otherwise, or do we require an epistemology very different from that underlying more traditional kinds of research?
- What kind of transformative change is required or expected to occur as a result of participatory research?[2]

The relevance of these questions lie in the fact that there are some tasks in which community participation is essential if we are at all serious about participatory research, but whose extent and nature of involvement is dependent on various structural factors and preferences of the key actors. When only researchers design and implement the various tasks of a typical research enterprise, we have traditional research, but when all the tasks are carried out by the relevant community, we have an instance of what may be termed communal research. While for some the ultimate objective of critical research is to produce autonomous, self-contained research communities, this is not an acceptable universal principle.

Feminist research frameworks

Feminist work in development has long struggled to redress systemic biases in data collection strategies that contribute to misrepresentation of the situation of women in the Third World by people charged with designing projects to help them. Decades of feminist work have resulted in undermining these misrepresentations and images. International development agencies such as the UN itself, the United Nations Educational, Social and Cultural Organization (UNESCO), the World Bank, USAID, the Ford Foundation, CIDA and so on have been major sites in which knowledge about women in the Third World is produced (Mueller 1986). Such knowledge, often produced by professionals and academics, is generated by and for these agencies with a focus on aid projects. The knowledge is limited to what is considered relevant for the aid bureaucracies and feeds into the objectives, rational decision making and management work of the international agencies. Additionally, the knowledge directs attention away from the local settings in which field workers and residents struggle directly with the overwhelming problems of poverty and underdevelopment. Local people are effectively excluded and silenced. Mueller (1986) argues that these processes are an important part of the mechanisms that subject Third World countries and their people to relations of ruling by the First World, which perpetuates a network of knowledge that sustains a discourse of relations of dependence. This discourse has succeeded in creating a type of underdevelopment that is politically and economically manageable (Escobar 1984).

In attempts to address criticisms levelled against them regarding their excessive control over development projects, international development agencies have, in the last few decades, adopted the concept of 'grassroots participation' in the implementation of some of their projects. Unfortunately, at the village level, this has been translated into practices that commonly give élite males control and veto power over projects intended for women. Barbara Rogers (1980) in looking at development programmes in several countries, showed that there is deep-seated sexism in the workings of development agencies, especially several of the United Nations bodies. She noted that

> one of the most important blocks to the development process that really hurts women is the blindness and rigidity of planners to needed changes, from the headquarters staff to those in the field, almost all of whom are men. Since they do not often deal professionally with women, they have little comprehension of women's real contribution to development, or even the fact that women may have needs that differ from those of men (Rogers 1980: 104).

The corollary of these practices is that development projects themselves have failed to make use of the potential resources, skills and expertise of women.

Feminist theorists (Mies 1983; Mies and Shiva 1993; Hoogvelt 1997) also agree that development policies based on promoting the market system have increasingly narrowed the entire social roles of women, their political empowerment and their capacity to generate income. As a result, society has also suffered by losing the household as an adaptive low-cost production centre that can shield its members from the vicissitudes of the market economy (Nash and Safa 1976). The areas reserved for women in development have been 'feminine' ones. For example, in a review of eleven major rural development projects in Nepal by Pradham (1979), it was found that because of the distortions in concepts such as 'housewife', 'head of household' and 'economic activities', the productive roles of women were completely ignored. In almost all the projects, women were either left out of all the major national development projects or included in peripheral activities. The exclusion of women from activities that were traditionally their domain, both as workers and decision makers, weakened their authority and status and diminished rather than enhanced their roles as contributors to the social and economic well-being of the community.

In the last fifteen years postcolonial feminists, consisting mostly of Third World female academics and researchers, have promoted a new discourse on development. Their focus on systemic biases includes those inherent in Western feminists' knowledge production processes regarding the Third World. This postcolonial discourse has highlighted the myths that abound in representations (both visual and descriptive) of Third World women as ignorant, poor, uneducated, tradition-bound and victimized dependants of men. In a remorselessly Foucauldian deconstruction of Western feminist writing on Third World women, Chandra Mohanty (1991) challenged their political effect as being no more than a 'prop' to a Western feminist colonial move. As Aihwa Ong (1988) puts it, 'when feminists look overseas, they frequently seek to establish their authority on the backs of non-Western women, determining for them the meanings and goals of their lives'. The postcolonial discourse has therefore pointed out the epistemological weakness of the strategy by Western feminists that has to do with the concept of Third World women as a unitary analytical category. The postmodern turn in feminist critique led to the problematizing of this assumption.

In order to constitute a legitimate forum for challenging weaknesses in Western feminist praxis, Development Alternatives with Women for a New Era (DAWN) was established in 1984 by a group of mostly Third World women researchers and activists. The main aim of this forum is to highlight and deconstruct, using a postcolonial discourse, the myths in representation of the Third World and to replace them with unbiased knowledge and methods for achieving justice, peace and development that is sustainable. These postcolonial, postmodern feminists found their voice through gender orientation mediated by class and race in development studies. Their discourse privileges the lived experiences of the subjects of research, thereby serving as a tool of empowerment. They rely on their possession of culturally relevant knowledge that Western feminists lack and they have pointed out that the emancipatory agendas of Western feminists are wholly inappropriate to the needs, day-to-day lives and struggles of Third World women. For example, Mohanty (1991) argues that Western feminists have a singular focus on gender as a basis for equal rights, while postcolonial feminists, consisting mostly of non-Western academics and researchers, are concerned with gender in relation to race and class as part of a broader liberation struggle.

Contemporary Western feminist researchers have had to shift their research methodology and tools for analyzing Third World women's role in development in response to criticisms from Third World feminists. Additionally, they are challenging new strategies emanating from international development institutions that focus on the role of the market and marginalize women. Both Third and First World feminists now engage in conversations in order to develop a better understanding of women on all sides through a focus on the 'personal as political'. They have come to the understanding that no outsiders can ever set the agenda for grassroots and oppressed people's practical or strategic needs. This means that all conceptual baggage must be thrown out if researchers are to understand and empower targets of development to take control of their lives. For this, listening will do as a first step.

What are the dilemmas?

In attempting to construct a postcolonial feminist framework for knowledge acquisition in development, several dilemmas need to be addressed. The main tenet of the framework is to make the actual lives and experiences of women the starting point. In this framework, women's experience becomes the basis of the practice that, in turn, legitimizes their roles and contributions to the development of the community and quality of life. But this can be difficult in the face of an increasing cultural resurgence of nationalism and/or fundamentalist religious groups that have restrictive notions of women. Moreover, the growth of the international women's movement has resulted in a global feminist framework that promotes a liberal feminist hegemony on human rights while locating indigenous feminism as the Other. But new developments in academic feminism have effected a shift in discourse on the notion of gender. Cultural constructions of gender redirect feminist language towards a greater recognition, for example, of the role of agents of empowerment and of the everyday struggles in which the subjects of empowerment are engaged. For the disadvantaged women of developing countries, participation within this new feminist discourse will need to include:

- Validating our own experience through self-reflection;
- Rethinking definitions of 'experts';
- Redefining objectivity *vis-à-vis* subjectivity;
- Demystifying the research process by identifying the role of agents;
- Research as a collective/collaborative process;
- Use of 'live' narratives in order to include women's voices;

- A holistic, interdependent research model;
- Linking research to women's empowerment.

Thus far these methodological aims have proved difficult but not impossible to implement.

In attempting to increase women's participation in development and to ensure partnerships, it is important to recognize and utilize the actual geographic and social location of the women. Where women are, how they structure their daily lives and how they spend their time impact on their ability to participate in development programmes and projects. Projects will need to be organized with these considerations in mind. The immense demands on women's time and energy to fulfil their social roles in the private and public spheres place a limitation on their ability to participate in development schemes.

If we are to form true partnerships and to empower women, it is necessary to enter into the arenas where the paid and unpaid employment occurs, especially the informal sector. Until recently women's roles as nurturers and social reproducers have meant they were invisible and excluded from consideration in development strategies, which defined development only in terms of economic considerations. These development strategies often had negative impacts on the quality of women's lives, increasing their workload, deepening their poverty and enhancing their vulnerability to market forces.

Notions of empowerment and participation rest on the assumption that women have some spare time to contribute to the project at hand. To facilitate their involvement, projects must address the actual needs of women within their spheres of activity. Development programmes will thus be able to address the actual needs of women within their everyday lives as well as encouraging their participation in projects that will enhance their quality of life.

The central themes of empowerment and participation mean starting from where women are and legitimizing their experiences. The different entry points would include an understanding of women's daily structures, as well as their emotions (including the pain of oppression and those that come with the different identities that define women – mother, wife, sister, daughter). Strategies adopted would encourage women's mobility; and take them out of their everyday roles. The role of the development agent would be reflexive research and involve double consciousness.

Alternative vision

With poverty, instability and environmental degradation on the increase in the wake of contemporary development strategies in most Third World countries, it is becoming increasingly clear that externally devised Eurocentric strategies for economic growth have failed to support sustainable development. This is because the strategies have often not taken into account the indigenous knowledge of the people that has ensured their survival for thousands of years. The resulting projects, designed by Western experts, have been sufficiently supportive neither of peasants who seek access to and control over their means of production and the results of their labour, nor of workers who seek the right to organize and to work under safe conditions. They have also failed to support women who seek the right to decide what and how they will produce. The need exists, therefore, for development processes that are centred on and directed by those they are supposed to benefit. This calls for a rethinking of the concept and its processes, and this brings into focus the roles of Third World people, their local knowledge inputs, their lived experiences and environments, and the use of appropriate technology.

In order to appreciate the limitations of Eurocentric development models as strategies for economic growth in developing countries, we need to look beyond the confines of industrialized societies in the West. We need to look at other cultures' concepts of the environment and sustainability, in historical societies like those of Pre-Columbian America, and in the technologically primitive societies which present-day development serves to undermine. This means that if development is truly meant to promote self-reliance and self-sufficiency of poor people through a process that is equitable and sustainable, then it ought to support and build upon the initiatives taken at grassroots level. As many developing countries, especially those in Africa, Asia, Latin America and the Caribbean, organize grassroots movements/organizations to challenge models of development that have brought them no progress, we need to revisit such models and revise them to include and advance knowledge that is rooted in local/indigenous ways of knowing and doing. Such models will promote and ensure the design of initiatives that underwrite social change sustained by the involvement, expertise and commitment of the majority of the people. Additionally, we will need to address and resolve the environmental crisis in the Third World, by reconfiguring ongoing capitalist-oriented development, according it the 'human face' that promotes the meeting of real human needs and the restoration of the environment to a sustainable healthy condition. How we do so is through taking the first step of participatory research that promotes equal participation of all players.

Conclusion

This chapter has analyzed critically the possibilities and limits of participatory research as a catalyst for social change towards equality in knowledge production. It has also explored the understanding of gender, class, race and community in the production of such knowledge and highlighted how this understanding may lead to (un)equal acknowledgment, valuation and inclusion/exclusion of the ideological practices from the trenches in the development discourse.

The model of development I have advocated in this chapter is one that reflects the lived realities and the goals and aspirations of the grassroots people of the community. It is a form of 'development' rooted in indigenous peoples' sense of moral and spiritual values, and the connections between the social and natural worlds. Critical perspectives on development argue that local communities should own and control the solutions to their own problems. But real and effective community control is possible only if the development agenda seeks to make indigenous knowledge systems critical in the search for solutions to human problems. This means articulating an alternative conception and praxis of development, one which does not reproduce the existing total local dependency on 'expert advice'. Local input must be from the grassroots and should tap the diverse views, opinions and interests manifested in the communities. How we can help to tap such local knowledge to assist the development process is our challenge.

The failure of various prescribed development strategies to improve impoverished Third World women's lives can be attributed partly to their excessive focus on industrialization and the importation of technology at the expense of human resource development. In general, the strategies have not adequately considered women's challenges (such as walking long distances to collect fuel and water, lack of child-care facilities, inadequate health care and lack of inheritance rights to land) as deserving serious commitment in terms of the allocation of scarce resources. Thus, women's needs are, for the most part, never met. Moreover, the male bias inherent in development processes has resulted in women's increased marginalization and undervaluation because of lack of equity for and participation by women (Elson 1991). According to Sen and Grown (1987),

> it is impossible to obtain sustainable improvement in women's economic and social position under conditions of growing relative inequality if not absolute poverty for both women and men. Therefore, equality for women is impossible within existing economic, political and cultural processes that reserve resources, power and control for small sections of people – usually men. (Sen and Grown 1987: 14)

Alternative development needs to elaborate new ways of understanding the world; to establish a balanced relationship between experience and expertise; and to value unquantifiable resources such as self-esteem and the everyday capacities of women. Empowerment within such a context would mean understanding the various parts of women's lives. The place of feminist discourse in valorizing women's experience will also need to be examined with regard to where balances are needed. Efforts will also be required to establish linkages between local and global issues and national frameworks.

Researchers, community workers, field practitioners and students of development must be able to unearth the specific nature of the linkage between local knowledge and grassroots participation in the development process. We must involve local peoples in all stages of the conception, planning, implementation and evaluation of local development activities. I would contend that if the idea of 'development' is to have any credibility at all, it must speak to the social, cultural, economic, political, spiritual and cosmological aspects of local people's lives, as well as to their specific needs and aspirations. Debates about development must be situated in appropriate social contexts that provide practical and social meaning to the actors as subjects rather than objects of development discourse.

Notes

1 The change in relation to the 'subject' is also called 'temporary affiliation'. See Oakley (1981: 30–61).

2 See Richer (1998).

13

Ethnographic Acts

Writing Women and Other Political Fields

Piya Chatterjee

Locations

Contemporary discussions about the politics of representation within anthropological writing have examined the creative possibilities of meshing poststructural and postcolonial critiques with feminist theorizing and practice.[1] These intersecting conversations about the politics and possibilities of a 'feminist ethnography' have opened up theoretical discussions around practice, politics and accountability inherent in the production of anthropological texts. Simply put, ethnography seeks to translate field experience into text. Yet, not so simply, these editorial and calligraphic acts are implicated in the 'actual' world which they seek to represent.[2] Is the relationship of such complex actualities to the ethnographic text something that remains safely in the dichotomy of world and text/theory? Can we enact a writing *practice* that extends through, and beyond, the scripts of worlds re/presented?[3]

This relationship of text to its context in anthropological production and practice is a profound one and oft discussed. For anthropologists, translation of ethnographic experience into text navigates the conceptual minefield of paradigmatic placements, editorial elisions and theoretical voicings. The 'field' and 'fieldwork' figure prominently within the text's frames. This framing, and the translations which enable the peopling of the textual field within, occur at multiple levels: from the oral to the literate, from language to language, meshing the visual with the literate, and so forth. Until the collective momentum of interventions – from postcolonial and feminist literary criticism, poststructuralist theories, writings on decolonization and imperial history, and feminist anthropology – anthropology remained comfortable with framing the field at a distance. Initiation rites of disciplinary training, for the most part, involved a 'going there' from 'here', making the strange familiar and *vice versa.* Natives remained native within such an analytic gaze and the knowledge base of Others, carefully crafted, marked an imperial epistemology.[4]

In the past decade, the interrogation of the 'there' – of a 'Third World' – as a primary site of investigation has been partly compelled by the changing face of disciplinary practitioners, many of whom have come from 'there' and themselves embody the absent, but still powerfully resonant, space of nativism. For many women anthropologists, trained in the US academy, who are from the 'there' of the dominant episteme, ethnographic production and writing is fraught with de/colonizing dissonance. How can the 'native' woman write within and against the 'here/there' without reifying the exoticism that she may embody for the paradigmatic gaze? How can she write herself, beyond the re-visions of such dichotomy, into the space of an integral, though not transparent, praxis? How can she be accountable to her privilege and the paradoxes of her own de/colonization?[5]

Coming to the writing voice, within and against the binary, is a process shot through with hybrid threads. The text it produces traverses the *here-there-here-there.* Its dance is an exquisite *ad infinitum.* Yet its voices may be dis/abled by the very oscillations that make them hybridities. These are not only calligraphic gestures to movements across maps. They speak through the body, in flight, traversing borders defined by global, national and regional state-power. Transnational anthropology is a given for those of us who came here to be trained, but our entry into the 'here' (of a US 'centre') from the 'there' (of the 'periphery') is itself compelled by specific postcolonial and imperial histories. Yet, such transnational moves are mediated by 'actual' power plays: the contradictions of class location, state and juridical power,[6] the politics of nation and citizenship. To then claim where we came 'from' as an ethnographic site, to engage the *home-as-field,* gestures to a counter-paradigmatic dance. Yet, its practice is implicated within the actualities of globalization and its imperial orders. It is simultaneously, and perhaps contradictorily, inflected by the bourgeois, feudal and regional particularities which are embedded within that larger matrix.[7]

In this chapter, I first look closely at the contradictions of my own fieldwork practice when I examined the history and politics of women and labour in the tea plantations of North Bengal, India. The most cursory glance suggests the first markers of authorial location and power: my own ethnic (Bengali), caste/class (Brahmin/upper-middle class) and gendered subject-position marks privilege in definitive ways. Except for gender (where class position did not always overwhelm a sense of secondary status within customary forms of patriarchy in North Bengal), my authorial location embodied the apex of socio-political power in North Bengal.

Second, I examine these contradictions of ethnographic production through the questions posed by subjects of my study – the women and men in the North Bengal plantation where I conducted my larger study. Third, I explore how efforts by plantation women to organize as a 'self-help group' open up the possibilities – and limitations – of doing collaborative and coalitional grassroots work. In brief, this chapter will ponder issues that continue to bedevil feminists and anthropologists who seek to bring into bolder relief the problematic and paradoxical politics of both re/presentation and pragmatic accountability when it comes to the communities they have chosen to study, or work within.

Keeping in mind Daphne Patai's strong cautionary note about claiming some ethically neutral (or ethically 'correct') feminist project,[8] this chapter does not seek to make facile claims about dialogue, collaboration and accountability. Indeed, it is very much a work-in-progress and its reflections are offered with the knowledge that the conditions of globalization, the paradoxes of postcolonial and diasporic location, and the enduring brutal nature of feudal power in rural India will mediate, and even break, the connections narrated therein. It is, in that light, just a fragment of an open-ended and continuous pedagogy about what it *might* mean to account for and write a history, and anthropology, about privilege and those who live their lives in its shadows.

Genealogies

I began my field research about women, labour and political culture in North Bengal tea plantations at the end of 1991. Though I had already begun archival research and interviews with tea planters in Calcutta in early 1991, I spent most of 1992 and early 1993 in North Bengal's plantation country. After returning to the United States, my journey back to the plantations was delayed for six years. This rupture of 'return', mediated by immigration and employment issues, constituted a significant break in my continuing relationships with a few of the plantation women who had befriended me, and who had become critical commentators on my ethnographic enterprise. I returned in the summer of 1998 when employment and immigration status within the United States ensured that I could move between India and the United States more easily. Since then, I returned to the plantations for further stints of fieldwork in early 1999 and the summer of 2000.

Bodily Economies

I was compelled to work on tea history and politics not only because of its significance in Chinese and British imperial trade, but because of its continuing importance in the postcolonial and national economy. Indeed, vast swathes of north-eastern and southern India are dominated by plantation enclaves which were started by the British in the mid-nineteenth century. While this specific postcolonial history is embedded within the larger matrix of global plantation economies,[9] I was particularly interested in how and why *adivasi*[10] and Nepali women emerged as primary workers in the tea fields.

Women's labour constitutes the backbone of an industry that has dominated regional, national and international trade for over a century and half. This fact of labour history was under-explained in the historical and anthropological literature. In addition, it appeared that this feminization of labour was underscored by a certain 'feminization of the commodity'[11] when tea circulated as a primary commodity of world trade. Not only is tea sold as the penultimate drink of genteel femininity, but the labour which produces it – as product and as commodity – is also fetishized as 'nimble'. Both fetishisms of commodity and labour were connected through women's bodies, linking in strange and powerful ways the feminized aristocratic, bourgeois and working-class bodies of empire and colony. Within labour practice, women's 'nimble fingers' were constituted through bodily essentialisms as 'natural' agility, and this came to mark the dominant discourse, and rationalization, of gendered fieldwork.

In my ethnographic research, I remained most interested in how these colonial, patriarchal forms of labour organization are constituted within the postcolonial factory, field and village. Indeed, how do women themselves articulate, through daily practice and talk, the effects of these inscriptions upon their bodies, families, and communities? What were their rituals of memory and resistance?

Though these larger analytical questions moved me through the field, as it were, I was not fully prepared for the important ways in which my location of difference and power would affect every encounter in the plantation. While such self-reflexive assertions about the privilege of anthropological location may appear banal and self-indulgent, I seek to push them into a space within which deeper epistemological issues might be probed. How does this location, and the methodology informed by it, inform the knowledge base – the epistemic domain – upon which the anthropological analysis is based?[12]

To wit, the narratives of patriarchy, patronage and labour which spin the cultural economies of plantation power were inextricably meshed to the contradictions of my socio-economic location. My own gender and status worked as a primary subtext within the analysis of plantation patronage and the terms of dominance, subordination, consent and resistance which enabled it. Indeed, the benevolence of a few senior planters made it possible for me to begin my sojourn in plantation country. At the outset, patronage defined both method and the larger theoretical claims of the ethnographic text to be produced.

Watching the Field. September 1991

This is my first trip into plantation country, past the forests and small towns, finally into the never-ending stretch of low green. It is a landscape of stunning illusion. From the distance of the car, the forest blends into an even emerald carpet. Only on closer inspection do you discern it as tamed jungle; the carpet, an unending vista of groomed tea bushes, maps with a euclidian exactness the slopes of the Himalayan foothills. Yet, the most curious aspect of this exquisitely cultivated landscape is the absence of people. It is as if – despite over a century of protracted taming of the natural forest, human endeavour and toil – the exacting labour of planting, tending and harvest remains utterly eclipsed.

On the right, suddenly rising from a field of tea bushes, is a palladian bungalow whose Grecian columns and high patio verandah manage to upstage the neighbouring, low-lying whitewashed factory buildings. This imposing abode, the director's bungalow seldom visited by the plantation's *maliks* (owners), is home for my initial sojourn into tea country. It could not, despite its grand emptiness, more concretely symbolize the absolute centre of the planter's world. From the verandah eyrie on the second floor, I see the factory and the staff houses lying in front and to the left respectively. On the right, the tea bushes begin.

The factory siren sounds loudly in the late afternoon, and I see groups of women hunched under heavily laden aprons walking through the factory gates. Through my elevated and ironic gaze, they are framed momentarily into a distant and colorfully bound stillness. I have described this tightly knit spatial clustering of factory, bungalow and *basha*, and the elevated Cartesian perspective of my glance, to gesture towards the contained locus of power symbolized by the arrangement of buildings, and my own location within that encirclement of power.[13]

Memsahib-in-Place

Four months after this initial gaze on the tea fields, I have found somewhere to stay. Benevolent patronage has allowed me to inhabit this place. It is an old bungalow on a plantation which I shall call *Sarah's Hope*. The sprawling two-bedroomed house, with an unused outhouse kitchen, is my abode for the year I remain in Dooars plantation country. The bungalow system of servitude ensures that, even if uninhabited, gardeners, watchmen and maids keep it outwardly groomed. Soon after my arrival, the perimeter of hedges grows wild and the goats graze on the lawn. My neighbour, an assistant manager, takes me to task: 'It is important that your garden is well kept. People from the road will see its untidiness and it will give the garden a bad name. Make sure the gardeners work. *Are they working?*'

Anjali Mirdha has worked in the plantation bungalow system for many years and we strike up an easy rapport. The news has gone across the village that a *memsahib* has arrived, without a *sahib*. Is she from the government? Is she a spy? Thus it is, within and beyond the small arc of soon-to-be-untidy lawn, that I finally begin to visit communities living on the other side of the fence. Anjali, assigned to the otherwise abandoned bungalow, lives five minutes from its borders, and it is with her and through her introductions to family and friends, that I enter *Sarah's Hope*'s villages.

Though no longer in the splendid isolation of a palladian second-floor verandah, and left mercifully to my own devices, there could be no mistaking my indelible marking as a *memsahib*. I am palpably aware of the bungalow's place of power. I am told by a *chota sahib* (assistant planter) to keep its lawns trimmed. I know my failure to supervise the gardeners will be one of many small signs of transgression for my uneasy patrons. Anjali and I ignore the order with a blithe spirit, and unlock the back gate.

The grandeur of planter lifestyles, and the leisured rhythms of their bungalows, are in stark contrast to the continuous and arduous work in the fields lying just on the other side of the bungalow walls. *Memsahibs*, the planters' wives, epitomize this leisured world and enact, in the most important ways, the rituals of neocolonial ladyship. In so doing, they create the foil for the planter's own masculinity: a vision of hardy, outdoors gentlemanliness which is tempered by the perfectly mannered 'inside' femininity of his wife, the *memsahib*.

My spatial and temporal rhythms are as leisured as hers and as a *memsahib* (albeit without a *sahib*) I am admonished by new acquaintances in the plantation's villages for walking without an umbrella and being seen so openly in public. The sun, I am told, will darken my complexion and make me like any other *coolie*.[14] Perceptions of my ascribed gender and status (whose placement I am told I must protect) register an openly racialized discourse, and understanding of the place of 'other women' whose stories I want to listen to.

It is ironic and telling that the ontologies of shared privilege mimic my neighbouring *memsahibs*' worlds, and border fences upon which I have stretched the tightrope of this research. It is a tightrope that winds around the analytic frames within which I come to some understanding of the complex and diverse cultural politics within the plantation 'labour lines'. To wit, my placement within the bungalow, where I territorially inhabit the status of *memsahib*, shapes the arc of all village encounters. Though I visit more distant lines and cross the borders of neighbouring plantations, it is a small area lying adjacent to the bungalow that becomes the focused site of plantation pedagogies. The bungalow location draws out the first lines of the cultural cartography of power.

Field/Work, Field/Research

My arrival in early 1991, during the last weeks of winter work, is fortunate in that Anjali, and the women I meet through her, have time to speak with me.

They are, as I am, aware how labour and time are inextricably connected. Though they are consistently generous with their time, which even in winter is packed with household tasks, I recognize that my research, and its demands for conversation, is itself dependent on leisure and its free and floating determinations. While conversation, a dialogical act, is certainly one place where a meaningful human encounter can occur, it cannot be excised from the conditions of its making. Indeed, since these conversations will sediment the knowledge base of my ethnography, the terms of their 'making' – who labours, who talks, who lies leisured – carve out the epistemic terrain.

As we become acquainted, that winter just before the call of harvest, I am aware of constant motion: bending over to stack the firewood carried miles from the forest; hitching the baby higher on her back; quickly making tea. Knowledge production is, I learn with some immediacy, also a process of extraction and the body – in both listening stillness, and in necessary movement – is implicated.

When I return, after seven years to the month of my first winter conversations with them, I remember this, and the relationship of their work, my research and its terms of leisured extraction. When I mention the issue of their 'giving time', Munnu Kujoor smiles. 'It was not that much trouble to talk, we did what we needed to do. But you see, with you there, I have an excuse not to work as well. Things won't be said, if you know what I mean.'

June is bursting with leaf and the pressure of work is constant. Some days, I walk into the field with Anjali Mirdha and we visit Bhagirathi Mahato's *dol* (labour gang). Even though they are welcoming, their exhaustion limits our conversation and we sit quietly in the shade. Many afternoons, I remain in the leisured isolation of my bungalow, venturing out in the late evening when I assume that the women will have completed their necessary chores. Yet again, the awareness of the sharp divide between my leisured privilege and their constant labour is acute.

To mull over that divide, in a feudal system within which structural inequity is a given, appears facile and indulgent. Yet, because of the basic tenets of ethnographic field research – participation and observation – I must carefully consider the historically specific terms within which my own experience and understanding of women's labouring takes place. To do so is not to resolve (or indeed absolve) myself of the inescapable conclusion that I reached about my fieldwork experience: that it is extractive, that my unease in 'taking time' both within the labouring field and in the village is ontologically and politically fraught by such extraction, and that it cannot be sidelined within ethnographic translations which make certain kinds of knowledge claims. In this specific instance, labour – as bodily discourse which defines plantation women's experiences – rests at the centre of narrative assertions about plantation disciplines and its complex, multiple patriarchies.

Philosophies of the 'Field'

The 'field' and 'fieldwork' take on a theoretical *double entendre* that cannot be obscured. In the plantation, the 'field' has a descriptive actuality that is created through bodily disciplines. Likewise, 'fieldwork' is realized by hard labour in which, agreeing to the terms of its feudal codes, I do not participate. The ethnographic 'field' – emptied of specificity into abstraction – is impossible to assert within a landscape which itself depends on an illusory absence of bodies coerced to labour. My own non-labouring body, and its observational stance, seems to reproduce the terms of that illusion within the text, in a language that may register the Cartesian logic of the disciplined landscape. I risk this splintered register in order to underscore the artifice of the ethnographic story: its production and manufacture and the kinds of bodily labour which are absent in its making. This ethnography cannot be about anything but labour. The story about fieldwork, like its tea, is a tale about the price of romance, its seductive disembodiments.

The plantation field is literally the site of bent labouring, and that upon which coercive labour regimes are enacted. It is a conceptual 'field' which is both 'home' and not-home in complex ways. And the 'field' of investigation is the site upon which the anthropologist-as-*memsahib* is continuously marked as she swims through the capillaries of the plantation's social body. The reflection on the situated-ness of this movement through space, and the places of power *always* inhabited in this movement, cannot be extricated from the larger analytic and theoretical claims about plantation politics. Indeed, the illustrations of field research are indelibly marked by the actualities of method and its contradictions.

Organizing/developments

Out of the rich tapestry of these encounters of contradiction and possibility, three women constituted a triage of temporary kinship through which I came to some understanding of plantation power and the ethnographic project implicated in it. Bhagirathi Mahato, Anjali Mirdha and Munnu Kujoor sketched the landscape of village pedagogies. They steered me through the minefields of anger and disdain with trenchant and humorous commentaries. They introduced me to other kinswomen, welcomed me into their actual labouring fields, took me across the borders and memories of their lives. Though I met many other generous women and men, Munnu, Anjali and Bhagirathi were my primary teachers and they feature prominently in the textual moments which follow. I have employed pseudonyms for some of the other characters. When I left, we knew that 'return' would be difficult. But we still spoke about the possibilities of change and collective work.

We kept in intermittent touch through letters, written by kinsmen and translated through Calcutta to the US, and I returned to the plantations only in mid-1998. During that brief visit, we discussed the possibility of beginning a women's organization, or *mahila samity*, which would be community-based and might focus on a range of issues including income generation, health and literacy projects. Through brief but intensive discussions (about leadership, organization, financial control and navigation within a highly charged political landscape) twelve women, all full-time fieldworkers, expressed interest in working collaboratively.

I returned in February 1999 to work with the group, which had already started a savings account and a small piggery. By early April 1999, this small self-help group called itself Tea Garden Women's Service Organization (Cha Bagan Mahila Sewa Samity). In numerous meetings in the village, we agreed that it was important to attain status as a not-for-profit society, making the group an official non-governmental organization within West Bengal state law.[15] While this has not yet happened, the organizing efforts of 1999 and 2000 focused entirely on micro-enterprise and developing 'trust' within the group when it came to monetary issues.

The *mantra* that emerged from numerous meetings was that the self-help group would raise money by running businesses 'for the *samaj* (society)'. Ideas for home-based businesses included the piggery, a small poultry farm, low-interest loan schemes, and a small informal school, a *balwadi.* The basic ethic about 'business' was to raise money (through profit) for a small primary health-care clinic – something 'good' for the *samaj.* Money, capital, fiscal control were almost immediately put on the table. But where were 'we' going to get money? What was my own vexed, but necessary, role in such fund raising? How could they raise money as full-time workers with a daily wage rate of less than one dollar?

What follows, then, is an analysis of how we might understand such meditations on *capital* in the discourses of *both* grassroots organizing and ethnographic production. I have purposefully combined the politics of textuality and organizing so as to underscore the ways in which they share an epistemic base. As a primary narrator of this plantation story-in-text, that politics of location not only presents the authorial 'problem' but also offers a dialogical critique posed by women, and men, in the plantation. Such critiques – of both textual production and organizing practice – mesh a symbolic and material understanding of the relationship between knowledge production and the possibilities of social change.

'Third World' circulations (or where does the buck stop?)

I am thinking, then, of the circulation of capital, and the international division of labour which creates the numerical hierarchy of *first–second–third*, but most of all *circulation* and *capital.* Capital is created within the full sense of the 'economic' understood as a web of symbolic, bodily, material and fiscal action. 'Capital' represents, and engages, issues of worth and value and is most ordinarily, yet potently, distilled in the form of currency. The circulation of currency, and its different valuations against the dollar, for example, mediate the hierarchies of global power.

These fundamental links between capital/circulation/value suggest other economies of circulation. The manufacture and circulation of the ethnographic text is embedded within the historical flows of what Benedict Anderson has defined as 'print capitalism'. In the late twentieth century, when the value of 'print' was itself being challenged by virtual economies, the manufacturing of text-as-value became a vexed but important arena of study.

For those of us who still work 'within' print, our currency of value is the tangible calligraphies of text. Its language of literate expression, English in this instance, charts a particular terrain of circulation. In its circuits, it gestures towards a value embedded within the colonial mediations of *first–second–third.*[16] Most simply, its literate-ness and its language constrain its 'return' to the communities that it claims to represent. For US-based anthropologists, the ethnography is situated within this larger matrix but its worth is also inflected by the market forces of publication and academic employment.

I would like to suggest more broadly, however, that interrogations of ethnographic manufacture and textual circulation – within a global economy – offer important openings for conversations about ethnographic accountability and practice. In the following reflections, I offer two (temporal) registers of interrogation. In one, I am questioned about circulation and production of text. In the second, I reflect on the power of dollar circulations and the cash economies upon which plantation women's organizing is based.

Register one

In the middle of 1992, six months into my sojourn at *Sarah's Hope*, a man who is prominent in a local union and well respected in the villages agrees to assist me with a questionnaire and survey. He sets up appointments with several families, though all the formal interviews occur with men who claim their status as heads of their families. I am taken to a few elders of the Santhal community in the village. The Santhals in the plantation, I hear, keep to themselves and are respected for their courage and history of radical political action. I am nervous but eager to meet these elders, all men. I meet them in a collective and they introduce themselves as community spokesmen: 'When you speak to us, you speak to all of us.' After a few preliminary courtesies, they begin to ask questions about my project. I present our dialogue from notes and memory. It is only part of the larger conversation about Santhali history and memory. (I rarely take tape recorders into homes of people who do not know me and the politics of their fear informs this decision.)

Mukhiya (Elder): So this is interesting, what you are doing. We are puzzled by it. You are collecting information about us and making it into a book. Is that correct?

Piya: Yes, that is right. Not a book right away but hopefully it will turn into one....

Mukhiya: When it becomes a book, will it be in America?

Piya: I am confused. You mean whether I will write this in America?

Mukhiya: Yes. What use will it be in America?

Piya: You are right. I don't know. I will write it there, but I will also write it here.

Mukhiya: But what I want to ask you is this, *memsahib*, what use is such a thing? Yes, if the story of our *samaj* (society) is deposited with the *sarkar* (government), maybe they will know who we are ... but in America ... what is the point?

Piya: This is not going to the government. It may indirectly but that is not its aim. It is a thesis. A professor will read it.

Mukhiya: If a professor is going to read it, you cannot stop a professor from showing it to someone else.

Piya: No, ultimately I cannot. Anyway, if something is published, then it sits on a bookshelf and anyone can pick it up. Or buy it.

Mukhiya: Where will the book be published? Here or in America?

Piya: I don't know. Probably America.

Mukhiya: Well, maybe it is not such a bad thing. Something written for after we are gone.

Piya: I know, but you raise the key questions. What purpose is this? Who will it benefit? I don't know anymore. I came thinking that telling stories is important but now I am not so sure. I do think stories should be told, but of course it is not that simple.

Mukhiya: Look, *memsahib*, don't mind these questions. We have agreed to speak with you because we have watched you and it does not seem you are doing any harm.

For reasons that remain unspoken, I appear to have satisfied them and we continue to discuss colonial history and resistance. Yet we don't meet again.

I have been in the plantation long enough to have had numerous other conversations about the 'book', the purpose of this research, and I am not surprised by the questions. They offer, however, an acute and critical understanding of the political effects of writing and publication; location of production; and audience. Because my research has been perceived as 'government' work, I intuitively interpret his positive gesture to governmental access as a test. When I disavow any connection with the government, he reveals his unease about 'anyone' reading the text. The fact of the language of literateness distances the text at two levels. First, it enacts the privilege of literacy that removes most of the plantation community from access to it. Second, it will be written in English.

Out of the small percentage of the community who are literate, very few will read or write in English. The politics of in/accessibility charts the first vector of value of the ethnography for this community. My location of writing in the United States, and the circulation of what I write as a thesis or published text, also informs the critique and inscription of value: the issue of 'benefit' is closely linked to their sense of remove from 'America', where the text will be written. To these Santhali men, the journey of a text from the plantation to 'America' places it into a space of both ambiguity and irrelevance. Their critique compels deeper reflection on the nature of global power and the textual economies embedded within it. In so doing, it also suggests spaces within which reconfigurations of anthropological practice – and textual value – can occur. If community critiques can imbue text and practice, then another kind of postcolonial and de/colonizing dissonance can inform the global circulation and the political economy of ethnographic practice and production.

Register two

Consider another moment in February 1999, almost seven years after the Santhali elders have interrogated ethnographic production. It is a moment which offers another kind of symbolic economy of text, one in which actual values of capital (as money) and circulation are considered. The *mahila samity*, the women's self-help group, has met enthusiastically, eager to move ahead with implementing ideas around income generation. In meetings in mid-1998, the twelve women, apart from myself, who constitute the group have started a savings account in a neighbouring town in Chamurchi, Bhutan, just across the permeable border between the two countries.

'We don't want to depend on what money you bring, *didi*,' Bhagirathi tells me then, 'if you can help us, fine. But we work hard and we will raise money even if it is 5 rupees (8 cents) a week. Why should we accept any charity? We work hard ourselves.' The women, all wage earners, have participated in an informal banking system, called *chit*, a common practice in the plantation. A group of kinswomen, often members of a *dol* (labour gang), will loan each other money in turn. They will agree, for example, to raising 50 rupees (just over one dollar) each and giving it to one woman in the group. If six women participate, the recipient gets 300 rupees (about 7 dollars) which is substantial savings for a daily wage of 32 rupees (90 cents) a day. Thus, the savings account of the *mahila samity* formalizes an ongoing customary savings practice of plantation women.

I have returned with some money, donated by those who prefer to remain anonymous, but who are based in the United States. Dollars are translated into rupees at the rate of $1 = Rs42,[17] and we now have $500 to work with. This is a considerable fortune for the women, about Rs21,000, though small change in terms of international aid for development projects. Because we have continuous and deeply honest conversations about money and accountability during many meetings, decisions about fiscal control – and the ambivalence about this large amount – are negotiated openly. By the end of March 1999 we have decided that only thirteen of us will be part of the group and that monetary decisions will be made by us and only us. The borders of control and exclusion are drawn.

As an NRI, or non-resident Indian, I am encouraged (by policies of the Indian state) to bring in US dollars to my State Bank of India account. The desire for the dollar is a state imperative: the location of the nation in the Third World is determined by the accumulation of dollars and debts. Within this larger imperative, I inhabit the twilight zone of dollared foreigner who is not foreign. I have a new state-manufactured acronym identity: NRI. I decide that I will use its label of privilege to open a local bank account in plantation country from which money can be transferred into the women's account in Chamurchi, Bhutan. A comedy of errors ensues as I try to do this. Despite my privileged NRI status, and because I am not a tea manager, and perhaps because I am a single woman, local banks do not want to open an individual savings account. I meet the manager at the Bank of Bhutan in another neighbouring border town, Samchi, and he agrees to take the small fund. A huge fee for the transaction will have to be paid.

Dizzy with the movement across these borders, and stunned by the difficulty of operating within the formal banking economy in the region, I finally persuade a locally prominent union member to recommend me to another branch of the State Bank of India. In the process, I have gained deep insight into how difficult it must be for rural and plantation women to access the formal banking structure in the region.[18] Finally, my NRI status and the patronage of the well-connected local man allow me to open an account. The money is deposited and we can continue organizing. The cash-economy is still the mode of monetary circulation. Once we decide that we will focus on low-interest-rate savings, the money is transferred in cash.

In the middle of February 1999 I meet a local plantation doctor who wants to collaborate on primary health care delivery for plantation women and their children. We have several conversations in which I emphasize that plantation women must be at the centre of decision making, and we agree to meet as a group. Since the meeting will take place on another plantation, it is an outing and the women who can make it are excited. Other women from the doctor's plantation sit with us and our discussion ranges around a clinic and important budgetary considerations. A yearly budget – including a fully but minimally paid staff, rent and equipment – totals Rs600,000 ($14,285). Since this is almost inconceivable to us, given our small capital base, we agree that starting a clinic might be premature, but the group will confer about what happened at the clinic meeting. After a few days, the women call a meeting with me. They have discussed the matter while working in the field, had called another meeting at Munnu's house, and decided that they would not work further on the clinic idea.

26 February 1999. Notes of Meeting, Cha Bagan Mahila Seva Samity

I begin the meeting by saying that Bhagirathi and I had talked and so I knew their doubts about the clinic. I also reiterate that my central concern is that they really feel right about any commitment they make. I tell them that I recognize fully the enormous pressures on time; they should feel 100 per cent right about it. I tell them that I am only learning this money business, so that is not an issue. Everyone is looking very sombre and upset and I recognize that this has been a difficult *bichar* (deliberation) for them.

Moniki Mosi: But what do you really feel about all this?

Piya: What I said. Look, I told you that anything I do with anyone outside, you are the centre of it. (I hold out my palm again and point to the centre of my palm.) So I want to hear from all of you, your *bichar* (deliberation) ... Bhagirathi was not at the meeting we had with the doctor, but she has told me basically about the meeting you guys had yesterday at Munnu's house....

Munnu: Didi, hum ko booohutt dukh laga (I felt a lot of sadness) when you all were talking about six lakhs[19] ... that is just money that is going to be lost....

Thakurmoni: What I did not like also was the way the doctor pointed you out as the person who would bring the money....

Moniki: ... And where are you going to get that kind of money....

Piya: ... No, no, what you did not understand is this – that was the maximum of what it might cost to run a clinic.

Moniki Mosi: ... But you are still talking about a lot of money – whether it is three lakhs or four lakhs....

Bhagirathi: I have told *didi* this (turning to me) ... *didi*, we are all women here, you are a woman, we are women. You bring and will bring money from distant places and people, and other people will pocket the money. Then we will just be laughed at. But to us, it is also about the efforts of many others who gave money and your efforts so and what happens to the money is the most important thing ... not *one* paisa can be lost. Not one. Why should we give rent money for the clinic land? Why should we simply throw that money away? Do you know how much that money is?

Piya: But again, as I have told you over and over, this is not *my* money – please don't think about this individually in that sense.... When money is going to be given to you ... like the application we worked on last week,[20] it will be given to you.... I am only a channel.... I have told you where the money has come from.... I will always be clear with you about that.

Bhagirathi: Yes, like you are clear with us we want to be clear with you. *Yeh bharosa ka bat he, na didi*? (This is a matter of trust, no *didi*?)

Piya: Yes, but not on *my* terms, on your terms....

Bhagirathi: Yes of course, but we want to remember that....

Thakurmoni: I have to say that I was very upset when the *daktar* (doctor) pointed to you as the person who is going to bring you money.... I remembered that ... why all this pressure on you? I did not like that at all.

Bhagirathi: Basically here is the thing...we have decided that we want to buy our own land...

Piya: And on that land, we can work on several things together....

Munnu: Yes, because if something is to continue, then we must keep it in our hands and not anyone else's hands.

Anjali: And then, we can build buildings and even have a small room and bathroom for *didi* so she does not have to stay with other people.

Bhagirathi: It will be in *our* name, that is the most important thing ... it will be ours.

Thakurmoni: The other thing we were talking about was that this clinic will be for people who can read and write, *burra aadmi* (big people) like those other women who were sitting there, they had some education ... they would get those salaries and the money ... and where would we be?

Gita: Yes, when you write Rs600,000 in English, like you and the doctor were doing, we won't even know what is being written.

Piya: Aha, this is why you guys must do your own education class ... what is happening with Kapil ... is the blackboard being made?... Can you learn mathematics?

Thakurmoni: But see, the thing is this, we have to think – will there be any benefit for us? Our children? There are many doctors in the town, this would just be another thing like that ... so a doctor comes from elsewhere ... it is the same old thing. Somebody else makes money off us. It will still be run by you *bara aadmi* (big people).

Piya: I agree with you, of course ... and why not ... if you are not comfortable with it....

Moniki Mosi: Didi, we could not open our mouths there. Look, the doctor is a good man, the other women are fine (referring to the women from another plantation who had attended the meeting), we will be happy to assist them but this is not the time to do this. This is *nothing* against them ... you do understand that....

Thakurmoni: Are we still going to the sewing centre thing on Sunday? (in reference to another small women-run business project in the same plantation where the meeting was held)

Piya: What do you want to do?

Bhagirathi: Of course we will go, that is a separate issue.

Piya: Yes, that is a separate issue.... (We schedule the trip.) There is another issue – what will we do about the big meeting planned on Wednesday the 10th? Do we cancel it?

Everyone: Oh yes....

Thakurmoni: Who will tell them?... You....

Piya: Whoever ... if we are going and Bhagirathi ... then if it comes up we will tell them. But I will also speak to the doctor separately.

(The meeting ends with a more extended conversation about land ownership.)

I have staged this vignette to underscore women's analysis and critique about what is often a typical community-based development idea: a primary health care clinic. I pursued the idea because of what I had learned about the state of medical treatment in the region. Though some tea plantations offer decent health care in 'garden hospitals', corruption and a lack of infrastructure in most plantations, and in regional medical centres, has resulted in extremely inadequate health care access and delivery. Indeed, women had emphasized this lack by telling me about gastro-intestinal epidemics during the monsoons and high rates of infant mortality. What I had envisioned was a small clinic in the nearby town of Banarhat in which plantation women were primary policy makers.

Their objections to the plan revolved around issues of fund raising and fiscal control. It is important to note, also, that the meeting with the doctor did not occur in their home plantation and involved women whom they did not know. The issue of knowing other women, of being from a familiar kinship space, was (I suspect) one reason for a collective unease – particularly with regard to issues of money. Indeed, in meetings which preceded the discussion of the clinic idea, and had to do with the organizational structure of the self-help group, women always emphasized the issue of trust and control around money-matters.

One of the first objections raised was the scale of the money required for a clinic. The doctor assumed, rightly, that with some effort I could get this funding (because of my access to US funding sources), but some women were resistant to this idea. Since they had also started saving money from their wages, and Bhagirathi had emphasized that they were not interested in 'charity', this issue of scale had much to do with their sense of having 'earned' the control of funding. Their resistance was also linked to an awareness that such large amounts of funding (particularly from abroad) would be open to both corruption and appropriation. Indeed, the doctor (who Moniki Mosi explicitly noted was a 'good man') was criticized for assuming that I could bring the amounts required. Even though I emphasized that, with time and careful grant writing, this might be possible, their objections were underwritten by a shrewd and pragmatic understanding that I, too, might be 'taken for a ride'. When it comes to money, and men, they emphasized repeatedly, you could not trust anyone. The scale of the project funding was connected to literacy ('we won't even know what is being written') and upper-caste/class privilege ('It will still be run by you *bara aadmi* (big people)').

Some women also voiced the importance of trust between all of us, as women – despite my own markedly outside and privileged positioning – and the importance of 'owning' the process so as to ensure that money was not wasted, especially if it came from 'elsewhere'. While I appreciated, and believed, the verbalized support of my own role in fund raising, I remained alert for the narratives-not-spoken. My role as a 'broker' is a vexed one, though in the thick of meeting and talk, I am not inclined towards philosophical reflections. I recognize most keenly that their rejection (of the clinic idea) has opened up other important discussions about the bottom-line of any effort such as this. Where does money come from? Who can script and read the terms of money? How much money? Who owns the process?

It is significant that the failure of the primary clinic idea led to productive discussions about micro-enterprise which would raise money for land, to be owned by the self-help group, upon which more self-sustainable development projects would take place. A self-help loan scheme, with low interest rates for women, was then implemented. However, its possibilities, and its failures, are part of another story.

Capital and pedagogy

I began this chapter with an extended discussion about the politics of anthropological writing. I then offered a literary and ethnographic scrutiny of the ways in which my own politics of location informed the knowledge base of a plantation ethnography. Yet, in offering such a scrutiny of ethnographic politics, I sought to push the current well-known debates about anthropological representation in a slightly different direction by juxtaposing both textuality and women's grassroots organizing within one theoretical field of engagement. I have suggested that capital – through its symbolic, textual, and material moments – articulates the terms of globality, and its circuits of power, when it comes to both ethnographic writing and community-based organizing practices. In searching through the thickets of this ethically fraught terrain of both representation and accountability, aware always of disavowal and failure, I recognize that through a pedagogy that links power to teaching/learning/dialogue, I can think of capital and its de/humanizing circulations in radical ways. The women in the plantation alert me, with their critique, to the importance of always connecting such abstract meditations to lessons on the ground. In that they present these lessons as a pedagogy, which reaches beyond easy and naïve claims about the politics of both representation and accountablity.

Thus, the academic anthropologist, who is also a postcolonial subject, constitutes her terrain of action with 'Third World women' through a complex dance of identification and distance. She is, within the First World of her textual production and institutional pedagogical practices, labelled as a 'Third World' woman. Placed within the contradictions of a class privilege which makes her not-so-Third World within the First, she seizes the category with a breathless desperation when pinned by the effects of a disciplining gaze which sees her as angry and native. In the 'Third World' of her roots, she represents the First, with her access to the currencies of a global superpower. But there are First Worlds within the Third which she inhabits as well, marked by an urban bourgeois privilege that can dance with MTV and carry a cell phone. These are worlds within worlds, within worlds. Writing 'Third World Women' is not a transparent task.

I work, like many others, in multiple spaces. I prefer to think of Three Worlds, inextricably connected, rather than 'the Third World' which assumes hierarchy, superior orders. But I cannot deny the actualities of power which have constituted the plantation as a 'Third World'. When I am in southern California, the orality of teaching and narrating the stories of the plantation comes close to the immediacy and power that only the spoken word has, whose cadences cannot be captured in text. Narrating the plantation story to my southern California students sometimes sparks stunning connections. When I speak about the labour of tea cultivation and the primacy of women in conducting that work, one young Chicana writes a brilliant essay about her own labour as a girl picking oranges in the citrus fields of southern California. I like to think that these are the coalition effects of two worlds coming into contact through the power of the spoken, bodied and textual imagination.

In Calcutta, my urban and bourgeois family, who have enabled my work in the most fundamental ways, patiently translate letters from Hindi into English and send them on e-mail to me. When I send an e-mail back, the same process happens the other way. The communication is intermittent but important still. Imagine this circulation between the oral, the written, the virtual. Where there is will to communicate, we find ways, even if it means leaping across three worlds of expression and three worlds of power. I would like to suggest that the anthropology is always in process and the written text is just one moment of these three worlds. It cannot be closed to its own historical movements. It is embedded always in a pedagogy – of teaching/learning/dialogue – which should, ideally, remain honest to its own artifice, its global traffic, its currencies of contradiction, power and hope.

Notes

1 For representative discussions about such 'new' theorizing, see Abu-Lughod (1990b: 7–27); Narayan (1993: 671–86); Savigliano (1995); Visweswaran (1988: 27–44).
2 I understand the relationship of the text and its 'actual' in Dorothy Smith's terms. She suggests that the 'text is the bridge between the actual and the discursive' and calls for 'a set of procedures of writing the social into texts, and hence of exploring the power of the textual to analyze and isolate dimensions of organization that are fully embedded in the actualities of living'. She argues for an understanding of textual relationality in which 'we are led back to outside the text in which living goes on and in which the text is being read' Smith (1992: 1, 92).
3 I am indebted here to Elizabeth Enslin's important critique (1994) of poststructuralist ethnographic writing, and its relationship to anthropological/ feminist practice and accountability.
4 For an early comprehensive discussion about the relationship between anthropology and colonialism, see Asad (1973); for another important extra-disciplinary critique, see Said (1989).
5 In posing these rhetorical questions, I am indebted to a growing literature on the relationship between postcolonial, feminist and anthropological theorizing. For a representative sampling of these, see John (1996: 5–28); Ong (1988); Savigliano (1995), especially her first chapter.
6 In this case, I refer quite specifically the US state's power, through immigration legal policy, to determine when and if one can enter, leave and return to the United States.
7 I have discussed these issues at greater length in the introductory chapter of my book (Chatterjee 2001).
8 Patai (1994: 21–43).
9 By 'global', I only gesture to the interconnections between plantation systems through labour emigration. For example, in the late nineteenth century, labour emigration from British India to Fiji and British Guyana fed the supply of labour for plantation systems in these areas.
10 By *adivasi*, I gesture to the lower and out-caste positionings of many plantation communities. I prefer not to use the 'tribe' as the more common nomenclature because of its colonizing homogeneity. Though *adivasi* is itself an overarching and homogenizing rubric, it is used self-referentially – though some communities, like the Nepalis, will define themselves explicitly against it.
11 This connection between labour and commodity is a central argument in my larger study. See Chapter 2 in Chatterjee (2001).
12 In posing these questions, I am indebted to the writings of gender standpoint theorists, and Sandra Harding's work on scientific method and its relation to epistemology.
13 This exact descripton is extended into a consideraton of the relationship between landscapes, memory and power in Chatterjee (2001).
14 The term *coolie*, often used disparagingly even when self-referential (as I am suggesting in this phrasing) is an artifact from the colonial era. It is a category not confined to tea plantations but used widely to signify 'manual labour' all over Asia.
15 For a succinct but comprehensive discussion of women's participation in and leadership of non-governmental organizations, see Silliman (1999: 133–62). To become an official NGO within West Bengal, this self-help group would have to achieve 'society' status within state law. This has not yet occurred.
16 In invoking the circulation within the international division of labour, I loosely follow Gayatri Chakravorty Spivak's important argument and suggestion that 'on the other side of the international division of labor, the subject of exploitation cannot know and speak the text of female exploitation, even if the absurdity of the nonrepresenting intellectual making space for

her to speak is achieved. The woman is doubly in shadow.... To confront them is not to represent (*vereten*) them but to learn to represent (*darstellen*) ourselves. This argument would take us into a critique of disciplinary anthropology and the relationship of elementary pedagogy and disciplinary formation.' Spivak (1988: 288–9).

17 This was the rate of exchange at the time of these deliberations, early 1999.

18 Two of the most significant mobilizations around women's banking in South Asia which have successfully countered the deep-seated prejudices and structural obstacles to poor women's fiscal autonomy are: the Self Employed Women's Association (SEWA) in Ahmedabad, Gujarat; and the Grameen Bank in Bangladesh. See Kalima Rose's *Where Women are Leaders* for a comprehensive account of how SEWA reworked the rules of banking so that women could become full participants and leaders in economic progress (Rose 1992). Recently, a movement by tribal women in Chattisgarh, Bihar, called the Didi [elder sister] Bank has led to the mobilization of thousands of tribal women. North Bengal plantation women are ready for this kind of mobilization because they are primary wage earners themselves.

19 A lakh is 100,000.

20 We had worked on a Global Fund for Women application the previous week.

14

Practising Theory through Women's Bodies

Public Violence and Women's Strategies of Power and Place

Ramona Pérez

> [T]he effects of extralocal and long-term processes are only manifested locally and specifically, produced in the actions of individuals living their particular lives, inscribed in their bodies and their words (Abu-Lughod 1991: 150).

Peering out of the window of a *colectivo* (community-based taxi) on my way back to the community that I have lived and worked in for several years, I sit back and try to see the community as I had when I first arrived: steeped in tradition, with distinct boundaries and rules on love and life. In the late afternoon, as the heat of the day dissipates, the roads fill up with people emerging from the coolness of their homes to run last-minute errands. Driving through the unmarked entrance to the official part of the *pueblo*, Atzompa appears as a sprawling yet traditional community. Carts pulled by burros or oxen share the road with cars, barefoot children in ragged clothes mill around small adobe homes on dirt roads, and herds of cows, bulls, goats, and burros are guided home through the main street of the town by young boys and their dogs. The community of Atzompa lies 8 kilometres outside the state capital, Oaxaca, and is a primary tourist destination for ceramic production, a result of their inclusion in the tourist development project of the Mexican state. Atzompa is a *cabacera* (municipal seat) for six *colonias* (neighbourhoods) and three *ranchos* (farming communities). It lies at the base of the ancient city of Monté Albán and traces its history back 2,500 years as the primary producer of ceramics for the area. The community is in a conscious state of flux, aware that they must retain their traditional history in order to survive in the tourist market as an independent community but also understanding that nothing will be the same as they move further and further into the global tourist and export markets. Men, women and children are cognizant of the negotiations they are making in carving out new forms of identity that must carry the next generation into a world dominated by Western ideals that offers much in terms of material gain but equally takes away from their social practices and lifestyle. The dynamic changes and negotiations are no longer obscure to me, as they were when I first arrived in 1993 and my vision was clouded by the images of stasis depicted in much of the existing ethnographic literature. Women and young girls scamper from their homes to a corner store, barefoot and dirty from the day's work, greeting other women in modern dress who have stopped at the store on their way home from work in the city – both are buying last minute items for *cena*, the late-night meal. Two huge tourist buses lumber down the main road, returning their passengers to Oaxaca after an all-day excursion into the so-called exotic world of indigenous artisans who, according to the Secretary of Tourism, still live an ancient lifestyle that has changed little in over 2,000 years.

What does it mean to be in an 'experimental moment' in anthropology (Vincent 1991: 58), to be given licence to write in diverse forms that defy old parameters, if we do not begin by reinventing the way in which we question, approach, conduct and frame our fieldwork analyses? These are especially important questions for those of us who are returning to places of origin for our work, where we have accepted the responsibility of writing ethnography that reflects an internal understanding of our lives and practices. Many of us wrestle with the question Spivak asked, can the subaltern speak? (1988) – especially since it is we, and not our subjects, who determine the subject of our writing. It is an important question, one we continue to wrestle with almost fifteen years after Spivak admonished us to contemplate it. Spivak has tried to make clear that her question is not one of words but of receipt:

> The actual fact of giving utterances is not what I was concerned about. What I was concerned about was that even when one uttered, one was constructed by a certain kind of psychobiography, so that the utterance itself – this is another side of the argument – would have to be interpreted in the way in which we historically interpret anything. (1996: 291)

So perhaps the other side of the question is one we should also answer: are we listening to the subaltern? Not just to their words but to their language, the full performance, of their lives?

As I read the ethnographic literature on Oaxaca, moving from gender-based ethnographies on craft production to ethnographies on religious practices, migration, and transnational strategies, I was taken aback by the lack of information on the actual dynamics of women's lives within the communities under study. Despite the move to place women in the forefront of ethnographic work in the Valley of Oaxaca, the restraints of the peasant discourse that continues to dominate the ethnography of Mexico today, resulted in a continuation of dichotomous categories in describing and analyzing the complexity of women's lived identity. Women and their communities remained trapped within a series of oppositional categories such as modern/traditional, peasant/proletarian, *indigena/mestiza*, rural/urban, core/periphery and public/private, among others (Cook and Binford 1990; Stephen 1991), preventing any kind of real description of the many issues that affect their world. The ethnographies are rich in detail about the economic impact of capitalism on community social structure. They provide a history of change in patterns of subsistence, market exchange, development projects, migration, fiesta sponsorship, religious practice and other such issues, but rarely offer more than a vignette or two about the dynamics, the day-to-day adjustments, behind the changes. The ethnographic literature of Oaxaca had moved from a framework of analysis based on dependency theory in the 1970s and 1980s to neo-Marxist analyses that, while placing women as the central subject, framed their lives as governed primarily by male-dominated economics and oppression. As I moved from 'guest' to 'participant' in Atzompa and became embroiled in the intense dynamics of the community fiesta system of power, politics and identity negotiations, I began to realize that the fiesta was an important social arena in their lives. The traditional religious fiesta, long held as a primary locus for male politics and power throughout Mesoamerica, became a space in which emerging gender identities and roles, a result of women's dominance in the tourist-based craft economy of Santa María Atzompa, were mitigated through the reinterpretation of existing practices, customs and spatial markers. It was, and is, a performance of power and rite, scripted not only by men but also by women.

Fiesta as tradition

The historical development and economic function of Mesoamerican fiestas, along with their social and symbolic significance and the excessive consumption of alcohol that is such an integral part of the ritual, has been given much scholarly attention (Bricker 1981; Cancian 1965, 1990; Earle 1992; Eber 1995; Greenberg 1981; Kearney 1970; Nash 1966; Rosenbaum 1993; Roseberry 1989; Stephen 1991; Vogt 1976; Wasserstrom 1983; Wolf 1966). These analyses have focused primarily on male negotiations of power and have not seen the fiesta as a legitimated social space for the gendered negotiations of power and place.[1] In this chapter I look at the fiesta as an ideological and physical space where religion, social roles and formal political relations are reaffirmed, while at the same time they are being contested. Eber (1995), Rosenbaum (1993), and Stephen (1991) have explored women's participation in religious cargos as a means for expressing women's symbolic power as representative of their family's status in community politics, but have done so within frameworks of class and economic privilege. My analysis expands our understanding of the fiesta as more than an arena for the affirmation or symbolic expression of class- or ethnic-based identities for family units and into an arena where the contestation, reinterpretation and modification of gender roles and identities of individual women, their families and the community are played out. I discuss how the suppressed hostilities toward women's emerging autonomy as primary economic providers manifests in male-initiated abuses against women, including physical violence, degradation and symbolic oppression of women within the social group. I also demonstrate how, consciously and unconsciously, women perpetuate the patriarchal structure of the fiesta as a means of containing and controlling the violence against them, which in turn allows them to reimagine and recreate social roles throughout the community. Expanding on Coward's notion that women's desires are often modes of sustaining male privilege (1985: 16), I argue that women in Atzompa (Atzompeñas) see the fiesta in terms of a symbolic space where they reaffirm their ties to traditional perceptions of marriage and household through long-term practices of food preparation and serving, spatial separation and a subordinate status in drinking and dancing. For many men and women, this reaffirmation justifies Atzompeñas' ability to break with other traditional roles, such as female confinement to the household, use of men as intermediaries in their craft sales and distribution, educational restrictions on their daughters and the inability to seek wage labour. I argue that Atzompeñas accept domestic violence as a natural reaction by men threatened by women's increasing autonomy. By moving the violence from the household to a public forum, such as the fiesta, communal traditions appear to be reaffirmed; family units are able to show their alignment with the community while creating new forms of household composition, economic activity, and male–female relationships. Finally, I discuss some women's perpetuation of these abuses as not only a compromise towards their growing autonomy but also as a perceived source of power gained through mimicking male behaviours. This is not an easy subject to address. Violence against women can never be justified, but it must be read and understood within the framework that produces and maintains it.

Social symbolism in the fiesta

Gendered violence and oppression are significant aspects of the fiesta experience. The fiesta, through its historic symbolism, is a stage from which people in the community act out their roles within the larger social group. The fiesta, as a safe haven for candid behaviour, literally becomes a theatrical production of individual stories played out against the community's story. It is a highly charged political microcosm of intra-community relations in which ritual and drinking serve to reaffirm power, prestige and harmony by removing the veil of formal relations and placing the negotiations between people within an arena of communal safety and refuge (Turner 1974). As Cohen argues, a communal festival '[a]lthough ... essentially a cultural, artistic spectacle ... is always political, intimately and dynamically related to the political order and to the struggle for power within it' (1993: 04). In the Mesoamerican fiesta, issues of disagreement or disharmony are played out within the fiesta due to the altered state of mind produced by the consumption of alcohol, which is believed to produce the 'true' feelings of the participants.[2] Thus, drunken individuals are not held accountable for actions that run contradictory to their own, or the community's, standards of acceptable behaviour.

A significant component of the fiesta, for those who use it as a forum for the resolution of conflict, is the power created by the attendance of almost all town officials at the celebration. Their participation renders the fiesta a political as well as ritual space. This rendering of power is extremely important to the issue of violence against women. Historically, women's only recourse against domestic violence has been the town council. When this legal body is present at the fiesta, any negative occurrence loses its significance as an overt act of hostility and becomes part of the larger ritual of communal identity. Domestic violence played out in this arena is no longer a private issue nor an individual act, but a public issue and a public act.

Gender and community identities

The melting boundaries between urban and rural, and between local and global, are evident throughout the world, but are especially evident in geographic spaces immediately surrounding major population centres. Access to wage employment, social services, media and telecommunications, land encroachment from the city, tourist traffic, and so forth, fan out, dispersing unequally as they melt into the fan of the next major population centre. Rural communities negotiate this expansion differently, some attempting to integrate with the major population centres, others creating boundaries that allow them to be identified as separate, and still others negotiating this distinction depending on context. Within the Valley of Oaxaca there are no clear physical distinctions between Oaxaca City and the surrounding communities, nor between them and national and transnational spaces. Instead, there is a constant blending or blurring of boundaries as people, ideas, objects and other things circulate within these spaces.

As communities become less dependent on agricultural subsistence they increase their participation and reliance on the production and distribution of crafts and petty commodities, wage labour, self-employment in both the formal and informal economies, and long term migration to other parts of Mexico and the United States. The effects of the dissolution of boundaries and the opening up of diverse alternatives have had profound implications for women in rural communities. Women in these communities increasingly find themselves at the heart of the solution to economic problems, while at the same time their participation and resulting autonomy creates disruptions in existing social and political structures. In addition, craft-producing communities must balance the image of being 'indigenous' or 'peasant' for the tourists with the increasing acquisition of Western or modern conveniences (Canclini 1982). This balancing act tends to manifest in the bodies of women, who physically represent the community to the outside world as well as to the community.

Women have been moving into the informal economy within Oaxaca for generations (Beltrán *et al.* 1991; Stephen 1991) through the extensive market system that has dominated Oaxacan commerce for centuries (Diskin 1969; Malinowski and de la Fuente 1982; Waterbury 1968). Within the last thirty years, as tourism has increased the demand for craft production, women have become more visible in the market as the image of the 'traditional indigenous woman' becomes synonymous with their craft products. This image of the traditional indigenous female artisan was commodified throughout Mexico and sold on the global tourist market (Canclini 1993; Novelo 1976), a situation that the women of Atzompa are extremely conscious of and have used in their negotiations of power over their craft production and marketing. In the early 1990s, the Mexican government established programmes aimed specifically at women in craft-producing communities (Nash 1993: 6). Nash points out that although the programmes were designed to give women greater 'autonomy and a political role in leadership positions … women have not asserted control over the profits nor taken as active a role in decision making as the organization allows' (*ibid.*: 9). Nash contends that this is due largely to patriarchal structures which 'encourage women to assign leadership roles to men' (*ibid.*: 11). To say that women 'have not asserted control' or 'taken an active role in decision making', in my opinion, dismisses the advances local women have made, however subtle in the eyes of women researchers, that mark moments of transition in local thought and practice. As indicated in many of the contributing essays in Nash, the issue appears to be more of a reflection of the conflict between the ideology of the local community and the Mexican nation state in terms of the management of development programmes. That is, local communities are still in the process of interpreting and incorporating these new economic programmes, which have internal structures that challenge local structures of gender roles and community identity. While the immediate response may indeed appear to move towards traditional patriarchal practices, contestation and renegotiation may be occurring at the same time, in different forms and expressions.

For Atzompa, as well as many craft communities in Mexico that have been immersed in the global tourist economy, there is confusion or a lack of cohesion in determining which of the many roles and identities being projected through the various media is the best for the community. A significant result of the indeterminacy and disagreement among community members as to the issues of identity is the destabilization of existing power structures. This instability creates further unrest and more insidious reactions to perceived changes within the social structure. Whereas histories and previous ethnographies of Mexico's participation in modernity indicate that new practices, ideas and perceptions were integrated into community social structure through existing power structures, such as the patriarchal political and religious hierarchies that surround the fiesta, now these structures are being challenged and new forms of group power, based on new processes, are being created.

Women's changing social status

Current social change in Oaxaca includes the renegotiation by women of their place and movement into mainstream positions of power. By moving into previously barred spaces and becoming more assertive, women of rural communities are challenging existing social structures that have formed both the imagined and real backbone of family structure in Oaxacan society. Specifically, Oaxaqueñas are outwardly challenging the mythical family structure that was based on female economic, political and social dependency on the male. Women's more active participation in arenas outside the household, such as producing incomes equal to or greater than men can earn, working outside the household compound and in many cases outside the community, holding offices as cooperative and union presidents, treasurers and secretaries, and negotiating and interfacing directly with the tourist trade, are negating many of the conditions of female dependency. For men, the recognition and subsequent acceptance of the economic need for women to be in these spaces has not been an easy transition. The turn toward violence and alcohol consumption as modes of expression of the tension associated with men's frustrations over female autonomy was a prominent theme in Gutmann's recent work on gender negotiations in Mexico City. He notes:

> Alcohol consumption and housework are realms in which limited degendering has taken place in Santo Domingo, just as the probable rise in domestic violence against women there is linked to an intensified engendering of aggression as some men seek to 'resolve' the contradictions and confusion in their masculinities resulting from women's increasingly declaring their independence from men. These emergent cultural practices taken as a whole describe and define gender relations and identities in Santo Domingo today. (1996: 244)

As the historically prevalent social space for negotiations of power and place, the fiesta has become a primary forum for the resolution of conflicts created by women becoming active partners in the economic and social position of the family, household and community.[3] Hostilities and anger regarding women's participation in spaces outside of the idealized are played out in the symbolically charged fiesta in the form of aggressive acts, both direct and indirect, against women and female children. I am arguing that the movement of gendered physical, emotional and mental abuse into a public space, such as the fiesta, is a clear indication that such behaviour is not only acceptable to the larger social unit, but sanctioned by it.

The fiesta

Historically, rural Mesoamerican fiestas were open to the entire town, especially the fiestas that honoured a saint or commemorated an important life passage for Jesus or the Virgin Mary. Although theoretical discussion as to the historical origin and purpose of the fiesta cycle continues, most scholars agree that since colonial times the fusion of public worship, familial sponsorship, social and political prestige, and excessive drinking has been at the heart of these extravaganzas. Today, as in the past, political offices are obtained only after serving multiple religious cargos. Each event is ranked in accordance with prestige, determined for the most part by the amount of wealth expended in order to pay adequate homage to the saint. Thus, issues such as the number of people in attendance, the length of each day's festivities, the amount, type and quality of food served, the availability of *mezcal* and beer, and the type and number of musical bands are extremely important to the prestige earned by the sponsors. Over the last sixty years, as *pueblos* have grown in population, the fiestas have become private affairs. Masses, processions, shrine decorations and other processes associated with the reverence and dedication to the saint continue to be conducted within public spaces and remain open to the general population. However, the continuation of ritual with food, alcohol, music and dance are by invitation only and serve to reaffirm alliances and establish new relationships.

In Atzompa, invitations are made through face-to-face visits by the *mayordomos* (sponsors) who visit each household at least two weeks before the event. Individuals who are unable to participate fully in the fiesta, specifically in the drinking that is such an integral part of the process, are obligated to express such problems during the visit. In most cases, the sponsors will excuse them from attending, accepting their inability to participate. The acquiescence to the declination to attend is seen by older, established families as an affirmation of their alliance with the sponsors and a relief from the pressure of drinking placed on the participants. Younger, up-and-coming families and female heads of households will not risk losing the opportunity to show publicly the extensions of their relationships, and will ignore health issues, personal problems associated with drinking, and employment constraints in order to participate. The fiesta and the concurrent ability to drink have become such strong political forces within the community that health risks ranging from recurrent dysentery to diabetic shock to physical abuse are considered normal repercussions of participation. The following vignette exemplifies this point.

Although I had been witness to numerous occasions of diabetic shock after my first few months in the *pueblo*, I had assumed they were unconscious incidents, a result of the person not being aware of their illness or its severity. I discovered through a good friend's negotiation with her own illness that it was not naïveté but a conscious choice.

Antonia had been struggling with severe diarrhœa for months. After several weeks of trying to cure herself with local remedies she finally went into the city to see a doctor. She was given a ten-day therapy of injectable antibiotics and vitamins. Four days into the therapy, I went over to see how she was, only to find out that she had not started the programme. She had a fiesta to attend that weekend and another the following. Since she could not drink and take antibiotics, she chose to participate in the fiestas. Angry, I challenged her on her decision, citing her position as a single mother responsible for her son as well as her aging mother. Antonia broke out into the laughter that always preceded one of her lectures on 'how life was in the *pueblo*' and motioned me to sit and listen:

> I am a single woman. I have been alone for seventeen years now. I have earned my place here, my presence is in demand at the fiesta. But if I do not go, if I am not strong, then I will lose. The others who wait to take my position will use this time to talk about me, to convince people that I cannot do my job because I am a weak woman. It is this way for all of us. A man, well, he can miss many fiestas before they begin to talk. But a woman, no, I cannot miss these fiestas. If I were a wife, I could stay home while my husband went to represent us. I have only myself and so I will go and my *pueblo* of worms [she pats her stomach], well, they can get drunk and dance before I kill them.[4]

In many ways I realized Antonia was right. Her power within the *pueblo* was a result of her ability to contract employment within the city as a ceramics teacher, thereby drawing tourists and professional artists to her home and, more importantly, to her work. As her personal wealth and outside fame grew, her position within the *pueblo* moved from being a pitied, abandoned woman to a source of political power. In recent years Antonia has held numerous high-ranking positions in the ceramics union, including her current position as president of the glaze cooperative. But in spite of her prestige and power, her position remains precarious, having to be re-established through constant participation in fiestas. This situation, as she explained, is not only unequal with men but exacting to the point of jeopardizing her health and life.

The need for women to constantly negotiate and affirm their power and prestige through fiesta participation is a form of subtle oppression that demonstrates how power relations are skewed in favour of male dominance. It expresses an undercurrent of hostility and control over women that is reflective of the bolder processes of aggressive and violent behaviour that are played out within the active space of the fiesta, an area I will discuss in a moment.

Another form of hostile control can be seen in the responsibility given to unmarried daughters for taking care of their fathers, grandfathers and childless uncles during the fiesta. The girls, ranging in age from seven to adolescence, are at the beck and call of the men. They run errands, help them off to the side to urinate or vomit, drag their passed-out bodies out of the way of other participants, and help them stumble home at the end of the night. Twice I witnessed young girls being slapped and castigated by their mothers when they refused to cater to their fathers' demands during a fiesta. After one such incident I asked Dominga, a friend who had always been vocal about men's abusive acts, why she had forced her daughter to help her husband the night before. Her response was defensive and indicative of the way in which women reproduce the cycle: 'Well, no, I don't like it, but it is the custom here and we cannot shame him in front of his friends. But he has shamed himself. Look, he cannot help but see the disgust in his daughter's eyes.' While I could see the tension between Elario and his daughter, it was all too obvious to me that the situation would fade into the normalcy of patterned behaviours within the household.

Spatial markers in the fiesta

Spatially, negotiations of control are played out through the return to clear-cut dichotomies in men's and women's roles in the making of the fiesta itself. Women, many of whom hold positions within the workforce and community equal to their spouses or fathers, are re-relegated to their previous positions of overt servitude as food preparers and servers. On a daily basis, women remain responsible for food preparation, but many men contribute to the workload by purchasing foodstuffs on their way home from work, setting the table, and watching the children while women finish the food preparation. Such is not the case during fiestas.

Facilities for food preparation are constructed the week before the fiesta by the male household members. Many households that have modern kitchens with concrete floors, refrigerators, and gas stoves will not use them during a fiesta. Other labour-saving devices such as blenders or large grinders will also not be utilized. Instead, women will revert to using the hastily constructed outdoor kitchens of cane and thatch within which they dig cooking pits and cover them with heavy ceramic pots. Rain, flies, mosquitoes and hungry dogs add to the work burden, all of which are accepted in order to maintain a certain ritual and historic symbolism in the food preparation for the fiesta. Justifications for these conditions by both men and women focus on the accommodation, both spatially and in shared labour, of the large groups of women who are symbolically required to participate. Streamlining food preparation through the use of modern kitchen facilities would eliminate the need for the groups of women, thereby ending a historic chain of labour exchange that has cemented alliances based on mutual need (see Stephen 1991). The maintenance of this communal bond is considered far more important than the quick preparation of food. Perhaps of more significance to the women are the hours spent together preparing the food. This provides an opportunity for gossip, joking and sharing of confidences; a time where relationships are re-solidified and new ones established. I learned more about women's lives in these three-day fiesta cycles than I did at any other time in my field experience. The hours of seeding peppers, grinding corn, stirring *atole* and wading ankle-deep in mud to serve the guests were indeed worth all the discomfort in terms of camaraderie and networking.

Within the arena of the fiesta, *mayordomos*, honorary male guests and participants sit at tables separate from women and children and are served immediately upon arriving. Throughout the day and into the night men will arrive, be fed and drink, while the women continue food preparation and serving, only taking breaks to eat. Women in the labour groups do not participate in the drinking or dancing until after 8 pm, when it is no longer customary to expect food upon your arrival. By this hour, the men are completely intoxicated and little to no socializing occurs between the women who prepared the fiesta and their spouses. As the final dishes are cleaned and food stored for the night, the women will be presented with a bottle of *mezcal* and usually, but not always, a case of beer by the *mayordomos*. This 'token of appreciation' was introduced in the last decade and is viewed by the women as a significant indicator of respect by the men. The women then join the couples who were not part of the labour force on the dance floor. It is normally at this point, when the women join the larger group, that the physical violence will begin. After I had witnessed my first display of domestic violence at a fiesta, I learned to anticipate the event through the mounting tensions of the men. This night, as I sat with the other *mayordamas* and their *comadres*, sipping our beer and ritually passing the *mezcal*, a screech from one of the women dancing reverberated through the crowd. The crowd parted to allow the visibility of the woman being slapped, full swing, by her husband. Forgetting all I had been taught about remaining neutral, I jumped from my chair towards the woman, but before I could push my way through the crowd, the woman was surrounded by a large group of women and children. Her mother-in-law faced off with her son, shoving him and admonishing him for his behaviour. He dipped and moved around her, trying to hit his wife over the heads of the other women, to no avail. The crowd around her was too deep and he was too conscious of not hurting any of these other women. After a few moments, he returned to his seat with the other men. The sequence of events was played out two more times before he gave up and sat weeping with the other men. He eventually made his way over to his wife, apologized for his behaviour and crawled onto her lap for forgiveness. I was shocked and could only sit and watch this whole spectacle play out. The next morning, I visited the woman, Angela, and found her with a bruised cheek and swollen lips. She tried to smile and offered me her understanding of the incident:

> I knew I was going to be the one last night. He has been mad at me for weeks because I went to Oaxaca to look for a job. I am not going to look anymore, he needs me to stay here for now. But after last night, he said I should look here in Atzompa for a job.

She paused, smiled, and asked, 'Did you see how my mother-in-law defended me?' (Field notes, 1996).

Breaking women's bodies

Physical violence tends to take two forms: husband/wife abuse and group attacks against a single male. In almost every situation of husband/wife abuse, the attacks are verbally provoked by the man, followed by blows directed toward the face as soon as the woman responds in any way. The pattern is so predictable that a woman will normally not suffer more than a few punches before her female relatives and children swarm to her defence. As described above, women form a ring around the woman and the dominant older female, in many cases the mother of the husband, becomes the spokeswoman, pushing him away while chastising him loudly and crudely. In the eight cases I witnessed, the spokeswoman was never struck, nor was any other woman. The abusive man continued to attempt to divert the group or convince the woman to leave the protective ring, until he had either passed out or grown bored. It was not unusual for the hostilities to continue over several hours with the wife receiving several blows at each resumption. If the husband had not grown powerless through intoxication, the couple was normally escorted home by a group of female relatives. Once inside the household, however, the woman was alone and unprotected. Many women state that the beating received inside the house was far worse than the beating they would have received had the male been permitted to continue at the fiesta. Despite the intensity of the postponed attack, most women stated that they enjoyed the public display of solidarity created by the protective ring of women.

Female children are active participants in the protection process and it is not unusual to see small girls pushing and hitting their fathers while the men slap the mother around once they are in the home. Young girls are rarely abused but adolescent girls may be seen with their mothers in much the same battered condition following an attack.

When interviewed, males involved in such attacks prove to be fairly uniform in their explanations and justifications. The man is usually remorseful but justifies his position by saying he was upset because his wife was not fulfilling her duty within the household and he could not stop his anger because of the alcohol. Such neglected duties included *comidas*, the heavy meal of the day, without meat or adequate tortillas; lack of sexual activity; excessive time outside the household; unescorted trips into the city; or frivolous spending – responses very similar to the ones Guttman received from men in Santo Domingo (1996: 190). My own *compadre*, who housed me within his compound, justified an attack against my *comadre* because she had sponsored a get-together with his sisters and me that included alcohol, and to which he was not invited. For him, the possibility that the neighbours knew that we were drinking and without male company degraded his position as head of household, leaving him no choice but to defend his honour publicly by attacking his wife at a fiesta. While we were talking about the incident, his two daughters, aged eight and ten, passed by hissing names at him of 'dog', 'pig' and 'beast', reducing him to tears. All of the men I interviewed were embarrassed by their loss of control but truly felt they had regained the respect of the community through the public castigation of their wives.

An equally prevalent form of violence occurs between groups of men and a single male, usually friends, and is inevitably the result of envy. In these situations, chiding begins early in the evening between one or two men and the victim. After several hours of drinking, the chiding becomes physical, with shoving and slapping accompanying the banter. The actual attacks occur outside the immediate fiesta space, usually as the victim attempts to leave. The form of husband/wife abuse is reversed,with the victim being surrounded by the attacking men and beaten and kicked around the group. In no situation did I ever witness another man breaking up such a fight. In all situations it was the responsibility of the female family members of the men involved to attempt to control the situation. Women would surround their male family member, whether he was the aggressor or the victim, and push him away from the group. The men rarely parted easily, resulting in the women receiving much of the physical attack meant for the other men. Beatings received in this forum proved to be worse than husband/wife abuse due to the sheer number of men involved and their use of knives and clubs.

Women's socially accepted responsibility for such protection was made clear to me by a murder case that took place in August 1994. A young man, aged nineteen, had recently received a recording contract and had a song on Oaxacan radio in the months before the annual patron saint festival. At the fiesta, he and a group of his friends began drinking. Shortly thereafter, several of the friends started chiding him about being a big-time star. His girlfriend joined him later in the night and the chiding was redirected toward her. It was at this point that the fight broke out between the young man and his friends. The mother of the two dominant aggressors, unable to stop her sons, panicked and picked up a two-by-four lying nearby and struck the victim on the back of the head, killing him. The beatings continued until the group realized the young man was dead. The two sons were arrested and recently tried and sentenced for the death of the young man. It is well known throughout the community that the mother was the actual killer but no one will accuse her. All agree that her sons are to blame and that her role was one of a mother only. Violence to this degree is not rare. A similar incident, in which I was involved, occurred over the Posadas or Christmas re-enactment, where I and several other women pulled a young man aged about twenty from the group. He suffered a broken nose, cheekbones and jaw, and received extensive internal injuries. The attack on him was provoked by his success in Phoenix, Arizona, where he had migrated two years earlier. In my attempt to remove him from the centre of the circle, I was punched in the right shoulder, and landed in a ditch. I was angry, hurt and embarrassed, but the amount of respect that I was given by both men and women after the incident is still a mystery to me, one that I hope never to encounter again. At the same time, I experienced the camaraderie and support the women speak of and it is energizing in its own way, a feeling that I continue to wrestle with and cannot interpret.

Atzompeñas' explanations

Women's reactions to these fields of violence and oppression vary. Almost all recognize and agree that the drinking associated with the fiesta is dangerous in the light of the prevalence of diabetes, anæmia and dysentery in the *pueblo*. They also recognize that the politically charged religious fiestas – as opposed to personal fiestas for baptisms, first communions, and weddings – produce the outbreaks of physical violence and gendered role dichotomies that are physically and emotionally exploitative of women. Yet most continue to support and participate in these events owing to the social prestige earned by the family and the freedom they receive to drink, smoke, dance and socialize without boundaries or repercussions: it is a personal freedom from behavioural constraints that still exist for women despite their movement into other social and political spaces.

Both men and women state that excessive drinking solidifies relationships by creating a sense of vulnerability and camaraderie among the participants. Many women have expressed a desire to end the cycle of violence but feel helpless to break a chain of behaviour that expresses communal identity to such a large degree. Yet some change is taking place. Several women who have been victims of violence during fiestas admit to turning the tables on their husbands once inside the household by physically beating them, tying them up through the night, or locking them inside the kitchen. Female children, encouraged by their mothers, have also proved merciless the next day, calling their fathers names as my *compadre's* daughters demonstrated, as well as recounting their father's antics over and over again, much to the chagrin of the men. Young unmarried women who have the economic and familial support to be more selective are choosing men who do not drink or who are from the city and do not want to participate in the fiesta cycle. In both situations, whether women choose a man who does not participate in the fiesta system or they choose to see the public violence as a social release for the larger community that in turn allows their individual negotiations to continue, women are changing their lives. The development of female-based cooperatives and movement into political offices, access to wage labour in the city, and the freedom to pursue education and professional careers are their long-term goals. Many cite the ability to sit and drink with the men to the point of oblivion, and to be the aggressor and not the pawn, as the true indication of women's acceptance by the community as equals, a practice that a decade earlier would not have occurred. Violence with its concomitant disfigurement of their bodies is not a sufficient deterrent for women to give up the opportunity to be a part of a world that has been forbidden to them for generations. Thus they will continue to support the constructs of violence and abuse within the fiesta, seeing their right to participate as an image of equality as opposed to oppression. The inability of women in the community to agree on what roles women should continue to be held accountable for, and what new modes of lifestyle are acceptable, prevents them from speaking with a unified voice against violence associated with the fiesta. Western notions of intervention remain outside their purview but the support and camaraderie the abused woman receives from others, along with the growth in female-based organizations and social circles, provide the support they need today.

Conclusion

Women in rural communities throughout Mexico are undergoing various forms and negotiations of autonomy and dependence. Their experiences, limitations and decisions are predicated on many things, including their community's social practices, geographic location, and participation in global processes.

Explanations that frame their lives within economic outcomes or as restricted by class provide an analysis of limitations, but fail to reflect the reality of women's everyday resolutions within their communities.

Atzompa is thus an example of a wider social process in which, with decreasing dependence on agricultural subsistence and male-based wage labour, the local economy is coming to rely on the participation of women and their production and distribution of crafts and petty commodities. It is in this way that Atzompeñas increasingly find themselves creating solutions to economic problems, while at the same time their empowerment and new-found freedom disrupts traditional social structures. Atzompeñas look to modernity for opportunity but understand that there is a price. They do not want to lose their family and community structure in favour of urbanized or Westernized lifestyles that leave women on the margins in their later years. The streams of single tourist women who pass through their markets are not seen as free and independent by the women of Atzompa; instead, they are alone, without husband and children. In addition, as we have seen, craft communities such as Atzompa must balance their 'indigenous' or 'peasant' identities, displayed for the tourists, with the increasing acquisition and influence of Western or modern conveniences, labour saving, ideas and desires (Canclini 1993). The outcome of this juggling act is the commodification of the bodies of women, who physically represent the community as 'traditional' to the outside world and their communities. Atzpompeñas, as well as many women throughout Latin America and many other countries, are perceived as the stabilizing unit of tradition and unity (Brydon 1989; de la Cadena 1995; Johnson 1992; Draper 1992; McAllister 1992; Miles 1992), mainly as a consequence of their responsibilities for biological and social reproduction. These perceptions of reproduction and stability – coupled with women's active involvement in determining and incorporating different images of, and roles for, themselves, their family, the household and the community – have a profound impact on the processes of identity formation and social change. Atzompeñas have no final answers as to what their world will look like in the future and approach their negotiations of power and place with great trepidation. In turn, men's perceptions of their lack of influence on these processes, coupled with their loss of control over the economic and political spheres resulting from the community's participation in global tourism and craft exportation, lead to their feelings of frustration, anger and loss. The release of men's emotions through alcohol into forms of dominance in the fiesta, and women's acquiescence to the resulting violence, produce a symbolic façade of normalcy between the genders. Thus, women's public assent to patriarchal control over their bodies through both symbolic and physical violence in the fiesta affirms long-term practices of male dominance and control, thereby mitigating the transitions of power from male-dominant to female-inclusive forms in their everyday lives. The transitions in power and place are subtle, marked by a time frame and an outcome that is owned by them and therefore not always listened to by those who write their stories. It is my hope that I have listened well enough to have given voice to a phenomenon that could be read as disempowering but may, in fact, be empowering.

Notes

1 See Eber 1995 and Rosenbaum 1993 for an in-depth analysis of women's participation in Maya religious cargos and fiestas.
2 See Kearney 1972 for an in-depth discussion of this belief in rural Mexico as well as Guttman 1996 for a discussion of the issue in urban Mexico. See also Pérez 2000 for a comparison between Western notions of drinking as being 'not one's self' and Mexican notions of finally being free of social constraints and therefore being 'one's true self'.
3 See Eber 1995 for a discussion of alcohol and violence toward women in a Maya community.
4 Field notes, February 1996.

Part VI
Other Bodies

15

Body Politics

Revisiting the Population Question

Wendy Harcourt

I

One of the major changes in development discourse has been the major paradigmatic shift in the area of population and development. The International Conference on Population and Development, held in Cairo in September 1994,[1] was a major effort to move the focus of population programmes away from demographic trends and fears that expanding population was preventing development, to the right of people, in particular women living in the global South, to make safer and more healthy life choices. Cairo placed women's empowerment and the right to reproductive health on the international development agenda in the face of opposition from the Vatican and other conservative religious states (Singh 1998; Corrêa 1994; Hartmann 1995; Bandarage 1997; Lassonde 1997; Stein 1997; and Demeny and McNicoll 1998). As the United Nations Family Planning Association (UNFPA) web site states, at Cairo

> 179 countries agreed that population and development are inextricably linked, and that empowering women and meeting people's needs for education and health, including reproductive health, are necessary for both individual advancement and balanced development. Advancing gender equality, eliminating violence against women and ensuring women's ability to control their own fertility were acknowledged as cornerstones of population and development policies. Concrete goals centred on providing universal education and reproductive health care, including family planning; and reducing infant, child and maternal mortality. (UNFPA, 2001)

Sadly, this major achievement has not been followed up. There have been changes at the community and national level on paper but not in practice. In the following chapter we explore problems that beset the Cairo agenda, despite all the hopes raised. We argue that these problems lie in the political limitations of what such an event as Cairo, and its sponsoring institutions, can deliver. The chapter aims to unsettle the current development trends, scientific approaches to medicine, health and cultural practices, and, ultimately, the institutions that defined and limited Cairo.

It is important to open up this debate analytically even if it focuses on what some might dismiss as the cooptative policy debates of governments, UN agencies and non-government organizations that such an international event as Cairo presents. Nevertheless, in a debate centred on development or post-development for women the claims Cairo makes cannot be dismissed easily. The vision of Cairo to empower huge numbers of women to exercise their reproductive rights and to achieve reproductive health is impressive. It opens up space for negotiation on a level that was not possible before, even though we need to take on board very seriously the limitations of such promises. The point of the chapter is to place Cairo in a wider analytical context that questions some of these promises and the assumptions behind them, but also to suggest ways in which the Cairo agenda can still be useful in a post-development analysis. In this sense, Cairo can be read as a discourse that through the interplay of different forms of knowledge and power structures has built up a view of population, gender relations, reproductive rights and health that is important for women's empowerment, even if, just as it places women's empowerment at the centre, its very reasoning obfuscates many of the mechanisms which are in fact disempowering women.

The chapter looks first at some of the problems inherent within the approach of Cairo, including the difficulty of follow-up by women's groups as a result. It then considers what the reading of Cairo could take from a post-development strategy that links body, place and globalization in the concept of the politics of place, and from that suggests how to reread the potential of the Cairo discourse. It does so in an atmosphere in which increasingly the women's groups that steered the success of the paradigmatic shift in Cairo are moving on to other development agendas, leaving in their wake a lack of strategic follow-up.

II

Cairo, in its eagerness to make the paradigmatic shift, zeroed in perhaps a little too far on getting a universal agreement on reproductive rights and health. Then, 'back home', it proved very hard to put such an agenda into action. Reproductive rights and health become slippery concepts when they are interpreted by diverse cultures and geopolitical positions, and are embedded in different economic situations. In order to produce international-level policy agreements these differences had been subsumed in the complex negotiation process that produced the Programme of Action. It appears, at least on paper, that Cairo brought about a transformation of cultural norms in relation to reproductive rights. But whose cultural norms set the basis for the agreement? The sophisticated concepts of sexual reproductive health and the autonomy of women can be read as a universalizing feminist agenda imposed through external mechanisms. The analytical framework that links gender relations, family, the public and private, and the micro and macro environment – which is so good on paper in big international meetings – can prove very difficult to use when translated back into reality to challenge established power and knowledge structures. Even if the insights into women's lives in the South, East and North led the conference and gave authority to the Cairo documents back at home, post-Cairo the authority has slipped away into entrenched bureaucratic systems. Up against both the backlash against women's groups from extremist traditional and religious positions and the deteriorating economic situation, rather unsurprisingly the Cairo consensus has faltered.

The problem was how to put into practice a participatory and empowering set of reproductive health practices given the limitations of traditional bureaucratic systems and medical practices and the concept of development aid itself. Cairo's message is clear – women of whatever background have to be the subjects not objects of reproductive health services. This makes the role of the expert outsider, doctor or nurse, woman or man, intervening into especially poor women's lives much more delicate. Medical practitioners, policy makers, community services workers and NGO activists have been challenged to provide reproductive health knowledge or services in order for poor girls and women (and boys and men) of all cultures to make self-determined choices. This implies a difficult task – of changing the prejudices, including gender blindness, of bureaucracies, medical establishments and well-meaning but insensitive agencies with a population policy agenda (and target) to push – in order to foster the self-esteem and provide real choices for those using the service.

Such considerations apply to another contentious issue: the ambiguity surrounding the use of modern reproductive technology as opposed to traditional customs. The efficacy of reproductive technology needs to be separated out from the oppressive delivery of techniques and service by medical and bureaucratic organizations. It is important to bring out the politics behind how a technology is conceived and practised. It is equally important to recognize the appropriateness of technology for different groups of women and men in their specific life stages and cultural contexts. In some cases this could mean rejecting today's reproductive technologies in favour of less interventionist tools. But recognizing the drawbacks of some medical technologies and their delivery does not mean celebrating the non-Western technological world of childbirth. This, in any case, hardly exists. The point is that in pursuing a reproductive health and rights framework we have to take on board the need to transform health and medical institutions in order to incorporate social and cultural requirements as defined by women at the local level. We may hope that such a political strategy will lead to a varied number of reproductive life patterns reflecting not only Western medical technology but past traditional practices which women feel are adaptable and still useful.

For example, the role of the community in life stage celebrations in Africa around menstruation can be recognized as positive, providing a supportive community of women that celebrates women's bodily functions. However, the practice of female genital mutilation, another life stage practice that many carry out to make women marriageable around the same time (though sometimes younger), is not healthy physiologically or psychologically in terms of reproductive health and empowerment. The practice is debilitating and life-threatening. The point, though, is not just to outlaw it but to see it in an economic, social and (local) political context. Men and women in the community have to understand it as dangerous but, at the same time, the life stage needs to be celebrated. Therefore the community has to be engaged in another way to mark entry into womanhood which is less destructive of women's health and well-being as a whole.

In shifting population policies towards a people-centred reproductive health framework the post-Cairo push was to create conditions where women and their community are not imposed upon but can build their own agenda with outside input. External intervention should be enriching, not overwhelming. That suggests, for any introduction of external ideas and practices, careful preparation and knowledge of the local environment in order to ensure that new information and technologies are conversant with local women and men's own experience and culture. Such an approach would include the need for long-term dialogue, discerning and informed, to effect change in communities. The ability of women to participate in practices that promote reproductive health – empowered to set priorities and make choices – demands a sense of direction and purpose within the community as well as the individual, implying a wider social and economic context.

Another concern is to what extent the rights discourse is grounded in Western notions of a rational, autonomous self that can clash with alternative notions of agency, for example of community. The claim is not that human rights is solely a Western discourse. There is clear evidence from the Cairo process that the feminist rights movement in the global South has spearheaded important changes for gender equality and women's bodily autonomy under the human rights flag, and in doing so correctly challenged the culture of masculinity underlying many forms of violence against women. Nevertheless there are still some uncomfortable questions about the extent to which the rights discourse can be taken up separately from other less positive connotations of the rights-based development framework. For example, the notion of property rights closely linked to individual rights is at the foundation of a neoliberal capitalist ideology and has been used to justify postcolonial greed and exploitation.

This leads us to one of the major criticisms levelled at Cairo – that the battle won over the reproductive rights agenda, based on a human rights and democratic framework, fatally pushed to one side the more politically contentious and difficult issues of the economic conditions and environment in which these rights would be realized. In the five-year review of Cairo the 'enabling environment' was looked at much more thoroughly – putting the framework of reproductive rights and women's empowerment within the context of the global economic crisis and questions around development itself. Unlike in Cairo, where economic growth at all costs was never questioned, post-Cairo the costs are all too evident. Governments that are forced by global imperatives to follow stringent market-oriented policies are unable to provide women with the reproductive rights and services that Cairo promised. Market stringencies, continued structural adjustment, cuts in the welfare state and the globalizing market all disrupt severely the provision of reproductive health, education and medical services for poor communities and especially for poor women and girls.

Another challenge, taking us to another political level, was how far issues can be raised in today's reactionary world of growing fundamentalism and uncertainty. How safe is it for women to raise publicly issues around reproductive health and rights? What must remain private? The 'personal is political' argument belongs to certain cultures and historical moments and cannot be applied to all women. Putting Cairo into action revealed that women's positions and political agendas are at different levels. While some women in some cultures can accommodate and actively promote an open discussion on sexuality and reproductive behaviour, others, for strategic reasons of survival, need to maintain a veil of silence. One of the most challenging issues within the international women's movement concerned with reproductive health and rights is how to accommodate the different parameters of private and public among cultures. Even if Cairo acknowledges that there is no one approach to creating women's access to safe and enjoyable reproductive rights and health practices, it is still a struggle to respect cultural diversity, particularly in the face of the such strong opposition from the Vatican and other religious states. What Cairo raises is how to create multiple safe spaces so that diverse women's views and choices can be aired and ultimately fed appropriately into their communities and national decision-making political spheres.

III

The arrival of the new holistic concept of reproductive health that embraces well-being, the breaking of taboos around sexuality, sexual health, and the discussions on autonomy, empowerment, gender and cultural difference on the international agenda were certainly major breakthroughs. They came, however, at the expense of leaving economic development issues unproblematized. How does one give effect to democracy and human rights given the neoliberal market stringencies? Women's rights have to encompass reproductive, economic and political rights. Women's rights and principles, respect for bodily integrity and security of person are not just fundamental to a human rights agenda but also pose a major challenge to global development policies. As Sonia Corrêa has put it,

> Transforming the population field in order to apply the reproductive rights and health framework is conditioned upon a virtual revolution in prevailing gender systems and development models.... [R]eproduction-related policies must be conceived and implemented as part of a renewed human development paradigm that fosters democratic institutions and most importantly, equitable economic policies. (Corrêa 1994: 9)

Studies done in the late 1990s by groups such as DAWN, one of the leading Southern-based women networks in the Cairo process, show that the Cairo agenda has been totally disrupted by an 'entirely unsatisfactory economic environment with deep inequality patterns and poverty levels' (Corrêa and Sen 1999), combined with a conservative reaction in some countries to the Cairo agendas. The DAWN network undertook studies in Bolivia, Brazil, Nicaragua, Peru, Puerto Rico, India, Malaysia, Thailand, Indonesia, Vietnam, Laos, Cambodia, the Philippines and Fiji. DAWN found that reproductive health policies were being implemented amidst state and health reforms, cuts in social investments and the privatization of services.[2]

The main problems that DAWN highlights are that effective improvement of reproductive health services is limited for the urban and rural poor. They also signal problems with the health sector reform packages pushed by the World Bank as 'agencies, managers and advocates involved with reproductive health programming are not interacting adequately with the sectors designing and implementing health reform. Given the current reduction in health budgets due to the economic crisis this has led to an uneasy bargaining power.' At the same time, Corrêa and Sen (1999) see the uncertainties and concerns being expressed about the impact of economic globalization on the poor as creating a space for bringing women's health concerns to the fore.

Two examples in Mexico and Zambia show how women's NGOs are trying to push the Cairo consensus. According to a study by Priya Nanda (1999) in Zambia, the constraints of the economic reforms mean that there is a major underfunding of the reproductive health delivery system in relation to staff capacity, skills, drugs and infrastructure. The study found that in the different districts the 'current economic context, differential access to income and other resources had deepened the sense of marginalization among many health workers'. Rural women can pay with maize but not with money, and even if a fee is paid there are no drugs or adequate facilities: 'our clinics do not even have privacy to insert IUDs'.

The NGOs are concerned that even if involved in the beginning they are increasingly excluded from government decisions, and that the lack of services jeopardizes poor women's lives. The study concludes that, despite the vision of equity in health care, the management of the reforms, combined with the shortage of medical supplies and service, has led to major constraints, and that the partnerships with the grassroots and women's NGOs have suffered as a consequence. It suggests that for poor countries even if globalization opens up possibilities for policy and programme development such as the Cairo initiative, which is welcomed, the greater risks – such as global financial insecurity or exposure to diseases such as AIDS – can undermine the vision of improved quality in health care delivery (Nanda 1999).

Grupo de Información en Reproducción Eelgida (GIRE), an NGO working on violence against women in Mexico, argues that the women's health movement could benefit from the Cairo agenda. Although the Mexican government has adopted the concept of reproductive health as a national policy, however, the simultaneous general budget cuts and service trimming that are part of Mexico's response to economic globalization are working directly against this process. Since 1994 privatization and liberalization have produced a reversal in the quality of life enjoyed by Mexicans. The number of people living in poverty has increased by 10.6 million to almost 80 per cent of the population, while 51 per cent are considered to be living in extreme poverty. This economic crisis has made the move from policy to practice in the field of reproductive health extremely difficult. Working mainly with the urban poor, GIRE has collaborated with the National Forum of Women and Population Policy (a network of 70 NGOs) in attempting to implement the official national programme of reproductive health and family planning – but with budgeted public resources for health declining by 37 per cent during the same period, the new gender approach and goal of more quality care has not seemed very realistic. Over 10 million Mexicans were without health services, and thousands more have only partial or insufficient access.

GIRE found that 'the globalization of the economy and its consequences on the Mexican health sector threaten the guarantee of a truly comprehensive reproductive health. The activities and consensus reached by international women's health advocates on violence as a major reproductive health issue have enabled a strong platform for local Mexican advocates.'

Both these examples show the problems resulting from not tackling the development model and economic climate undergirding Cairo. At the heart of the problems with Cairo was the lack of understanding of power and knowledge. A focus on development and empowerment, on social organization and equality was needed as much as a concentration of factors thought to be more directly related to health (Stein 1997: 259). We need to recognize that what is required is a major social and economic shift. The inequitable organisation of society in terms of social justice and economic resources is 'not a separate layer or strand of the web that somehow undergirds other strands, but rather an integral, controlling, fundamental part of all the tangled strands' (Stein 1997: 250).

IV

In order to understand the failures of the Cairo agenda we need to look much more carefully at these contradictory economic and social trends of today's globalization as well as at the potential of women's groups to resist and shape globalization. While pointing out some of the failures of Cairo we also need to recognize what the Cairo process revealed in potential for change once the economic and political context is restored. The alliances women have made – along with the gender approach to body politics, the economy and broader political processes – provide some important strategic approaches for change.

The number of participants in the women's movements engaged in Cairo is part of the profound shifts in gender relations and new forms of cultural expression that are emerging in response to economic globalization. Women working at the grassroots in different economic, social and cultural positions are creating a new form of politics that is changing women's sense of self and their place in the community, and opening up new public spaces for negotiating gender, economic and social justice. Despite the backdrop affecting many women – increasing economic poverty, exploitation and state restructuring – women are resisting strongly the negative impact of economic globalization on their lives through a place-based politics around the body, community and the public arena. In engaging in a politics of place, women are redefining political action to take into account gender concerns based on their own needs and responses to globalism as it is experienced at the level of their daily lives. At the same time this placed-based politics links localities into significant 'glocal' configurations, redefining possibilities for women's sense of self, position in the community and access to the public arena and decision-making venues. Glocal networks are creating alternative configurations of culture, power and identity that are not determined solely by the global, but also by place-based practices.

In mainstream and critical debates alike, globalization is presented as a totalizing economic and cultural phenomenon with no alternative possible. Globalization is seen as driven by global capitalist processes advanced under the rubric of neoliberal principles – particularly those of free trade (trade liberalization under the World Trade Organization), privatization of all economic activities, significant dismantling of welfare state policies, and the overall deregulation of the economy, which gives unprecedented power to transnational corporations. Second, globalization is understood in terms of the increased interconnectedness of social groups worldwide in ways that are greatly uneven (in terms of types and intensity of connections), culturally driven (that is, dominated by cultures of European origin, particularly North American culture), and fundamentally facilitated by new information and communication technologies (ICTs). Many people assume that these two facets of what we might call neoliberal capitalist globalization dominate all that we do. And therefore, the best strategy for women at the national, regional or local level is to negotiate for better terms of connection to the global economy and the global society, via the production of commodities or information that fit into the dominant social dynamic. This essentially is the Cairo strategy and process.

Another understanding that might lead to a different set of strategies is to see how women are negotiating globalization. In this approach women's groups respond to and shape globalization through their strategies in defence of place. Here we understand political struggles around place as a source for a strategic vision that provides us with a much stronger basis for women's autonomy and self-empowerment.

Building on the recent studies of place by feminist geographer Doreen Massey and historian Arif Dirlik, we can develop a useful framework for understanding the politics of place. For Massey (1997) it is possible to speak of a 'global sense of place'. This is not a contradiction in terms, as it might at first appear, but rather an indication of the fact that the role of place in social life has changed. Places are no longer isolated, nor are they pure, static, or just traditional. The places that we now inhabit are clearly produced in their encounter with the global – but this does not render places irrelevant for people's lives. Dirlik suggests something similar, although starting with a different observation: that there is a fundamental asymmetry between 'the local' and 'the global' in most of the debates on globalization (1998). This asymmetry simply means that there is always the hidden assumption in these debates that 'the global' is where power resides, and that 'the local' – and place – can only adapt or perish. Instead, we need to look at how local specificity and global construction are intertwined.

V

We can explore gender specificities in relation to place, politics and globalization at three spatial levels.

Women's bodies are the first place that defines political struggle – for autonomy, for reproductive and sexual integrity and right, for safe motherhood, for freedom from violence and sexual oppression. The body is the site for many struggles over different modern/traditional – or hybrid – identities.

A second place is that of *the home and the environment* that for many women still define their primary social and cultural identity, the lived domain of immediate economic and political struggle within the family, and the site of everyday work in the home and on the land. The home and the immediate community and environment are the safe places for women's political and economic activity, though also the places where violence and oppression can be the most savage.

The third place is the *social public space* – the male-dominated domain to which most women still have limited access, and where many women find their gender-based concerns silenced or missing. For many years, women's movements have been creating diverse avenues for entry into that space, even if they are still marginal to the pulse of dominant forms of political power.

A place-based strategy for women recognizes that political change can only come about by changes in power relations so that women are able to act on all three levels of place in their everyday life activities, fostering their current questionings of hierarchies, resistance to male domination and confidence in their own creativity.

The first level is where women have defined their identity and their most gender-specific fight for social justice. The bodily experience of particular bodies perceived and lived as female construct a concept of self and place that has a political meaning and is based on fleshly experience. As feminists it is important to validate this specific bodily experience, constructing a concept of self and place that forms the basis for political actions. In writing about the experiences of globalization from the perspective of women's lives we need to explore the different cultural and ideological constructs of the body in its fleshly political being, with the body being understood as not bound to the private and to the self but linked integrally to material expressions of community and public space. In this sense there is no neat divide between the corporeal and the social; there is instead what has been called 'social flesh' (Beasley and Bacchi 2000). In this sense, the body is understood as a political site or place that mediates the lived experiences of social and cultural relationships. What is interesting is how the theorizing of place can speak to the concepts of political embodiment, aware of the uneasiness still in feminist theorizing around the body. While avoiding the pitfalls of essentialism and biologism and the seductiveness of the abstract theorizing of the body as narrative or metaphor, we cannot avoid the importance of the body as we analyze material inequities, racism/ethnicities or disabilities. We still need to work against the concept of an essential Other, and to refuse to see women, in all their diversities of history, race, experience and age, 'being lashed to their bodies' at one remove from a 'true' self, as Adrienne Rich (1976) described it.

This theorizing of the body aims to move beyond the dualism of body/mind, body/spirit, body/politics, able/disabled, reproductive/productive, public/private, to look at lived experiences of bodies as part of social, cultural and political institutions. It tries to work with tensions in the constructions of power/knowledge around the particularities of female bodies, their fleshly capacity to nurture another life, acknowledging that the body for women is a conscious and material entry point to their political identity. Women deal with the material result of being sexualized subjects.

Feminist writers (such as Liz Grosz) since the 1970s have theorized the body as the place 'closest in', an important political terrain for women's identity and politics. Using their work we can look at the relationship of 'being in the body' and 'being in place'. The body in most political theories is not a subject of politics but an object of political control, and is the exteriorized terrain of public regulation. There is an implicit disconnection from the 'private' experience of the lived body and a person's subjectivity. Instead a feminist theory of the body builds on a Foucauldian understanding of the body as critical to modern operations of power. Bodies are not separate from politics but rather their very embodiment: their corporeal, fleshly, material existence determines our relations. In calling attention to bodies as political subjects, we recognize that 'we are our bodies'. The political self is not distinct from the body, or, to put it another way, the body is the place 'closest in'. Our experience of ourselves, our cultural, political and social identity, is a lived one, determined by our relations to other bodies. In order to lodge bodies in their physical and social particularities, theoretically we have to move from the instrumentalizing of the body as an object, to understanding the body as a subject, central to power, gender and culture. Focusing on the fleshly bodies of women – on birth, breasts, breast milk, menstruation, their material experience of sex, pregnancy, violation, rape – is not dismissing the experiences of bodies as outside political discourse. It is taking women's lived experiences as participating subjects in politics. This understanding reverses the suggestion that a body 'conventionally regarded as mired in biology' (Beasley and Bacchi 2000) is disqualified from politics. The body is inherently part of social and political participation. Female, black, disabled bodies do not have biological limitations to overcome or to be negotiated; their fleshliness is present and integral to political subjectivity.

An example of a modern defence of place by women is the active involvement of Bal Rashmi, a Jaipur-based NGO, in the struggle for women's autonomy and rights and against women's sexual exploitation through child marriage, rape, dowry deaths and wife torture – a struggle that drew the negative attention of the conservative state government of Rajasthan. The government filed bogus criminal cases and the leaders of Bal Rashmi were arrested. In fighting back, Bal Rashmi members used the Internet to contact international human rights and women's networks in India, South Asia, Europe and North America. Their call set off an appeal that within a few weeks led to faxes and letters flooding into the National Human Rights Commission, the Rajasthan state and the Indian government. The Internet campaign forced a legal investigation of the cases and within a few months they were quashed.

This example illustrates different levels of a gendered, place-based politics. First, there is the defence of women's body as the first level of place. Bal Rashmi aims to protect and defend women's sexual autonomy – to stop sexual abuse, child marriage, rape in prisons and the like – in the 'feudal', conservative second level of place (community or environment) of Jaipur, Rajasthan. When the group was directly and forcibly challenged – false cases made against them, arrest and imprisonment by a corrupt political authority – they used networking to defend their political action by moving to the third level of place, the public social place where they reached out through networking to women's groups worldwide that are also fighting to defend women's bodies against patriarchal oppression. This is an important example of a unique political place-based action by women's groups that succeeded because they could harness the Internet's potential for rapid networking and support. Interestingly, Bal Rashmi found more support at the third level of place than at the second, where the community environment constrained other women's movement groups from openly joining their struggle once the crackdown began. Alice Garg, the secretary of the organization, underlines this dilemma in a recent article (Garg 2001) that emphasizes the local and global connections as the strengthening line of support.

Bal Rashmi illustrate the complex connections among the various levels at which place operates in global times. A political defence of place by these women focuses not just on the defence of a community's land or environment or traditional culture in the face of global change, but also on a struggle for women's freedom and right to bodily integrity, autonomy, knowledge and identity that is a mix of modern and traditional discourses. The politics of women's groups defending their place, their body or their right is not limited to the local level, but is intermeshed with national and international networks; the political work performed by these networks is geared towards pushing for women's economic, social and political rights.

Women's 'politics of place' is a description of how different women's groups are engaging in complex multilevel strategies of the politics of place: changing their sense of self, their place in the community and their cultural identity, and opening up new types of public political spaces to negotiate gender, economic and social justice as part of a local and global process. As the examples suggest, 'place-based politics' is not purely a matter of resistance to modernization or modern capital in the defence of traditional culture and land. It involves multiple political activities carried out by women around the body, the environment, the community and the public arena – all the places where women's groups are redefining political action to take into account gender concerns based on their own needs and in response to various forms of globalization as it is experienced at the level of their daily lives. This process of place-based politics links localities horizontally to other political activities by women's groups that may be located in other places, building networks that are creating new configurations of culture, power and identity that are not determined solely by global, but also by place-based practices. There is, then, a network component to the politics of place: place is not simply local, nor is its politics place-bound, even if it continues to be fundamental to people's daily lives.

VI

In focusing on women's particular experience of place, and on what is new in globalization for women in shaping those places, we can take place as a new site of politics that allows for a rethinking of globalization and disrupts notions of a binary relationship between 'the' local and global. Key to that analysis is to explain how women's politics around the body, the environment and public place is reconfiguring globalization. In exploring the historical continuities and discontinuities of today's experience of globalization, we are also exploring ways to create counter-imaginaries to the dominant view of globalization as all-encompassing and immobilizing for women's political activity.

What is interesting is how this post-development analysis allows us to move outside the development discourse based on national arrangements to explore how women's networking of specific experiences of place can link different sites of power and knowledge through and around traditional development institutions.

In this reading we can take up the Cairo agenda again and see it in a different light. In terms of 'fleshly politics' Cairo has catalogued many of the areas of body politics in which women have been actively engaged – violence against women, autonomy and control of the body, choices throughout the life stage. In responding to the Cairo discourse women have pushed to move away from repressive technological intervention and medicalized concepts of the female body. This is a struggle over recognition of the intersection of women's productive and reproductive lives in terms of well-being, with economic, social and cultural aspects. It seems that horizontal linking among local women's groups around reproductive rights and health issues, in particular violence against women, has been producing interesting new possibilities in reconfiguring power and knowledge. The Internet is starting to play a very important role, enabling women to move around the backlash and resistance at the community level. Resistance to the violence against women – the Bal Rashmi case is one example, but there are many others (Hamm 2001; Harcourt 2001) – shows the strength of these 'glocalities'.

It is at the second level of place that Cairo's vision is lacking. The impact of economic change, structural adjustment, environmental degradation and the lack of education and other services finds women again linking up to understand how they can deal with the impact of globalization, constructing alliances that move beyond the state. It is here that there is a wealth of information on economic and environmental shifts that needs to be brought into the analysis of how to guarantee reproductive health and rights. Alliance building at this political level, beyond the state, can take on board the wider economic environment and help to make good the failures of Cairo. That rethinking includes consideration of economic activities outside of mainstream neoliberal capitalism in which creative energy and strategies for livelihood abound. Many of these examples need to be taken as serious alternatives to mainstream development projects to link local markets with global markets.[3]

The last level of place is the entry of these concerns into the social public space. Here Cairo has already opened up many avenues, making inroads in medical establishments and population agencies, creating a space for a globalized culture of the body politic. The important issue here is to ensure that both the negative and positive sides of this shift are recognized – the commodification of women's bodies along with the fight to change oppressive practices at the global level. The visibility of rape of women in war, the campaigns against female genital mutilation and Nestlé's promotion of artificial milk, or international concern about the trafficking of young women are important examples of women's fleshly politics entering the public domain. The promotion of white, thin Barbie dolls as the universal image of women, however, or of smoking among young women in the global South, or of universal brands of consumerism are negative forms of the same trend. It is important to have a complex understanding of the hybridities that globalization creates – the entry points into modernity that bring with them dislocating identities and discontinuities with tradition that can have a mixed result for the women involved.

We need to bring out the sites of conflict and tension among these different levels of place, and to map out what constitutes different kinds of bodily experience for women in various cultures and environments. This information provides vital coordinates in women's diverse and creative political and economic struggles. In this way we look at the relationships forming women's places: the relations of their bodies/places to modernity, the dialectics, the need for linking and delinking, the entry points, the escaping, the reconfigurations and the strategies of recovery. Cairo is part of a continuum in these stories. As such it cannot be entirely dismissed; the limitations need to be revealed, the difficulties acknowledged, but the entry points need to be used and transformed. The stale negotiations of the development machinery must yield to the deployment of strategic tools in women's place-based politics.

Notes

1 Referred to in the chapter as 'Cairo' following the trend of most discussions of the big UN meetings held in the 1990s to refer to the city where they were held; a familiar example is how the Fourth UN Conference on Women held in Beijing in September 1995 is usually referred to as 'Beijing'.

2 Nevertheless, the studies showed a movement forward, with efforts to overcome lack of integration between different components of reproductive health and greater attention to maternal mortality. Other achievements are that violence is being taken as a serious health issue, and a paradigmatic shift from a narrow family planning approach to a holistic approach to reproductive health can be seen as a having started in these countries. The studies also noted 'striking and positive examples of institutional arrangements in which governments, non-governmental organizations and international agencies were coming together to implement the post-Cairo reproductive health agenda'. Brazil, Peru, Bolivia and Uruguay were cited as particularly impressive.

3 The Society for International Development is currently compiling many of these experiences in its sustainable livelihoods programme.

16

Reproductive Technologies

A Third World Feminist Perspective

Esther Wangari

High fertility rates in the Third World are blamed for lack of economic growth, environmental degradation, and the low status of women, among other ascribed effects. Sustainable development, according to the World Bank, the IMF and donor countries, can only be achieved by controlling fertility rates and lifestyles. Globally, people of African descent in general, and particularly women, are blamed not only for high fertility rates and their lifestyles, which some consider to be responsible for poverty and environmental degradation, but also for high rates of HIV–Aids. Because these debates, whatever their precise focus, are framed within the context of lifestyle, they deflect and obscure the interconnectedness of policies imposed by the state, international financial institutions, the family planning establishment, donor countries, and the apparatus of resource control and power at a global level. It also shifts the responsibility of resource conservation and consumption patterns to people in the Third World.

This chapter addresses some of the interconnectedness between fertility rates and reproductive technologies in the Third World. The argument does not treat access to reproductive technologies on the basis of individual rights to one's body as the only means to improving empowerment or status. Factors such as social, economic and political structures, state policies, gender biases, racism, today's globalization of the market and culture and the prevalence of wars may be more fundamental barriers to one's individual rights. For example, in developing countries, Raymond points out that

> it is not always the rights of all individuals that are in need of protection from the state. For example, many people in Third World countries are faced with tremendous poverty and hunger. This is not caused by the governments

> restricting the rights of individuals *per se* but rather by governments allowing a certain class of individuals to flourish at the expense of others. Thus it is important to consider which classes or groups of individuals are in need of rights. This can only be done if the material differences, that is, the specific inequalities of certain individuals in relation to others, are incorporated into visions and declarations of human rights. For women, this means talking about gender inequality. Failure to make tangible the ideals of freedom and dignity for specific women in society means these ideals will be expressed in abstract, Western, and male terms. (1993: 196)

Although some feminists have articulated and expanded upon the discourse of family planning in the Third World, greater commitment is required in the examination of the racist, class, and gender biases inherent in Western hegemony and control of resources. Looking at reproductive technologies within the context of state policies, most of which are imposed at the behest of the family planning establishment, the IMF or the World Bank, this chapter discloses abuses, class issues, gender biases and racism embedded in the application of these technologies. Looking through a Third World lens, the chapter discusses some ambiguities and contradictions in the family planning approach. The examination of such programmes within the context of state policies underscores why various other macro-economic programmes implemented in the Third World in general, and in Africa in particular, have not been beneficial to a majority of people. For instance, the education system in Kenya still adheres to colonial policies by which entry to high school or universities is limited. If women fail the entrance exams, the only alternatives left are becoming domestic workers, getting married or joining others in the urban informal sectors, where they are subject to police harassment for the use of public space without licences – often expensive and acquired only if one has the right political connections (Wangari 1997: 32–3). Other women become prostitutes catering to the locals and Western tourists. None of the various activities women get involved in generate sufficient resources to empower them and their families. Given these conditions, women who find themselves in the sex industry, for instance, do not choose prostitution in order to feel liberated – contrary to the sexual and reproductive liberals who support prostitution as a liberating act.

> What kind of choices do women have when subordination, poverty, and degrading work are the options available to most? The point is not to deny that women are capable of choosing within contexts of powerlessness, but to question how much real power these 'choices' have.... They do not make them under conditions they create but conditions and constraints that they are often powerless to change. (Raymond 1990: 110)

Traditional gender biases, as exemplified by the Kenyan land reforms under the Swynnerton Plan of 1954 and subsequent policies, deny women individual rights to land ownership. 'Title deed, a land collateral for obtaining credits from financial institutions such as commercial banks and particularly the Agricultural Finance Cooperation (AFC), disqualifies women as potential borrowers' (Wangari 1993: 172–3). Gender-neutral policies, which were supposed to benefit both men and women in the Third World, have not been beneficial to the majority of women in Africa. Gender-neutral policies for economic development obscure gender biases that discriminate against women as women because of gender differences imposed by some of the static theories such as culture, religion and biology (Schor 1994: xv; Sapiro 1994: 84). The equality of neutrality denies women their rights as individuals. The 'trickle down effect' of economic policies has different streams based on gender, class and race/ethnicity, as evidenced by the current situation in Kenya. Some of the theories used to justify gender biases have also been applied in discrimination against people of colour and especially people of African descent. 'In assessing the impact of science upon eighteenth- and nineteenth-century views of race, we must first recognize the cultural milieu of a society whose leaders and intellectuals did not doubt the propriety of racial ranking – with Indians below whites, and blacks below everybody else…' (Gould 1993: 85). These socially constructed racial and gender differences deprive some people of their rights as human beings.

These differences have national and international policy implications in terms of global resource allocation and blame for the loss of biodiversity in the 'global village'. Policies that work in other countries are assumed to work in Africa regardless of different historical experiences, cultures and ecosystems. Failure to consider these factors in policy implementations has led to the failure of policies such as structural adjustment advocated by the IMF and the World Bank. The rights of those affected by these policies are ignored, not only by these institutions but also in some analyses coming from those Western women who perceive Third World women as a homogeneous group, regardless of their colonial and postcolonial experiences, and their cultural and economic differences.

> All women as women share common interests around which to organize and mobilize, but women of relative privilege, especially, must guard against constricting the meaning of women's empowerment to gender relations alone.… Development organizations enabling women's empowerment must confront all sources of women's subordination, for they are interconnected. To do that will require tremendous resources, but only then will women be treated as equal in society. (Young 1990: 94)

The discussion of women's different experiences, especially in the Third World, is paramount to understanding their needs and their rights as human beings.

'Many white feminists have been so eager to emphasize their common womanhood and equality with African-American women that they have ignored or denied race-based differences in their histories, experiences, and perspectives that make real differences in their lives' (Sapiro 1996: 91).

This chapter is also about the double standards of reproductive technologies. In the West, reproductive technologies have been a cause of celebration for many women. The successful treatment of infertility, amniocentesis to discover disabilities, successful pregnancy for post-menopausal women, selective abortions, gestational motherhood, artificial insemination, *in vitro* fertilization and embryo transfer, and the use of chemical abortifacients such as RU 486/PG, Mifepristone (Callahan 1995) have all been praised by women in the West. On the other hand, reproductive technologies in the Third World are mainly focused on reducing fertility rates. Soon new technologies, such as Lunelle, Ortho Evra and the improvement of hormonal IUD (Mirena), will increase Western women's options. For example, 'Tanga's hit–and–miss record ended three years ago after she enrolled in clinical trial of once-a-month contraceptive injection' (*US News & World Report*, 2 April 2001: 58). The convenience of having a shot once a month reduces time taken from women's busy schedules and eliminates the daily chance of missing taking an oral pill. About 16 per cent of oral contraceptive users miss 'two or more pills in any three months' (*ibid.*). Yet, overall, reproductive technologies have been hailed as a liberating measure for giving a woman autonomy over her reproductive system. 'Birth control places in the hands of women the only effective instrument whereby they may reestablish the balance in society, and assert, not only theoretically but practically as well, the primary importance of the woman and the child in civilization' (Sanger 1967: 257). This liberating effect of individual ownership of one's body is questionable in situations in which the individual's rights, understood as one's bodily rights, are manipulated by scientific reproductive methods or by pornography; or when these rights are embodied within the whole community. The community, as the custodian of culture and norms, limits one's rights as an individual.

My purpose in this chapter is not to get into the discourse of individual rights, or rights of ownership of one's body, or to agree or disagree with various brands of feminism on applications of the new and the old reproductive technologies. It appears to me that the individual rights debate, framed within the context of the sexual and reproductive liberalism, deflates the discourse on what constitutes the rights of an individual as a human being. To argue that engaging in pornography or surrogacy gives women freedom may seem as ridiculous to women in the Third World as burning one's bra to declare one's liberation (Kemp *et al.* 1995: 138). For many Third World people, having shelter, clean water, clean air, food, health care and fuel may define what it means to enjoy individual rights. According to Raymond (1990: 111), 'there's a conscious manipulation of language and reality that happens when defenders of surrogacy use the rhetoric of "procreative liberty", knowing that many women will resonate with this phrase because of the feminist emphasis on reproductive choice articulated around the abortion issue'. My objective here is to offer a critique of the position taken by the family planning establishment, international financial institutions and donor countries in justifying the use of reproductive technologies in the Third World. I do not disagree with the use of the reproductive technologies; it is with the rationales and unsafe or banned procedures used on people of colour that I wish to take issue. I am also concerned about the negative effects of reproductive technologies on people and especially women in the Third World.

My perspective on reproductive technologies is shaped by my experiences in both Kenya and the US. As a Kenyan woman I have observed, through my research on the effects of land tenure policies (1996) and my ongoing study of the impact of rice irrigation production on health and the environment in Kenya (2000), the enormous hardships women experience in rural areas. The lack of access to health care delivery or clean water frequently leads to waterborne diseases such as typhoid, ameobiasis, bilharzia and malaria. Lack of fuelwood and infrastructure further make daily struggles and strategies of survival more demanding on women's lives and time. The women and their families have experienced the imposition of international and national policies that leave their conditions worse. Neither agricultural production of cash crops nor family planning policies have benefited the majority of women in Kenya. The powers that imposed family planning and structural adjustment should not then blame the lack of economic development or environmental degradation on fertility rates. My perspective has also been informed by my experiences in the US and in the higher education system there, where I have been exposed to Western feminism in both theory and practice. The struggle of white 'first-' and 'second-wave' feminists to create a space in their society still reflects Western privilege and a position of power and control that diminishes positive interactions with women of colour or poor white women. That some white feminists fail to reflect on their own privilege – at times made possible by the exploitation of people of colour – diminishes the effective articulation by women of colour of their experiences within the context of the history of colonialism,the postcolonial state, imperialism, class, gender and racism at a global level. According to bell hooks, for most American women

> the first knowledge of racism as institutionalized oppression is engendered either by direct personal experience or through information gleaned from conversations, books, television or movies. Consequently, the American woman's understanding of racism as a political tool of colonialism and imperialism is severely limited. (hooks 1981: 119)

Both my Kenyan and US experiences have left me ambivalent about the policies of family planning and how some feminists articulate the need for population control, basing their position on Western women's experiences and failing to embrace the concept of difference among and between women globally. I have also become highly suspicious of any policy prescription for the Third World. Such policies are exemplified by various deployments of reproductive technology in the Third World as a solution to high fertility rates. As Callahan points out, 'we need to be suspicious of *all* technologies that are applied to women's reproductive capacities' (Callahan 1995: 12). The International Women and Health Meeting, organized by the International Women's Health Movement, which opposed the use of RU 486 in developing countries, at its sixth meeting in the Philippines in 1990, has taken such a stand (*ibid.*: 288). In addition to this, I feel we should be suspicious of any policies such as the structural adjustment policies imposed on the Third World by the World Bank and the IMF. These policies have shifted labour and land to the production of cash crops in the name of economic growth. However, the production of cash crops catering to the West and the élites of the Third World has led to hunger and environmental degradation. The scapegoat for the failed or misguided policies is then found in the lifestyles of the general population of the Third World, in particular with regard to fertility rates, that need to be controlled by any means necessary, whether they are safe or not.

The debate over rampant HIV–Aids infections in Africa has taken the same turn, often scapegoating the lifestyles of Africans and, in the US, of African-Americans. According to a World Bank report (1999: 1) 'HIV is already widespread in many countries in sub-Saharan Africa and may be on the verge of exploding in other regions'. Both this report and that of the Economic and Social Council (UN 1999: 17) argue that more than 90 per cent of African cases of HIV–Aids deaths are due to risky behaviour, including sexual 'orientations', as the cause of this epidemic trend of HIV–Aids deaths. 'Behavioral studies show that observable individual characteristics, such as occupation, age, or sexual orientation, can partially predict risk behavior' (World Bank 1999: 5). Sex workers, the military and the police, according to the report, are responsible for the spread of the virus, since they tend to have more sexual partners than the rest of the population. The Economic and Social Council also sees rural–urban migration as a factor that is spreading HIV, since men, away from their wives, seek other sexual partners. 'When they return to their rural households and re-establish sexual relationships, they increase the possibility of HIV transmission being carried back to their wives and home communities' (UN 1999: 19). Women's entry into the workforce in economic sectors such as manufacturing and tourism, 'form[s] new sexual networks without the protective and supportive features of families and village communities, thus increasing their vulnerability to STD and HIV infection' (*ibid.*). Such is the literature by the 'experts' on Africa, describing why Africa has such a high morbidity and mortality. The cure is policy interventions to teach Africans how to behave and to be 'civil'. These arguments do not address the social, economic, historical and political factors that, for example, make people move from rural to urban areas. For instance, no connections are made between previous apartheid policies of forced labour and high HIV–Aids rates in South Africa. These policies confined families, and especially women, within Bantustans (impoverished rural areas similar to the reserves to which they were confined in colonial Kenya) while their husbands, fathers and sons migrated into urban areas. Men were put in hostels where families were not allowed (Wangari 2000: 6). The colonial policies of segregation and racism, and the subsequent policies of the postcolonial state, have to be blamed. The power ingrained in gender biases that makes older men take advantage of younger women is an issue that degrades and pollutes women's bodies and should be addressed seriously from a global perspective. Tourism as a policy to increase foreign exchange – in Thailand, for example – is connected to high rates of HIV–Aids (Usher 1994: 10). In other cases, policies geared to capitalist agricultural production have wiped out resources and denied women land ownership.

The campaigning literature regarding fertility rates, and justifying the use of reproductive technologies, continues to circulate among the family planning establishment, the donor countries and the experts on economic growth, hailed as a solution to environmental degradation and a means of empowering women and improving their status in the Third World. 'In 1985, at the height of a major drought, Colorado Governor Richard D. Lamm wrote in the *New York Times* that the United States should stop giving emergency relief to African countries that failed to reduce their population growth, since such aids would "merely multiply empty stomachs"' (Hartmann 1995: 15). The rights of Africans, as individuals, are beyond comprehension among the experts on Africa. The debates fail to make connections between Western hegemony and domination of global resources and negative consequences as a result. Additionally, these policies do not include prior consultation with the people who will receive the services as to their needs and whether these policies are consistent with their cultural norms. 'The new reproductive technologies have increased the ability of the privileged race, class, and gender to make policy decisions about who will live and who will not, as Phillida Bunkle's account of the international politics of birth control shows' (Harding 1993: 273). People of colour, whether in Africa or in the US, have been more often than not the 'targets' of the new technologies. They have been used as guinea pigs to perfect medical interventions. For instance, Dr Sims operated on slave women without anaesthesia to find the cure 'for cases of vaginal-vesico fistula' (Leidholdt and Raymond 1990: 85). To support or not to support the old or the new technologies is definitely a big challenge, in my view. The literature on the misuse of reproductive technologies on people of colour, defined as less human, is not only deplorable but also sickening. The use of fertility rates as justification for abusive reproductive techniques obscures the rationale for the control of resources and profit by the West.

At UNCED in Rio in 1992, '[w]hen worn-out development talk prevailed, attention centred on the South and its natural treasures and not on the North and its industrial disorder. There were conventions on biodiversity, climate and forests, but no conventions on agri-business, automobiles or free trade' (Sachs 1995: xvi). The re-examination of justifications for and controversies over reproductive technologies in the Third World shifts the root of the problems women face to state policies and Western influence in the power structure of the Third World.

Reproductive technologies: justifications and controversies

Inherent in the birth control rationale is the argument that population growth, if not controlled, results in resource scarcity that would affect future generations negatively. The United Nations Family Planning Association (UNFPA) in its *State of the World's Population 1992*, asserts that high fertility rates in developing countries have been responsible for around 70 per cent of deforestation, 72 per cent of arable land expansion and 69 per cent of growth in livestock (Hartmann 1995: 26–7). Hence funds are needed to control fertility rates in these countries. What these statistics do not reveal are the underlying issues behind patterns of consumption of resources by Western countries, corruption, and macro-policies borrowed from developed countries. These statistics do not look at the history and legacy of colonialism and postcolonial policies in 'developing' countries. For example, in Kenya, the colonial state not only destroyed African tenure and farming systems that retained and generated soil fertility, but also put Africans and their livestock into marginal lands. This resulted in the devastation of the environment and people's physical as well as mental health. Hartmann points out that the United Nations Research Institute for Social Development (UNRISD) has disputed the blame placed on impoverished migrants as destroyers of forest, since it ignores the larger underlying factors – such as the expansion of large-scale commercial farming, ranching, logging and mining – that are forcing migrants into forest areas. The study finds no correlation between deforestation and rates of either total or agricultural population growth. The production of export-oriented crops such as tea, cotton, tobacco and coffee has also contributed to environmental devastation and the corruption of state officials. The Nyao Tea Zone at the foot of the Mount Kenya, and the fight led by Wangari Mathai (the founder of the Green Belt Movement in Kenya) and others against the destruction of Karura Forest in the name of development are examples of such corruption and greed, and of the struggle against their impact. People are pushed away from the base of their livelihoods in the name of economic development. The relationship between environmental degradation and scarcity can only be seen within the context of global economy, power and control of resources – and population control is not the only solution. 'The key to development and prosperity doesn't lie in attempting to control the reproduction of those considered least desirable and a burden to a society. Rather they lie in reforming the social and economic conditions which breed destitution for segments of a society' (Callahan 1995: 258).

Another argument is that high fertility rates in 'developing' countries limit economic growth. The family planning establishment and the World Bank perceive uncontrolled fertility rates as the cause of poverty and as a factor that lowers women's status (Hartmann 1995). The root of the problem, however, could be articulated within the corruption of state officials as a privileged class that forms alliances with the international family planning establishment and donors. In other words, the problem is inherent in the national and international power structure that controls resource allocation. Appropriation and overconsumption of resources by Western countries should not be blamed on the majority of the Third World population. The control of women's and some men's reproductive systems through the use of sterilization, Depo-Provera or Norplant, and IUDs is not a solution to either environmental degradation or economic growth. Pumping pills or inserting IUDs into their bodies in the absence of gynaecological examinations, follow-up examinations, or information about side-effects will not bring 'sustainable development' but degradation of women's bodies – which, given the division of labour, affects their families and the economy.

Solutions lie in redefining and rejecting misleading imported policies that infringe people's livelihoods. Economic growth does not guarantee an equal distribution of resources. By the end of the 1960s, 'the richest 20 per cent of Kenyans received 68 per cent of the country's annual income, the bottom 40 per cent only 10 per cent' (Hartmann 1995: 84). The Kenyan land reforms under the Swynnerton Plan in 1954, characterized by the privatization of land ownership, left many families landless and others unemployed. Women were the most affected by the reform, since they lost the right to use land. This led to rural–urban migration and poverty. Young women who could not and still cannot make it to colleges or universities are left with limited alternatives. Some of them get married while others join the rural–urban drift to seek jobs as domestic workers, get into the informal sector or engage in prostitution (Wangari 1997: 32). The roots of their problems lie not in fertility rates that need to be controlled but in power and economic structures that determine resource allocation. 'So-called population problems are not genuine population problems, but interlocking problems of sexual, racial, or ethnic, and classist biases which governments are slow to rectify because states are run by those of privileged sex, class and race or ethnicity' (Callahan 1995: 258). Thus the state in Africa, during the colonial period and since, has been the worst enemy of the people because it victimizes not only men but also women and children.

Silenced voices

Wacera's experience with reproductive technology as an 'acceptor' is an example of such a nightmare. Through the International Planned Parenthood Federation (IPPF) campaign to control fertility rates in rural Kenya, Wacera became a statistic of the pill 'acceptor'. Being a mother of five children who left her abusive husband, and being in a country where child support, child care, welfare and social security are not enforced, Wacera felt family planning would improve her life. However, Wacera was given the pill without a gynaecological check-up. Her journey to 'controlling her body' took her over twenty miles every month to pick up the pills from a family planning centre. The campaign for birth control did not include information about possible side-effects and health care delivery. Issues of Wacera's transport, food and time were not considered. Since there were no follow-up examinations, Wacera was hospitalized three times with heavy bleeding and her health was negatively affected, leaving her with mental anguish (interview with Wacera, 21 February 2001). Wacera had no right to choose. As in the case of many other Third World women, her right to choose to have or not to have a baby was mediated and determined by reproductive technology experts and by race, class and gender. For millions of women like Wacera, suing is out of the question since information about their personal rights is not available to them. The hegemony of Western countries in determining the global distribution of resources, and their influence and support for pharmaceutical companies to distribute banned reproductive technologies and test some of the new ones on people in the Third World, has been a major factor in women's daily experience of mental and physical anguish.

> Large numbers of poor women have been sterilized in Puerto Rico, Brazil, Bangladesh and India. This has taken place in the absence of proper information, adequate facilities, of consideration for desires, circumstances and health status of the women in question.... Since the 1960s, new contraceptives have been tested on women in developing countries, frequently with very limited, if any, information being imparted to them or to health workers.... (Smyth 1998: 221)

This is blunt racism against the people of colour. Their bodies and their families become nothing but testing and dumping grounds for the new and banned reproductive technologies of the West.

It is not fertility rates that are destroying resources, nor are they responsible for women's lack of empowerment or improvement of well-being. After all, a family of five in the Third World may consume fewer resources than a family of two in the West. It is Western countries, it appears to me, that need 'family consumption planning clinics'. But of course the debate on fertility rates in the Third World obscures the consumption patterns, power, economic structures, racism and class issues which limit economic development and women's empowerment. Hartmann points out that US pharmaceutical companies, using foreign subsidiaries, have been able to export drugs not approved by their own country's Food and Drug Administration (FDA), using the Third World as a dumping ground. '[I]n the contraceptive research business, the Third World has long been an important laboratory for human testing. From 1980 to 1983 at least one fifth of contraceptive research and development and safety evaluation projects were located in developing countries, with India, China, Chile, Mexico, and Brazil the major locations' (Hartmann 1995: 183). Implementation of reproductive technologies in the Third World does not require rigorous standards, with suitable provision of information about side-effects. The state and its élites, the pharmaceutical companies and the family planning establishment reap the benefits of the policies, which apply double standards. Safety regulations are required or implemented in the West while denied in the Third World. The argument for this double standard is that deaths caused by contraceptives are less than those caused by pregnancies or childbirth. The issues which lead to deaths in pregnancy or childbirth are not addressed. The fundamental factors of poor health or malnutrition leading to death in pregnancy or childbirth are not issues of interest to the population control establishment. No connections are made between women's poor health and agricultural production of cash crops. Traditional staple foods, such as millet, sorghum, legumes and varieties of beans among others, which provided nutrition for pregnant women and their families, have been replaced by cash crops. Cutting trees for the production of coffee, tea, tobacco and cotton has resulted in the loss of minerals and vitamins due to soil erosion. For instance, in the case of tobacco curing the loss of trees and traditional farming systems which sustained the environment has led to the depletion of vitamins, iron and iodine. Frequent use of pesticides and fertilizers, together with sewage contamination, leads to a lack of iodine that 'in pregnant women can result in miscarriages or the necessity for abortion, stillbirths, birth of cretinous or hypothyroid babies, deaf-mutes, or babies with psychomotor retardation' (Shiva 1994: 62). Cultivation of cash crops has replaced vegetables, fruit and food grains, leading to a lack of vitamins (*ibid.*). Environmental degradation translates to the degradation of the body, and especially of women's bodies. 'The solution to unwanted births lies not in bringing more powerful contraceptive technologies into the market nor in adopting more and more coercive population control methods, but enabling women to take at least some decisions affecting their lives' (*ibid.*). Most of the policies implemented in the Third World, and especially reproductive technologies, have been influenced by racism, class and gender bias, which tainted earlier family programmes in the West. That is how the positive effect celebrated by Western women becomes a nightmare to millions of women in the Third World. The 'acceptors' of birth control are made to believe that their living conditions and empowerment will be achieved through family planning. For the majority of women in rural areas and in urban slums, however, the liberating effect experienced by some women in the West becomes a tool for the exploitation of their bodies. For example, 'in South Africa, adolescent black girls have been injected with Depo-Provera without their consent, and black women have been required to document their use of birth control as part of their application for jobs' (Callahan 1995: 257). 'The government targeted almost exclusively black and mixed-race women as part of its effort to reduce the growth rate of the African population (and concurrently increase the number of whites)' (Hartmann 1995: 206).

What would explain this act of crassness toward one group of people while whites are exempted? International financial donors and the family planning establishment often blame the poor and uneducated for high fertility rates, which are perceived as barriers to economic growth. Furthermore, they also blame them for environmental degradation and sanitation problems. Women, and especially women of colour, are perceived as irresponsible 'baby producers' whose irrational behaviour has to be controlled (Barroso and Bruschini 1991: 156). They are often subject to family planning measures that violate their reproductive systems and leave their bodies crippled by poor health and a perpetually nervous condition.

> While millions of women have benefited from contraceptive services, some policies and programmes to limit (or increase) population growth have had negative effects, especially on poor women. In many countries, abuses such as pressure to use specific types of contraceptives, sterilization, inadequate attention to contraceptive safety, poor-quality services that ignore women's multiple reproductive health needs, and barriers to access to contraceptives and safe abortion have jeopardized women's rights and health. (Garcia-Moreno and Claro 1994: 47).

The proclaimed litany of improved status and empowerment of women by the family planning establishment, donors and some women's movement organizations has failed millions of women in the Third World. 'Improved status' simply does not factor in their daily experiences. It is an alien term exclusively for the privileged.

When Margaret Sanger was conducting her crusade in the 1930s, eradicating procreation for those unfit and advocating it for those fit, she was blind to racial and class issues that 'informed her eugenicism or the basic incoherence in a view calling for both reproductive freedom and eugenics' (Callahan 1995: 257). This is an important point when re-examining the contemporary family planning establishment. In most cases, the establishment views people in the Third World as illiterate, poor, irrational and unable to make decisions concerning their own lives. As such, they have to be organized and controlled. This paternalistic attitude is inherent in the history of colonialism in Africa. While not all family planning authorities think this way, it remains justifiable for people in the Third World to have suspicions about birth control programmes implemented in Africa.

While feminists have been engaged in a continuous fight for women to have the right to make choices over their bodies and experience safety in reproductive technology delivery, this fight, for the majority of women from the Third World, has been inflected by injustice at the hands of the family planning establishment. Forced sterilization of some men and women, IUDs, Depo-Provera and Norplant, among other dubious interventions by the IFPP and international funding institutions, deny the majority of Third World women their voice. We need to hear voices calling with a global reach for a fair distribution of resources, gender equity, and the dismantling of parameters of the state that are oppressive not only to women but also to their men. The collusion of the state with the international family planners and donor agencies has left many women with no say in matters that concern their livelihoods and empowerment. The notion of Africans devastating the environment and the world's dwindling resources removes the moral blame from those who in truth consume resources recklessly, and sets out their justification for controlling global procreation. The bodies of women of colour become the target of that control.

Challenges to feminisms

My educational experiences in both postcolonial Kenya and the United States have exposed me to how deeply Eurocentric and North American perspectives have constructed and defined who we are in Africa. Africa, to some people in the West, including some feminists, is perceived as a continent with no variations in terms of history, culture, politics, economics, and ecosystems. People are perceived as homogeneous, without differences. In comparison to Western societies, we are backward, primitive and underdeveloped, among other things. Most feminist literature and ideological theorizing on the need for fertility control in

Africa is influenced by how the West perceives Africans. As Chandra Mohanty points out, feminists writing in the West should be understood within the context of the power and control the West has on scholarship (Mohanty 1991: 55). At times their focus on patriarchal oppression and the need for policy interventions through development or control of fertility rates to improve women's status is shaded with racism. Reproductive interventions as solutions to women's oppression in the Third Word fall short when it comes to explaining the causes of the problems. The occupation of some Third World countries by some Western countries, from the slave trade through the colonial state and neocolonialism to today's global economy, has a lot to do with the negative experiences facing African people. Feminists who are proponents of reproductive technologies as measures to improve women's status in the Third World should be aware of the continuing destruction wrought by the West's policies of globalization of the market and culture. There are no guarantees that in contemporary times the application of scientific methods will be immune to subjecting people to abuses and exploitation. As Harding points out,

> Western sciences clearly have been and continue to be complicit with racist, colonial, and imperial projects. Not surprisingly, Westerners fail to situate their understandings of both nature and sciences within maximally realistic and objective world histories. Full acknowledgement and analysis of these Eurocentric tendencies leads to the recognition that racially marginalized groups, at least, may have good reasons to avoid sciences that have had undoubted good effects for those in a position to benefit from them, but nevertheless, in other respects appear to be effectively committed to increasing consumerism and profit, maintaining social control, and legitimating the authority of élites. (Harding 1993: 3)

Ingrained hegemonic aims mean that some of the programmes implemented in the Third World lack compassion and concern for the people they are supposed to be helping. Their actions are justified on the basis of the quantity of targeted acceptors versus the quality of people's health. Statistical numbers become the norm for future funding and evaluation of the family planning programmes. Investing in people in terms of human rights that include – as first priorities – accessibility of health care, clean water, food, infrastructure, energy, opportunities and overall well-being would provide the basis of empowerment. However, this is only the necessary but not a sufficient remedy. The treatment of people of colour as inferior by some people working for the family planning establishment, and by those of colour in the high echelons of Third World states whose success depends upon and echoes the West, also has to change. Racism, paternalistic attitudes toward people of colour, and the power over and distribution of resources on a world scale are concerns of anyone fighting for justice and gender equity. The fight should transcend boundaries and Eurocentric perspectives so as to reflect on how those involved in the fight could also be contributing to the fight *against* the rights of women in the Third World.

> Western feminist scholarship cannot avoid the challenge of situating itself and examining its role in such a global economic and political framework. To do any less would be to ignore the complex interconnections between First and third world economies and the profound effect of this on the lives of women in all countries. (Mohanty 1991: 54)

Western feminists have to challenge policies which appear as beneficial to people of colour yet embody racism. While Margaret Sanger contributed remarkably to the birth control movement in the US, 'still, there was simply no way to avoid the fact of endemic racism among many activists in the birth control movement, let alone among the white public health officials in the South on whom the success of any voluntary effort ultimately depended' (Chesler 1992: 388). These attitudes on the part of Western policy makers have not changed as far as the Third World is concerned. The rhetoric on the reduction of fertility rates in the Third World obscures the motives behind Western hegemony in its domination of the world economy and its contribution to the problems faced by women and their families.

An individual right to make choices expressing autonomy over one's body is not a right one can fully claim, given the economic, social, political and global structures which embody gender biases, racism, war and the privileges of Western hegemony. These factors shape or prevent choices people make. It seems that our rights as human beings are under the receivership of the global economy and the scientific world. To argue that family planning in the Third World would improve women's status fails to examine critically enough those factors that would prevent or facilitate the process of empowering women.

17

Gender, Bodies and Cosmos in Mesoamerica

Sylvia Marcos

> ...Look now, don't choose from among the men the one that seems the best to you like those who shop for mantas in the market ... and don't carry on like people do when the new corn is just fresh, looking for the best and tastiest cobs... *Florentine Codex,* Chapter VI

Introduction: a conceptual re-visioning

Body perceptions are embedded in both gender and culture. Mesoamerican sources are particularly revealing of that relationship. Concepts like equilibrium and fluidity are fundamental to grasping perceptions and constructions of bodies in ancient Mexico. A review of some of the primary sources for the history of ancient Mexico manifests a conception of corporeality that could be called 'embodied thought'.

By Mesoamerican thought, which provides the context of this chapter, I am referring to the highly developed complex of ideas and beliefs that constituted the prevalent epistemological framework among the Nahuas of Central Mexico. The Mayas and all other cultural groups in the region participated in the same basic belief system.[1]

The main sources for the present study are Books III and VI of the *General History of the Things of New Spain (Florentine Codex).* Researchers have pointed out their depth and richness – especially Book VI – and their value in bringing us closer to the moral vision and thought of the ancient Nahuas. The contributions of Lopez Austin and Leon-Portilla to the understanding of the Mesoamerican philosophical world are of great importance for the interpretation of these primary sources. Excerpts from the *Royal Palace Matritense Codex*, and especially Leon-Portilla's recent translation of it, were also examined.[2]

Duality in the Mesoamerican universe

The original duality

The feminine–masculine dual unity was fundamental to the creation of the cosmos, its (re)generation and its sustenance. The fusion of feminine and masculine in one bipolar principle is a recurring feature of Mesoamerican thinking. This principle, both singular and dual, is manifested by representations of gods in pairs.[3] Several Mesoamerican deities were pairs of gods and goddesses, beginning with Ometeotl, the supreme creator whose name means 'double god' or dual divinity. Dwelling beyond the thirteen heavens, Ometeotl was thought of as a feminine–masculine pair. Born of this supreme pair, other dual deities, in their turn, incarnated natural phenomena. A brief manuscript from the sixteenth century attributed by Angel Garibay to Fray Andres de Olmos records this concept of duality. It is precisely its quality that marks this work by one of the first Christian chroniclers as one of the least-altered primary sources (Olmos 1973).

The cultures of Mesoamerica, says Lopez Austin, 'view the world ordered and put in motion by the same divine laws, adore the same gods under different names' (Lopez Austin 1984b). Thus the concept of 'dual oneness' is found in the entire Mesoamerican region. Thompson (1975), for example, speaks in the same terms of Itzam Na and his partner Ix Chebel Yax in the Mayan region. Las Casas (1967) mentions the pair made up by Izona and his wife; and Diego de Landa (1966) refers to Itzam Na and Ixchel as the god and goddess of medicine. For the inhabitants of the Michoacan area, the creator pair was Curicuauert and Cuerauahperi.

The specificity of Mesoamerican duality

Omecihuatl and Ometeculi are the feminine and masculine halves of the divine duality Ometeotl. According to an ancient Nahua myth, they had a fight during which they broke dishes, and from every shard that hit the ground a new dual divinity sprang up. While some Mexicanists have inferred that this legend was used to explain the multiplicity of gods, it also illustrates how the prime duality in its turn engenders dualities. Perhaps, then, gender itself – the primordial, all-pervasive duality – could be seen as 'engendering' the multiple specific dualities for all phenomena.

Life/death is an example of the duality that pervades the Mesoamerican world. That life and death are but two aspects of the same dual reality is dramatically expressed by a type of figure from Tlatlilco with a human head that is half living face and half skull. Or, to turn to the cosmos, the sun and the moon are regarded as a dynamic masculine–feminine complementarity (Baez-Jorge 1988). Likewise, during the ritual bathing of new-borns, feminine and masculine water are invoked (Sahagun 1969, 1989). Cosmic duality is reflected in everyday life: corn, for example, was in turn feminine (*Xilonen-Chicomeocoatl*) and masculine (*Cinteotl-Itztlacoliuhqui*).

Just as space was structured in polar pairs (above and below, east and west, far and near, etcetera), so was time itself. Duality, the essential ordering force of the cosmos, was reflected in the ordering of time: time was kept by two calendars. One was a ritual calendar of 260 days (13 x 20) which some regard as linked to the human gestation cycle, while the other was an agricultural calendar of 360 days (18 x 20) (Olmos 1973). Five days were added to adjust it to the astronomical calendar.[4]

Even the arts of poetry and oratory reflected the dual make-up of the universe: metaphorical verses were repeated twice with minimal but significant changes. Leon-Portilla calls this rhetorical form 'di-phrasing' (Leon-Portilla 1984; Garibay 1953; Sullivan 1983). Poets alternated pairs of verses whose order varied but whose elements could not be separated. Among Mexicanists, Alfred Lopez Austin stands out for his perception that Mesoamerican thought was *totally* permeated by dualities (Lopez Austin 1984b). Thelma Sullivan echoes this understanding when she speaks of 'redundant pairs' as an oratorical and narrative device (Sullivan 1983).

What kind of duality was Mesoamerican duality? How does it differ from the binary ordering found in feminist gender theory? Many have commented on the qualities of Mesoamerican duality. For example, both Frances Karttunen and Gary Gossen describe it as a dynamic duality (Karttunen 1986; Gossen 1986). To the polar ordering of opposites other authors add a complementarity that gives duality a certain 'reversibility of terms or movement to the concept'.[5] Fluidity deepens the meanings of bipolarity by giving a permanently shifting nature to feminine and masculine. With fluidity, femininity is always in transit to masculinity and vice-versa.

Fluid equilibrium

The idea of duality, discussed above, was enhanced by another concept equally pervasive in Mesoamerican thought: that of 'equilibrium'. This equilibrium is not, however, the static repose of two equal masses. Rather, it is a force that constantly modifies the relation between dual and/or opposite pairs. Like duality itself, equilibrium or balance not only permeated relations between men and women, but also relations among deities, deities and humans, and elements of nature. When we consider that the constant search for this balance was vital to the preservation of order in every area from daily life to the activity of the cosmos, it is clear that equilibrium was as fundamental as duality itself.

To understand how equilibrium affects duality, we can begin by acknowledging how this concept differs from and is foreign to our own traditions of thought. I will start with a consideration of classical Greek thinking in order to see how Mesoamerican thought is conceived, and then move to an examination of oral traditions, because the sources examined here are essentially the products of an oral culture; finally, I will discuss metaphor, one of the characteristics of the oral tradition and a key element in Nahua thought.

Plasticity and dynamism: qualities of balance

Duality in Nahuatl thought is conceptualized differently than it is in ancient Greek thought (Lloyd 1966). To speak of dualities and polarities evokes classical Greek thought, wherein polarities are regarded as excluding a third position (*tertium non datur*) and leading to 'either/or' situations (what logicians call 'disjunctions'). Some authors stress the link between this type of 'clear-cut logic' with the development of alphabetic writing at the beginning of the fifth century BC, while others have opposed it to the 'fluidity' of oral thought (Lord 1975). Nahuatl thought shows the eminent fluidity characteristic of oral cultures.

Nahuatl thought, with the plasticity and dynamism that characterize its poles and keep them 'pulsating', as it were, is clearly beyond the classical Greek cultural horizon. Discussion of Nahuatl thought in terms of what it is not brings us directly to its 'otherness'. The following comment by Jacques Soustelle, on the other hand, presents an understanding of the Nahuatl universe in terms of what it is:

> Thus [in] Mexican thought ... what characterized [it] is precisely the connecting of traditionally associated images. The world is a system of symbols that mutually reflect each other.... We are not in the presence of 'long chains of reason' but of an implicit and continuous reciprocity of various aspects of a whole. (Soustelle 1940)

Oral thought and oral narrative

The texts on which this study is based are 'hybrid' or mixed texts belonging both to oral and written narrative forms or styles. Through a comparison of oral narrative and the written text I can better understand the specific character of the Nahuatl concept of 'balance'. The various versions of Sahagun's work consist of transcribed oral narratives and include epic stories such as that of *Tohuenyo*, which I analyze below, and speeches consisting of moral and practical advice. As transcriptions of traditional oral discourses, they probably correspond to what Parry and Dorson (Parry 1971) term 'authentic texts' – the first transcriptions of narrations that previously were exclusively oral.[6]

Oral narrative cannot be reduced to categories of (written) literature. It belongs to another order of reality. While an oral narrative is never the recitation of a 'text' learned by memory, neither is it the completely original creation of the narrator. According to Parry, it is a *rhapsodia*, a Greek word meaning a patchwork or woven sort of composition based on groupings of traditional formulas. The reciter of a fixed, memorized text unrolls a prefabricated tapestry, as it were, in front of the listeners. The oral narrator, in contrast, weaves the tapestry as he goes along, using elements familiar to his audience. The narration, punctuated by breathing, is given the pauses required by speaking (Tedlock 1983). In oral recitation, epic actions of heroes are glorified, divine interventions are celebrated, codes of proper behaviour are presented, and repetition is used for emphasis throughout. In fact, repetition of the same episode with the same or different formulas enhanced by numerous metaphors is one of the most notable characteristics of the Nahuatl 'texts'. This is due largely to the fact that they are transcriptions of oral narratives. Sahagun, in an attempt to gather information about the civilization his own people had conquered and almost eradicated, drew up a questionnaire in Nahuatl and sent out assistants to interview the old people in villages around Mexico City (Sullivan 1983; Leon-Portilla 1980).

The amblings of oral thought, its circular and unpredictably innovative flow, remind us of the river that Heraclitus spoke of – ever the same and ever changing. Its waters flow incessantly, murmuring over stones, disappearing down a ravine or flowing freely toward the sea that embraces them. The thought behind oral narrative resembles water that flows swiftly at times and quietly at others, changing course unpredictably but always remaining the same river.

A large part of the material that makes up the *General History of the Things of New Spain* and the *Codex* consists of epic and poetic songs, chronicles and stories, human and ritual discourses, all destined to be declaimed in public. These gems of knowledge and oral tradition are called *chalchihuitl*, or pieces of jade, indicating that in the collective memory they were regarded as having jade's permanence and value. 'A scattering of jades' is the metaphor for the discourses of the wise old women and men *(ilamatlatolli* and *huehuetlatolli)* and expressed the imperative need to remember (Sullivan 1983; Leon-Portilla 1984).

Even though the texts studied here are predominantly oral in character, they are cut, synthesized, transformed and arranged by Sahagun in the process of adapting them to certain guidelines of his era related to book writing (Lopez Austin 1971). This combination of oral transcription and literary manipulation in Sahagun gives us a view in miniature of the confrontation between the two worlds. In this respect, several scholars have pointed out the immense value of these texts as 'dia-logic', expressions of a dialogue established between the old and new worlds (Karttunen 1986; Burkhart 1989; Klor de Alva 1988a). Comparing the Nahuatl version of the *Matritense Codex* with the translation and adaptation that Sahagun had done in 1577, elements of this dialogue and confrontation between the two logics appear.

In the discussion of the Mesoamerican concept of equilibrium by other Mexicanists, I find the following comments concerning its implications for living life correctly. Gingerich writes, in relation to the Nahuatl metaphor used to express a proper life that appears in the *ilamatlatollis,* that 'The doctrine of the middle way, therefore, was a central principle in the formulation and interpretation of the ethic ... this middle way definitely is not the Aristotelian golden mean. This concept (is) profoundly indigenous' (Gingerich 1988: 522).

Mesoamerican thinking was based on the concept of opposing dualities and the search for the balance between them. Equilibrium, thus defined, required that each individual in all circumstances seek the central hub of the cosmos and orient himself or herself in relation to it. To maintain this balance is to combine and recombine opposites. This implies not negating the opposite but rather advancing toward it, embracing it in the attempt to find the fluctuating balance. The principle of the excluded middle – the *tertium non datur* of formal classical logic – definitely has no place in the Nahuatl universe. In this realm of thought, opposites are integrated: cold and hot, night and day, sun and moon, sacred and profane, feminine and masculine. The extremes, although they did not have to be completely avoided, did have to be offset one with the other (Burkhart 1989).

This fluid position made up the equilibrium of the cosmos. The fusion/tension of contraries in the Mesoamerican cosmos was the measure and means of achieving the fundamental, primordial equilibrium.

Cosmic and moral equilibrium

The collective responsibility of not only sustaining balance but also participating in its achievement produced a very particular set of moral codes. The best expression of these moral codes is found in the *huehuetlatolli* and *ilamatlatolli.* As mentioned above, many Mexicanists regard Book VI of the *Florentine Codex* of Sahagun as a sort of *summa* of Nahuatl thought. It is the work which probes most deeply into the beliefs and rules of this society. The *ilamatlatolli* contained in Book VI of the *Florentine Codex* are explicitly about the type of equilibrium required in the conduct of the women and men.[7]

(D)o not walk hurriedly nor slowly ... because walking slowly is a sign of

> pompousness and walking quickly shows restlessness and little sense. Walk moderately.... Do not walk with your head lowered or your body slouched, but also do not carry your head overly high and upright because this is a sign of bad upbringing. (Sahagun 1969)

> When you speak, do not speak rapidly ... do not raise your voice nor speak too softly.... Don't use a thin, high voice in speaking and greeting others, do not speak through your nose, but let your voice be normal. (*Ibid.*)

In the *huehuetlatolli* we find this constant of Nahuatl thought as it is incarnated in daily life, in relations between the genders and bodily attitudes. 'If a harmonious balance is established, the individual can derive great benefit from the inclinations and tendencies that the *tonally* [see p. 320] was given...' (Lopez Austin 1984b). These recommendations, we will recall, are normative and do not necessarily permit direct inferences to be drawn concerning everyday behaviour. Nonetheless, existing documents show that women occupied social spaces of power. They were experts in medicine and exercised ritual power as priestesses. Their belief system regarded the originating force of the universe as feminine; divine forces were female and male, and the overall importance of the feminine was engraved in every aspect of their symbolic reality. Both Susan Kellogg and Frances Karttunen find evidence of non-hierarchical gender relations in their analyses of legal documents that deal with property and inheritance and indicate that women owned, administered and inherited property. These behaviours and attitudes cannot be linked to Spanish practices in Mexico at that time (sixteenth century) (Kellogg 1984, Karttunen 1986). Further, the importance of textile (*manta*) production is shown in *Historia de los Mexicanos por sus Pinturas* (Garibay 1973). The production of textiles, which were used in ancient Mexico as a form of exchange, was the preferred domain of women.

The Mesoamerican body: permeable corporeality

In dominant traditions, the very concept of body has been formed in opposition to mind. It is defined as the place of biological data, of the material, of the immanent. It has also been conceptualized since the seventeenth century as that which marks the boundaries between the interior self and the external world (Bordo and Jaggar 1989; Duden 1991).

In the Mesoamerican tradition, on the other hand, the body has characteristics that are very different from those of the anatomical or biological body. In this tradition exteriority and interiority are not separated by the hermetic barrier of skin. Between the outside and inside, permanent and continuous exchange occurs. Material and immaterial, external and internal are in permanent interaction while the skin is constantly crossed by all kinds of entities. Everything leads toward a concept of corporeality in which the body is open to all dimensions of the cosmos. It is a body conceived of as both singular and dual; it incorporates solids and fluids in permanent flux, and generally immaterial 'airs' or volatile emanations in the dynamic confluence of multiple entities, both material and immaterial; often seemingly contradictory and unpredictable, this body combines and recombines in endless play.

Bodies – feminine and masculine – echo each other and, united, they mirror the universe: their duality reflects cosmic duality. In turn this cosmic duality reflects the duality of the masculine and feminine imbricated in each other and both incorporated in the universe. Body and cosmos reflect each other and are complementary. The head corresponds to the heavens, the heart as the vital centre corresponds to the earth, and the liver to the underworld. These interrelations are immersed in a permanent reciprocal movement, characterized by an ebb and flow between the universe and the body, and also between a cosmic duality and the bodies of women and men, such that it pours back from the feminine to the masculine body, and from this duality to the cosmos.

Three animic entities

In addition to the visible body, the Mesoamerican body is made up of 'animic entities' as Lopez Austin calls them (1984b). These entities can materialize or not, and transit between the inside and the outside of the permeable body in a fluid interchange. Furthermore, the body is open to inclusions from the outer world. There are three pre-eminent entities: the *tonally*, the *teyolia* and the *ihiyotl.* Each has its privileged – but not unique – location within the physical body. The *tonally*, whose principal residence is the head, travels at night during sleep. It can also leave the body during coitus; occasionally an unusual or frightening event can cause it to leave. The *tonally* travels along the paths of supernatural beings. The travelling, mobile *tonally*, identified with the hair and head, is thus located at the customary place of respect. Thelma Sullivan translates several metaphors from Nahuatl that express the importance of the head which, according to Viesca, is synonymous with the *tonally* in Nahuatl culture (1984). 'Where have I gone over the hair, over the head of our lord?' means: 'Have I offended God in any way for him to send me such misfortune?' Likewise, 'Cover your hair, cover your head' means: 'Protect your honour and your good name' (Sullivan 1983).[8]

The *teyolia* resides in the heart. Contrary to our concepts of mental activities taking place in the head, the *teyolia* was the centre of memory, knowledge and intelligence. Further, when the *teyolia* leaves the body, death occurs. Likewise, what is today called 'personality' was, according to Leon-Portilla, described by the Nahuatl as 'a face and a heart' (1963).

The *ihiyotl* (breath or *soplo*, according to Simeon) which is associated with the liver, can produce emanations that harm others (1977). It is divisible and can leave the body voluntarily or involuntarily. Individuals with supernatural knowledge and abilities can seem to be the work of evil spirits and cause illness. The *ihiyotl* is the vital centre of passion and feeling. But, says Lopez Austin, 'the most elevated thoughts and the passions most related to the preservation of human life originated in the heart and not in the liver nor in the head' (Lopez Austin 1984b: 219).

It is as part of this play of multiple emanations and inclusions that the body is conceptualized in Mesoamerican thought (Ortiz 1993). Emanations include all the material and non-material entities that can leave the body. The *tonally*, for example, travels to the upper and lower worlds, while the *ihiyotl* sends out emanations that can affect and harm others (Lopez Austin 1984b). 'Inclusions' refer to those external entities – at times regarded as material – which enter the body from other domains of nature, from the spirit world, and at times from the realm of the sacred. The heart, *teyolia,* is open to the gods, according to Lopez Austin (*ibid.*). Frequently, sickness is conceptualized as an intrusion into the body of harmful elements that, when expelled, take the form of animals and material objects (Viesca 1984). Health and ill-being for the Mesoamericans is defined by a balance between the opposing forces and elements whose totality gives the individual his or her characteristics.

Multiple body components

The animic centres and their flow of vital forces hardly exhaust the totality of what makes up an individual. The body, teeming with activity in the greater and lesser centres that emanate and receive forces and entities, reflects, of course, the multiplicity of the cosmos of which it is a part. There are many forces that can move in from the outside, merge with internal forces and then leave the body as emanations. The joints are regarded as centres of dense life force. It is at the joints that supernatural beings (of a cold nature) can attack and thus impede bodily movement (Lopez Austin 1984b). All these entities are discernible to the Mesoamerican, as evident to them as their own faces, hands, arms, legs and genitals.

The Nahua mode of being in the world

The world, for the Nahuas, is not 'out there', established outside of and apart from them. It is within them and even 'through' them. Actions and their circumstances are much more imbricated than is the case in Western thought, where the 'I' can be analytically abstracted from its surroundings. Using a grammatical comparison, it could be said that the circumstantial complement of place and that which defines the modes of action are inseparable: all spatial location implies modalities of action, and vice versa.

Further, the body's porosity reflects an essential porosity of the cosmos, a permeability of the entire 'material' world that defines an order of existence characterized by continuous transit between the material and the immaterial. The cosmos emerges literally, in the conceptualization, as the complement of a permeable corporeality. Klor de Alva writes that 'the Nahuas imagine their multidimensional being as an integral part of their body and of the physical and spiritual world around them' (1988). He adds that the 'conceptual being' of the Nahua was much less limited than that of Christians at the time of the Conquest and more inclined toward forming 'a physical and conceptual continuum with others, with the body and with the world beyond it' (*ibid.*).

Metaphors and the flesh

Metaphors not only abound in Mesoamerican thought, they make up its very fabric. Almost immediately after the first contact between Spain and Tenochtitlan, Sahagun, Duran and Olmos commented on the rich metaphorical language of the inhabitants of America. At times they complain of its extensive use when the ever-present metaphors complicated their attempts to understand the inhabitants of these lands. At the same time, however, they marvelled at the metaphorical complexity of speech (Duran 1980; Klor de Alva 1988). Fray Bernardino de Sahagun called them 'metaphors delicate in their declarations' and he is the first to record a glossary of Nahuatl metaphors and their equivalents in the language of the time.[9]

In 1650 Jacinto de la Serna wrote that 'the words used of old cannot be explicated, nor the force of the metaphors they made use of, to give them all the signification they had in former times'. Leon-Portilla, in *Nahuatl Philosophy*, defines Nahua thought as the 'culture and philosophy of metaphors' (1956: 322). Metaphor, to Lakoff and Johnson, 'is not only a rhetorical embellishment but part of everyday language that affects how I perceive, think and act. Metaphors impregnate our language.' They add that 'the most fundamental values of a culture will be consistent with the metaphorical structure of its fundamental concepts' (Lakoff and Johnson 1986).

Metaphors such as bodies of men described as juicy, tender ears of corn convey not only the culture's fundamental values but also a distinctive attitude toward carnal pleasure. This metaphor and the others analyzed below are found in discourses and narratives from Books III and VI of Sahagun's *General History of the Things of New Spain*. Studying them offers the possibility of understanding Mesoamerican corporeality more fully.

The metaphors of the body discussed appear mainly in certain teaching discourses which were learned by memory at the Calmecac, the schools where Nahua children (mainly boys, but also girls) were sent. Leon-Portilla says the following about these schools:

> In the Calmecac and Telpuchalli … the students had to systematically memorize long chronicles, hymns to the gods, poems, myths and legends…. Thus through this double process of transmission and systematic memorization of the chronicles, the hymns, poems and traditions … the religious leaders and elders preserved and propagated their religious and literary heritage. (Leon-Portilla 1984: 15)

It is important to emphasize that the discourses were didactic and used for instruction. What the student in the Calmecac memorized also served as models for their own conduct.

Many metaphors are also found in the *ilamatlatolli* or *huehuetlatolli,* the discourses of the elders, which were central to the rite of initiation into adult life among the Nahuas.[10] They were, furthermore, rhetorical and ritual admonitions that played a very important role throughout the lives of the Mesoamericans and ritualized many kinds of social events. Each significant event in the life of the Aztec people, regardless of whether it referred to a religious celebration, the installation of a new government, the start of battle, the selection of a spouse, the introduction of a midwife to a pregnant women, or the beginning of an adult life, was accompanied by long and eloquent discourses (Sullivan 1986).

My objective here, however, is to present some of the metaphors for the feminine and masculine body that are found in the *ilamatlatolli* and *huehuetlatolli* in Book VI of *General History of the Things of New Spain (Florentine Codex).* Full of metaphors, they are a rich source for the analysis of gender relations because they define the conduct considered appropriate both for women towards men and vice versa (see Marcos 1991).The discourses, recited publicly when children became adolescents, contain metaphors fundamental to Mesoamerican thought and morals.

> [F] rom the time of the lord of Tetzcuco, named Netzahualcoyotzin … who asked them [the older women], saying: 'Grandmothers, tell me, is it true that you have desire for fleshly pleasure … old as you are? The old women replied with a long explanation ending in a metaphor: '… [Y]ou men when you become old no longer desire carnal delights … but we women never tire of these doings nor do we get enough of them because our bodies are like a deep abyss, a chasm that never fills up; it receives everything … desiring more and asking for more….' (*Florentine Codex 382*)

In Book XVIII, there is the following advice for daughters:

Look now, don't choose from among the men the one that seems the best to you like those who shop for mantas in the market ... and don't carry on like people do when the new corn is just fresh, looking for the best and tastiest cobs.... (*Ibid.*: 369).

These metaphors about the bodies of women and men reveal aspects of the culture that were selectively eliminated by the first chroniclers because they clashed with their own moral values. The metaphors surviving in everyday language, however, probably seemed innocent enough and passed for mere poetic adornment of language. Sahagun would qualify them as 'very delicate and exact and adequate'.

Metaphor carries the imprint of the conceptual system. For example, socially accepted desire for the body of another is evident in the use of the metaphor 'the best and tastiest cobs'. It is evident likewise in the image of women's bodies as 'a deep abyss, a chasm that never fills up'. Such abundance of metaphors carries the imprint of orality.

These metaphors, along with the *Tohuenyo* narrative analyzed below, give us an idea of the sorts of pleasures accepted in the Mesoamerican world. *Tlalticpacayotl*, translated as carnality or sex, literally means 'that which pertains to the surface of the earth' (Lopez Austin 1984b). As with all that pertains to the earth's surface, erotic pleasure belongs to earthly identity. Not only is it accepted, but it defines the inhabitants of Mesoamerica as dwellers in the four intermediate levels of earth's surface. This abode of women and men is the place of the flesh, its joys and concerns. The earth would be inconceivable without the corporeal dimension. Perhaps this was the reason why Mesoamericans regarded the negation of carnal activities as abnormal since, without them, one didn't belong to the earth. To speak cosmically of eroticism is to speak of the dimensions belonging to 'the surface of the earth' and its central position in the Nahua cosmos.

Narrative and metaphor: Nahua corporeality in the Florentine Codex

The narrative of *Tohuenyo* (the Foreigner) is a choice example for understanding body and gender in Nahua thought. Found in Book III of the Florentine Codex, it forms part of the wealth of documentation in Nahuatl about sixteenth century Mexican culture. The story was collected from indigenous informants by Fray Bernardino de Sahagun in Tepepulco (Tezcoco region), and in Tlatelolco in and after 1547. The 'normative discourses' of the *huehuetlatolli* cannot be understood without narratives such as this in which the cosmic meaning of pleasure manifests itself. The story, part of epic narratives concerning divinities, is surprising for its images and metaphors, as it was for the prominent place given to desire and carnality as expressed by a young girl. Leon-Portilla comments:

> It has been said at times concerning our indigenous culture that there is a lack of erotic themes .... But, contrary to those who think this way, there are some old texts in Nahuatl, collected from native lips at the time of the conquest. (1980)

Tohuenyo concerns the erotic ardour that, without hyperbole, overcame a Toltec princess.[11] Here at length, in Leon-Portilla's recent translation, is the story of The Foreigner.

The Story of Tohuenyo

...
He went about naked, his thing just hanging,
He began selling chillies,
Setting up his stand in the market, in front of the palace.
...
So then, the daughter of Huemac, very appealing [*cenca quali*], was desired and sought after by many of the Toltecan men who wanted her as a wife.
But Huemac ignored them all.
He wouldn't give his daughter to any of them.
...
So then that daughter of Huemac looked toward the market and saw the Tohuenyo: there with his thing hanging.
As soon as she saw him, she went into the palace.
Then, because of this, the daughter of Huemac fell sick.
She became filled with tension, she entered into great heat, feeling herself deprived of the Tohuenyo's bird – his manly part –
And the lord Huemac, seeing this, gave orders and said,
'Toltecs, look for the chilli vendor, find the Tohuenyo.'
And immediately they went about looking for him everywhere.
...
They turned all Tula upside down
And even though they made every effort,
They didn't see him anywhere.
So they came to tell the lord that they hadn't seen Tohuenyo anywhere.

But a little later Tohuenyo appeared on his own,
He just came to set up
Where he had been seen the first time.
Huemac asked him: 'Where is your home?'

The other answered:
I am a Tohuenyo (foreigner).
I am here selling chillies.
And the lord said to him:
'What kind of life is yours, Tohuenyo?
Put on a loincloth, cover yourself.'
To which the Tohuenyo responded,
'This is how I live.'
Then the lord said to him:
'You have awakened that yearning in my daughter, you will cure her.'
...
And right away they cut his hair,
They bathed him and after this
They rubbed him with oils, put a loincloth on him and tied on a cloak.
And when Tohuenyo went to see her, he immediately stayed with her
and with this she got well at that moment.
Soon after, Tohuenyo married the lord's daughter.[12]

Tohuenyo later won the recognition of the Toltecs and led them to victory in many battles. The story of his extraordinary deeds becomes part of an epic myth about the adventures of supernatural beings of whom Tohuenyo is one. In the middle of these heroic deeds comes this 'curious story of the Tohuenyo' as Leon-Portilla calls it (1980). Curious it is, even for those most expert in ancient Mexico. It still surprises scholars that, despite the moral scrutiny and expurgation that the vestiges of erotic Nahua art suffered at the hands of the clerical chroniclers, this has survived.

Text and context

The Tohuenyo figure is itself an example of mythic fluidity between contradictory conditions and situations. But the narrative is also a political history in which carnality plays an important role.

It is interesting to recall that this narrative was probably one of 'those old Nahuatl "texts" with a certain rhythm and measure that was learned by heart in the Calmecac or other Nahua centres of superior education' (Leon-Portilla 1980). Nahuatl youth in these centres received a polished education, an intellectual training, as they listened to the *tlamatinime* (the wise men and women, or philosophers) express the highest values of their culture. It was also a place of training for the priesthood. '[T]here is no doubt that the teachings directed at the most select of Nahuatl youth included the highest thinking, often contained in the songs and discourses learned by memory' (Leon-Portilla 1980).

To find a text with an explicitly carnal content in such a context leads us to another level of understanding about the role of desire, the body and pleasure in Nahuatl thought and culture. These New World expressions are very far from any sort of fear of the power of feminine desire, or from the fear of inexhaustible sexuality as found in Europe in the *Malleus Maleficarum.*[13] Interestingly, Garibay places the *Tohuenyo* narrative between 1430 and 1519, dates that also bracket the great witch hunt in the Old World.

Generally, history has emphasized the disciplined and to a certain degree repressive (as I would say) character of Aztec culture. Without a doubt, norms and disciplinary demands with respect to sex existed. At the same time, we cannot simply declare that no space existed for eroticism. In a culture and thought produced by duality, by the alternating presence of opposites in motion, the demands of discipline are enriched by the possibility of and esteem for carnality. The one-sided chronicling emphasis on rigour and discipline is more a product of the values of the missionary historians than a true reflection of the data and realities of that ancient world. What Sahagun recorded in Chapter 7 of Book VI of the *Florentine Codex* balances the picture:

> They worshipped Tlazulteotl, the deity of lust, the Mexicans did, especially the Mixtecs and Olmecs … and the Cueztecs worshipped and honoured Tlazulteotl, and didn't accuse themselves of lust before him, because for them lust was not a sin. (1969).

Conclusion

The emphasis here has been to view metaphors of pleasure and eroticism in their relation to gender. In these texts women are not only presented as valuable because their designated sphere is giving birth in Aztec society.[14] They are not respected solely because they represent fertility and the possibility of new life, even though this is the case in the great majority of agrarian societies and civilizations. It is appropriate to emphasize that in these Mesoamerican concepts, not only are women's bodies recognized and venerated for their reproductive capacity, but they also appear as 'subjects of desire' (Laqueur 1990). I have reviewed the case of one woman – the young daughter of Huemac – whose desire provoked concern and action and affected the mythic and political history of her time.

The body, an abode and axis of delight and pleasure, the dual body of women and men, a fluid and permeable corporeality, the principle of being on earth in fusion with the immediate surroundings and with the origin of the cosmos: this feminine and masculine body manifests itself in epic poetry, songs, narratives and metaphors. Finding even vestiges of it can begin to reveal incarnate universes that escape the master narrative of spirit over flesh.

Notes

1 See Lopez Austin 1984b, Kirchoff 1968 and Marcos 1991 for in-depth presentations.

2 The *Royal Palace Matritense Codex* is the collection in Nahuatl by Sahagun and his assistants of the material they gathered from informants. See Sahagun 1984. For a discussion of the origin of Sahagun's work and the complexity of dealing with the sources, see Marcos 1991. I will try to interpret the sources with the help of concepts derived from the sources themselves. In other words, when studying the healing rites described by Sahagun, I consciously suspend the 'certainties' derived from the modern medicine and the biological sciences as I try to perceive elements of the Mesoamerican thought system embedded in the sources. It is now understood that modern scientific certainties are not universals but are themselves historical constructions (Petchesky 1988; Duden 1990; Katz-Rothman 1994). This permits a less confined way of looking at the Mesoamerican world. From this perspective, some of the analytical tools mentioned above prove inadequate for approaching this universe. Among them, especially, is the separation of biology (sex) from culture (gender). Concepts of duality, equilibrium and corporeality are also considered here as specific dissonances between critical gender theory and Mesoamerican thought.

3 Olmos 1973; González Torres 1991; Sahagun 1969; Lopez Austin 1984b.

4 '{T]hey counted by twenty days from the first day, which was their month; they counted up one year then left five days, thus a year only had three hundred and sixty days…' (Olmos1973).

5 This complementarity means that every pole is the other's referent: masculinity, for instance, is only defined in relation to femininity and vice versa. The same holds true for the secondary dualities such as hot/cold, right/left, day/night. Hence the mutual distance between the poles determines the distinctness of their opposition, with a growing distance allowing for diminishing contrast, for ambiguity and even the reversibility of one ('hot', for example) into the other ('cold'). That proximity and distance rule polar oppositions and their range of shadings seems to be confirmed by one of the names for the divinity: Tloque-nahuaque – 'the near, the far'. Like many other cultures, the Nahua world considered the divine as the point at which hierarchies can be reversed. This fluidity allows a certain permanent shifting from one pole to the other.

6 Parry and Dorson (Parry 1971) elaborate criteria to distinguish a text – that is a writ composed pen in hand – from an epic oral narrative, and call the first transcription of an epic narrative by a scribe an 'authentic text'. By this standard, the *Iliad* and the *Odyssey* have the characteristics of authentic texts.

7 The *huehuetlatolli* and *ilamatlatolli* are ritual admonitions of fathers and mothers to boys and girls during their ceremonial passage to adulthood.

8 In traditional medicine, hair is often used as an ingredient or component due to its association with the head of *tonally* (Viesca 1984).

9 Sahagun, *Historia de las cosas de Nueva Espana (Codice Florentino)*, Book VI, Chapter 53, Nahuatl version 1547, his translation into Spanish 1577.

10 Gingerich (1988). Gingerich says that in Book VI of the *Florentine Codex* both the terms *ilamatlatolli*, or admonitions of the 'old women, the white-haired and wise grandmothers', and *huehuetlatolli*, or admonitions of the old men, are used. The historical tradition written in Spanish in which the generic masculine encompasses and in a certain sense annuls the feminine has led to the disuse of the term *ilamatlatolli*. Thus, today the discourse of wise old people, both women and men, is called *huehuetlatolli*. This favours an interpretation which sees only old men as the givers of these discourses. Gingerich speaks of these discourses and says that they were both didactic and rhetorical (Sullivan 1986). In addition, he says that in the original Nahuatl the terms *Intlatol ilamatque* ('the voices of old women') and *Intlatol ueuetque* ('the words of old men') are used. These terms appear in the last discourse in Chapter 40 of Book VI of the *Florentine Codex*. These discourses were those spoken by the mothers and fathers to their sons and daughters before they entered the Calmecac or school for religious training.

11 Garibay (1953).

12 Leon-Portilla (1980).

13 *Malleus Maleficarum* (The Hammer of Witches), in Latin, by Heinrich Kramer and James Sprenger, both Dominicans, appeared in 1484 (or 1486 according to some authors). From this sadly renowned document, written to help hunt 'witches' and later condemn them to the Inquisition's fire, comes the idea of women envious of masculine genitals, insatiable, and thus dangerous to men. The work almost implies that all men are near-saints and that only the evil influence of women keeps them from dedicating their lives to the service of God or to the elevated (bodiless) activities of the mind. The document is an unrestrained harangue against the body and its activities.

14 Women who died giving birth for the first time were deified by the Nahuas as the *Cihuateteo.* This deification has been used as a proof of the metaphorical equivalence between war and birth, which gave women access to similar avenues of prestige as men had as warriors. When a woman died in this way, warriors would try to obtain hair or cut off the middle finger of the left hand, or even the left arm. 'And the soldiers watched to try to steal the body because they regarded it as something sacred or divine....' If the warrior obtained the body part and carried it with him into battle, he became extraordinarily powerful and brave. In the context of a society that made wars sacred, we can deduce the value assigned to the bodies of these women (Sahagun 1969).

References & Bibliography

AAWORD (Association of African Women for Research and Development) (1985) *Women in Rural Development in Africa*, Dakar: AAWORD.

Abu-Lughod, L. (1990a) 'The romance of resistance: tracing transformations of power through Bedouin women', *American Ethnologist* 17.

—— (1990b) 'Can there be a feminist ethnography?' *Women and Performance* 5, 1: 7–27.

—— (1991) 'Writing against culture' in R. Fox (ed.), *Recapturing Anthropology: Working in the Present*, Santa Fe: School of American Research Press.

—— (1999) *Veiled Sentiments: Honor and Poetry in a Bedouin Society*, Berkeley: University of California Press.

Addelson, K. P. (1994) *Moral Passages: toward a Collectivist Moral Theory*, New York: Routledge.

Afshar, H. (ed.) (1998) *Women and Empowerment: Illustrations from the Third World*, London: Macmillan.

Agarwal, B. (1994) *A Field of One's Own: Gender and Land Rights in South Asia*, New York: Cambridge University Press.

Aggarwal, R. (1995) 'Shadow work: gender and the marketplace in Ladakh', *Anthropology of Work Review* 16, 1–2.

Aguirre Beltran, G. (1980) *Medicina y Mágica,* Mexico: INAH.

Ahdab-Yehia, M. (1977) 'Reflections on the conference on women and development', in Wellsley Editorial Committee (1977).

Ahmed, L. (1992) *Women and Gender in Islam*, New Haven and London: Yale University Press.

Ahmed, M. (1996) '"We are Warp and Weft" – Nomadic Pastoralism and the Tradition of Weaving in Rupshu (Eastern Ladakh)', unpublished PhD. thesis, Oxford University.

Alarcon-Gonzalez, D. and T. McKinley (1999) 'The adverse effects of structural adjustment on working women in Mexico', *Latin American Perspectives* 26, 3: 103–17.

Al-Azmeh, A. (1993) *Islam and Modernities*, London: Verso.

Albers, P. C. (1989) 'From Illusion to Illumination: Anthropological Studies of American Women', in S. Morgan (ed.), *Gender and Anthropology: Critical Reviews for Research and Teaching,* Washington, DC: American Anthropological Association.

Allione, T. (1984) *Women of Wisdom*, Boston: Routledge and Kegan Paul.

Althusser, L. (1977) *For Marx*, London: New Left Books.

Altink, S. (1995) *Stolen Lives: Trading Women into Sex and Slavery,* London: Scarlet Press.

Amadiume, I. (1987) *Male Daughters, Female Husbands*, London: Zed Books.

Ambrogi, T. (1999) 'Jubilee 2000 and the campaign for debt cancellation', *National Catholic Reporter* (July).

Amin, S. (1974) *Accumulation on a World Scale,* translated by B. Pearce, New York: Monthly Review Press.

—— (1985) 'Apropos the Green Revolution', in H. Addo *et al.* (eds.), *Development as Social Transformation,* Boulder CO: Westview Press.

Angmo, S. (1999) 'Women's Development in Ladakh', in M. van Beek, M. K. Bertlesen and P. Pederson (eds.), *Ladakh: Culture, History and Development between Himalaya and Karakoram,* Aarhus: Aarhus University Press.

Antrobus, P. (1992) 'South women lead the debate', *Dawn Informs* 2.

Apaza, J. T. (1998) 'Conversación ritual entre las familias del agua y los miembros de la Comunidad Humana en Conima y Tilali', in J. T. Apaza, V. C. Gordillo and S. F. Cutipa (eds.), *La Crianza Mútua en las Comunidades Aymaras,* Puno and Lima, Peru: Chuyma Aru and PRATEC.

Apffel-Marglin, F. (1990) 'Smallpox in Two Systems of Knowledge', in F. Apffel-Marglin and S. Marglin (eds.), *Dominating Knowledge: Development, Culture and Resistance,* Oxford: Clarendon Press.

—— (1995) 'Gender and the unitary self: looking for the subaltern in coastal Orissa', *South Asia Research* 15, 1: 78–130.

—— (1996) 'Rationality, the Body and the World: from Production to Regeneration', in F. Apffel-Marglin and S. Marglin. (eds.), *Decolonizing Knowledge: from Development to Dialogue,* Oxford: Clarendon Press.

Apffel-Marglin, F. and S. Simon (1994) 'Feminist Orientalism and Development', in W. Harcourt (ed.), *Feminist Perspectives on Sustainable Development,* London: Zed Books, pp. 26–45.

Appendini, K. (1995) 'Revisiting women wage-workers in Mexico's agro-industry: changes in rural labor markets', *CDR Working Papers,* 95, 2.

Arriata, M. and L. Sanchez (1998) 'Crianza de la vida en comunidades campesinas Andinas', *Informe del Taller de Género, Regeneración y Biodiversidad,* Cochabamba, Bolivia: CAIPACHA, CAM, PRATEC.

Asad, T. (ed.) (1973) *Anthropology and the Colonial Encounter,* New York: Humanities Press.

Ashby, J. A. and L. Sperling (1995) 'Institutionalizing participatory, client-driven research and technology development in agriculture', *Development and Change* 27: 753–70.

Avoseh, M. B. M. (2000) 'Adult education and participatory research in Africa: in defence of tradition', *Canadian Journal of Development Studies* 21: 565–78.

Babb, F. (1989) *Between Field and Cooking Pot,* Austin: University of Texas Press.

Baez-Jorge, F. (1988) *Los oficios de las diosas,* Xalapa: Universidad Veracruzana.

Bandarage A. (1997) *Women, Population and Global Crisis: a Political-Economic Analysis,* London: Zed Books.

Barad, K. (1996) 'Meeting the Universe Halfway: Realism and Social Constructivism without Contradiction', in L. H. Nelson and J. Nelson (eds.), *Feminism, Science and the Philosophy of Science,* Dordrecht, Boston and London: Kluwer Academic Publishers, pp. 161–94.

—— (1998) 'Getting Real: Technoscientific Practices and the Materialization of Reality', *Differences: a Journal of Feminist Cultural Studies* 10, 2: 87–128.

Barlow, T. (1997a) 'Woman at the Close of the Maoist Era in the Polemics of Li Xiaojiang and her Associates', in L. Lowe and D. Lloyd (eds.), *The Politics of Culture in the Shadow of Capital,* Durham: Duke University Press.

—— (1997b) 'Theory and political development in non-reductionist gender history', unpublished draft paper, November.

—— (2000) 'Spheres of debt and feminist ghosts in area studies of women in China', forthcoming in *Traces* 1, 1.

—— (forthcoming (a)) *The Question of Woman in Chinese Feminism,* Durham: Duke University Press.

—— (forthcoming (b))'The question of women in Chinese feminism of the 1920s and 1930s',

Gendai shiso (in Japanese).

Barrientos, S., A. Bee, A. Matear and I. Vogel (1999) *Women and Agribusiness: Working Miracles in the Chilean Fruit Export Sector,* Houndmills, Basingstoke: Macmillan Press.

Barroso, C. and C. Bruschini (1991) 'Building Politics from Personal Lives: Discussion on Sexuality among Poor Women in Brazil', in C. Mohanty, A. Russo and L. Torres (eds.), *Third World and the Politics of Feminism,* Bloomington: Indiana University Press.

Basch, L., N. Glick Schiller, and C. Szanton-Blanc (1994) *Nations Unbound: Transnationalized Projects and the Deterritorialized Nation-State,* New York: Gordon and Breach.

Basu, A. (2000) 'Globalizaton of the local/localization of the global: mapping transnational women's movement', *Meridians: Feminism, Race, Transnationalism,* 1, 1.

Bataille, G. (1991) *The Accursed Share: an Essay on General Economy,* New York: Urzone Inc.

Batliwala, S. (1994) 'The Meaning of Women's Empowerment: New Concepts from Action', in G. Sen, A. Germein and L. Cher, *Population Policies Reconsidered,* Boston: Harvard University Press.

Beasely, C. and C. Bacchi (2000) 'Citizen bodies: embodying citizens – a feminist analysis', *International Feminist Journal of Politics,* 2, 3: 337–58.

Becker, G.S. (1981) *A Treatise on the Family,* Massachusetts: Harvard University Press.

Bello, W. (1998) *A Siamese Tragedy: Development and Disintegration in Modern Thailand,* London: Zed Books.

Beltrán, E., M. L. Calleros, M. E. Jimenez and J. Norienga (1991) 'La mujer en el trabajo', in M. Dalton (ed.), *La mujer Oaxaqueña: un análisis de su contexto,* Oaxaca: Consejo Estatal de Población del Estado de Oaxaca.

Benería , L. (1992) 'The Mexican Debt Crisis: Restructuring the Economy and the Household', in L. Benería and S. Feldman (eds.), *Unequal Burden: Economic Crises, Persistent Poverty and Women's Work,* Boulder CO: Westview Press, pp. 83–105.

Benería, L. and M. Roldán (1987) *The Crossroads of Class and Gender: Industrial Homework, Subcontracting and Household Dynamics in Mexico City,* Chicago and London: University of Chicago Press.

Benería, L. and S. Feldman (eds.) (1992) *Unequal Burden: Economic Crises, Persistent Poverty and Women's Work,* Boulder CO: Westview Press.

Benjamin, J. (1988) *The Bonds of Love: Psychoanalysis, Feminism and the Problem of Domination,* New York: Pantheon Books.

Bennholdt-Thomsen, V. and M. Mies (1999), *The Subsistence Perspective,* London: Zed Books.

Bernal, E., S. Bissell, and A. Cortes (1999) 'Effects of globalization on the efforts to decriminalize abortion in Mexico', *Development,* 42, 4: 130–3.

Bernstein, H., B. Crow, M. MacKintosh and C. Martin (1990) *The Food Question: Profit Versus People?* London: Earthscan Publications.

Bertelsen, K. (1996) 'Our Communalized Future: Sustainable Development, Social Identification and Politics of Representation in Ladakh', unpublished PhD thesis, Aarhus University, Denmark.

Bever, J. D. (1994) 'Feedback between their plants and their soil communities in an old field community', *Ecology,* 75.

Bever, J. D., K. M. Westover and J. Antonovics (1997) 'Incorporating the soil community into plant population dynamics: the utility of the feedback approach', *Journal of Ecology,* 85.

Bezaury, J. A. (ed.) (1988) *Las mujeres en el campo,* Institute for Sociological Research, Autonomous University of Benito Juárez, Oaxaca.

Bishop, R. and L. Robinson (1998) *Night Market: Sexual Cultures and the Thai Economic Miracle,* New York: Routledge.

Bonacich, E., L. Cheng, N. Chinchilla, N. Hamilton and P. Ong (eds.) (1994) *Global Production: the Apparel Industry in the Pacific Rim,* Philadelphia: Temple University Press.

Booth, W. (1999) 'Thirteen charged in gang importing prostitutes', *Washington Post,* 21 August.

Bordo, S. and A. Jaggar (eds.) (1989) *Gender/Body/Knowledge. Feminist Reconstructions of Being and Knowing,* New Brunswick: Rutgers University Press.

Bose, C. E. and E. Acosta-Belen (eds.) (1995) *Women in the Latin American Development Process: from Structural Subordination to Empowerment,* Philadelphia: Temple University Press.

Boserup E. (1970) *Woman's Role in Economic Development*, New York: St Martin's Press.

Boserup, E. and C. Liljencrantz (1975) *Integration of Women in Development: Why, When, How*, New York: United Nations Development Programme.

Bossen, L. (1983) 'Sexual Stratification in Mesoamerica', in C. Kendall, J. Hawkins and L. Bossen (eds.), *Heritage of Conquest: Thirty Years Later*, Albuquerque: University of New Mexico Press, pp. 35–72.

Botchway, K. (2001) 'Paradox of empowerment: reflections on a case study from Northern Ghana', *World Development* 29, 1: 135–53.

Bourdieu, P. (1990) *In Other Words: Essays Towards a Reflexive Sociology*, Stanford: Stanford University Press.

Bourguignon, C. (1995) Address at ARISE workshop, Auroville, India, April 1995.

Boyd, M. (1989) 'Family and personal networks in international migration: recent developments and new agendas', *International Migration Review* 23: 638–70.

Braathen, E. (2001) 'New social corporatism: a discursive-critical review of the WDR 2000/1, "Attacking Poverty"', *Forum for Development Studies* 2 (2000): 331–50.

Braathen, E., B. Morten and G. Sæther (eds.) (1999) *Ethnicity Kills? The Politics of War, Peace and Ethnicity in Sub-Saharan Africa*, Basingstoke: Macmillan.

Bradshaw, Y., R. Noonan, L. Gash and C. Buchmann (1993) 'Borrowing against the future: children and third world indebtness', *Social Forces* 71, 3: 629–56.

Braidotti, R., E. Charkiewicz, S. Häusler and S. Wieringa (eds.) (1994) *Women, Environment and Sustainable Development: towards a Theoretical Synthesis*, London: Zed Books.

Bray, J. (1985) *The Himalayan Mission*, Leh: Moravian Church.

Brenner, S. (1998) *The Domestication of Desire: Women, Wealth, and Modernity in Java*, Princeton: Princeton University Press.

Bricker, V. (1981) *The Indian Christ, the Indian King: the Historical Substrate of Maya Myth and Ritual*, Austin: University of Texas Press.

'Brides from the Phillippines?' www.geocites.co.jp/Milkyway-Kaigan/5501/ph7.html

Bright, C. (1999) 'Invasive species: pathogens of globalization', *Foreign Policy*, 116: 51.

Brohman, J. (1996) *Popular Development: Rethinking the Theory and Practice of Development*, Oxford: Blackwell.

Brown, L. R. and L. Haddad (1995) 'Time allocation patterns and time burdens: a gendered analysis of seven countries', International Food Policy Research Institute, Washington DC.

Brundtland Report (1987) *Our Common Future*, report of the World Commission on Environment and Development, Delhi, Oxford and New York: Oxford University Press.

Brydon, L. (1985) 'The Avatime Family and Migration 1900–1977', in R. M. Prothero and M. Chapman (eds.), *Circulation in Third World Countries*, New York: Routledge and Kegan Paul.

Brydon, L. and S. Chant (1993) *Women in the Third World: Gender Issues in Rural and Urban Areas*, New Brunswick: Rutgers University Press.

Buchmann, C. (1996) 'The debt crisis, structural adjustment and women's education', *International Journal of Comparative Studies*, 37, 1–2: 5–30.

Burke, M. J.and J. P. Grime (1996) 'An experimental study of plant community invisibility', *Ecology* 77: 776–90.

Burkhart, L. (1989) *The Slippery Earth: Nahua–Christian Moral Dialogue in Sixteenth Century Mexico*, Tucson: University of Arizona Press.

Burris, B. *et al.* (1973) 'The Fourth World Manifesto' in A. Koedt, E. Levine and A. Rapone (eds.), *Radical Feminism*, New York: Quardrangle.

Butler, J. (1992) 'Contingent Foundations: Feminism and the Question of "Postmodernism"', in J. Butler and J. Scott (eds.), *Feminists Theorize the Political*, New York: Routledge.

Buvinic, M. (1983) *Women and Poverty in the Third World*, Baltimore: Johns Hopkins University Press.

Cagatay, N. and S. Ozler (1995) 'Feminization of the labor force: the effects of long-term development and structural adjustment', *World Development* 23, 11: 1883–94.

Callahan, J. C. (ed.) (1995) *Reproduction, Ethics, and the Law: Feminist Perspectives*, Bloomington:

Indiana University Press.
Canadian Labour Congress (1999) *The Morning NAFTA: Labour's Voice on Economic Integration*, 14 (May): 1–10 (http://www.clc-ctc.ca/publications/index.html).
Cancian, F. (1965) *Economics and Prestige in a Maya Community: the Religious Cargo System in Zinacantan*, Stanford: Stanford University Press.
—— (1989) 'Participatory and Working Women: Democratizing the Production of Knowledge', paper presented at the annual meeting of the American Sociological Association, San Francisco, August.
—— (1992) *The Decline of Community in Zinacantan: Economy, Public Life and Social Stratification, 1960–1987,* Stanford: Stanford University Press.
Canclini, N. G. (1993) *Transforming Modernity: Popular Culture in Mexico,* translated by Lidia Losano, Austin: University of Texas Press.
Casper, M. (1994) 'Reframing and grounding nonhuman agency: what makes a fetus an agent?' *American Behavioral Scientist* 37, 6: 839–56.
Castells, M. (1996) *The Rise of the Network Society*, Oxford: Blackwell.
—— (1996–8). *The Information Age: Economy, Society and Culture*, Vols 1–3, Oxford: Blackwell.
Castles, S. and M. J. Miller (1998) *The Age of Migration: International Population Movements in the Modern World,* 2nd edition, New York: Macmillan.
Castro, M. (ed.) (1999) *Free Markets, Open Societies, Closed Borders?* Miami: University of Miami, North–South Center Press.
Chakravarti, U. (1989) 'Whatever Happened to the Vedic *Dasi*? Orientalism, Nationalism and a Script for the Past', in K. Sangari and S. Vaid (eds.) *Recasting Women: Essays in Colonial History*, New Delhi: Kali for Women.
Chambers, R. (1994a) 'The Origins and Practice of Participatory Rural Appraisal', *World Development* 22, 7: 953–69.
—— (1994b) 'Participatory Rural Appraisal (PRA): analysis of experience', *World Development* 22, 9: 1253–68.
—— (1994c) 'Participatory Rural Appraisal (PRA): challenges, potentials and paradigm', *World Development* 22, 10: 1437–54.
—— (1997) *Whose Reality Counts? Putting the First Last,* London: Intermediate Technology Publications.
Chaney, E. and M. Garcia Castro (198?) *Muchachas No More: Household Workers in Latin America and the Caribbean*, Philadelphia: Temple University Press.
Chang, G. (1998) 'Undocumented Latinas: the New "Employable Mothers"', in M. Andersen and P. Hill-Collins (eds.), *Race, Class and Gender*, 3rd edition, Wadsworth.
Chant, S. (ed.) (1992) *Gender and Migration in Developing Countries*, London and New York: Belhaven Press.
Chatterjee, P. (2001) *A Time for Tea: Women, Labor and Post/Colonial Politics on an Indian Plantation,* Durham: Duke University Press.
Chesler, E. (1992) *Women of Valor,* New York: Simon and Schuster.
Chin, C. (1997) 'Walls of silence and late twentieth-century representations of foreign female domestic workers: the case of Filipina and Indonesian house servants in Malaysia', *International Migration Review*, 31, 1: 353–85.
Chinas, B. (1973) *The Isthmus Zapotecs: Women's Roles in Cultural Context,* New York: Holt, Rinehart and Winston.
Chossudovsky, M. (1997) *The Globalisation of Poverty*. London: Zed Books/TWN.
Chowdhry, P. (1994) *The Veiled Women: Shifting Gender Equations in Rural Haryana, 1880–1990*, New Delhi: Oxford University Press.
Chuang, J. (1998) 'Redirecting the debate over trafficking in women: definitions, paradigms and contexts', *Harvard Human Rights Journal*, 10 (Winter).
Chuyma, A. (1998) 'Rituales de la crianza de las semillas', in PRATEC (ed.), *Crianza ritual de semillas en los Andes*, Lima: PRATEC.
Cixous, H. and C. Clement (1991) *The Newly Born Woman,* translated by B. Wing, Minneapolis:

University of Minnesota Press.

Clark, G. (1994) *Onions Are My Husband: Survival and Accumulation by West African Market Women*, Chicago: University of Chicago Press.

Cleaver, F. (1999) 'Paradoxes of participation: questioning participatory approaches to development', *Journal of International Development* 11: 597–612.

Coalition to Abolish Slavery and Trafficking (Annual) Factsheet, www.traffickedwomen.org/fact.html

Coats, D. (1989) *Old MacDonald's Factory Farm*, New York: Continuum.

Code, L. (1991) *What Can She Know? Feminist Theory and the Construction of Knowledge*, Ithaca NY: Cornell University Press.

Cohen, A. P. (1985) *The Symbolic Construction of Community*, New York: Routledge Press.

Cohen, A. (1993) *Masquerade Politics: Explorations in the Structure of Urban Cultural Movements*, Berkeley: University of California Press.

Collier, J. and M. Rosaldo (1987) *Marriage and Inequality in Classless Societies*, Stanford: Stanford University Press.

Collier J. and S. Yanagisako (1987) *Gender and Kinship: Essays Toward a United Analysis*, Stanford: Stanford University Press.

Comaroff, J. and J. Comaroff (1988) 'Through the looking glass: colonial encounters of the first kind', *Journal of Historical Sociology* 1, 1: 6–32.

Connelly, P. *et al.* (2000) 'Feminism and Development: Theoretical Perspectives', in J. Parpart, P. Connelly and E. Barriteau (eds.), *Theoretical Perspectives on Gender and Development*, Ottawa: International Research Development Centre.

Cook, S. and L. Binford (1990) *Obliging Need: Rural Petty Industry in Mexican Capitalism*, Austin: University of Texas Press.

Cooper, F. and R. Packard (eds.) (1997) *International Development and the Social Sciences*, Berkeley: University of California Press.

Copjec, J., and M. Sorkin (eds.) (1999) *Giving Ground*, London: Verso.

Corbridge, S. (1998) 'Beneath the pavement only soil', *The Journal of Development Studies* 34, 6 (August): 138–48.

Corrêa, S. with R. Reichmann (1994) *Population and Reproductive Rights: Feminist Perspectives from the South*, London: Zed Books.

Corrêa, S. and G. Sen (1999) 'Cairo Plus 5: Moving Forward in the Eye of the Storm', *Social Watch 1999 Report*, Uruguay: Social Watch.

Coward, R. (1985) *Female Desires: How They Are Sought, Bought and Packaged*, New York: Grove Press.

Cowen, M. and R. Shenton (1995) 'The Invention of Development' in J. Crush (ed.) *Power of Development*, London: Routledge.

Craig, C. and M. Mayo (eds.) (1995) *Community Empowerment*, London: Zed Books.

Crawley, H. (1998) 'Living up to the Empowerment Claim? The Potential of PRA', in I. I. Guijt and M. K. Shah (eds.), *The Myth of Community*, London: ITT Publications.

Crush, J. (ed.) (1995) *Power of Development*, London: Routledge.

Cruz, H. María de los (1988) 'La mujer indígena y el trabajo artesanal', in J. A. Bezaury (ed.), *Las mujeres en el campo*, Oaxaca: Institute for Sociological Research, Autonomous University of Benito Juárez.

Dahlerup, D. (1994) 'Learning to live with the state – state, market and civil society: women's need for state intervention in East and West', *Women's Studies International Forum* 17: 117–27.

Dai, J. 'Woman, Demon, Human: A Woman's Predicament', trans. K. Denton, in Jing Wang and T. Barlow (eds.) *Cinema and Desire: The Feminist Marxism of Dai Jinhua*, London: Verso.

Dankelman, I. and J. Davidson (1988) *Women and Environment in the Third World: Alliance for the Future*, London: Earthscan Publications.

Darwin, C. (1927) *The Formation of Vegetable Mould through the Action of Worms with Observations on their Habits*, London: Faber and Faber.

David, N. (1999) 'Migrants made the scapegoats of the crisis', *ICFTU Online*, International

Confederation of Free Trade Unions: www.hartford-hwp.com/archives/50/012.html
DAWN (Development Alternatives with Women for a New Era) (1995) *Markers on the Way: the DAWN Debates on Alternative Development,* DAWN Publications.
Dayan, S. (2000) 'Policy Initiatives in the US Against the Illegal Trafficking of Women for the Sex Industry' (Committee on International Relations, University of Chicago), on file under author.
de Beauvoir, S. (1961) *The Second Sex,* New York: Bantam Books.
de Lauretis, T. (1990) 'The Practice of Sexual Difference and Feminist Thought in Italy', introduction to Milan Women's Bookstore Collective, *Sexual Difference, a Theory of Social-Symbolic Practice,* Bloomington: Indiana University Press.
—— (1991) 'La tecnologia del género', in C. Ramos (ed.), *El género en perspectiva: de la dominación universal a la representación multiple,* Mexico: UAM Iztapalapa.
Deere, C. D. (1976) 'Rural women's subsistence production in the capitalist periphery', *Review of Radical Political Economy* 8, 1: 9–17.
de la Cadena, M. (1996) 'The political tensions of representations and misrepresentations: intellectuals and *mestizas* in Cuzco', *Journal of Latin American Anthropology* 1 (Autumn): 112–47.
Delahanty, J. and M. K. Shefali (1999) 'Improving women's health and labour conditions in the garment sector', *Development,* 42, 4: 98–102.
Demeny, P. and G. McNicoll (eds.) (1998) *Population and Development,* London: Earthscan.
Derrida, J. (1978) *Writing and Difference,* Chicago: University of Chicago Press.
—— (1981) *Disseminations,* Chicago: University of Chicago Press.
—— (1992) 'Force of Law: the Mystical Foundation of Authority', in D. Cornell, M. Rosenfelt and D. G. Carlson (eds.), *Deconstruction and the Possibility of Justice,* New York: Routledge.
—— (1993) *Aporias,* Stanford: Stanford University Press.
—— (1996) *The Gift of Death,* Chicago: University of Chicago Press.
de Walt, B. (1979) 'Drinking behavior, economic status, and adaptive strategies of modernization in a highland Mexican community', *American Ethnologist* 6, 3: 510–30.
Dirlik, A. (1998) 'Globalism and the politics of place', *Development* 41, 2: 7–14.
Diskin, M. (1969) 'Estudio estructural del sistema de plaza en el valle de Oaxaca, *América Indígena* 29, 4 (October): 1077–99.
Douglas, M. (1982) *Natural Symbols,* New York: Pantheon.
Draper, P. (1975) '!Kung Women: Contrasts in Sexual Egalitarianism in Foraging and Sedentary Contexts', in R. R. Reiter (ed.), *Toward an Anthropology of Women,* New York: Monthly Review Press.
Drew, F. (1875) *The Jummoo and Kashmir Territories: a Geographical Account,* London: Edward Stanford.
Duden, B. (1991) *The Woman Beneath the Skin,* Cambridge MA and London: Harvard University Press.
Du Fangqin (1988) *Nüxing guannian de yanbian* (Evolution of the Woman Concept), Zhengzhou: Henan University Press.
—— (1993) *He Xuangqing ji,* Tianjin: Zhongzhou guji chubanshe.
—— (ed.) (1996) *Faxian funü de lishi: Zhongguo funü shi lunji,* Tianjing: Tianjin shehui koxu xueyuan chubanshe.
Duffield, M. (2001) 'Durable Disorder: Governing the Global Margins', paper presented at Conference on New Regionalism and New/Old Security Issues, Goteborg, Sweden, 31 May–2 June.
Dumont, L. *Essais sur l'individualisme: une perspective anthropologique sur l'idéologie moderne.* Paris: Seuil, 1983.
Duran, D. de (1980) *Ritos y Fiestas (1576–1578),* Mexico: Editorial Cosmos.
Earle, D. (1990) 'Appropriating the Energy: Highland Maya Religious Organization and Community Survival', in L. Stephen and J. Dow (eds.), *Class, Politics and Popular Religion in Mexico and Central America,* Society for Latin American Anthropology Publication Series, Vol. 10.
Eber, C. (1993) '"That We May Serve Beneath Your Flowery Hands and Feet": Women and

Weavers in Highland Chiapas, Mexico', in June Nash (ed.), *Crafts in the World Market: the Impact of Global Exchange on Middle American Artisans*, Albany: State University of New York Press.

—— (1995) *Women and Alcohol in a Highland Maya Town*, Austin: University of Texas Press.

Economist, The (1987) 'Buttercup Goes on Hormones', 9 May.

Ehlers, T. (1991) 'Debunking marianismo: economic vulnerability and survival strategies among Guatemalan wives', *Ethnology* 30: 1–16.

Ehrenreich, B. and D. English (1979) *150 Years of the Experts Advice to Women*, New York: Anchor Books.

Eisenstein, Z. (1996) 'Stop stomping on the rest of us: retrieving publicness from the privatization of the globe', *Indiana Journal of Global Legal Studies* 4, 1 (Autumn), Special Symposium on Feminism and Globalization: the Impact of The Global Economy on Women and Feminist Theory.

El Fisgón (pseudonym of Rafael Barajas) (1996) *Cómo sobrevivir al neoliberalismo sin dejar de ser Mexicano*, Mexico: Grijalbo.

Elias, N. (1978) *The Civilizing Process: the Development of Manners in Early Modern Times*, translated by E. Jephcott, New York: Urizen Books.

Elson, D. (ed.) (1995) *Male Bias in Development*, 2nd edition, Manchester: Manchester University Press.

Elton, C. S. (1959) *The Ecology of Invasion by Animals and Plants*, London: Methuen & Co.

Enloe, C. (1988) *Bananas, Beaches, and Bases*, Berkeley: University of California Press.

Enslin, E. (1994) 'Beyond writing: feminist practice and the limitations of ethnography', *Cultural Anthropology* 9, 4: 537–68.

—— (1998) 'Imagined Sisters: the Ambiguities of Women's Poetics and Collective Actions', in D. Skinner, A. Pach and D. Holland (eds.), *Selves in Time and Place: Identities, Experience, and History in Nepal*, Boulder CO: Rowman and Littlefield Publishers.

Escobar, A.. (1984) 'Discourse and power in development: Michel Foucault and the relevance of his work to the Third World', *Alternatives* 10: 377–400.

—— (1992a) 'Reflections on development: grassroots approaches and alternative politics in the Third World', *Futures*, 24: 411–34.

—— (1992b) 'Imagining a post-development era? Critical thought, development and social movements', *Social Text* 31/32: 20–36.

—— (1995) *Encountering Development: the Making and Unmaking of the Third World*, Princeton: Princeton University Press.

—— (2001) 'Culture sits in places: anthropological reflections on globalism and subaltern strategies of globalization', *Political Geography*, 20: 139–74.

Escobar, A. and W. Harcourt (1998) 'Creating "glocality"', *Development* 41, 2: 2–5.

Fals-Borda, O. and A. Rahman (eds.) (1991) *Action and Knowledge: Breaking the Monopoly with Participatory Action-Research*, New York: Apex Press.

Farrior, S. (1997) 'The international law on trafficking in women and children for prostitution: making it live up to its potential', *Harvard Human Rights Journal*, 10 (Winter).

Ferguson, J. (1991) *The Anti-Politics Machine*, Minneapolis: University of Minnesota Press.

Fernandez-Kelly, M. P. (1983) *For We Are Sold, I and My People: Women and Industry in Mexico's Frontier*, Albany: University of New York Press.

Fischer, W. (1996) 'Race and Representation in Participatory Research', unpublished MA research proposal, Department of Adult Education, Ontario Institute for Studies in Education, Toronto.

Flax, J. (1990) *Thinking Fragments: Psychoanalysis, Feminism, and Postmodernism in the Contemporary West*, Berkeley: University of California Press.

Foster, G. (1967) *Tzintzuntzan: Mexican Peasants in a Changing World*, Boston: Little, Brown & Co.

Foucault, M. (1973) *The Order of Things*. New York: Vintage Books.

—— (1977) *Discipline and Punish: the Birth of the Prison*, New York: Pantheon.

—— (1978) *The History of Sexuality,* Vols I–IV, New York: Pantheon.

—— (1980) *Power/Knowledge: Selected Interviews and Other Writings, 1972–1977,* edited and translated by C. Gordon, Brighton: Harvester Press.

—— (1982) 'The Subject and Power', in H. L. Dreyfuss and P. Rabinow (eds.), *Beyond Structuralism and Hermeneutics,* Chicago: Chicago University Press.

—— (1991) *The Foucault Reader: an Introduction to Foucault's Thought,* edited by P. Rabinow, Harmondsworth: Penguin.

Fox-Genovese, E. (1991) *Feminism without Illusion: a Critique of Individualism,* Chapel Hill and London: University of North Carolina Press.

Frank, A. G. (1967) *Capitalism and Underdevelopment in Latin America,* New York: Monthly Review Press.

Franklin, S. (1995) 'Science as culture, cultures of science', *Annual Review of Anthropology* 24: 163–84.

—— (1997) *Embodied Progress: a Cultural Account of Assisted Reproduction,* London and New York: Routledge.

Fraser, N. (1995) 'From redistribution to recognition? Dilemmas of justice in a "post-socialist" age', *New Left Review* 212 (July/August).

Freeman, J. (1975) *The Politics of Women's Liberation,* New York: David McKay.

Freedman, J. (2000) *Transforming Development,* Toronto: University of Toronto Press.

Freire, P. (1970) *Pedagogy of the Oppressed,* New York: Continuum.

Freud, S. (1989) *Inhibitions, Symptoms and Anxiety,* New York: W. W. Norton & Co.

Friedmann, J. (1992) *Empowerment: the Politics of Alternative Development,* London: Zed Books.

Friends of the Earth (International) (1995) *Towards Sustainable Europe,* London: Friends of the Earth.

Frischmuth, C. (1998) 'From Crops to Gender Relations: Transforming Extension in Zambia', in I. Guijt and K. M. Shah (eds.), *The Myth of Community: Gender Issues in Participatory Development,* London: Intermediate Technology Publications.

Furst, P. T. (1986) 'Human Biology and the Origin of the 260-day Sacred Alamanac: the Contribution of Leonhard Schultze Jena (1872–1955)' in G. H. Gossen (ed.), *Symbol and Meaning beyond the Closed Community: Essays in Mesoamerican Ideas,* Albany: Institute for Mesoamerican Studies, State University of New York.

Gabriel, C. and L. Macdonald (1994) 'NAFTA, women and organizing in Canada and Mexico: forging a "feminist internationality"', *Millennium* 23, 3: 535–62.

Gal, S. (1991) 'Between Speech and Silence: the Problematics of Research on Language and Gender', in M. di Leonardo (ed.), *Gender at the Crossroads of Knowledge,* Berkeley: University of California Press.

Gallop, J. (1988) *Thinking Through the Body,* New York: Columbia University Press.

Gandhi, M. (1995) 'The Crimes of Al-Kabeer', *People for Animals Newsletter,* May.

Garcia-Merono, C. and A. Claro (1994) 'Challenges from the Women's Health Movement: Women's Rights versus Population Control', in G. Sen, A. Germain and L. C. Chen (eds.), *Population Policies Reconsidered: Health, Empowerment, and Rights,* Cambridge MA: Harvard University Press.

Gardiner, H. (1993) *Frames of Mind: The Theory of Multiple Intelligences,* New York: Basic Books.

Garfinkel, H. (1967) *Studies in Ethnomethodology,* Englewood Cliffs NJ: Prentice Hall.

Garg, A. (2001) 'Countering violence against women in Rajasthan: problems, strategies and hazards', *Development* 44, 3.

Garibay, A. M. (1953) *Historia de la literatura Nahuatl,* Mexico: Porrua.

—— (ed.) (1973) 'Historia de los Mexicanos por sus pinturas', in *Teogonia e historia de los Mexicanos. Tres opusculos del siglo XVI,* Mexico: Porrua.

George, S. (1985) *Operation Flood,* Delhi: Oxford University Press.

Gereffi, G. (1996) 'The Elusive Last Lap in the Quest for Developed-Country Status', in J. Mittelman (ed.), *Globalization: Critical Reflections,* Boulder CO: Lynne Rienner.

Gewertz, D. (1984) 'The Tchambuli view of persons: a critique of individualism in the works of

Mead and Chodorow', *American Anthropologist,* 86: 615–29.
—— (1987) *Cultural Alternatives and Feminist Anthropology*, Cambridge: Cambridge University Press.
Gingerich, W. (1988) 'Cipahuacanemiliztli, the "Purified Life" in the Discourses of Book VI, *Florentine Codex*', in J. Kathryn Josserand and K. Dakin (eds.), *Smoke and Mist: Mesoamerican Studies in Memory of Thelma Sullivan,* London: BAR International Series 402.
Ginzburg C. (1985) *Night Battles: Witchcraft and Agrarian Cults in the Sixteenth and Seventeenth Centuries,* New York: Penguin Books.
Global Survival Network (1997) 'Crime and Servitude: an Exposé of the Traffic in Women for Prostitution from the Newly Independent States', www.globalsurvival.net/femaletrade.html (November).
Goebel, A. (1998) 'Process, perception and power: notes from "participatory" research in a Zimbabwean resettlement area', *Development and Change* 29, 2: 277–305.
Goethe, J. W. *Scientific Studies,* edited by Douglas Miller, New York: Suhrkamp.
Goetz, A. M. (1991) 'Feminism and the Claim to Know: Contradictions in Feminist Approaches to Women and Development', in R. Grant and K. Newland (eds.), *Gender and International Relations,* Bloomington: Indiana University Press.
—— (1995) 'Institutionalizing women's interests and gender-sensitive accountability in development', *IDS Bulletin* 26, 3: 1–10.
—— (ed.) (1997) *Getting Institutions Right for Women in Development,* London: Zed.
Gomel Apaza, Z. (1998) 'Regeneración de la colectividad humana', *Informe del Taller de Género, Regeneración y Biodiversidad,* Cochabamba, Bolivia: CAIPACHA, CAM, PRATEC.
González González, M., H. E. Rodríguez and J. M. Contreras Urbina (1997) *Impacto de la crisis 1993–1995: estadísticas sobre el mercado de trabajo femenino,* Mexico: Instituto de Investigaciones Económicas–UNAM.
González, S., O. Ruiz, L. Velasco and O. Woo (eds.) (1995) *Mujeres, migración y maquila en la frontera norte,* Mexico: El Colegio de la Frontera Norte and El Colegio de Mexico.
González Torres,Y. (1991) *Directionario de mitologia y religion de Mesoamerica,* Mexico: Larousse.
Goodeve, T. N. (1999) *Donna J. Haraway: an Interview with Thyza Nichols Goodeve,* London: Routledge.
Goodson, I. F. and J. M. Mangan (1996) 'Exploring alternative perspectives in education research', *Interchange* 27, 1: 41–59.
Gossen, G. H. (1986) 'Mesoamerican Ideas as a Foundation for Regional Synthesis', in G. H. Gossen (ed.), *Symbol and Meaning Beyond the Closed Community: Essays in Mesoamerican Ideas,* Albany: Institute for Mesoamerican Studies, State University of New York.
Gould, S. (1993) 'American polygeny and craniometry before Darwin: blacks and Indian as separate, inferior species', in S. Harding (ed.), *The 'Racial' Economy of Science: toward a Democratic Future,* Bloomington: Indiana University Press.
Gowan, P. (1999) *The Global Gamble: Washington's Faustian Bid for World Dominance*, London: Verso.
Gramsci, A. (1971) *Selections from the Prison Notebooks,* translated and edited by Q. Hoare and G. Nowell Smith, New York: International Publishers.
Grant, R. and K. Newland (eds.) (1991) *Gender and International Relations,* Bloomington: Indiana University Press.
Grasmuck, S. and P. Pessar (1991) *Between Two Islands: Dominican International Migration,* Berkeley: University of California Press.
Greenberg, J. (1981) *Santiago's Sword: Chatino Peasant Religion and Economics,* Berkeley: University of California Press.
Grimshaw, A. (1994) *Servants of the Buddha: Winter in a Himalayan Convent,* Cleveland: Pilgrim Press.
Grist, N. (1985) 'Ladakh, a Trading State', in C. Dendaletsche and P. Kaplanian (eds.) *Ladakh Himalaya Occidental: Ethnologie, Ecologie,* Pau: Centre Pyrenéen de Biologie et Anthropologie des Montagnes.

Grosz, E. (1996) *Space, Time and Perversions: Essays on the Politics of the Body,* New York: Routledge.

Groves, R. H. and J. J. Burdon (eds.) (1986) *Ecology of Biological Invasions: an Australian Perspective,* Canberra, Australia: Australian Academy of Science.

Guayaquil, E. 'Invisible Adjustment…' Vol. 2. … UNICEF.

Guha, R. (1997) *Dominance without Hegemony: History and Power in Colonial India,* Cambridge MA: Harvard University Press.

Guijt, I. and M. K. Shah (eds.) (1998) *The Myth of Community: Gender Issues in Participatory Development,* London: Intermediate Technology Publications.

Guijt, I., T. Kisadha and G. Mukasa (1998) 'Agreeing to Disagree: Dealing with Gender and Age in Redd Barna Uganda', in I. Guijt and M. K. Shah (eds.), *The Myth of Community: Gender Issues in Participatory Development,* London: Intermediate Technology Publications.

Gupta, A. (1998) *Postcolonial Developments: Agriculture in the Making of Modern India,* Oxford: Oxford University Press.

Gutchow, K. (1998) 'An Economy of Merit: Women and Buddhist Monasticism in Zangskar, Northwest India', unpublished PhD thesis, Harvard University.

Gutmann, M. C. (1996) *The Meanings of Macho: Being a Man in Mexico City,* Berkeley: University of California Press.

Guyer, J. (1984) 'Women in African Rural Economies: Contemporary Variations', in J. Hay and S. Stichter (eds.), *African Women South of the Sahara,* London: Longman.

Gyatso, J. (1987) 'Down with the Demoness: Reflections on a Feminine Ground in Tibet', *The Tibet Journal* 12 (4): 38–53.

Hall, B. (1993) 'Introduction', in P. Parks, M. Brydon-Miller, B. Hall and T. Jackson (eds.), *Voices of Change: Participatory Research in the United States and Canada,* Toronto: OISE Press.

Hamm, S. (2001) 'Information communications technologies and violence against women', *Development* 44, 3.

Haque, S. M. (1999)*Restructuring Development Theories and Policies: a Critical Study,* Albany: State University of New York.

Haraway, D. (1985) 'A manifesto for cyborgs: science, technology, and socialist-feminism in the 1980s', *Socialist Review,* 80: 65–108.

—— (1988) 'Situated Knowledges: the science question in feminism as a site of discourse on the privilege of a partial perspective', *Feminist Studies* 14 (3): 575–680.

—— (1991) *Simians, Cyborgs, and Women: the Reinvention of Nature,* New York: Routledge.

—— (1997) *Female Man© – Meets – Onco Mouse™,* New York: Routledge.

Harcourt, W. (2000) 'Rethinking Difference and Equality: Women and the Politics of Place', afterword in R. Prazniak and A. Dirlik (eds.), *Places, Identities and Politics in an Age of Globalization,* NewYork: Rowan and Littlefield.

—— (2001) 'The personal and the political: women using the Internet', *Kommuikation Global* 14, 2: 30–3.

Hardiman, D. (1986) 'From Custom to Crime: the Politics of Drinking in Colonial South Gujerat', in R. Guha (ed.), *Subaltern Studies IV,* Delhi: Oxford University Press.

Harding, S. (1991) *Whose Science, Whose Knowledge?* Ithaca NY: Cornell University Press.

—— (ed.) (1993) *The 'Racial' Economy of Science: toward a Democratic Future,* Bloomington: Indiana University Press.

—— (1998) *Is Science Multicultural? Postcolonialisms, Feminisms and Epistemologies,* Bloomington: Indiana University Press.

Harrington, M. (1992) 'What Exactly's Wrong with the Liberal State as an Agent of Change?', in V. S. Peterson (ed.), *Gendered States: Feminist (Re)Visions of International Theory,* Boulder CO: Lynne Rienner.

Hartmann, B. (1995) *Reproductive Rights and Wrongs: the Global Politics of Population Control,* Boston MA: South End Press.

Havnevik, H. (1994) 'The Role of Nuns in Contemporary Tibet', in R. Barnett and S. Akiner (eds.), *Resistance and Reform in Tibet,* Bloomington: Indiana University Press.

Hay, J. and S. Stichter (eds.) (1984), *African Women South of the Sahara,* London: Longman.

Hazari, T. (1992) Court Judgement passed on 23 March, Case No. 2267/90, Delhi.

Heath, D. B. (1988) 'Emerging Anthropological Theory and Models of Alcohol Use and Alcoholism', in C. D. Chaudron and D. A. Wilkinson (eds.), *Theories on Alcoholism,* Toronto: Addiction Research Foundation.

—— (1991) 'Women and alcohol: cross-cultural perspectives', *Journal of Substance Abuse* 3: 175–85.

Heber, A. and K. Heber (1926) *In Himalayan Tibet: a Record of Twelve Years Spent in the Topsy-Turvy Land of Lesser Tibet,* Philadelphia: J. B. Lippincott Company.

Hegel, G. W. F. (1977) *Hegel's Phenomenology of the Spirit,* translated by A. V. Miller, London: Oxford University Press.

Hekman, S. (1995) 'Subjects and Agents: the Question for Feminism', in J. K. Gardiner (ed.), *Provoking Agents: Gender and Agency in Theory and Practice,* Chicago: University of Illinois Press.

Held, D., A. McGrew, D. Goldblatt and J. Perraton (1999) *Global Transformations: Politics, Economics and Culture,* Cambridge: Polity Press.

Hennessy, R. (1993) *Materialist Feminism,* London: Routledge.

Heron, B. (1996) PhD research proposal, Department of Sociology, Ontario Institute for Studies in Education (OISE), Toronto.

Herrnstein, R. and C. Murray (1994) *The Bell Curve: Intelligence and Class Structure in American Life,* New York: Free Press.

Hess, D. (1995) *Science and Technology in a Multicultural World: the Cultural Politics of Facts and Artifacts,* New York: Columbia University Press.

Heyzer, N. (1994) *The Trade in Domestic Workers,* London: Zed Books.

Hindu, The (1996) '*The Hindu* Survey of Indian Agricuture'.

Hirshman, M. (1995) 'Women and Development: a Critique', in M. Marchand and J. Parpart (eds.), *Feminism/Postmodernism/Development,* London: Routledge.

Hodges, T. (2001) *Angola from Afro-Stalinism to Petro-Diamond Capitalism,* Oxford: James Currey.

Hondagneu-Sotelo, P. (1994) *Gendered Transitions,* Berkeley: University of California Press.

Hoogvelt, A. (1997) *Globalization and the Post-Colonial World: the New Political Economy of Development,* London: Macmillan Press.

hooks, b. (1981) *Ain't I a Woman?: Black Women and Feminism,* Boston: South End Press.

—— (1984) *Feminist Theory: From Margin to Center,* Boston: South End Press.

—— (1990) *Yearning: Race, Gender and Cultural Politics,* Boston: South End Press.

Hooper, C. (2000) 'Masculinities in Transition: the Case of Globalization', in M. H. Marchand and A. S. Runyan (eds.), *Gender and Global Restructuring: Sightings, Sites and Resistances,* London: Routledge.

Howard, G. (1993) *Frames of Mind: the Theory of Multiple Intelligences,* New York: Basic Books.

Hubbard, R. (1990) *The Politics of Women's Biology,* New Brunswick: Rutgers University Press.

Huang, S. (director). *Woman, Demon, Human* (Ren, gui, qing), Nanhai (USA) inc.

Huber, T. (1997) 'Green Tibetans: a Brief Social History', in F. Korom, *Tibetan Culture in the Diaspora,* Vienna: Verlag der Osteriechischen Akademie der Wissenschaften.

Ibhawoh, B. (2001) 'Cultural relativism and human rights: reconsidering the Africanist discourse', *Netherlands Quarterly of Human Rights* 19, 1: 43–62.

India, Government of (1995) 'New Livestock Policy', Section 2.10 on 'Meat Production', Department of Animal Husbandry, Ministry of Agriculture.

INS (Immigration and Naturalization Service of the United States) (1999) Annual Report, Washington DC: Government Printing Office.

IOM (International Office for Migration) (Various years) *Trafficking in Migrants,* quarterly bulletin, Geneva: IOM.

Ismi, A. (1998) 'Plunder with a human face', *Z Magazine* (February).

Itzkoff, S. (1994) *The Decline of Intelligence in America: A Strategy for National Renewal,* Westport, CT: Praeger.

Jackson, C. (1997) 'Post poverty, gender and development?' *IDS Bulletin* 28, 3: 145–55.

Jacobson, D. (1996) *Rights Across Borders,* Baltimore: Johns Hopkins University Press.
Jahan, R. (1995) *The Elusive Agenda: Mainstreaming Women in Development* London: Zed Books.
Jiménez Sardón, G. (1995) *Rituales de vida en la cosmovision Andina,* Convenio, Editorial Secretariado Rural Peru–Bolivia, Centro de Informacion para el Desarrollo, La Paz, Bolivia.
John, M. E. (1996) *Discrepant Dislocations: Feminism, Theory and Postcolonial Histories,* Berkeley: University of California Press.
Johnson, J. J. (1980) *Latin America in Caricature,* Austin:University of Texas Press.
Johnson, P. L. (1992) *Balancing Acts: Women and the Process of Social Change,* Boulder CO: Westview Press.
Jones, E. (1999) 'The gendered toll of global debt crisis', *Sojourner* 25, 3: 20–38.
Jordanova, L (1989) *Sexual Visions,* Madison: University of Wisconsin Press.
Juday, D. (1998) 'Intensification of Agriculture and Free Trade', paper presented at Eighth World Conference on Animal Production, Seoul, Korea, 28 June–4July.
Judd, D. and S. Fainstein (1999) *The Tourist City,* New Haven: Yale University Press.
Kabeer, N. (1995) *Reversed Realities: Gender Hierarchies in Development Thought,* London: Verso.
Kabria, N. (1993) *Family Tightrope,* Princeton: Princeton University Press.
Kaldis, Nick (1999) 'Huang Jianxing's "Cuowei" and/as aesthetic cognition', P*ositions: East Asia Cultures Critique* 7, 2.
Kamat, S. (2001) 'Rediscovering the noble savage', *Cultural Dynamics* 13, 1.
Kapchan D. (1996) *Gender on the Market: Moroccan Women and the Revoicing of Tradition,* Philadelphia: University of Pennsylvania Press.
Kaplanian, P. (1981) *Le Ladakhi du Cachemire,* Paris: Hachette.
Karttunen, F. (1986) 'In Their Own Voice: Mesoamerican Indigenous Women Then and Now', Austin: Linguistics Research Center, University of Texas.
Kaul, S. and H. N. Kaul (1992) *Ladakh through the Ages: towards a New Identity,* New Delhi: Indus Publishing Company.
Kearney, M. (1970) 'Drunkenness and religious conversion in a Mexican village', *Quarterly Journal of Studies on Alcohol* 31: 132–52.
—— (1972) *The Winds of Ixtepeji: World-View and Society in a Zapotec Town,* Illinois: Waveland Press, Inc.
—— (1996) *Reconceptualizing the Peasantry,* Boulder CO: Westview Press.
Kellogg, S. (1984) 'Aztec Women in Early Colonial Courts: Structure and Strategy in a Legal Context', in R. Spores and R. Hassig (eds.), *Five Centuries of Law and Politics in Central Mexico,* Nashville: Vanderbilt University Publications in Anthropology (No. 30).
Kelly, P. and W. Armstrong (1996) 'Villagers and outsiders in cooperation: experiences from development praxis in the Philippines', *Canadian Journal of Development Studies* 12, 2: 241–59.
Kemp, A., N. Madlala, A. Moodley and E. Salo (1995) 'The dawn of a new day: redefining South African feminism', in A. Basu (ed.), *The Challenges of Local Feminism: Women's Movement in Global Perspective,* San Francisco: Western Press.
Kempadoo, K. and J. Doezema (1998) *Global Sex Workers: Rights, Resistance, and Redefinition,* London: Routledge.
Kim, Myung Mi (1996) *The Bounty,* Minneapolis: Chax Press.
Kirby, S. and K. McKenna (1989) *Experience, Research, Social Change: Methods from the Margins,* Toronto: Garamond Press.
Kirchoff, P. (1968) 'Mesoamerica: Its Georgraphic Limits, Ethnic Composition and Cultural Characteristics', in S. Tax (ed.), *Heritage of Conquest: the Ethnology of Middle America,* New York: Cooper Square Publishers.
Klein, A. (1995) *Meeting the Great Bliss Queen: Buddhist, Feminist, and the Art of the Self,* Boston: Beacon Press.
Klor de Alva, J. (1988a) 'Sahagun and the Birth of Modern Ethnography: Representing, Confessing, and Inscribing the Native Other', in J. Klor de Alva, H. B. Nicholson and Q. E. Keber (eds.), *The Work of Bernardino de Sahagun, Pioneer Ethnographer of Sixteenth-Century Aztec Mexico,* Albany: State University of New York.

—— (1988b) 'Contar vidas: la autobiografia confesional y la reconstrucción del ser Nahua', in *Arbor* 515–16, Madrid.

—— (1989)'European spirit and Mesoamerican matter: Sahagun and the "crisis of representation" in Sixteenth-Century ethnography', in David Carrasco (ed.), *The Imagination of Matter: Religion and Ecology in Mesoamerican Traditions,* Oxford: BAR International Series.

Knab, T. (1986) 'Metaphors, Concepts, and Coherence in Aztec', in G. H. Gossen (ed.), *Symbol and Meaning beyond the Closed Community: Essays in Mesoamerican Ideas,* Albany: Institute for Mesoamerican Studies, State University of New York.

Kneen, B. (1987) 'Biocow', *Ram's Horn: Newsletter of the Nutrition Policy Institute* (Toronto) 40 (May).

Knop, K. (1993) 'Re/Statements: feminism and state sovereignty in international law', *Transnational Law and Contemporary Problems* 3 (Autumn): 293–344.

Koczberski, G. (1998) 'Women in development: a critical analysis', *Third World Quarterly* 19, 3: 395–409.

Krais, B. (1993) 'Gender and Symbolic Violence: Female Oppression in the Light of Pierre Bourdieu's Theory of Social Practice', in *Bourdieu: Critical Perspectives,* Chicago: University of Chicago Press.

Krishna, A., N. Uphoff and M. J. Esman (eds.) (1997) *Reasons for Hope: Instructive Experiences in Rural Development,* West Hartford, CT.: Kumarian Press.

Kristof, N. (1998) 'With Asia's economies shrinking, women are being squeezed out', *New York Times,* 11 June.

Kromhout, M. (2000) 'Women and Livelihood Strategies: a Case Study of Coping with Economic Crisis through Household Management in Paramaribo, Suriname', in M. H. Marchand and A. S. Runyan (eds.), *Gender and Global Restructuring: Sightings, Sites and Resistances,* London: Routledge, pp. 140–56.

Lacan, J. (1977) *Écrits: a Selection,* New York: W. W. Norton & Co.

—— (1981) *The Four Fundamental Concepts of Psychoanalysis,* New York: W. W. Norton & Co.

Lacey, R. W. (1994) *Mad Cow Disease: the History of BSE in Britain,* Channel Islands: Cypsela Publications Ltd.

Lacqueur, T. (1990) *Making Sex: Body and Gender from the Greeks to Freud,* Cambridge MA: Harvard University Press.

Lakoff, G. and M. Johnson (1986) *Metaforas de la vida cotidiana,* Madrid: Ediciones Catedra.

Lamphere, L. (1991) 'Feminismo y antropologia' in C. Ramos (ed.), *El género en perspectiva: de la dominación universal a la representación multiple,* Mexico: UAM Iztapalapa.

Landa, D. de (1966) *Relación de las cosas de Yucatan,* introduction by A. Garibay, Mexico: Ediciones Porrua.

Las Casas, B. de (1967) *Apologetica historia,* Mexico: National Autonomous University of Mexico, Institute of Historical Research.

Lassonde L. (1996) *Coping with Population Challenges,* London: Earthscan.

Latin American Regional Reports, Mexico and NAFTA Report (1999) January, RM-99-01, London: Latin American Newsletters.

Latouche, S. (1993) *In the Wake of the Affluent Society: an Exploration of Post-Development,* London: Zed Books.

Latour, B. (1993) *We Have Never Been Modern,* Cambridge MA: Harvard University Press.

Lazreg, M. (1988) 'Feminism and difference: the perils of writing as a woman on women in Algeria', *Feminist Studies* 14, 1 (Spring): 81–107.

—— (ed.) (2000) *Making the Transition Work for Women in Europe and Central Asia,* World Bank Discussion Paper No. 411.

Leacock, E. and J. Nash (1982) 'Ideologies of Sex: Archetypes and Stereotypes', in L. L. Adler (ed.), *Cross-Cultural Research at Issue,* New York: Academic Press.

Lehmann, D. (1997) 'An opportunity lost: Escobar's deconstruction of development', *Journal of Development Studies* 33, 4: 568–78.

Leidholdt, D. and J. G. Raymond (eds.) (1990) *The Sexual Liberals and the Attack on Feminism,*

Oxford: Pergamon Press.
Lennie, J. (1999) 'Deconstructing gendered power relations in participatory planning: towards an empowering feminist framework of participation and action', *Women's Studies International Forum* 22, 1: 97–112.
Leon-Portilla, M. (1963) *Aztec Throught and Culture,* Norman and London: University of Oklahoma Press (translation of *La filosofia Nahuatl,* Mexico: UNAM, 1956).
—— (1980) *Toltecayotl, aspectos de la cultura Nahuatl,* Mexico: FCE.
—— (1984) *Literaturas de Mesoamerica,* Mexico: SEP Cultura.
Lewis, W. A. (1955) *The Theory of Economic Growth,* London: Allen and Unwin.
Li, X. (1989) *Xing Gou is Beijing* (The Sex Gap), Sanlian shudian.
Lim, L. (1998) *The Sex Sector: the Economic and Social Bases of Prostitution in Southeast Asia,* Geneva: International Labour Office.
Lin, C. (1996) 'Citizenship in China: the gender politics of social transformation' in *Social Politics* 3: 2 (Summer/Autumn).
Lin, L. and W. Marjan (1997) *Trafficking in Women, Forced Labor and Slavery-like Practices in Marriage, Domestic Labor and Prostitution,* Utrecht and Bangkok: Foundation against Trafficking in Women (STV) and Global Alliance Against Traffic in Women (GAATW).
Lingzhen, W. (1999) 'Retheorizing the person: identity, writing and gender in Yu Luojin's autobiographical act', P*ositions: East Asia Cultures Critique* 6, 2 (Winter): 395–438.
Lloyd, G. (1993) *The Man of Reason,* Minneapolis: University of MinnesotaPress.
Lloyd, G. E. R. (1966) *Polarity and Analogy: Two Types of Argumentation in early GreekThought,* Cambridge University Press.
Loerch, S. (1991) 'Efficiency of plastic pot scrubbers as a replacement for roughage in high concentrate cattle diets', *Journal of Animal Science* .60: 2321–8.
Longworth, R. (1998), *Global Squeeze: The Coming Crisis for First World Nations,* Chicago: Contemporary Books.
Lopez Austin, A. (1971) *Medicina Nahuatl,* Mexico: SepSetentas, 1971.
—— (1984a) *'Cosmovision y salud entre los Mexicas'* in A. Lopez Austin and C. Viesca (eds.), *Historia general de la medicina en Mexico,* Book 1, Mexico: UNAM, Faculty of Medicine.
—— (1984b) *Cuerpo humano de Ideologia,* 2 vols, Mexico: UNAM/IIA.
Lord, A. (1975) 'Perspectives on recent work on oral literature', in J. J. Duggan (ed.), *Oral Literature: Seven Essays,* New York: Barnes and Noble.
Lorde, A. (1984) *Sister Outsider:* Freedom CA: Crossing Press.
Lowe, L. and D. Lloyd (eds.) (1997) *The Politics of Culture in the Shadow of Capital,* Durham: Duke University Press.
MacCormack, C. and M. Strathern (1980) *Nature, Culture and Gender,* New York: Cambridge University Press.
Mack, R. N. (1981) 'Invasion of Bromus tectorum L. into western North America: an ecological chronicle', *Agro-Ecosystems* 7.
Mack, R. N, N. D. Simberloff, W. M. Lonsdale, H. Evans, M. Cloud and F. Bazzaz (2000) 'Biotic invasions: causes, epidemiology, global consequences and control', *Issues in Ecology* 5 (Spring).
Maguire, P. (1987) *Doing Participatory Research: a Feminist Approach,* Amherst MA: Center for International Education.
Mahler, S. (1995) *American Dreaming: Immigrant Life on the Margins.* Princeton NJ: Princeton University Press.
Mahoney, M. (1996) 'The problem of silence in feminist psychology', *Feminist Studies* 22, 3: 603–25.
Malinowski, B. and J. del Fuente (1982) *Malinowski in Mexico: the Economics of a Mexican Market System,* London: Routledge and Kegan Paul.
Malkki, L. H. (1995) 'Refugees and exile: from "Refugee Studies" to the national order of things' *Annual Review of Anthropology* 24: 495–523.
Mama, A. (2001) 'Gender and research', *Nordic Africa Institute Newsletter.*
Mander, J. (1995) *In the Absence of the Sacred,* Sierra Club Books.
Mani, L. (1989) 'Contentious Traditions: the Debate on Sati in Colonial India', in K. Sangari and

S. Vaid (eds.) *Recasting Women: Essays in Colonial History*, New Delhi: Kali for Women.

Manning, K. (n.d.) 'Making Gendered Sense of Political Transition' (unpublished manuscript).

March, K. (1987) 'Hospitality, Women and the Efficacy of Beer', *Food and Foodways* 1, 4.

Marchand, M. H. (2000) 'Globalization and the Rearticulation of Identities: Cosmopolitanism on the Rise?', paper presented at the annual meeting of the Royal Irish Academy, Dublin, 23–24 November.

—— (2002) 'Regionalismes concurrents en Amérique du Nord: contestation, spatialisation et l'emergence des identités frontières', *Revue Quebecois de Sociologie.*

Marchand, M. and J. Parpart (eds.) (1995) *Feminism/Postmodernism/Development,* London: Routledge.

Marchand, M. H. and A. S. Runyan (eds.) (2000) *Gender and Global Restructuring: Sightings, Sites and Resistances,* London: Routledge.

Marcos, S. (1991) 'Gender and moral precepts in ancient Mexico: Sahagun's texts', *Concilium* 6.

—— (1993) 'Missionary Activity in Latin America: Confession Manuals and Indigenous Eroticism', in L. Martin (ed.), *Religious Transformations and Socio-Political Change,* New York: de Gruyter.

—— (1998) 'Embodied Religious Thought: Gender Categories in Mesoamerica', *Religion,* 28 (41), October.

Martin, E. (1987) *The Woman in the Body,* Boston: Beacon Press.

Martin, L. *et al.* (1989) *Technologies of the Self: a Seminar with Michel Foucault,* Amherst MA: University of Massachusetts Press.

Massey, D. (1997) 'A Global Sense of Place', in A. Gray and J. McGuigan (eds.), *Studying Culture,* London: Edward Arnold.

Mathews, H. H. (1985) '"We are Mayordomo": a reinterpretation of women's roles in the Mexican cargo system', *American Ethnologist* 17: 285–301.

Mazumdar, V. (1977) 'Reflections on the conference on women and development', in Wellsley Editorial Committee (eds.), *Women and National Development: Complexities of Change,* Chicago: University of Chicago Press.

Mayoux, L. (1995) 'Beyond Naivety: women, gender inequality and participatory development', *Development and Change* 25: 497–526.

—— (1998) 'Gender Accountability and NGOs: Avoiding the Black Hole' in C. Miller and S. Razavi (eds.), *Missionaries and Mandarins: Feminist Engagement with Development Institutions,* London: Intermediate Technology Publications.

Mbiliny, M. (1990) 'Structural Adjustment: Agribusiness and Rural Women in Tanzania', in H. Bernstein *et al.* (eds.), *The Food Question: Profit Versus People?* London: Earthscan.

McAllister, C. (1992) '"It's Our Adat": Capitalist Development and the Revival of Tradition among Women in Negeri Sembilan, Malaysia', in P. L. Johnson (ed.), *Balancing Acts: Women and the Process of Social Change,* Boulder CO: Westview Press.

McClelland, D. C. (1976) *The Achieving Society,* New York: Irvington.

McCormick, A. (1895) *An Artist in the Himalayas,* London: T. F. Unwin.

Mehra, R. (1997) 'Women, empowerment and economic development', *Annals of the American Academy of Political and Social Science* (November): 136–49.

Mei, S. (1933/4) Funü Wenti Taolun Ji (The Debate Over the Chinese Women Question) Sanghai: New Culture Press (Shanghai: Shanghai xin whenhua shushe).

Melrose, D. (1999) 'Two Steps Forward, One Step Back: Experiences of Senior Management' in F. Porter *et al.* (eds.), *Gender Works: Oxfam Experience in Policy and Practice,* London: Oxfam.

Meng, E. (1994) 'Mail order brides: gilded prostitution and the legal responses', *University of Michigan Journal of Law Reform* (Autumn).

Meng Y. (1993) 'Female Images and National Myth', in T. E. Barlow (ed.), *Gender Politics in Modern China: Writing and Feminism,* Durham: Duke University Press.

Merchant, C. (1980) *The Death of Nature: Women, Ecology, and the Scientific Revolution,* San Francisco: Harper and Row.

Michelet, J. (1842) *La Femme,* Paris: Grevin.

Mies, M. (1983) 'Towards a Methodology for Feminist Research', in G. Bowles and R. D. Klein (eds.), *Theories of Women's Studies*, New York: Routledge and Kegan Paul, pp. 117–39.

Mies, M. and V. Shiva (1993) *Ecofeminism*, Halifax: Fernwood Publications.

Miles, A. (1992) 'Pride and Prejudice: the Urban Chola and the Transmission of Class and Gender Ideologies in Cuenca, Ecuador', in P. L. Johnson (ed.), *Balancing Acts: Women and the Process of Social Change*, Boulder CO: Westview Press.

Milkman, R. (1987) *Gender at Work: The Dynamics of Job Segregation by Sex During WWII*, Champaign: University of Illinois Press.

Mittelman, J. (ed.) (1997) *Globalization: Critical Reflections*, Boulder CO: Lynne Rienner.

Moghadam, V. M. (2000) 'Economic Restructuring and the Gender Contract: a Case Study of Jordan', in M. H. Marchand and A. S. Runyan (eds.), *Gender and Global Restructuring: Sightings, Sites and Resistances*, London: Routledge, pp. 99–115.

Mohan, G. and K. Stokke (2000) 'Participatory development and empowerment: the dangers of localism', *Third World Quarterly* 21, 2: 247–68.

Mohanty, C. (1988) 'Under Western eyes: feminist scholarship and colonial discourses', *Feminist Review* 30: 61–88; also in C. Mohanty, M. A. Russo and L. Torres (eds.) (1991) *Third World Women and the Politics of Feminism*, Bloomington: Indiana University Press.

Mohanty, M. (1995) 'On the concept of "empowerment"', *Economic and Political Weekly* (17 June): 1434–36.

Mooney, H. A and J. A. Drake (1986) *Ecology of Biological Invasions of North America and Hawaii*, New York: Springer Verlag.

Moreau, T. (1982) *Le Sang de l'histoire: Michelet, l'histoire et l'idée de la femme au XIXième siècle*, Paris: Flammarion.

Morokvasic, M. (1984) Contribution to Special Issue on Women Immigrants, *International Migration Review* 8, 4.

Moser, C. (1989a) 'Gender planning in the Third World: meeting practical and strategic gender needs', *World Development* 17, 11: 1799–1825; also in R. Grant. and K. Newland (eds.) (1991), *Gender and International Relations*, Bloomington: Indiana University Press.

—— (1989b) 'The impact of recession and structural adjustment policies at the micro-level: low-income women and their households in Guayaquil, Ecuador', *Invisible Adjustment*, vol. 2 (UNICEF).

—— (1993) *Gender Planning and Development: Theory, Practice and Training*, London: Routledge.

—— (1997) 'The Impact of Recession and Structural Adjustment Policies at the Micro-level: Low Income Women and Their Households' in J. Mittelman (ed.), *Globalization: Critical Reflections*, Boulder CO: Lynne Rienner.

Mosse, D. (1994) 'Authority, gender and knowledge: theoretical reflections on the practice of participatory rural appraisal', *Development and Change* 25: 497–526.

Mueller, A. (1986) 'The bureaucratization of feminist knowledge: the case of women in development', *Resources for Feminist Research* 15, 1 (March): 36–8.

Munck, R. (1999) 'Deconstructing Development Discourses: of Impasses, Alternatives and Politics', in R. Munck and D. O'Hearn (eds.), *Critical Development Theory: Contributions to a New Paradigm*, London: Zed Books.

Munshi, K. M. (1951) 'Towards Land Transformation', Government of India, Ministry of Food and Agriculture.

Myerhoff, B. (1976) 'Shamanic equilibrium: balance and mediation in known and unknown worlds', *Parabola* 1.

Nanda, M. (1991) 'Is modern science a Western, patriarchal myth? A critique of the neo-populist orthodoxy', *South Asia Bulletin* 11.

—— (1997) 'History Is What Hurts: a Materialist Feminist Perspective on the Green Revolution and Its Ecofeminist Critics', in R. Hennessy and C. Inghram (eds.), *Materialist Feminism: a Reader in Class, Difference and Women's Lives*, New York: Routledge.

—— (1999) 'Who needs post-development? Discourses of difference, the green revolution and agrarian populism in India', *Journal of Developing Societies* 15, 1: 5–31.

—— (forthcoming) 'A "Broken People" defend science: reconstructing the Deweyan Buddha of India's Dalits', *Social Epistemology*.

Nanda, P. (1999) 'Global agendas, health sector reforms and reproductive health and rights: opportunities and challenges in Zambia', *Development* 42, 4: 59–63.

Nandy, A. (1988) *Science, Hegemony and Violence: a Requiem for Modernity*, New Delhi: Oxford University Press.

—— (1993) *The Intimate Enemy*, New Delhi: Oxford University Press.

Narayan, K. (1993) 'How "Native" is a "Native" Anthropologist?' *American Anthropologist* 95 (1993): 671–86.

Nash, J. (ed.) (1993) *Crafts in the World Market*, New York: State University of New York Press.

Nash, J. and H. Safa (eds.) (1976) *Sex and Class in Latin America*, New York: Praeger.

Nash, M. (1966) *Primitive and Peasant Economic Systems*, San Francisco: Chandler Publishing Co.

Nathan, D. (1999) 'Work, sex and danger in Ciudad Juárez', in *Contested Terrain: the US–Mexico Borderlands*, special issue of *NACLA Report on the Americas* 33, 3 (November/December): 24–30.

Ndungu, N. S. (1999) 'Gender-based violence within the African region: an overview', *WILDAF News* 1: 7–10.

Ngunjiri, E. (1998) 'Participatory methodologies: double edged swords', *Development in Practice* 8, 4: 466–70.

Novelo, V. (1991) *Artesanías y capitalismo en México*, Mexico City: SEP–INAH.

Norberg-Hodge, H. (1991) *Ancient Futures: Learning from Ladakh*, London: Rider.

Nzomo, M. (1995) 'Women and Democratization Struggles in Africa: What Relevance to Postmodern Discourse?', in M. Marchand and J. Parpart (eds.), *Feminism/Postmodernism/Development*, London: Routledge.

O'Connor, M. and R. Arnoux (1993), introduction to *In the Wake of the Affluent Society: An Exploration of Post-Development*, by S. Latouche, London: Zed Books.

Olds, K., P. Dicken, P. F. Kelly, L. Kong, H. Yeung and W. Chung (eds.) (1999) *Globalization and the Asian Pacific: Contested Territories*, London: Routledge.

Oakley, A. (1981) 'Interviewing Women: a Contradiction in Terms', in H. Roberts (ed.), *Doing Feminist Research*, Boston: Routledge and Kegan Paul, pp. 30–61.

Oglesby, E. (2001) 'Machos and Machetes in Guatemala's Cane Fields', *NACLA Report on the Americas* 34, 5 (March/April).

Okin, S. M. (1994) 'Gender inequality and cultural differences', *Political Theory* 22, 1: 5–24.

Oldenburg, V. (1987) *Spirits of Resistance and Capitalist Discipline: Factory Workers in Malaysia*, Albany, New York University Press.

—— (1990) 'Lifestyles as resistance: the case of the courtesans of Lucknow, India', *Feminist Studies*, 16, 2.

Olmos, A. de (1973) 'Historia de los Mexicanos por sus pinturas', in A. Garibay (ed.), *Teogonia y historia de los Mexicanos, tres opusculos del siglo XVI*, Mexico: Porrua.

Omvedt, G. (1993) *Reinventing Revolution: New Social Movements and the Socialist Tradition in India*, New York: M. E. Sharpe.

Ong, A. (1988) 'Colonialism and modernity: feminist re-presentations of women in non-Western society', *Inscriptions* 3, 4: 79–83.

—— (1996) 'Globalization and women's rights: the Asian debate on citizenship and communitarianism', *Indiana Journal of Global Legal Studies* 4, 1 (Autumn), Special Symposium on Feminism and Globalization: the Impact of the Global Economy on Women and Feminist Theory.

Ong, A. and D. Nonini (eds.) (1997) *Underground Empires: the Cultural Politics of Modern Chinese Transnationalism*, New York: Routledge.

Ortiz, S. (1993) 'El cuerpo y el trance entre los espiritualistas Trinitarios Marianos', presentation at the symposium on Symbol and Performance in Healing: the Contributions of Indigenous Medical Thought, CICAE Congress, July.

Ortner, S. (1995) 'Resistance and the problem of ethnographic refusal', *Comparative Studies in*

Society and History 37.

Ortner, S and H. Whitehead (eds.) (1989) *Sexual Meanings: the Cultural Construction of Gender and Sexuality,* Cambridge: Cambridge University Press.

Oxfam (1999) 'International submission to the HIPC debt review' (April), www.caa.org/au/oxfam/advocacy/debt/hipcreview.html.

Pala, A. O. (1977) 'Definitions of Women and Development: an African perspective', in Wellsley Editorial Committee, *Women and National Development: Complexities of Change,* Chicago: University of Chicago Press.

Pallis, M. (1939) *Peaks and Lamas,* London: Cassell and Co. Ltd.

Panya, C. (1998) quoted in D. Juday, 'Intensification of Agriculture and Free Trade', paper presented at Eighth World Conference on Animal Production, Seoul, Korea, 28 June–4 July.

Paretti, J. (1998) 'Nativism and nature: rethinking biological invasions', *Environmental Values* 7, 2.

Parpart, J., S. Rai and K. Staudt (eds.) (2002) *Rethinking Empowerment: Gender and Development in a Global/Local World,* London: Routledge.

Parry, M. (1971) *The Making of Homeric Verse,* Oxford: Clarendon Press.

Parsons, T. (1960) *Family, Socialization and Interaction,* Glencoe, IL: Free Press.

Paso y Troncoso, F. (1906) *Codice Matritense del Real Palacio,* Vol. 7, Madrid: Hausery Menet.

Patai, D. (1994) 'US Academics and Third-World Women: Is Ethical Research Possible?' in S. O. Weisser and F. Fleischner (eds.), *Feminist Nightmares, Women at Odds: Feminism and the Problem of Sisterhood,* New York and London: New York University Press, pp. 21–43.

Payer, C. (1975) *The Debt Trap: the IMF and the Third World,* Harmondsworth: Penguin.

—— (1991) *Lent and Lost: Foreign Credit and Third World Development,* London: Zed Books.

Payne, A. (2001) 'The global politics of development: towards a new research agenda', *Progress in Development* 1, 1: 5–20.

Pérez, R. (1997) 'Moulding Our Lives from Clay: the Redefinition of Gender and Community in the Artisan Pueblo of Santa María Atzompa, Oaxaca', unpublished dissertation, University of California, Riverside.

—— (2000) 'Fiesta as tradition, fiesta as change: ritual, alcohol and violence in a Mexican community', *Addiction* 95 (3): 365–73.

Pessar, P. (1995) 'On the homefront and in the workplace: integrating immigrant women into feminist discourse', *Anthropological Quarterly* 68, 1: 37–47.

Petchesky, R. (1987) 'Fetal images: the power of visual culture in the politics of reproduction', *Feminist Studies* 13, 2.

Peterson, V. S. (ed.) (1992) *Gendered States: Feminist (Re)Visions of International Relations Theory,* Boulder CO: Lynne Rienner.

Peterson, V. S. and A. S. Runyan (1993) *Global Gender Issues,* Boulder CO: Westview Press.

Philippines Information Service (1999) 'Filipina Brides' www.pis.or.jp/data/tothug.htm

Pieterse, J. N. (1998) 'My paradigm or yours? Alternative development, post-development, reflexive development', *Development and Change* 29, 3: 343–73.

—— (2000) 'After post-development', *Third World Quarterly,* 21, 2: 175–91.

Pietilä, H. and J. Vickers (1994) *Making Women Matter: the Role of the United Nations,* London: Zed Books.

Ping-Chun Hsiung (1998) 'Transformation , Subversion, and Feminist Activism: Report on the Workshops of a Developmental Project, Xian, China', unpublished report, Department of Sociology, University of Toronto at Scarborough.

Porter, F., I. Smyth and C. Sweetman (eds.) (1999) *Gender Works: Oxfam Experience in Policy and Practice,* London: Oxfam.

Pradham, B. (1979) *The Status of Women in Nepal,* Kathmandu, Nepal: Trubhuran University.

Public Citizen's Global Trade Watch (1998) 'NAFTA at Five: School of Real-Life Results Report Card', www.citizen.org/pctrade/nafta/reports/5years.htm, December, pp. 1–26.

Quarterly Monitor (1995) No. 13, special issue on 'Reverence for Life'. New Delhi: Research Foundation for Science, Technology and Natural Resource Policy.

Quezada, N. (1975) *Amory magia amorosa entre los Aztecas,* Mexico: Universidad Autonoma de

Mexico.

Rahman, A. (1999) 'Micro-credit initiatives for equitable and sustainable development: who pays?' *World Development* 27, 1: 67–82.

Rahnema, M. (1990) 'Participatory action research: the "Last Temptation of Saint" development', *Alternatives* 15: 199–226.

Rahnema, M. and V. Bawtree (eds.) (1997) *The Post-Development Reader,* London: Zed Books.

Rai, S. (2002) 'Political Representation, Democratic Institutions and Women's Empowerment: the Quota Debate in India', in J. Parpart, S. Rai and K. Staudt (eds.), *Rethinking Empowerment: Gender and Development in a Global/Local World,* London: Routledge.

Rathgeber, E. (1990) 'WID, WAD, GAD: trends in research and practice', *Journal of Developing Areas* 24 (1990): 489–502.

Raymond, J. G. (ed.) (1990) *The Sexual Liberals and the Attack on Feminism.* Athene Series: Pergamon Press.

—— (1993) *Women as Wombs: Reproductive Technologies and the Battle over Women's Freedom,* San Francisco: Harper.

Razavi, S. (1998) 'Becoming Multilingual: the Challenges of Feminist Policy Advocacy', in C. Miller and S. Razavi (eds.), *Missionaries and Mandarins: Feminist Engagement with Development Institutions,* London: Intermediate Technology Publications.

Reis, R. (1983) 'Reproduction or Retreat: the Position of Women in Ladakh', in D. Kantowsk and R. Sander (eds.), *Recent Research on Ladakh*, Munich: Weltforum Verlag.

Renato Ruggiero, R. (1998) speech given at 'Policing the World Economy' Conference, held at Geneva, 23–25 March.

Rengifo, G. (1998) 'The Ayllu', in F. Apffel-Marglin (ed.) with PRATEC, *The Spirit of Regeneration: Andean Culture Confronting Western Notions of Development*, London: Zed Books, pp. 89–123.

Reno, W. (1998) *Warlord Politics and African States*, Boulder CO: Lynne Rienner.

Ribot, J. C. (1996) 'Participation without representation: chiefs, councils and forestry law in the West African Sahel', *Cultural Survival Quarterly*: 40–44.

—— (1999) 'Decentralisation, participation and accountability in Sahelian forestry: legal instruments of political-administrative control', *Africa* 69, 1: 23–65.

Richards, P. (1983) 'Ecological change and the politics of African land use', *African Studies Review* 26, 2.

Rich, A. (1976), *Of Woman Born: Motherhood as Experience and Institution*, London: Virago.

Richer, S. (1998) 'Explorations in Participatory Research: towards Equality in the Production of Knowledge', 29th Sorokin Lecture delivered 28 January at the University of Saskatchewan, Canada.

Richter, M. (1999) 'Europe and the Other in Eighteenth-Century Thought', in J. Rizvi, *Trans-Himalayan Caravans: Merchant Princes and Peasant Traders in Ladakh*, New Delhi: Oxford University Press.

Rist, G. (1997) *The History of Development: from Western Origins to Global Faith,* London: Zed Books.

Rizvi, J. (ed.) *Trans-Himalayan Caravans: Merchant Princes and Peasant Traders in Ladakh*, New Delhi: Oxford University Press.

Robinson, J. (1996) 'Searching for the "Community" in Community-Based Conservation: a Case Study of a Zimbabwe Campfire Project', Masters dissertation in Environmental Studies, Dalhousie University, Halifax, Nova Scotia.

Rocheleau, D., B. Thomas-Slayter and E. Wangari (eds.) (1996) *Feminist Political Ecology, Global Issues and Local Experiences.*

Rogers, B. (1980) *The Domestication of Women in Developing Countries*, London: Tavistock.

Rose, K. (1992) *Where Women Are Leaders: the SEWA Movement in India*, London: Zed Books.

Roseberry, W. (1989) *Anthropologies and Histories: Essays in Culture, History and Political Economy*, New Brunswick: Rutgers University Press.

Rosenbaum, Brenda (1993) *With Our Heads Bowed: the Dynamics of Gender in a Maya Community,* Austin: University of Texas Press.

Rosenfelt, D. (1998) 'Think globally, teach locally', *Women's Review of Books*, 15, 5: 28–9.

Rostow, W. (1960) *The Stages of Economic Growth*, Cambridge: Cambridge University Press.

Rowlands, J. (1997) *Questioning Empowerment: Working with Women in Honduras,* Oxford: Oxfam Publications.

—— (1998) 'A Word of the Times, but What Does It Mean? Empowerment in the Discourse and Practice of Development,' in H. Afshar (ed.), *Women and Empowerment: Illustrations from the Third World*, London: Macmillan.

Rubin, G. (1975) 'The Traffic in Women: Notes on the "Political Economy" of Sex', in R. Reiter (ed.), *Toward an Anthropology of Women,* New York: MonthlyReview Press.

Ruiz de Alarcon, H. (1987) 'Tratado de las supersticiones de los naturales de esta Nueva Espana', in P. Ponce, P. Sanchez Aguilar *et al.* (eds.), *Et alma encantada,* Mexico: FCE–INI.

Rupert, M. (2000) *Ideologies of Globalization: Contending Visions of a New World Order,* London: Routledge.

Sachs, W. (1999) *Planet Dialectics: Explorations in Environment and Development,* London: Zed Books.

—— (ed.) (1992) *The Development Dictionary: a Guide to Knowledge and Power*, London: Zed Books.

—— (ed.) (1993) *Global Ecology: a New Arena of Political Conflict,* London: Zed Books.

Sæther, G. (2001) 'Inequality, security and violence', *The European Journal of Development Research* 13, 1: 181–92.

Safa, H. (1995) *The Myth of the Male Breadwinner: Women and Industrialization in the Caribbean,* Boulder CO: Westview Press.

Sagoff, M. (2000) 'Why exotic species are not as bad as we fear', *Chronicle of Higher Education* 46, 42 (June).

Sahagun, B. de (1969) *Florentine Codex: General History of the Things of New Spain,* translation of original Nahuatl text by A. Anderson and C. Dibble, Salt Lake City: School of American Research, University of Utah.

—— (1989) *Historia general de las cosas de Nueva Espana,* Books I and II, introduction and paleography, etc., edited by A. Lopez Austin and J. Garcia Quintana, Mexico: Consejo Nacional para la Cultura y las Artes.

Said, E. (1989) 'Representing the colonized: anthropology's interlocutor', *Critical Inquiry* 15, 2 (Winter): 202–25.

Sanchez, L. (1998) 'La agenda oculta de género', in *Informe del Taller de Género, Regeneración y Biodiversidad,* Cochabamba, Bolivia: CAIPACHA, CAM, PRATEC.

Sanchez, L. and M. Arratia (1996) 'Género y riego en comunidades campesinas de los Andes: una approximación conceptual', Cochabamba, Bolivia: National Programme for Irrigation (PRONAR).

Sangari, K. and S. Vaid (1989) 'Recasting Women: an Introduction', in K. Sangari and S.Vaid (eds.), *Recasting Women: Essays in Indian Colonial History*, New Delhi: Kali for Women.

Sanger, M. (1967) *The Pivot of Civilization,* New York: Maxell Reprint Company.

Sapiro, V. (1994) *Women in American Society: an Introduction to Women's Studies,* 3rd edition, Mountain View, California: Mayfield Publishing Co.

Sassen, S. (1988) *The Mobility of Labour and Capital*, Cambridge: Cambridge University Press.

—— (1998) *Globalization and its Discontents: Essays on the Mobility of People and Money*, New York: New Press.

—— (1999a) *Guests and Aliens,* New York: New Press.

—— (1999b) 'Global financial centers', *Foreign Affairs* 78, 1: 75–87.

—— (2001) *The Global City* (revised edn), Princeton: Princeton University Press.

Savigliano, M. (1995) *Tango and the Political Economy of Passion: Exoticism and Decolonization,* Boulder CO: Westview Press.

Sawicki, J. (1991) *Disciplining Foucault: Feminism, Power and the Body,* New York: Routledge.

Schapin, S. and S. Schaffer (1985) *Leviathan and the Air-Pump: Hobbes, Boyle and the Experimental Life,* Princeton: Princeton University Press.

Schiebinger, L. (1982) *The Mind Has No Sex? Women and the Origins of Modern Science,* Cambridge MA: Harvard University Press.

Scholte, J. A. (2000) *Globalization: a Critical Introduction,* Houndmills, Basingstoke: Palgrave.

Schor, N. (1994) 'Introduction', in N. Schor and E. Weed (eds.), *The Essential Difference,* Bloomington: Indiana University Press.

Schor, N. and E. Weed (1994), *The Essential Difference,* Bloomington: Indiana University Press.

Schumacher, E. F. (1973) *Small is Beautiful: a Study of Economics as if People Mattered,* London: Blond and Briggs.

Schuurman, F. (1993) *Beyond the Impasse: New Directions in Development,* London: Zed Books.

Scoones, I. and J. Thompson (1993) 'Challenging the Populist Perspective: Rural People's Knowledge, Agricultural Research and Extension Practice', *IDS Bulletin,* University of Sussex, Discussion Paper No. 332.

Sen, G. (1997) 'Globalization in the Twenty-first Century: Challenges for Civil Society', University of Amsterdam Development Lecture, University of Amsterdam, 20 June.

Sen, G. and C. Barrosos (1996) 'After Cairo: Challenges to Women's Organizations', paper presented at the Workshop on Reproductive Health, Rights and Women's Empowerment, Centre for Development Studies, Bangalore.

Sen, G. and C. Grown (1987) *Development, Crisis, and Alternative Visions: Third World Women's Perspectives,* New York: Monthly Review Press.

Serna, J. (1987) 'Manual de ministros de Indios', in P. Ponce, P. Sanchez Aguilar *et al.* (eds.), *El alma encantada,* Mexico:FCE–INI.

Serres, M. and B. Latour (1995) *Conversations on Science, Culture and Time,* Ann Arbor: University of Michigan Press.

Shah, M. K. (1998) 'Addressing Gender Issues in Participatory Program Implementation', in I. Guijt and M. K. Shah (eds.), *The Myth of Community: Gender Issues in Participatory Development,* London: Intermediate Technology Publications.

Shannon, S. (1999) 'The global sex trade: humans as the ultimate commodity', *Crime and Justice International* (May): 5–25.

Shaw, M. (1994) *Passionate Enlightenment: Women in Tantric Buddhism,* Princeton: Princeton University Press.

Shiva, V. (1988) *Staying Alive: Women, Ecology and Development,* London: Zed Books.

—— (1995) *The New Livestock Policy: a Policy of Ecocide of Indigenous Cattle Breeds and a Policy of Genocide for India's Small Farmers,* New Delhi: Research Foundation for Science, Technology, and Ecology.

—— (1999) 'Ecological Balance in an Era of Globalization', in Nicholas Low (ed.), *Global Ethics and Environment,* London: Routledge.

—— (2001) *Stolen Harvest: The Hijacking of the Global Food Supply,* London: Zed Books.

—— (ed.) (1994) *Close to Home: Women Reconnect Ecology, Health and Development Worldwide,* Philadelphia: New Society Publishers.

Shousun, C. (1929) *Shehui Wenti Cidian* (Dictionary of Social Problems), Shanghai: Minzhi Shujyu.

Silliman, J. (1999) 'Expanding Civil Society, Shrinking Political Spaces: the Case of Women's Nongovernmental Organizations', in J. Silliman. and Y. King (eds.), *Dangerous Intersections: Feminist Perspectives on Population, Environment and Development,* Cambridge MA: South End Press, pp. 133–62.

Silverblatt, I. (1987) *Moon, Sun and Witches: Gender Ideologies and Class in Inca and Colonial Peru,* Princeton: Princeton University Press.

Simeon, R. (1977) *Dictionario de la lengua Nahuatl o Mexicana,* Mexico: Siglo Veintiuno Editores. (First edition in French, *Dictionaire de la langue Nahuatl ou Mexicaine,* 1885).

Simone, T. M. (1989) *About Face: Race in Postmodern America,* New York: Autonomedia.

Singh, J. S. (1998) *Creating a New Consensus on Population,* London: Earthscan.

Sinha, M. (1995) 'Gender in the Critiques of Colonialism and Nationalism: Locating the "Indian Woman" ', in J. Scott (ed.), *Feminists amd History,* Oxford: Oxford University Press.

Slater, D. (1997) 'Geopolitical imaginations across the North–South divide: issues of difference, development and power', *Political Geography* 16, 8: 631–53.

Smith, D. (1992) 'Sociology from women's experience: a reaffirmation', *Sociological Quarterly* 10.

Smith, J. and I. Wallerstein (eds.) (1992) *Creating and Transforming Households: the Constraints of the World-Economy,* Cambridge and Paris: Cambridge University Press and Maison des Sciences de l'Homme.

Smyth, I. (1998) 'Gender Analysis of Family Planning: beyond the "Feminist vs. Population Control" Debate', in C. Jackson and R. Pearson (eds.), *Feminist Visions of Development: Gender Analysis and Policy,* London: Routledge.

—— (1999) 'A Rose by Any Other Name: Feminism in Development NGOs', in F. Porter, I. Smyth and C. Sweetman (eds.), *Gender Works: Oxfam Experience in Policy and Practice,* London: Oxfam.

SNDR (Secretaria Nacional de Desarrollo Rural) (1995) Government document, La Paz, Bolivia.

Snyder, M. (1995) *Transforming Development: Women, Poverty and Politics,* London: Intermediate Technologies Institute Publications.

Sonam Phuntsog (1993) 'gLe grong khyer gyi sngon rabs', *Ladags Melong* 1.

Soustelle, J. (1940) *La Pensée cosmologique des anciens Mexicans,* Paris: Herman et Cie.

Soysal, Y. (1994) *Limits of Citizenship*, Chicago: University of Chicago Press.

Spelman, E. (1988) *Inessential Woman*, Boston: Beacon Press.

Spivak, G. (1988a) 'Can the Subaltern Speak?' in C. Nelson and L. Grossberg (eds.), *Marxism and the Interpretation of Culture*, Urbana: University of Illinois Press. Also in P. Williams and L. Chrisman (eds.), (1994) *Colonial Discourse and Postcolonial Theory: a Reader,* New York: Columbia University Press.

—— (1988b) *In Other Worlds. Essays in Cultural Politics*, New York: Routledge.

—— (1996) *The Spivak Reader: Selected Works of Gayatri Chakravorty Spivak*, D. Landry and G. MacLean (eds.), New York: Routledge.

—— (1997) 'Teaching for the Times', in A. McClintock *et al.* (eds.), *Dangerous Liaisons,* Minneapolis: University of Minnesota Press.

Standing, G. (1999) 'Global feminization through flexible labor: a theme revisited', *World Development* 27, 3: 583–602.

Staudt, K. (1998) *Policy, Politics and Gender: Women Gaining Ground,* West Hartford CT: Kumarian Press.

—— (ed.) (1990) *Women, International Development and Politics: the Bureaucratic Mire,* revised edition (1997), Philadelphia: Temple University Press.

Staudt, K., S. Rai and J. Parpart (2001) 'Protesting world trade rules: can we talk about empowerment?', *Signs: Journal of Women in Culture and Society*, 26, 4 (Summer): 1251–8.

Steady, F.C. (1986) 'Research Methodology and Investigative Frameworks for Social Change: The Case for African Women', in *AAWORD, Seminar on Research on African Women: What Type of Methodology?*, 5–9 December 1983, Dakar, Senegal: AAWORD.

Stein, J. (1997) *Empowerment and Women's Health*, London: Zed Books.

Stephen, L. (1991) *Zapotec Women*, Austin: University of Texas Press.

Subramaniam, B. (2001) 'The aliens have landed! Reflections on the rhetoric of biological invasions', *Meridians: Feminism, Race, Transnationalism* 2, 2.

Suleiman, S. R. (ed.) (1985) *The Female Body in Western Culture,* Cambridge MA: HarvardUniversity Press.

Sullivan, T. (1983) *Compendio de la gramatica Nahuatl,* Mexico: UNAM, IIH.

—— (1986) 'A Scattering of Jades: the Words of the Aztec Elders', in G. H.Gossen, *Symbol and Meaning Beyond the Closed Community: Essays in Mesoamerican Ideas,* Albany: Institute for Mesoamerican Studies, State University of New York.

Summers, L. (1999) quoted in V. Shiva, 'Ecological Balance in an Era of Globalization', in N. Low (ed.), *Global Ethics and Environment*, London: Routledge.

Suski, L. (1997) 'Voices and Absences: the Subjects of Development Discourse', paper presented at the Canadian Association for Studies in International Development, St Johns, Newfoundland.

Sylvester, C. (1994) *Feminist Theory and International Relations in a Postmodern Era,* Cambridge: Cambridge University Press.

Tedlock, D. (1983) *The Spoken Word and the Work of Interpretation,* Philadelphia: University of Pennsylvania Press.

Tetreault, M. K. T. (1993) 'Classrooms for Diversity: Rethinking Curriculum and Pedagogy', in I. A. Banks and C. A. M. Banks (eds.), *Multicultural Education: Issues and Perspective,* 2nd edition, Boston: Allyn and Bacon.

Tharoor, S. (1998) *India: From Midnight to Millennium,* New York: Harper.

Therien, J-P. and C. Lloyd (2000) 'Development assistance on the brink', *Third World Quarterly* 21, 1: 21–38.

Thomas-Slayter, B. (1992) 'Implementing effective local management resources: new roles for NGOs in Africa', *Human Organization* 51: 136–43.

Thompson, E. (1975) *Historia y religion de los Mayas,* Mexico: Fondo de Cultura Economica.

Thompson, J. (1995) 'Participatory approaches in government bureaucracies: facilitating the process of institutional change', *World Development* 23, 9: 1521–54.

Tiessen, R. (1997) 'A Feminist Critique of Participatory Development Discourse: PRA and Gender Participation in Natural Resource Management', paper presented at the International Studies Association, Toronto.

Tilly, L. and J. Scott (1987) *Women, Work and Family,* New York: Methuen.

Tinker, I. (ed.) (1990) *Persistent Inequalities: Women and World Development,* New York: Oxford University Press.

Tomes, N. (2000) 'The making of a germ panic, then and now', *American Journal of Public Health* 90, 2 (February).

Toulmin, S. (1990) *Cosmopolis: the Hidden Agenda of Modernity,* New York: The Free Press.

Toussaint, E. (1999) 'Poor countries pay more under debt reduction scheme?', July, www.twnside.org.sg/souths/twn/title/1921-cn.htm

Tshomo, T. (1992) 'Bu mo rnams gyi rgyan chas gos' (The Jewellery and Dress of Women), *Sheeraza* 14, 5–6.

Turner, V. (1974) *Dramas, Fields, and Metaphors: Symbolic Action in Human Society,* Ithaca NY: Cornell University Press.

Tyner, J. (1999) 'The global context of gendered labor emigration from the Phillipines to the United States', *American Behavioral Scientist* 42, 40: 671–94.

UNFPA (2001) *ICPD Reports,* www.unfpa.org/icpd.reports.htm

Usher, A. D. (1994) 'After the forest: AIDS as ecological collapse in Thailand' in V. Shiva (ed.), *Close to Home: Women Reconnect Ecology, Health and Development Worldwide,* Philadelphia: New Society Publishers.

United Nations (1999) 'Commission on Population and Development', Economic and Social Council, United Nations.

United States Agency for International Development (USAID) (1982) 'Women in Development', USAID policy paper, Washington DC: USAID.

Vanaik, A. (1990) *The Painful Transition: Bourgeoise Democracy in India,* London: Verso.

van Beek, Martijn (1996) 'Identity Fetishism and the Art of Representation in Ladakh: the Long Struggle for Regional Autonomy in Ladakh', unpublished PhD thesis, Cornell University.

—— (2000) 'Lessons from Ladakh? Local Responses to Globalization and Social Change', in J. Dragsbaek Schmidt and J. Hersh (eds.), *Globalization and Social Change,* London: Routledge.

Viesca, C. (1984) 'Prevención y terapeuticas Mexicas', in A. Lopez Austin and C. Viesca (eds.), *Historia general de la medicina en México,* Book 1, Mexico: UNAM, Faculty of Medicine.

Vincent, J. (1991) 'Engaging Historicism', in R. Fox (ed.), *Recapturing Anthropology: Working in the Present,* Santa Fe: School of American Research.

Viramma, J. and J. L. Racine (1997) *Viramma: Life of an Untouchable,* London and Paris: Verso and UNESCO Publishing.

Visweswaran, K. (1988) 'Defining feminist ethnography', *Inscriptions* 5, 4: 27–44.

Visweswaran, K. (1996) 'Small Speeches, Subaltern Gender: Nationalist Ideology and Its

Historiography', in S. Amin and D. Chakrabarty (eds.), *Subaltern Studies IX*, New Delhi: Oxford University Press.

Vitousek, P. M and L. R.Walker (1989) 'Biolgocal invasion by Myrica faya in Hawaii: plant demography, nitrogen fixation, ecoosystem effects', *Ecological Mongraphs* 59.

Vogt, Evan C. (1976) *Tortillas for the Gods: a Symbolic Analysis of Zinacantan Rituals*, Cambridge MA: Harvard University Press.

Walby, S. (1989) *Theorizing Patriarchy*, London: Blackwell.

Walker, L. R and S. D. Smith (1997) 'Impacts of invasive plants on community and ecosystem properties', in J. O. Luken and J. W. Theeret (eds.), *Assessment and Management of Plant Invasions,* New York: Springer Verlag.

Wallace, T. (1999) 'GADU Remembered: Some Reflections on the Early Years', in F. Porter, I. Smyth and C. Sweetman (eds.), *Gender Works: Oxfam Experience in Policy and Practice,* London: Oxfam.

Wangari, E. (1993) 'Sustainable development in arid and semi-arid ecosystems with reference to Mbeere in Kenya', International Consultation to Advance Women in Ecosystems, Environmentally Sustainable Development, World Bank.

—— (1997) 'The effects of Kenyan land policies on female headed households', *Towson University: Journal of International Affairs 33,*1 (Autumn).

—— (2000) 'The Effects of Rice Irrigation Production on Health in the Mwea Irrigation Scheme, Kenya', draft of an interim report for a research project, Towson University.

Ward, K. (1991) *Women Workers and Global Restructuring*, Ithaca NY: Cornell University Press.

Ward, K. and J. Pyle (1995) 'Gender, Industrialization and Development', in Christine E. Bose and Edna Acosta-Belen (eds.), *Women in the Latin American Development Process: from Structural Subordination to Empowerment*, Philadelphia: Temple University Press, pp. 37–64.

Wasserstrom, R. (1983) *Class and Society in Central Chiapas*, Berkeley: University of California Press.

Waterbury, R. (1968) 'The Traditional Market in a Provincial Urban Setting', dissertation, University of California, Los Angeles.

Watkins, J. (1996) *Spirited Women: Gender, Religion, and Cultural Identity in the Nepal Himalayas*, New York: Columbia University Press.

Weiss, R. (1997) 'Gene Enhancements' Thorny Ethical Traits', *Washington Post,* 11 October.

Welbourn, A. (1996) 'RRA and the analysis of difference', *RRA Notes* 14: 14–23.

Wellsley Editorial Committee (Ximena Bunster *et al.*) (1977) *Women and National Development: Complexities of Change,* Chicago: University of Chicago Press.

West African Workshop (1999) 'Report on the West African Workshop on Women in the Aftermath of Civil War, 11–13 December 1998', *Review of African Political Economy* 26, 79: 123–31.

White, S. C. (1996) 'Depoliticising development: the uses and abuses of participation', *Development and Practice* 6, 1: 6–15.

White, T. (1961) *The Making of the President*, New York: Atheneum.

Whitehead, A. (1990) 'Food Crisis in the African Countryside', in H. Bernstein *et al.* (eds.), *The Food Question: Profit Versus People?* London: Earthscan.

WIDE, NAC, Alt-WID, CRIAW (1994), 'Wealth of Nations – Poverty of Women', framework paper prepared for Globalization of the Economy and Economic Justice for Women Workshop, NGO Forum of the ECE Regional Preparatory meeting of the Fourth World Conference for Women, Vienna, 13–15 October.

Wieringa, S. (1994) 'Women's interests and empowerment: gender planning reconsidered', *Development and Change* 25: 829–48.

Williams, L. (1999) 'Women's Eyes on the World Bank: Integrating Gender Equity into Advocacy Work', in F. Porter, I. Smyth and C. Sweetman (eds.), *Gender Works: Oxfam Experience in Policy and Practice,* London: Oxfam.

Wiltshire, R.. (DAWN) (1992) *Environment and Development: Grassroots Women's Perspective,* DAWN Publications.

Wolf, E. R. (1966) *Peasants*, New Jersey: Prentice-Hall, Inc.

World Bank (1980) *World Development Report,* New York: Oxford University Press.

—— (1990) *World Development Report: Poverty*, New York: Oxford University Press.

—— (1995) *World Bank Participation Source Book,* Washington, DC: World Bank, Environment Department Papers.

—— (1997a) *South Asia's Integration into the World Economy,* Washington DC: World Bank.

—— (1997b) *Confronting AIDs: Public Priorities in a Global Epidemic,* Washington DC: World Bank.

—— (1999) *World Development Report,* New York: Oxford University Press.

—— (2000) World Bank figures in 'Global Loan Agencies Buckle Up for Washington Turbulence', *New York Times*, 16 April, p. 6.

—— (2000/1) *World Development Report: Attacking Poverty*, New York: Oxford University Press.

World Trade Organization (1994) *GATT Agreement*, Geneva.

Yeoh, B., S. Huang and J. Gonzalez III (1999) 'Migrant female domestic workers: debating the economic, social and political impacts in Singapore', *International Migration Review* 33, 1: 114–36.

Young, G. (1990) 'Hierarchy and Class in Women's Organizations: a Case from Northern Mexico', in K. Staudt (ed.), *Women, International Development, and Politics,* Philadelphia: Temple University Press.

Young, I. M. (1985) 'Humanism, gynocentrism and feminist politics', *Women Studies International Forum* 8: 173–83.

Yuthok, D. (1990) *House of the Turquoise Roof,* Ithaca: Snow Lion Publications.

Zajonc, A. (1993) *Catching the Light: the Entwined History of Light and Mind,* Oxford: Oxford University Press.

Index